Rick Steves'

Europe
Through
the
Back Door

THIRTEENTH EDITION

John Muir Publications
Santa Fe, New Mexico

JMP travel guidebooks by Rick Steves

Asia Through the Back Door (with Bob Effertz)
Rick Steves' Europe Through the Back Door (formerly *Europe Through the Back Door*)
Europe 101: History, Art, and Culture for the Traveler (with Gene Openshaw)
Kidding Around Seattle
Mona Winks: Self-Guided Tours of Europe's Top Museums (with Gene Openshaw)
Rick Steves' Country Guides (formerly 2 to 22 Days Itinerary Planners)
   Rick Steves' Best of the Baltics and Russia (with Ian Watson)
   Rick Steves' Best of Europe
   Rick Steves' Best of France, Belgium, and the Netherlands
   (with Steve Smith)
   Rick Steves' Best of Germany, Austria, and Switzerland
   Rick Steves' Best of Great Britain
   Rick Steves' Best of Italy
   Rick Steves' Best of Scandinavia
   Rick Steves' Best of Spain and Portugal
Rick Steves' Foreign Language Phrase Books (formerly Europe Through the Back Door Phrase Books)
   Rick Steves' French Phrase Book
   Rick Steves' German Phrase Book
   Rick Steves' Italian Phrase Book
   Rick Steves' Spanish and Portuguese Phrase Book
   Rick Steves' French/German/Italian Phrase Book

Rick Steves' PBS TV series (*Travels in Europe with Rick Steves*), travel seminar, and tour schedules are available from Europe Through the Back Door, Box 2009, 120 4th North, Edmonds, WA 98020 (telephone 206-771-8303; BBS: 206-771-1902, 1200 to 2400, 8/N/1; Compuserve: 73552,300).

John Muir Publications, P.O. Box 613, Santa Fe, NM 87504

Thirteenth Edition. First printing January 1995
Printed in the United States of America

Library of Congress Cataloging-in-Publications Data
Steves, Rick, 1955–
   [Europe through the back door]
   Rick Steves' Europe through the back door. — 13th ed.
     p.   cm.
   Includes index.
   ISBN 1-56261-193-3
   1. Europe—Guidebooks.   I. Title.
D909.S83 1995
914.04'559—dc20   94–33352
                                          CIP

Distributed to the book trade by
W. W. Norton & Company, Inc.
New York, N.Y.

Editor: Risa Laib
Production: Kathryn Lloyd-Strongin, Chris Brigman
Editorial Support: Elizabeth Wolf, Nancy Gillan, Dianna Delling
Cover Design: Tony D'Agostino
Interior Design: Linda Braun
Illustrations: Melissa Meier
Maps: Dave Hoerlein
Photography: Rick Steves
Typesetting: Marcie Pottern
Printer: Quebecor/Kingsport
Cover Photo: Leo de Wys Inc./Steve Vidler

Although the author and publisher have made every effort to provide accurate, up-to-date information, they accept no responsibility for loss, loose stools, injury, or inconvenience sustained by any person using this book.

To the People of Europe

Photo by Rich Sorensen

Acknowledgments

Thanks to Gene Openshaw, Dave Hoerlein, Steve Smith, and Anne Steves for research assistance. And to Carl, Ruth, Gene, Greg, Patty, Dave, Mike, the minibus tours, my parents, and my wife, Anne, for sharing with me the excitement of European travel. And thanks to the following for help in their fields of travel expertise: Dave Hoerlein (Europe, in general, and editing); Risa Laib (travel savvy and editing); Matthew Nolan (tours); Dale Torgrimson (travel agent, flights, insurance); Joan Marsden (guidebooks); the staff at Rail Europe (train travel); Richard Walters (biking); Ruth Kasarda, Claire McIntyre, Suzanne Hogsett, Gail Morse, and Pam Negri (women traveling); Craig Karpilow, M.D. (health for travelers); Arlan Blodgett (photography); Ian Watson (Baltic States and Russia); and Anne Steves (travel with kids). Thanks also to Pat Larson, Sandie Nisbet, John Givens, and Dick Dahl at Small World Productions for introducing so many travelers to this book through our PBS-TV series, "Travels in Europe with Rick Steves."

Contents

Preface

The average American traveler enters Europe through the front door. This Europe greets you with cash registers cocked, $5 cups of coffee, and service with a purchased smile.

To give your trip an extra, more real dimension, come with me through the back door. Through the back door a warm, relaxed, personable Europe welcomes us as friends, not as part of the economy. Traveling this way, we become temporary Europeans, part of the family—approaching Europe on its level, accepting and enjoying its unique ways of life. We'll demand nothing, except that no fuss be made over us.

This "Back Door-style" travel is better because of—not in spite of—your budget. Spending money has little to do with enjoying your trip. In fact, spending less money brings you closer to Europe. A lot of money forces you through Europe's grand front entrance, where people in uniforms greet you with formal smiles. But the back door is what keeps me in my wonderful European rut.

I've spent the last 22 summers exploring Europe. For the first five trips I traveled purely for kicks. Then it became clear: each trip was going smoother . . . I must be learning from my mistakes. And I saw people making the same mistakes I had made . . . costly in time, money, and experience. Then it occurred to me that if I could package the lessons I've learned into a class or book, others could learn from my mistakes rather than their own and enjoy maximum travel thrills per mile, minute and dollar. (And I'd have a good excuse to go back to Europe every summer to update my material.) For the last 17 years I've been doing just that—traveling with my teaching in mind, making mistakes, taking careful notes, losing my traveler's checks just to see what will happen, ordering a Margarita and getting pizza. And this book, which has evolved over 13 editions, is my report to you.

My readers, many whose grandkids warned, "You shouldn't be doing this," are having great trips and coming home with money in the bank for next summer. I'm careful not to send people to Europe with too much confidence and not enough money, reservations, or skills. If I did, travelers would suffer and I'd hear about it. But judging from the happy postcards my road scholars send me, it's clear that those who equip themselves with good information and expect themselves to travel smart, do.

The first half of this book covers the skills of Back Door European travel—packing, planning an itinerary, finding good hotels, getting around, and so on. The second half gives you keys to my favorite discoveries, places I call "Back Doors," where you can dirty your fingers in pure Europe—feeling its fjords and caressing its castles. It'll raise your travel dreams to their upright and locked positions. Happy travels!

Rick Steves' Back Door Travel Philosophy

Travel is intensified living—maximum thrills per minute and one of the last great sources of legal adventure. Travel is freedom. It's recess, and we need it.

Experiencing the real Europe requires catching it by surprise, going casual . . . "Through the Back Door."

Affording travel is a matter of priorities. (Make do with the old car.) You can travel—simply, safely, and comfortably—anywhere in Europe for $50 a day plus transportation costs. In many ways, spending more money only builds a thicker wall between you and what you came to see. Europe is a cultural carnival, and time after time, you'll find that its best acts are free and the best seats are the cheap ones.

A tight budget forces you to travel close to the ground, meeting and communicating with the people, not relying on service with a purchased smile. Never sacrifice sleep, nutrition, safety, or cleanliness in the name of budget. Simply enjoy the local-style alternatives to expensive hotels and restaurants.

Extroverts have more fun. If your trip is low on magic moments, kick yourself and make things happen. If you don't enjoy a place, maybe you don't know enough about it. Seek the truth. Recognize tourist traps. Give a culture the benefit of your open mind. See things as different but not better or worse. Any culture has much to share.

Of course, travel, like the world, is a series of hills and valleys. Be fanatically positive and militantly optimistic. If something's not to your liking, change your liking. Travel is addicting. It can make you a happier American, as well as a citizen of the world. Our Earth is home to nearly six billion equally important people. It's humbling to travel and find that people don't envy Americans. Europeans like us, but with all due respect, they wouldn't trade places.

Globe-trotting destroys ethnocentricity. It helps you understand and appreciate different cultures. Travel changes people. It broadens perspectives and teaches new ways to measure quality of life. Many travelers toss aside their hometown blinders. Their prized souvenirs are the strands of different cultures they decide to knit into their own character. The world is a cultural yarn shop. And Back Door Travelers are weaving the ultimate tapestry. Come on and join in!

PART ONE
Basic Travel Skills

Photo by Andrea Hagg

Europe

500 KM
300 MI

N

LAPLAND
ARCTIC CIRCLE

Trondheim
NORWAY
SOGNE FJORD
FINLAND
Bergen
Oslo
Helsinki
Turku
St. Petersburg
Stockholm
Tallinn
RUSSIA
SWEDEN
BALTIC
ESTONIA
SCOTLAND
Moscow
DENMARK
SEA
Riga
LATVIA
Edinburgh
NORTH
Copenhagen
LITHUANIA
IRELAND
N. IRE.
Dublin
York
Vilnius
DINGLE PENINSULA
WALES
ENGLAND
SEA
RUSS.
Lübeck
BELARUS
POLAND
London
Amsterdam
Berlin
Warsaw
Bath
NETH.
GERMANY
Bruges
Brussels
Krakow
Kiev
Mont St. Michel
BELG.
RHINE
Prague
UKRAINE
ATLANTIC
NORMANDY
MOSEL
CZECH.
LUX.
Paris
ROM. ROAD
SLOVAK.
BRITTANY
ALSACE
Munich
Vienna
MOLDOVA
Colmar
BAVARIA
Budapest
LOIRE
Salzburg
OCEAN
FRANCE
Bern
AUST.
HUNG.
ROMANIA
BLACK
SWITZ.
BERN. OBER.
TIROL
DORDOGNE
DOLO-MITES
SLOV.
Belgrade
Bucharest
Chamonix
Milan
CRO.
SEA
Venice
BOSNIA-HERZ.
PROVENCE
CINQUE TERRE
Florence
SERBIA
Sofia
Carc.
Arles
SAN MARINO
Dubrovnik
BULG.
MONACO
UMBRIA
ANDORRA
Nice
ADRIATIC SEA
ALB.
Istanbul
SPAIN
CORSICA
Rome
ITALY
GREECE
CAPPA-DOCIA
PORTUGAL
Madrid
Barcelona
AEGEAN
TURKEY
Lisbon
Toledo
Naples
CORFU
Athens
Ephesus
SARDINIA
AMALFI COAST
Seville
Gran.
MEDITERRANEAN
PEL. PEN.
SEA
ALGARVE
ANDALUSIA
SICILY
MOROCCO
ALGERIA
TUNISIA
SEA
CRETE

DCH

1
Planning

A European adventure is a major investment of time and money. Those who think of the planning stage as part of the experience invest wisely and enjoy tremendous returns. A well-planned trip is more fun, less expensive, and not necessarily more structured. Planning means understanding your alternatives, preparing to be spontaneous.

Tour versus Independent Travel

One of the first big decisions to make is whether to travel independently or with a tour. Consider the pros and cons of each. Do you want the security of knowing that all your rooms are reserved and that a trained guide will take you smoothly from one hotel to the next? Do you require consistently good hotels and restaurant meals, wishing at the same time to be as economical as possible? Will you forgo adventure, independence, and the challenge of doing it on your own in order to take the worry and bother out of traveling? Is sitting on a bus with the same group of tourists an acceptable way to spend your vacation? Is observing rather than experiencing good enough? If the answer to these questions is "yes," then you need a good European tour company. There's a tour for just about every travel dream. Your travel agent can help you.

For many people with limited time and money, tours are the most efficient way to see Europe. Without a tour, three restaurant meals a day and a big, modern hotel are very expensive. Large tour companies book thousands of rooms and meals year-round and can, with their tremendous economic clout, get prices that no individual tourist could even come close to. For instance, on a recent Cosmos tour (one of the largest and cheapest tour companies in Europe), I got fine rooms (with private bath), three hot meals a day, bus transportation, and the services of a European guide—all for $80 a day. Considering that many of the hotel rooms alone would have cost the tourist off the street $80, that all-inclusive tour price per day was great. Such comfort without a tour is very expensive.

Eight and forty tourists baked in a bus

There are, however, cheaper ways to see Europe than from the tinted windows of a tour bus. The cheapest and—for me—the best way to see Europe is to travel independently. If you've read this far, you've got what it takes intellectually to handle Europe on your own.

Europe is amazingly well organized. For instance, many cities sell a "Key to the town." For $15 you get 24 hours of free entrance to all the sights; free use of all the subways, buses and boats; a booklet explaining everything; and a map. It's all very straightforward and usually in English. If you're inclined to figure things out, it's clear. But some people are not inclined to figure things out. They do that to earn their living for fifty weeks a year, and that's not their idea of a good vacation. These people should travel with a tour . . . or a spouse. But if you enjoy the challenge of tackling a new great city, you can do it.

The tour groups that unload on Europe's quaintest towns experience things differently. They are treated as an entity, a mob to be fed, shown around, profited from, and moved out. Tours drink *at* Europe while the individual traveler drinks *with* Europe.

This book focuses on the skills necessary for do-it-yourself European travel. If you're destined for a tour, read on anyway (especially the section on bus tour self-defense). Even on a bus with fifty other people, you can and should be in control, equipped with a guidebook and thinking as an independent traveler. Your trip's too important for you to blindly trust an overworked and underpaid tour guide.

Alone or with a Friend?

The independent traveler must decide whether to travel alone or with a friend. Here are some pros and cons.

Traveling alone gives you complete freedom and independence. You never have to wait for your partner to pack up; you never need to consider a partner's wishes when you decide what to see, where to go, how far to travel, how much to spend, or even when the day has been long enough. You go where you want to, when you want to, and you can get the heck out of that stuffy museum when all the Monets start looking alike.

You meet more people when you travel alone because you're more approachable in the eyes of a European, and loneliness will drive you to reach out and make friends. When you travel with someone, it's easy to focus on your partner and forget about meeting Europeans.

Solo travel is intensely personal. Without the comfortable crutch of a friend, you're more likely to know the joys of self-discovery and the pleasures found in the kindness of strangers. You'll be exploring yourself as well as a new city or country.

But traveling alone can be lonely. Hotel rooms become lifeless cells, and meals are served in a puddle of silence. Big cities can be cold and

Traveling on your own, you'll have the locals dancing with you—not for you

ugly when the only person you have to talk to is yourself. Being sick and alone in a country where no one even knows you exist is, even in retrospect, a miserable experience.

Europe is full of lonely travelers, and there are some natural meeting places. You're likely to find a vaga-buddy in youth hostels, in museums (offer to share your *Mona Winks* chapter), on one-day bus tours, and on trains. Eurailers buddy up on the trains. If you're carrying a Cook Timetable, leave it lying around, and you'll become the most popular kid on the train. Travel as a student, whatever your age: they have more fun, make more friends, and spend less money than most travelers. Board the train with a little too much of a picnic—and share it with others. Be bold; if you're lonely, others are, too.

Traveling with a partner overcomes many of these problems. Shared experiences are more fun, and for the rest of your life, there will be a special bond between you. The confident, uninhibited extrovert is better at making things happen and is likelier to run into exciting and memorable events. And when I travel with a partner, it's easier for me to be that kind of "wild and crazy guy."

Traveling with a partner is cheaper. Rarely does a double room cost as much as two singles. If a single room costs $30, a double room will generally be around $40, a savings of $10 per night per person. Picnicking is cheaper and easier when you share costs, as are travel guides, banking, maps, magazines, taxis, storage lockers, and much more. Besides expenses, partners can share the burden of time-consuming hassles, such as standing in lines at train stations, banks, and post offices.

Remember, traveling together greatly accelerates a relationship—especially a romantic one. You see each other constantly, making endless decisions. The niceties go out the window. Everything becomes very real, and you are in an adventure, a struggle, a hot-air balloon for two. You can jam the experiences of years into one summer.

I'd highly recommend a little premarital travel. A mutual travel experience is a good test of a relationship—often revealing its ultimate course.

Your choice of a travel partner is critical. It can make or break a trip. Traveling with the wrong partner can be like a two-month computer date. I'd rather do it alone. Analyze your travel styles and goals for compatibility. Consider a trial weekend together before merging dream trips.

Choose a partner carefully. One summer I went to Europe to dive into as many cultures and adventures as possible. I planned to rest when

Many single travelers pick up a partner in Europe

I got home. My partner wanted to slow life down, to get away from it all, relax and escape the pressures of the business world. Our ideas of acceptable hotels and the purpose of eating were quite different. The trip was a near disaster.

Many people already have their partner—for better or for worse. In the case of married couples, minimize the stress of traveling together by recognizing one another's needs for independence. Too many people do Europe as a three-legged race, tied together from start to finish. Have an explicit understanding that there's absolutely nothing selfish, dangerous, insulting, or wrong with splitting up occasionally. This is a freedom too few travel partners allow themselves. Doing your own thing for a few hours or days breathes fresh air into your togetherness.

Traveling in a threesome or foursome is usually troublesome. With all the exciting choices Europe has to offer, it's often hard for even a twosome to reach a consensus. Without a clear group leader, the "split and be independent" strategy is particularly valuable.

Another way to minimize travel partnership stress is to go communal with your money. Separate checks, double bank charges, and long lists of petty IOUs in six different currencies are a pain. Pool your resources, noting how much each person contributes, and just assume everything equals out in the long run. Keep track of major individual expenses, but don't worry who got an extra postcard or gelato. Enjoy treating each other to taxis and dinner out of your "kitty," and after the trip, divvy up the remains. If one person consumed $25 or $30 more, that's a small price to pay for the convenience and economy of communal money.

Our Travel Industry

Travel is a huge business. Most of what the industry promotes is decadence: lie on the beach and be catered to; hedonize those precious two weeks to make up for the other fifty; see if you can eat five meals a day and still snorkel when you get into port. That's where the money is, and that's where most of the interest is. The name of the game is to get people's money here for travel thrills over there. You (anyone who's read this far in this book) are a fringe that fits the industry like a snowshoe in Mazatlán.

Understand what shapes the information that shapes your travel dreams. As a newspaper travel columnist, I've learned that it takes a bold (or, some would say, foolish) travel editor to run articles that may upset advertisers. Travel newspaper sections are possible only with the support of travel advertisers. And advertisers are more interested in filling cruise ships or tour buses than in turning people free to travel independently. In fact, when I first started running my weekly travel column, it was called "The Budget Traveler." Within a month of its appearance, that travel section's major advertisers met with the editor and explained they would no longer buy ads if he continued running a column called "The Budget Traveler." Hastily, the editor and I found a new name. To save the column we called it "The Practical Traveler"—same subversive information but with a more palatable title.

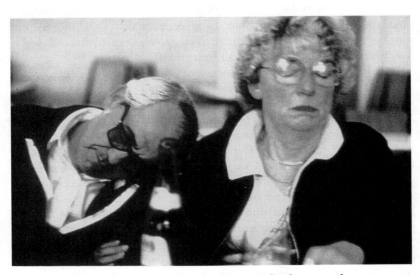

Not all tours are as exciting as their brochures make them sound

Most travel agents don't understand travel "through the Back Door." The typical attitude I get when I hobnob with bigwigs from the industry in Hilton Hotel ballrooms is: "If you can't afford first class, save up and go next year." I'll never forget the bewilderment I caused when I turned down a free room in Bangkok's most elegant Western-style hotel in favor of a cheap room in a simple Thai-style hotel.

Of course, these comments are generalizations; there are many great travelers in the travel industry. These people will understand my frustration because they've also dealt with it.

Travel can mean rich people flaunting their affluence, taking snapshots of black kids jumping off white ships for small change. Or it can promote understanding, turning our American perspective into a human perspective and making our world more comfortable in its smallness. What the industry promotes is up to all of us—writers, editors, agents, and travelers.

WHY YOU NEED A TRAVEL AGENT, AND HOW TO CHOOSE ONE

I'm not "anti travel agent." My travel agent is my vital ally. And I've never gone to Europe without the help of my agent. But there are a lot of flat-out bad travel agents. And I am "anti bad travel agent." As a tour organizer, it's frustrating to have someone who wants to join one of my ETBD tours but can't find an affordable airplane ticket. Many times, with customers from every part of the U.S., I've said, "Don't give up. Let me see if I can find you something." And my Seattle travel agent beats their hometown agent's price by several hundred dollars (as could any good agent in their town). You don't need *my* agent. But you do need a *good* agent.

What do I need from an agent? Travel agents are, or should be, experts on getting there, getting around over there, and tour options. I use an agent for my plane ticket, train pass, or car rental, and nothing else.

Although many agents can give you tips on Irish B&Bs and sporadic advice on the best biking in Holland, you'll generally do better if you use your travel agent to get you to your destination and after that, rely on a good guidebook. Travel agents generally have to handle their clients with kid gloves. Don't let their caution clamp a ball and chain onto your travel dreams.

It takes a full-time and aggressive travel professional to keep up with the constantly changing airline industry these days. You won't save money by going directly to the airlines. Most airline representatives barely know what they're charging, much less their competitors' rates and schedules. Only your agent would remind you that leaving two days earlier would get you in on the end of shoulder season—and save you $100. And nowadays, "consolidator tickets" enable your travel agent to beat an airline's price on its own tickets (explained later).

Agents charge you nothing. They make their money from commissions paid by the airlines, not by marking up your tickets. Take advantage of their expertise. A good agent explains to her client how there's no free lunch in the airline industry. Normally, for every dollar you save, you're losing a dollar's worth of comfort, flexibility, or reliability. Rather than grab the cheapest ticket to Europe, I go with my agent's recommendation for the best combination of reliability, economy, and flexibility for my travel needs.

Car rentals are cheaper when arranged before departure through your agent. Eurail, and most country railpasses, must or should be purchased before you leave home. To get good service on small, tedious items like these, do all your trip business through the agent who made a good commission on your air ticket.

When do I buy? Survey the ticket situation with your agent as soon as you know where you're going. Buy your plane tickets as soon as you're ready to firmly commit yourself to flight dates and ports. As you delay, dates sell out and prices may rise. Ask your agent if you can reserve a seat now but pay later, in case the price drops. Once you buy your ticket, you fix the price. Remember, cheap tickets are expensive to change.

From whom do I buy? If people would spend as much energy finding the right agent and cultivating a loyal relationship with him or her as they do shopping around for the cheapest ticket, they'd be much better off. A good agent can get you almost any ticket, and dumping your agent for a $30 savings from a discount agent down the street is a bad move. (See Chapter 3, Transportation, for flight information.)

These days, many people milk good agents for all they're worth and then buy tickets from their sister's friend's agency around the corner. Because of this, it's tough to get good advice over the phone, and "browsers" usually get no respect. I enjoy the luxury of sitting down with my agent, explaining travel plans, getting a briefing on my options, and choosing the best flight. I don't have time to sort through all the frustrating, generally too-good-to-be-true ads that fill the Sunday travel sections.

If you have a travel specialty, find an agency with the same focus. In the fast-paced and deregulated airline industry, your agency should be have access to consolidator tickets. Big or specializing agencies have more clout with the airlines and can often exercise a little more flexibility with airline rules and prices. Big-city agencies have a closer working

Know Thy Travel Agent—A Quiz

One way to be sure your travel agent is properly suited to helping you with your trip is to ask him or her a few questions. Here's a little quiz—complete with answers.

1. What is "open-jaws"?
a) Yet another shark movie sequel.
b) A tourist in awe of the *Mannekin Pis*.
c) A special-interest tour of Romania's dental clinics.
d) An airline ticket that allows you to fly into one city and out of another.

2. Which international boat rides are covered by the Eurailpass?
a) Poland to Switzerland.
b) All of them.
c) Ireland to France, Sweden to Finland, Italy to Greece, Germany to Denmark, and Sweden to Denmark.

3. What's the Youth Hostel membership age limit?
a) Five.
b) As high as 30 if you like rap music.
c) There is none, except in Bavaria, where it's 26.

4. What is the most economical way to get from London's Heathrow Airport into London?
a) Walk.
b) In a Youth Hostel.
c) Don't. Spend your whole vacation at Heathrow.
d) By subway or airbus.

5. What is an ISIC card?
a) A universal way to tell foreigners you're not feeling well.
b) It beats three-of-a-kind.
c) The International Student Identity Card, good for many discounts at sights and museums.

6. Is there a problem getting a bed and breakfast in England's small towns without a reservation?
a) Not if you live there.
b) Yes. Carry No-Doz in England.
c) No.

7. How much does a Hungarian visa cost?
a)"How much you have, comrade?"
b) You can just charge it on your Visa card.
c) More than a Grecian urn.
d) It's not required.

relationship with airlines and, therefore, a slight advantage. But a hard-working smaller agency might give you more personal attention and be less distracted. The travel agency chains are best suited to help the business traveler. Often, but not always, the discounting agencies make too little per ticket to properly serve their masses. I'd choose a no-frills flight, not a no-frills agency. Travel agency recommendations from other travelers provide excellent leads.

But the right agency doesn't guarantee the right agent. You need a particular person—someone whose definition of "good travel" matches yours. Consider his or her attitude and experience. Are you a Love Boat, shuffleboard-and-bad-magic-acts-after-dinner traveler? Or do you travel to leave behind rather than flaunt your Americanness?

Once you find the right agent, nurture your alliance. Be loyal, keep your traveling eggs together in the correct basket, and travel with this expert on your side. Send her a postcard.

Travel Insurance—To Insure or Not to Insure

Travel insurance is a way to buy off the considerable financial risks of traveling. These risks include accidents, illness, missed flights, canceled or interrupted tours, lost baggage, and emergency evacuation. Each traveler's risk and potential loss varies, depending on how much of the trip is prepaid, the kind of air ticket purchased, your and your loved ones' health, value of your luggage, where you're traveling, what health coverage you already have, and the financial health of the tour company or airline. For some, insurance is a good deal; for others, it's not.

Travel agents will recommend travel insurance because they make a commission on it, because they can be held liable for your losses if they don't explain insurance options to you—and maybe because it's right for you. But the final decision is yours. What are the chances of needing it, how able are you to take the risks, and what's peace of mind worth to you? (Like most kinds of insurance, the commission is big—in this case, a whopping 30%.)

You can design your own coverage by ordering à la carte through a policy like Access America's or Mutual of Omaha's. This insurance menu includes four sections: medical, baggage, trip cancellation, and flight insurance. Tailor it to your needs, then compare it with the package deal explained below.

Baggage insurance costs about $2 or $3 per day per $1,000 coverage, occasionally with some serious limitations on coverage of items such as cash, eye wear, and photographic equipment. Since this is the industry's least profitable kind of insurance, it can be difficult to purchase alone. If you've left your valuables either in your money belt or at home, this coverage is unnecessary. Your homeowners insurance may cover your possessions overseas.

Trip cancellation or interruption insurance covers your losses if: (1) you, your travel partner or a family member cannot travel due to sickness or a list of other acceptable reasons; (2) your tour company or airline goes out of business or can't perform as promised; (3) a family member at home gets sick, causing you to cancel; or (4) for a good reason, you miss a flight or need an emergency one. In other words, if, on the day before your trip, you or your travel partner breaks a leg, you can both bail out and neither of you will lose a penny. And if, one day into the tour, you have an accident, both of you will be flown home, and you'll be reimbursed for the emergency one-way return flight (which usually costs far more than your economy round-trip fare) and whatever portion of the tour you haven't used. This insurance costs about 5½ percent of the amount you want covered. (For example, $1,500 tour and $500 airfare can be insured for $110. Even if you buy a $2,000 policy for $110, there are worst-case fly-home-in-a-hurry scenarios where you could need more coverage.) This is a good deal if you figure there's a better than 1-in-20 chance you'll need it. The rugged, healthy, unattached, and gung-ho traveler will probably skip this coverage. I have for 20 trips, and my number has yet to come up. Someone with questionable health (but no "pre-existing conditions") or a loved one in frail health taking an organized tour (which is very expensive to cancel) should get this coverage.

Flight insurance (crash coverage) is a statistical rip-off that heirs love. More than 60,000 airplanes take off and land safely every day. The chances of being in an airplane crash are minuscule.

There are **package insurance** deals (such as Travel Guard's) that give you everything but the kitchen sink for 8 percent of your prepaid trip cost (airfare, car rental, Eurail ticket, tour cost, etc.). This can be a better deal for travelers with less of the trip prepaid (those without tours) because coverage is the same regardless of the premium you pay. This covers any deductible expense your existing medical insurance plan doesn't cover. And it also gives you a supplemental collision damage waiver (CDW) on rental cars which can, in itself, make this policy a great value (see below).

The problem with a Travel Guard-type package is that you must take the whole works—dental care, hotel overbooking, CDW supplement and all—whether you need it or not. It's comprehensive but not necessarily the cheapest coverage.

Your travel agent has insurance brochures. Ask your agent which he or she recommends for your travels and why. Study the brochures. Consider how insurance fits your travel and personal needs, compare its cost to the likelihood of your using it and your potential loss—and then decide.

THE COLLISION DAMAGE WAIVER (CDW) RACKET

In the past, the insurance on a rental car normally had a $1,000 deductible clause. Car companies charged a ridiculous fee to waive this deductible, so travel insurance companies and credit card companies were offering more reasonable CDW supplement deals to people renting cars. Lately, car rental companies (which "self-insure" their cars) have raised their "deductible" to as much as the entire value of the car, far beyond the CDW coverage offered by the more reasonable alternatives. And the car renter has one way to drive without this huge deductible hanging over his or her head: pay the roughly $10 a day the car rental companies charge for CDW. Ask your travel agent about ways to avoid this fee. While some "gold" credit cards promise to give you free CDW coverage if you charge it through them, you'll go without CDW as far as the rental company is concerned. If you are using your credit card, ask to have the worst-case scenario explained to you. A possible problem is that you'll need a line of credit big enough to cover the

Luckily, he paid extra for full insurance

value of the car. If you have an accident, you may have to settle with the rental company and then fight to get reimbursed by your credit card company when you get home. Also, many companies are going to all-inclusive rental plans which include a more reasonable CDW. Ask your travel agent about this. CDW is most expensive when purchased at the rental desk. Those renting a car for over three weeks should ask their agent about leasing, which skirts many tax and insurance costs.

If you do pay the car company, remember that the rental rates are so competitive that, to make a reasonable profit, these companies have had to make a killing on the CDW. If it's any consolation, think of your CDW fee as half for CDW and half money that you should have paid on the rental fee.

Regardless of how tough CDW is on the pocketbook, I get it for the peace of mind. It's so much more fun to hold your own on the road with Europe's skilled maniac drivers, knowing you can return your car in an unrecognizable shambles with an apologetic shrug, saying, "S-s-s-sorry," and lose no money.

Red Tape—Passports, Visas, Shots, and Such

The only document a U.S. citizen needs to travel through Western Europe is a passport. For most travelers, the only complicated border crossing and the only time any customs official will look at you seriously is at the airport as you reenter the United States. Most European border crossings are a wave-through for U.S. citizens.

Passports, good for 10 years, cost $65 ($55 for a renewal). Apply for one at the U.S. Passport Agency, any federal or state courthouse, or some post offices. You can telephone a recording for complete details. Although they say applications take several weeks (and you should be prepared for delays), most passports are processed within a few days. If you can prove you're in an emergency situation and go in person, they'll do it while you wait.

Losing your passport while traveling is a major headache. Contact the police and the nearest U.S. consulate or embassy right away. You can get a short-term replacement, but you'll earn it. A photocopy of your passport can speed the replacement process.

As you travel, take good care of your passport. But Americans, notorious passport-grippers, need to relax when it comes to temporarily giving it up. As you cross some Eastern European borders by train, a usually unofficial-looking character will come down the aisle picking up all the passports. Relax, you'll get it back later. When you sleep in a *couchette* (night-train sleeping car) that crosses a border, the car attendant will take your passport so you won't be disturbed when the train crosses the border at 3:00 a.m. And hotels routinely take your passport "for the night" so they can register you with the police. This bookwork must be done for foreign guests throughout Europe. Receptionists like to gather passports and register them together when things are quiet. Although it's unreasonable to expect them to drop whatever they're doing to register you right now, I politely ask if I can pick up my passport in two hours. I just don't like my passport in the top drawer all night long. A passport works well for collateral in cases when you don't have the cash right now (hefty deposits on bike rentals, hotels that don't trust you, etc.).

Visas are not required for Americans traveling in Western Europe and most of the East (except in Romania and the former USSR). A visa is a stamp placed on your passport by a government, allowing you to enter their country. A few countries technically require a visa, but they stamp it in without delay as you enter. Since things can always change, get up-to-date information on visa requirements from your travel agent or the U.S. Department of State.

If you do need to get a visa, it's usually best to get it at home before you leave. If you forget, every European country has an embassy or consulate (which can issue visas) in the capital of every other European country.

At this time, shots are not required for travel in Europe. But this can change, so check the inoculation requirements before you leave home. Remember that countries "require" shots in order to protect their citizens from you and "recommend" shots to protect you from them. If any shots are recommended, take that advice seriously.

Customs is not a concern unless you plan to buy more than $1,400 worth of souvenirs. Your first $400 are duty-free, and the next $1,000 are dutied at a flat 10 percent rate. If you buy less than $400 worth of goods, you simply say so as you reenter the United States.

The ISIC card, the only internationally recognized student ID card, will get you lots of discounts on transportation, entertainment, and sightseeing throughout Western Europe and even some travel insurance. If you are a full-time student or have been one in the last year (and can prove it), get one. (The cost is $15 from your CIEE student travel agency or university foreign study office.) Teachers (of any age) are promised student-type discounts with an "ITIC" (International Teacher Identification Card) but this is often not honored. Non-student travelers under age 26 can get a youth card for similar discounts.

Information Sources

GUIDEBOOKS

Guidebooks are $15 tools for $3,000 experiences. Many otherwise smart people base the trip of a lifetime on a borrowed copy of a three-year-old guidebook. As a writer of guidebooks, I am a big fan of their worth. When I visit someplace as a rank beginner—a place like Belize or Sri Lanka—I equip myself with a good guidebook and expect myself to travel smart. I travel like an old pro, not because I'm a super traveler but because I have good information and I use it. I'm a connoisseur of guidebooks. I buy several for each country I visit, rip them up, and staple the chapters I want together into my own personalized hybrid guidebooks. My trip is my child. I love her. And I give her the best tutors money can buy.

Too many people are penny-wise and pound-foolish when it comes to information. I see them every year, stranded on street corners in Paris—hemorrhaging money. It's flipping off them in $20 bills. Con-artists smell the monied blood and circle anxiously. These vacations are disasters. Tourists with no information run out of money, go home early, and hate the French. With a good guidebook you can come into Paris for your first time, go anywhere in town for a dollar on the subway, faster than a taxi can take you, sleep in a clean and friendly $40 double room in a hotel with a singing maid, on a pedestrian-only street in village Paris seven blocks from the Eiffel tower, and enjoy a memorable $15 bistro dinner. All you need is a good guidebook covering your destination.

Before buying a book, study it. How old is the information? The cheapest books are often the oldest—no bargain. Who wrote it? What's the author's experience? Does the book promote the tourist industry or smart travel? Does it give hard opinions or just superlatives? To whom is it written? Is it readable? It should have personality without chattiness.

Don't believe everything you read. The power of the printed word is scary. Most books are peppered with information that is flat-out wrong. Incredibly enough, even this book may have an error. Many "writers" succumb to the temptation to write guidebooks based on hearsay, travel brochures, other books, and wishful thinking. Many writers are met at the airport by an official from the national tourist board. They learn tips handy only for others met at the airport by an official from the national tourist board.

Bookstores that specialize in travel books have knowledgeable salespeople and the best selection. If you have a focus, there's a book written just for you. There are books written for those traveling with toddlers, pets, grandparents, and wine snobs. There are books for vegetarians, galloping gluttons, hedonists, cranky teens, nudists, pilgrims, gays, bird-watchers, music lovers, campers, hikers, bikers, and motorcyclers. Some are for the rich and sophisticated, others are for the cheap and sleazy. Here's a rundown of my favorite guidebooks:

Let's Go: Europe—Aptly subtitled *The Bible of the Budget Traveler*, *Let's Go* covers the big cities, towns, and countryside of all European countries as well as North Africa and Russia. You'll find listings of budget accommodations and restaurants; information on public transportation; capsule social, political, and historical rundowns; and a refreshingly opinionated look at sights and tourist activities. It doesn't teach "Ugly Americanism," as do many prominent guidebooks.

Although written by Harvard students for young train-travelers on tight budgets, it's the best book available for anyone wanting to travel as a temporary European in search of cultural intimacy on a budget. *Let's Go* is the best book out for the youth/alternative nightlife scene and youth hosteling. *Let's Go* is updated each year (hits the bookstores in January) and sold in Europe for 50 percent over its U.S.A. price. Always use the current edition. If you've got more money, stick to its higher-priced listings. The only problem with *Let's Go* is that every young North American traveler has it, and the flood of backpacker business it sends can overwhelm a formerly cozy village, hotel, or restaurant and give it a whopping Daytona Beach hangover.

Let's Go also publishes books covering these countries individually: Britain, Ireland, France, Germany/Switzerland, Austria, Spain/Portugal/Morocco, Greece/Turkey, Italy, and Israel/Egypt. If you'll be spending two weeks or more in any of these areas and like *Let's Go*'s style, invest in these more focused editions. With ten times the information and one-tenth the readership of *Let's Go: Europe*, they don't have the negative impact that the big Europe book has on their listings. For me, these are the best guides available for these countries.

Berkeley Guides—The success of the Harvard students' *Let's Go: Europe* series has attracted several hungry travel publishers. Fodor, declaring that *Let's Go* is "tired," has brought out the Berkeley Guides, a super-hip West Coast series that claims to "put the funk" back into travel. Written by Berkeley students, this series is fresh, accurate, and hard-hitting. But it seems uninspired, offering forced opinions and no improvement over *Let's Go*.

Lonely Planet guidebooks are the dominant series for travel in the Third World. Published in Australia, these are the best independent budget travel guidebooks for most countries in Asia, Africa, and South America. Their long-anticipated invasion of Europe began with huge, expensive, and overlapping Western, Eastern, and Mediterranean Europe editions. Lonely Planet's approach to Europe is more mature than *Let's Go*'s student style but, as Napoleon and Hitler learned, conquering Europe is harder than wanting to. Lonely Planet is introducing country guides for most of Europe. These more focused and portable books will fill a niche.

Rough Guides, a fast-growing British series (formerly the Real Guides) includes books about every part of Europe, several city guides, and a fat all-Europe edition. They're a great source of hard-core go-local-on-a-vagabond's-budget information. While the hotel listings are skimpy, uninspired, and often sloppy, these books are written by Europeans who understand the contemporary and social scene better than American writers. Rough Guides are particularly strong on Eastern European countries.

Frommer Guides—Arthur Frommer's classic guide, *Europe on $5 a Day*, is now up to $50 a day. It's great for the 26 most important big cities but ignores everything else (and there's so much more!). It's full of reliable and handy listings of budget hotels, restaurants, and sightseeing ideas compiled by the father of budget independent travel himself. Every year I rip up an edition and take along chapters as supplemental information on the cities I plan to visit.

Frommer books on specific countries cover regions, towns, and villages as well as cities but are not as good as Frommer's Europe book. Arthur sold his name and that's the only thing "Frommer" about these guides. Frommer's *$X a Day* books have a budget focus, whereas his *Dollarwise* guides are for pricier travel. Frommer guidebooks give good advice on which sites are essential when time is short. And they are especially well-attuned to the needs of older travelers but handle many with unnecessary kid gloves.

Karen Brown's Country Inn series is great for people with a few extra bucks and an appetite for doilies under thatch. Her recommended routes are good and her listings are excellent if you plan on spending $100 a night for your double rooms.

Michelin Green Guides, the famous tall green books, available in dryly translated English all over Europe, ignore hotels and eating but are a gold mine of solid, practical information on what to see. A French publication (English editions are available in Europe for about the same price as in the U.S.A.), Michelin has English editions covering some regions of France and most countries of Europe. French-speakers will find more editions available. Each book includes small but encyclopedic and practical chapters on history, lifestyles, art, culture, customs, and economy. These books are a tour guide's best friend. All over Europe tour leaders are wowing their busloads by reading from their Green guide. ("And these are fields of sugar beets. Three-quarters of Austria's beet production lies along the banks of the Danube, which flows through 12 countries draining an area the size of the Sudan.") A wonderful and unique feature of the Green Guides is their handy "worth a journey/worth a detour" maps. The prominence of a listed place is determined by its touristic importance rather than its population. So a cute visit-worthy village (like Rothenburg) appears bolder than a big, dull city (like Dortmund). These books are filled with fine city maps and designed for drivers, ideally on Michelin tires.

The **Michelin Red Guides** are the hotel and restaurant connoisseur's bible. But I don't travel with a poodle and my taste buds weren't designed to appreciate $100 meals.

The **Blue Guides** (which have nothing to do with European brothels) take a dry and scholarly approach to the countries of Europe. Blue Guides are ideal if you want to learn as much about a country's history, art, architecture, and culture as you possibly can. With the *Blue Guide to Greece*, I had all the information needed about any sight in Greece and never needed to hire a guide. Scholarly types actually find a faint but endearing personality hiding between the sheets of their Blue Guides.

Access Guides offer the ultimate in-depth source of sightseeing information for London, Paris, Venice, Florence, and Rome. They are creatively put together, but information overkill for most speedy travelers. Two pricey new series, **Eyewitness** and **Knopf**, also cover the big cities. They offer a futuristic, hi-tech, visually super-friendly layout and lots of fine cultural and historical information. Knopf is the more highbrow of the two. While each of these narrates walking tours, the granddaddy of the walking tour guidebooks, *Turn Right at the Fountain*, is still the best for those who would enjoy a couple of pleasant do-it-yourself historic strolls through Europe's greatest cities.

Cadogan (rhymes with toboggan) guides are readable and thought-provoking, giving the curious traveler a cultural insight into many regions. Editions cover Scotland, Ireland, Italy, Italian islands, Umbria and Tuscany, Spain, Portugal, Morocco, the Greek islands, Turkey, and more (published by Globe Pequot). If you're traveling alone and want to understand tomorrow's sightseeing, Cadogan gives you something productive to do in bed.

Work, Study, Travel Abroad, published by the Council on International Educational Exchange (CIEE), is the best sourcebook for work or study in Europe. CIEE, the biggest and most energetic student travel service in the United States, is worth taking advantage of. (For a catalog, contact a local office or send $1 to CIEE, 205 E. 42nd St., New York, NY 10017-5706, tel. 212/661-1450.) The CIEE travel agency, Council Travel, has 47 offices around the United States (800-2-COUNCIL for flight information). CIEE also publishes *Going Places*, a guide for teens in search of work and study. Susan Griffith's **Work Your Way Around the World** (ISBN 1-85458-023-X, published by Vacation Work) is heavy on Europe and better than the CIEE guide for non-students.

RICK STEVES' BOOKS

Rick Steves' Country Guides (Santa Fe, N.M.: John Muir Publications, 1995)—Formerly my 2 to 22 Days series, each of these eight titles has been thoroughly updated and overhauled for maximum use, flexibility, and user-friendliness. The series is aptly subtitled, *Making the Most Out of Every Day and Every Dollar*. These books cut through all the superlatives. Yes, I know "you can spend a lifetime in Florence," but you've only got 1½ days—here's how to spend them. I update each book in person each year and give you all my favorite hotels, restaurants, local characters, and sightseeing ideas. The Best of Country guides target each country's or region's top 10 to 15 big-city, small-town, or countryside "destinations."

The largest book in the series, *Rick Steves' Best of Europe*, offers step-by-step coverage of Europe's 30 greatest destinations: big cities, small towns, and regions. It lays out the most efficient and exciting mix of "must see" sights, intimate nooks, and offbeat crannies, with lots of great budget places to eat and sleep. It's your blueprint for enjoying the best of Europe, including most of the "Back Doors" described in the last half of this book, complete with city maps, day plans, train schedules, and everything you'll need to get the most out of every day and every dollar.

The seven other titles in the Rick Steves' Best of Country series cover, respectively, the Baltics and Russia; France, along with Belgium and the Netherlands; Germany, Austria, and Switzerland; Great Britain; Italy; Spain and Portugal; and Scandinavia. (Turn to the Appendix for exact destinations covered in each book and information on ordering these and other Rick Steves' titles.)

Europe 101: History and Art for the Traveler, by Gene Openshaw and Rick Steves (4th ed.; John Muir Publications, 1990), is the only fun travelers' guide to Europe's history and art. It's full of boiled-down, practical information to carbonate your sightseeing. Written for smart people

Two Rick Steves art guides to make your sightseeing more meaningful

who were sleeping in their art history classes before they knew they were going to Europe, *101* is the perfect companion to all the survival guides. *Europe 101* is your passport to goosebumps in a practical and easy-to-read manual. After reading five *101* pages on Gothic you can step into a Gothic cathedral and excitedly nudge your partner and say, "Isn't this a great improvement over Romanesque!"

Mona Winks: Self-Guided Tours of Europe's Top Museums, by Rick Steves and Gene Openshaw (John Muir Publications, 1993) gives you a breezy, step-by-step, painting-by-sculpture walk through the best two hours or so of Europe's 20 most overwhelming and exhausting museums and cultural obligations. It covers the great museums of London, Paris, Venice, Florence, Rome, and more. Museums can ruin a good vacation . . . unless you're traveling with *Mona*. Don't assume you can buy good English guidebooks on the spot for Europe's sights and museums. Museum guidebooks available in Europe are too big, too expensive, and so dry that if you read them out loud your lips will chap.

Rick Steves' Phrase Books for French, Italian, German, and Spanish/Portuguese (John Muir Publications) are the only phrase books designed by a guy who speaks only English. That's why they're so good. They're based on 20 years of experience traveling with other phrase books. These are both fun and practical with a meet-the-people and stretch-the-budget focus. Mr. Berlitz knew the languages but he never stayed in a hotel where you needed to ask, "At what time is the water hot?"

Although adequate travel information keeps you afloat, too much information can sink the ship. Rip up your books (bend them over to break the spine and pull chapters out with the gummy edge intact, or just butcher and staple), bringing with you only the applicable pages. There's no point in carrying 120 pages of information on Scandinavia to dinner in Barcelona. When I finish seeing a country, I give my stapled-together chapter on that area to another traveler or leave it in my last hotel's lounge. Consider binding your own hybrid city or region guides by stapling together the same chapters from all the guidebooks you're using. This gives you one small, perfectly focused, disposable "guide-book" to each stop on your trip.

Your hometown library has a lifetime of valuable reading on European culture. (Dewey gave Europe the number 914.) A book on the court of Louis XIV brings Versailles to life. Consider some trip-related recreational reading. After reading *The Agony and the Ecstasy*, you'll visit friends in Florence—who lived there 500 years ago. Paging through photo essays on places you'll be visiting can give you some great, often untouristy, sightseeing ideas. If travel partners divide up their studying, they can take turns being "guide" and do a better job. Your local travel-bookstore stocks good travel literature as well as guidebooks.

MAPS

Drivers need first class maps. Excellent, up-to-date maps with the European place-names spelled as you'll see them in your travels are on sale throughout Europe. I buy the Michelin 970 Europe map at home for overall planning. I pick up the Michelin maps for each region (1/200,000, $3 or $4 each) at gas stations, book shops, and tourist shops as I go. Drivers should consider the popular and inexpensive road atlases for each country (1/200,000 with city maps and indexes).

Spend half a traffic jam learning the key. Handy sightseeing informa-tion such as scenic roads and towns, ruined castles, youth hostels, moun-tain huts, view points, and costs and opening schedules of remote roads can be found on good maps by good map readers.

By train, you can pretty much wing it with the free Eurail map that comes with your pass, and the very cheap little maps of each town that you'll pick up at the local tourist offices as you go.

Maps double as handy excuses to communicate with new friends. You can haul out the map and show them where you've been and where you're going.

TALK WITH OTHER TRAVELERS—IN PERSON OR
THROUGH YOUR COMPUTER

Both in Europe and here at home, travelers love to share the lessons they've learned. Learn from other tourists. Firsthand, fresh information can be good stuff. Keep in mind, however, that all assessments of a place's touristic merit are a product of that person's personality and time there. It could have rained, he could have shared an elevator with the town jerk, or she may have been sick in "that lousy, overrated city." Or he might have fallen in love in that "wonderful" village. Every year, I find travelers hell-bent on following miserable travel advice from friends at home. Except for those found in this book, treat opinions as opinions.

Many great guidebooks are not sold in the United States. Take advantage of every opportunity (such as train or bus rides) to swap information with travelers you meet from other parts of the English-speaking world. This is particularly important when traveling beyond Western Europe.

Cyberspace is filled with on-line travel talk these days. Anyone with access to the Internet can get on-line and share travel information. Compuserve, for instance, offers global weather, news, visa, "Easy Sabre" on-line flight and hotel reservations service, and travel advisory information, plus a travel forum where vagabonds hang out between trips. If you have a particular concern or need, you can get a world of advice through your computer modem. Many travel writers are getting involved with various forums and bulletin board systems. I'm on Compuserve. At Europe Through the Back Door we run a free ETBD bulletin board for travelers wishing to download travel information updates (ETBD BBS: 206-771-1902, 1200 to 2400, 8/N/1). Be wary, however, of mainstream on-line services that sell information. These tend to be little more than infomercials from the tourist industry. Information from a front-door publisher, even from a snazzy on-line service, is still front-door.

Another way to share information with travelers is through newsletters. At ETBD, we publish a free, 64-page quarterly newsletter filled with articles, book updates, and letters from what we call our "Road Scholars." For a free subscription, call 206/771-8303.

CLASSES

The more you understand something, the longer it stays interesting. Those with no background in medieval architecture are the first to get "cathedraled out." Whether you like it or not, you'll be spending lots of time browsing through historic buildings and museums. Those who read or take trip-related classes beforehand have more fun sightseeing in Europe.

There are plenty of worthwhile classes on many aspects of Europe. Although you can get by with English, a foreign language—even a few survival phrases—can only make Europe more fun. History makes Europe come alive. A basic modern European history course makes a dull museum fun. An Eastern European studies class will bring a little order to that demographic chaos.

Art history is probably the most valuable course for the prospective tourist. Don't go to Europe—especially Italy or Greece—without at least having read something on art and architecture.

Many universities have "free" or "experimental" colleges which offer informal classes to the public on travel and foreign languages. I support a handful of "European travel resource centers" throughout the U.S.A. (listed in the ETBD newsletter) which have my latest class, research, and video material; give classes; and do consulting for people planning Back Door European trips much as I do in Seattle.

TRAVEL VIDEOS

The world is anxiously waiting for good travel videos. So far, most travel videos are uninspired destination picture-books or cheesy promos sponsored by tourist boards or hotel groups. Most local TV travel shows shamelessly sell segments and are little more than disguised ads.

I'm doing my best to change this. My 39-week public television series, *Travels in Europe with Rick Steves*, filmed over nine months in Europe (which airs on over 250 PBS stations in the U.S.A.), is now available in fifteen 55- to 80-minute home videos (see Back Door Catalog). Our third 13-week season will air on public television throughout 1995 (scheduling varies; call your local station for air times in your city).

All 24 hours of my slideshow/lectures are now available on 12 different simple but clean, information-packed video slideshows. This includes my one-hour "How to Use Your Railpass" class, a four-hour European-art-for-travelers video slideshow, and two-hour classes on each region of Europe. (See Back Door catalog.)

NATIONAL TOURIST OFFICES

Tourism is an important part of Europe's economy. Each country has a National Tourist Office in the United States with a healthy promotional budget. Switzerland, for instance, figures you'll be doing Alps but you've yet to decide if they'll be French, Swiss, or Austrian Alps. They are happy to send you a free package of promotional information to get you into a Swiss Alps frame of mind. Just send a postcard to the office of each country you plan to visit. Ask for specific information to get more than the general packet. If you want to sleep in a castle on the Rhine, river-raft in France, or hut-hop across Austria, there's a free brochure for you. Ask for an English-language schedule of upcoming events and maps for the country and for each city you'll be visiting. I find it's best to get answers to specific questions by telephone.

European National Tourist Offices in the U.S.A.

Austrian National Tourist Office, P.O. Box 491938, Los Angeles, CA 90049, 310/477-3332, fax 310/477-5141; Box 1142 Times Square, New York, NY 10108-1142, 212/944-6880, fax 212/730-4568. Ask for their "Vacation Kit" map.

Belgian National Tourist Office, 780 3rd Ave., New York, NY 10017, 212/758-8130, fax 212/355-7675. Elaborate phone tree.

British Tourist Authority, 551 5th Ave., 7th Floor, New York, NY 10176, 212/986-2200, fax 212/986-1188. Free maps of London and Britain, which otherwise cost.

Bulgaria-Balkan Holidays, 41 E. 42nd St., New York, NY 10017, 212/573-5536, fax 212/573-5538. Scanty information but friendly advice over the phone.

Denmark (see Scandinavia)

Finland (see Scandinavia)

French Tourist Office, 610 Fifth Ave., #222, New York, NY 10020-2452, may move in 1995; 9454 Wilshire Blvd., #303, Beverly Hills, CA 90212-2967. Rather than mess with their flaky 900 number, write a card with your requests.

German National Tourist Office, 122 E. 42nd St., 52nd Floor, New York, NY 10168, 212/661-7200, fax 212/661-7174; 11766 Wilshire Blvd., Suite 750, Los Angeles, CA 90025, 310/575-9799, fax 310/575-1565. Germany map, Romantic Road map, city maps, Rhine schedules, events, very helpful.

Greek National Tourist Organization, 645 Fifth Ave., 5th floor, New York, NY 10022, 212/421-5777, fax 212/826-6940; 168 N. Michigan Ave. Chicago, IL 60601, tel. 312/782-1084, fax 312/782-1091; 611 West 6th St. #2198, Los Angeles, CA 90017, 213/626-6696, fax 213/489-9744. General how-to booklet, map of Athens, plenty on the islands and ferries.

Hungarian Tourist Board, 1 Parker Plaza, #1104, Fort Lee, NJ 07024, 201/592-8585, fax 201/592-8736.

Irish Tourist Board, 345 Park Ave., 17th floor, New York, NY 10154, 800/223-6470, 212/418-0800, fax 212/371-9052.
Italian Government Travel Office, 630 Fifth Ave., #1565, New York, NY 10111, 212/245-4822, fax 212/586-9249; 12400 Wilshire Blvd., #550, Los Angeles, CA 90025, 310/820-0098, 310/820-6357. Ask for their great art book and city maps.
Luxembourg National Tourist Office, 17 Beekman Place, New York, NY 10022, 212/935-8888, fax 212/935-5896.
Netherlands National Tourist Office, 225 North Michigan Ave., #326, Chicago, IL 60601, tel. 312/819-0300, fax 312/819-1636.
Norway (see Scandinavia)
Polish Tourist Office, 275 Madison Ave., #1711, New York, NY 10016, 212/338-9412, fax 212/338-9283. Regional and city maps.
Portuguese National Tourist Office, 590 Fifth Ave., New York, NY 10036, 212/354-4403.
Scandinavian National Office, 655 3rd Ave., 18th Floor, New York, NY 10017, 212/949-2333, fax 212/983-5260. Good general book on all four countries but be sure to ask for city maps and specifics.
Spanish National Tourist Office, 665 Fifth Ave., New York, NY 10022, 212/759-8822, fax 212/980-1053; 845 N. Michigan Ave., Chicago, IL 60611, 312/642-1992, fax 312/642-9817; 8383 Wilshire Blvd., Suite 960, Beverly Hills, CA 90211, 213/658-7188, fax 213/658-2061.
Sweden (see Scandinavia)
Swiss National Tourist Office, 608 Fifth Ave., New York, NY 10020, 212/757-5944, fax 212/262-6116; 150 North Michigan Ave., #2930, Chicago IL 60601, 312/630-5840, fax 312/630-5848; 222 North Sepulveda Blvd., #1570, El Segundo, CA 90245, 310/335-5980, fax 310/335-5982. Great maps and service.
Turkish Tourism Office, 821 United Nations Plaza, New York, NY 10017, 212/687-2194, fax 212/599-7568.

Middle Eastern and North African Tourist Offices in the U.S.

Egyptian Tourist Office, 630 Fifth Ave., Suite 1706, New York, NY 10111, 212/332-2570, fax 212/956-6439.
Israel Government Tourist Office, 350 Fifth Ave., New York, NY 10118, 212/560-0650 (relocating in 1995).
Moroccan National Tourist Office, 20 East 46th St., #1201, New York, NY 10017, 212/557-2520, fax 212/949-8148.

Pack Light Pack Light Pack Light

The importance of packing light cannot be overemphasized, but for your own good, I'll try. You'll never meet a traveler who, after five trips, brags, "Every year I pack heavier." The measure of a good traveler is how light he or she travels. You can't travel heavy, happy, and cheap. Pick two.

Limit yourself to 20 pounds in a carry-on-size bag. A 9" x 22" x 14" bag fits under most airplane seats. That's my self-imposed limit. At ETBD we've taken thousands of people of all ages and styles on tours through Europe. Half of them are my parents' age. We allow only one carry-on bag. For many, this is a radical concept. "9 by 22 by 14 inches? That's my cosmetics kit!" But they manage and they're glad they did. Now these former nonbelievers are the fanatical nucleus of my pack-light cult. And after you enjoy that sweet mobility and freedom, you'll never go any other way.

You'll walk with your luggage more than you think you will. Before leaving home, give yourself a test. Pack up completely, go into your hometown, and be a tourist for an hour. Fully loaded, you should enjoy window shopping. If you can't, stagger home and thin things out.

When you carry your own luggage, it's less likely to get lost, broken, or stolen. (Many travelers claim that airline employees rifle through checked luggage.) A small bag sits on your lap or under your seat on the bus, taxi, and airplane. You don't have to worry about it, and when you arrive, you leave immediately. It's a good feeling. When I land in London, I'm on my way downtown while everyone else still stares anxiously at the luggage carousel. When I fly home, I'm the first guy the dog sniffs.

Too much luggage marks you as a typical tourist. It slams the Back Door shut. Serendipity suffers. Changing locations becomes a major operation. Con artists figure you're helpless. Porters are a problem only to those who need them. With one bag hanging on your back, you're mobile and in control. Take this advice seriously.

BACKPACKADEMIA—WHAT TO BRING?

How do you fit a whole trip's worth of luggage into a small suitcase or rucksack? The answer is simple: bring very little.

Spread out everything you think you'll need on the living room floor. Pick up each item one at a time and scrutinize it. Ask yourself, "Will I really use this snorkel and fins enough to justify carrying them around all summer?" Not "Will I use them?" but "Will I use them enough to feel good about carrying them through the Swiss Alps?" I'd buy them in

Greece and give them away before I'd carry that extra weight through the Alps.

Don't pack for the worst scenerio. Risk shivering for a day rather than taking a heavy coat. Think in terms of what you can do without—not what will be handy on your trip. When in doubt, leave it out. I've seen people pack a whole summer's supply of deodorant, nylons, or razors, thinking you can't get it there. The world's getting awfully small; you can buy Dial soap in Sicily. Tourist shops in major international hotels are a sure bet whenever you have difficulty finding some personal item.

Whether I'm traveling for three weeks or three months, I pack exactly the same. Rather than take a whole trip's supply of toiletries, I take enough to get started and look forward to running out of toothpaste in Bulgaria. Then I have the perfect excuse to go into a Bulgarian department store, shop around, and pick up something I think might be toothpaste. . . .

RUCKSACK OR SUITCASE?

Whether you take a rucksack or a small soft-sided suitcase with a shoulder strap is up to you. Packing light applies equally to rucksack or suitcase travelers. Hard-sided suitcases with one-inch wheels are impractical. Bobbling down the cobblestones of Rothenburg, you'll know what I mean. (Those physically unable to lug a bag around manage well by bungee-cording their bag to a collapsible trolley with larger wheels.)

Older travelers traveling like college kids—light, mobile, footloose and fancy-free, wearing their convertible suitcase rucksacks—have nothing to be ashamed of

Most young-at-heart travelers go the rucksack route. If you are a suitcase person who would like the ease of a rucksack without forgoing the "respectability" of a suitcase, use the new and popular convertible suitcase/rucksacks with zip-away shoulder straps. These carry-on-size bags give you the best of both worlds. I live out of one of these for three months at a time. (See the Back Door Catalog at the back of this book.)

Unless you plan to camp or sleep out a lot, a sleeping bag is a bulky security blanket. Even on a low budget, bedding will be provided. I'd rather risk being cold one or two nights out of the summer than carry a sleeping bag just in case I might need it. Don't pack to camp unless you're going to camp.

Without a sleeping bag, a medium-size rucksack is plenty big. Start your trip with it only two-thirds full to leave room for picnic food and souvenirs. Sturdy stitching, front and side pouches, padded shoulder straps, and a low-profile color are rucksack virtues. Many travelers figure an internal frame and a weight distribution hip belt are worth the extra money and get a more high-tech bag for around $130. Packing very light, I manage fine without the extra weight and expense of these fancier bags.

Entire books are written on how to pack. It's really quite simple: use stuff bags (one each for toiletries, underwear and socks, bigger clothing items and towel, chocolate, camera gear and film, and miscellaneous stuff such as a first-aid kit, stationery, and sewing kit). Be careful to choose clothes that either don't wrinkle or look good wrinkled. (Give everything a wet rehearsal by hand-washing and drying at home.) Roll and rubber-band clothes or zip-lock in airless baggies to minimize wrinkles.

CLOTHING

The bulk of your luggage is clothing. Minimize by bringing less and washing more often. Every few nights you'll spend ten minutes doing a little wash. This doesn't mean more washing, it just means doing it little by little as you go.

Bring dark clothes that wash and dry quickly and easily. You should have no trouble drying clothing overnight in your hotel room. I know this sounds barbaric, but my body dries out a damp pair of socks or shirt in a jiffy. It's fun to buy clothes as you travel—another reason to start with less.

For winter travel, I pack just about as light. The only difference is a down or pile coat, long johns (capeline), mittens, hat, and an extra pair of socks and underwear since things dry slower. Pack with the help of a climate chart. (See the Appendix.) Assume you'll be outside in the cold for hours at a time.

Recommended Clothing
(for summer travel)

Two pairs of long pants; one lightweight cotton and another super-lightweight for hot and muggy big cities and churches with modest dress codes. Jeans are too hot for summer travel. Linen is great.

Walking shorts with plenty of pockets—doubles as a swimsuit for men.

Two T-shirts or short-sleeved shirts, cotton/polyester blend.

Two long-sleeved shirts, same blend.

Dark, warm sweater—for warmth and for dressing up; it never looks wrinkled and is always dark, no matter how dirty it is.

Light, water-resistant windbreaker jacket. Gore-tex is good if you expect rain.

Underwear and socks—five sets, quick-dry.

One pair of shoes—sturdy vibram-type sole, good traction, well broken in, light, cool. I like Rockports or Easy Spirits. Sturdy, low-profile-colored tennis shoes with a good tread are fine, too.

A tie (instant respectability), cheap necklace, colorful scarf, pair of lime green socks and suspenders. Anything lightweight that can break the monotony and make you look snazzy.

Especially for women—summer dress or skirt, swimsuit, sandals, robe or nightshirt.

The tourists' Europe is casual. I have never felt out of place at symphonies, operas, or plays wearing a decent pair of slacks and a good-looking sweater. Cultural events are more formal outside of the tourist season. Of course, there are situations where more formal attire would be in order, but the casual tourist rarely encounters these. Wear color-coordinated clothing. Layer it for warmth.

Many travelers are concerned about appropriate dress. European women wear dresses more often than pants. American women generally feel fine in pants, but in certain rural and traditional areas, they'll fit in better and may feel more comfortable in a skirt or dress. Tennis shoes and jeans mark you as an American. Frankly, so what? Europeans will know anyway. I fit in and am culturally sensitive by watching my manners, not the cut of my pants.

A handful of sacred places, mostly in southern Europe (such as St. Peter's in Rome), have modest dress requirements: basically, no short pants or bare shoulders. Although these dress codes deserve respect, they are rarely enforced. If necessary, it's usually easy to improvise some modesty (a hairy-legged man can wear a nearby tablecloth as a kilt and his partner in a sleeveless blouse can wear maps on her shoulders).

Go casual, simple, and very light. Remember, in your travels you'll meet two kinds of tourists—those who pack light and those who wish they had. Say it once out loud: "PACK LIGHT."

OTHER THINGS TO PACK

Indicates items available through Back Door Catalog at end of book.

*Hostel sheet. Youth hostels require one. You can bring your own or rent a sheet there for $2 to $5. If you plan to do a lot of hosteling, bring your own regular bedsheet or buy a regulation hostel sheet (basically, a normal bedsheet sewn together like a sleeping bag, $18) at the first hostel you visit. This sheet can double as a beach or picnic blanket, is handy on overnight train rides, shields you from the dirty blankets in mountain huts, and will save you money in other dorm-type accommodations, which often charge extra for linen or don't provide it at all.

Poncho or parka. Hard-core vagabonds use a plastic poncho, large enough to protect you and your pack in a rainstorm, that can open flat to serve as a ground cloth for sleeping on or for a beach or picnic blanket. Otherwise, a good weatherproof parka is your best bet. For summer travel, I wing it without rain gear. But pack for rain in Britain.

*Small day-pack. A small nylon day-pack is great for carrying your sweater, camera, literature, picnic, and so on, while you leave your large bag at the hotel or train station. Fanny-packs (small bags with thief-friendly zippers on a belt) are a popular alternative but should not be used as money belts.

A good paperback. There's plenty of empty time on a trip to either be bored or enjoy some good reading. Books such as *Iberia* for Spain and Portugal, *The Agony and the Ecstasy* for Italy, *The Greek Treasure* (Stone) for Greece and Turkey, a book of Wordsworth poems for England's Lake District, and *Trinity* for Ireland are real trip bonuses.

*European map. An overall map best suited to your trip's needs. Get maps for specific local areas as you go.

*Money belt. Essential for the peace of mind it brings; you could lose everything except your money belt, and the trip could still go on. Lightweight, low-profile beige, and water-resistant is best.

Money. Bring travelers checks, a credit card, driver's license, a few personal checks, and some hard cash. Bring American dollars (Europeans get a kick out of seeing George Washington fold up into a mushroom) for situations when you want to change only a few bucks and not a whole traveler's check. I bring a few $1, $10, and $20 bills. And bring one foreign bill worth about $50 for each country you plan to visit so you can function easily until you can get to a bank. (See Chapter 5, Finances and Money, for details.)

Picnic supplies. A small tablecloth to give your meal some extra class (and to wipe the knife on), salt and pepper, a cup, a damp facecloth in a baggie for cleaning up, and a Swiss Army-type knife with a corkscrew and can opener.

Water bottle. The plastic half-liter mineral-water bottles sold throughout Europe are reusable and work great.

*Earplugs. If night noises bother you, you'll grow to love a good set of plugs such as Sleep-well. Europe has more than its share of night noises.

Zip-lock baggies. 1,001 uses; great for leftover picnic food, containing wetness, and bagging potential leaks before they happen. Bring a variety of sizes. The two-gallon jumbo size is handy for packing.

First-aid kit. (See Chapter 7, Health.)

Medicine. In original containers, if possible, with legible prescriptions.

Wristwatch. A built-in alarm is handy. Otherwise, pack a small travel alarm clock, too. Cheap hotel wake-up calls are unreliable.

Extra eyeglasses, contact lenses, and prescriptions. Many find their otherwise-comfortable contacts don't work in Europe. Bring your glasses just in case.

*Toiletries kit. Sinks in cheap hotels come with meager countertop space and anonymous hairs. With a small, easy-to-hang-on-a-hook-or-mirror zipper bag this is no problem. Put all squeeze bottles in zip-lock baggies, since pressure changes in flight cause even good bottles to leak. Consider a vacation from cosmetics. Bring a little toilet paper.

Soap. Not all hotels provide soap. A plastic squeeze bottle of concentrated, multi-purpose, biodegradable liquid soap is handy for laundry and much more.

*Clothesline. For hanging up clothes to dry in your hotel room. The handy twist kind needs no clips.

Small towel. You'll find small bath towels at all moderate hotels, most cheap hotels, and no youth hostels. Although $30-a-day travelers will often need to bring their own towel, $60-a-day folks won't. I bring a thin hand-towel for the occasional need. Face towels are rare in Europe. Many recommend the quick-drying "Sport Sponge" which is like a chamois in a plastic box.

Sewing kit. Clothes age rapidly while traveling. Your flight attendant may have a freebie for you.

Travel information (minimal). Rip out appropriate chapters, staple them together, store in a zip-lock baggie. When you're done, give them away.

Postcards or small picture-book from your hometown, and family pictures. A zip-lock baggie of show-and-tell things is always a great conversation piece with Europeans you meet.

Address list. For sending postcards home and collecting new addresses. Taking a whole address book is not packing light. Consider typing your mail list onto a sheet of gummed address labels before you leave. You'll know exactly who you've written to, and the labels will be perfectly legible.

Journal. An "empty book" filled with the experiences of your trip will be your most treasured souvenir. Use a hardbound type designed to last a lifetime, rather than a spiral notebook. Attach a photocopied calendar page to visualize your itinerary and jot down reminders; keep a traveler's check and expenses log in the appendix.

Mini radio or cassette player. Partners bring one, with Y-jacks for two sets of earphones. Many travelers enjoy a microcassette recorder to record things such as pipe organs, tours, and journal entries. And some recorders have radios, which add a whole new dimension to your experience.

Small notepad and pen. A tiny notepad in your back pocket is a great organizer, reminder, and communication aid (on sale in European stationery stores).

Camera and film, protective and polarizing lens, mid-range zoom lens, cleaning tissue, and a trip's worth of film all stored not in a camera bag but in a low-profile nylon stuff bag.

Consider these options: a pillowcase (cleaner and possibly more comfortable to stuff your own), inflatable pillow (or "neck nest") for sunsnoozing, light warm-up suit (for pajamas, evening lounge outfit, instant modest street wear, smuggling things, and going down the hall), Teva-type sandals or thongs, small "squeeze-me"-type flashlight, collapsible cup, stronger light bulbs (buy in Europe to give your cheap hotel room more brightness than the 25- to 40-watt norm), an envelope of envelopes, paper, tiny miscellaneous office supplies, safety pins, sunglasses. Bug juice for France and Italy. Gifts (local kids love T-shirts and baseball cards; gardeners appreciate flower seeds).

Electricity: Try to go without electrical gear. Travelers requiring electricity need a converter to let their American appliance work on the dif-

One carry-on-size bag?? Here's exactly what I traveled with for two months (photos taken naked in a Copenhagen hotel room): convertible 9" x 22" x 14" suitcase/rucksack; lightweight nylon day-bag; ripped-up sections of three guidebooks, notes, maps, journal, tiny pocket notepad; wristwatch; tiny Swiss Army knife; pocket-size radio with earplugs; money belt (with one credit card, driver's license, passport, plane ticket, train pass, cash, traveler's checks, sheet of phone numbers and addresses); toiletries stuff bag (with squeeze bottle of shampoo, soap in a plastic container, battery shaver, toothbrush and paste, comb, nail clippers, travel alarm clock, squeeze bottle of liquid soap for clothes); camera gear stuff bag (with camera, polarizer lens, cleaning tissues, film); miscellaneous bag with family photos, tiny odds and ends; Gore-tex rain jacket in a stuff bag; long khaki cotton pants (button pockets, no wallet), super-light long pants, shorts, five pairs of socks, three underpants, long-sleeved shirt, two short-sleeved shirts, T-shirt; stuff bag with sweater, half a bath towel, plastic laundry bag; a light pair of shoes (Rockports).

ferent European current (many travel accessories come with a built-in converter) and an adapter to let the American plug fit into the European wall. British plugs have three big flat prongs. Continental European plugs have two small round prongs. Many sockets in Europe are recessed into the wall. Your adapter should be small enough to fit into this hole in order for your prongs to connect. Cheap converters with built-in adapters have prongs that are the right size but are unable to connect. Many cheap hotel rooms have only one outlet, occupied by the lamp. Hardware stores sell cheap three-bangers which let you keep the lamp on and still plug in your toothbrush and Game Boy.

2

Designing an Itinerary

If you have any goals at all for your trip, make an itinerary. I never start a trip without having every day planned out. Your reaction to an itinerary may be, "Hey, won't that shackle me to a rigid plan at the expense of spontaneity and freedom!" Not necessarily. Although I always begin a trip with a well-thought-out plan, I maintain my flexibility and make plenty of changes. An itinerary forces you to see the consequences of any spontaneous change you make while in Europe. For instance, if you spend two extra days in the sunny Alps, you'll see that you won't make it to, say, the Greek Isles. With the help of an itinerary, you can lay out your goals, maximize their potential, avoid regrettable changes, and impress your friends.

By planning an itinerary, you can deal thoughtfully with issues like weather, crowds, culture shock, health maintenance, fatigue, festivals, and inefficient transportation. The result is a more enjoyable trip.

An Efficient Plan

Establish a logical flight plan. You can avoid needless travel time and expense by flying "open-jaws." With open-jaws, you fly into one port and out of another at no extra expense. You usually pay just half the round-trip fare for each port. Even if your open-jaws flight plan is more expensive than the cheapest round-trip fare, it may save you lots of time and money when surface connections are figured in. For example, you could fly into London, travel east through whatever interests you in Europe, and fly home from Athens, eliminating the costly and time-consuming return to London. Your travel agent will know where flying open-jaws is economical.

Moderate the weather conditions you'll encounter. Match the coolest month of your trip with the warmest area, and vice versa. For example, for a spring and early summer trip, enjoy comfortable temperatures through-

A romantic stroll through St. Mark's Square in July. Venice is sinking under its peak-season crowds.

out by starting in the southern countries and working your way north. If possible, avoid the midsummer Mediterranean heat. Spend those weeks in Scandinavia or the Alps. (See the Appendix for climate charts.)

Avoid tourist crowds. Europe is most crowded in July and August. Try to avoid this peak season crush by scooting your trip into the more relaxed shoulder months (May, early June, and September). Or arrange your activities to minimize crowds.

Consider, for instance, a six-week European trip beginning June 1, half with a Eurailpass to see the famous sights and half visiting relatives in Scotland. It would be wise to do the Eurail section first, enjoying those precious last three weeks of relatively uncrowded shoulder season, and then spend time with the family during the last half of your vacation, when Florence and Salzburg are teeming with tourists. Salzburg on June 10 and Salzburg on July 10 are two very different cities.

Although the tourist crowds can generally be plotted on a bell-shaped curve peaking in July and August, there are odd glitches that individual country guidebooks normally explain. For instance, Paris is empty and easy during its July and August holiday season, while a busy convention schedule packs it out in September. And hotels in Scandinavia are cheapest in the summer when travel—which, up there, is mostly business travel—is down.

In much of Europe (especially Italy and France), cities are partially shut down in July and August when local urbanites take their beach break. You'll hear that these are terrible times to travel but it's really no big deal. You can't get a dentist and many laundromats are shut down, but tourists are basically unaffected by Europe's mass holidays unless they happen to be caught on the wrong road on the 1st or 15th of the month (when vacations often start or finish) or are crazy enough to compete with all of Europe for a piece of Riviera beach.

Punctuate a long trip with rest periods. Constant sightseeing is grueling. Schedule a peaceful period every two weeks. If your trip is a long one, schedule a vacation from your vacation in the middle of it. Most people need several days in a place where they couldn't see a 42museum or take a tour even if they wanted to. A stop in the mountains or on an island, in a friendly rural town, or a visit with a relative is a great way to revitalize your tourist spirit. Alternate intense big cities with villages and countryside (for example, break your tackling of Venice, Florence, and Rome with easygoing time in the hill towns or on the Riviera).

Leave some slack in your itinerary. Don't schedule yourself too tightly (a common tendency). Everyday chores, small business matters, transportation problems, constipation, and planning mistakes deserve about one day of slack per week in your itinerary.

Don't overestimate your powers of absorption. Especially on your first trip, European travel can be intense, bombarding your senses from all sides day after day. Each day is packed with experiences and memories. It may be thrilling, but you can take only so much. You have a saturation point. Rare is the tourist who doesn't become somewhat jaded after several weeks of travel. At the start of my trip, I'll seek out every great painting and cathedral I can. After two months, I find myself "seeing" cathedrals with a sweep of my head from the doorway, and I probably wouldn't cross the street for a Rembrandt. Don't burn out on mediocre castles, palaces, and museums. Sightsee selectively. Look ahead on your itinerary. Save your energy for the biggies.

See countries in order of cultural hairiness. For instance, if you plan to see Britain, the Alps, Greece, and Turkey, do it in that order so you'll grow steadily into the more intense and crazy travel. England, compared to any place but the U.S.A., is pretty dull. Don't get me wrong–it's a great place to travel. But go there first, when cream teas and roundabouts will be exotic. And you're more likely to enjoy Turkey if you work gradually east.

Save your good health. Visit countries that may be hazardous to your health (North Africa or the Middle East) at the end of your trip so you won't needlessly jeopardize your healthy enjoyment of the safer countries. If you're going to get sick, do it at the end of your trip so you can recover at home, missing more work—not vacation.

Assume you will return. This Douglas MacArthur approach is a key to touristic happiness. You can't really see Europe in one trip. Don't even try. Enjoy what you're seeing. Forget what you won't get to on this trip. If you worry about things that are just out of reach, you won't appreciate what's in your hand. I'm planning my twentieth three-month European vacation, and I still need more time. I'm happy about what I can't get to. It's a blessing that we can never see all of Europe.

The nine factors listed above must be weighed and thoughtfully juggled until you arrive at a plan that best fits your needs. There are several trade-offs (for instance, you may have to choose between optimal weather and minimal crowds). You can't have the best of each point.

Your Best Itinerary in Eight Steps

1. Read up on Europe, talk to travelers, study. You must have some friends who'd love to show you their slides. What you want to see is determined by what you know (or don't know). Identify your personal interests. World War II buffs will study up on battle sites, and McGregors will locate their clan in Scotland.

2. List all the places you want to see, keeping these factors in mind:

a) Minimize redundancy. On a quick trip, focus on only one part of the Alps. Oxford and Cambridge are redundant. Choose one (Cambridge).

b) Have a reason for every stop. Don't go to Casablanca just because it's famous.

c) Minimize travel time required. When you must cut something, cut to save the most mileage. For instance, if Amsterdam and Berlin are equally important to you and you don't have time for both, cut the destination which saves the most miles, Berlin.

d) Minimize clutter. A so-so sight (San Sebastian) breaking a convenient night train (Paris-Madrid) into two half-day journeys is clutter. Once you've settled on a list, be satisfied with your efficient plan and focus any more study and preparation only on places that fall along your proposed route.

Step 2 example: Places I want to see:

London	Alps	Bavaria	Florence	Amsterdam
Paris	Rhine	Rome	Venice	Greece

3. Establish a general structure or framework. Decide on the length of your trip and where you'll fly into and out of. Research flights for the cheapest and most convenient dates and ports.
Step 3 example: I can escape for 23 days. Cheapest places to fly to: London, Frankfurt, Amsterdam.

4. Determine your mode of transportation. Do this not solely on economical terms but by analyzing what is best for the trip you envision.
Step 4 example: Since I'm traveling alone, going so many miles, and spending the majority of my time in big cities, I'd rather not mess with a car. I'll use a Eurailpass.

5. List the sights you want to see in a logical geographical order. Consider minimizing miles, an open-jaws flight plan, your mode of transportation, getting maximum overnight train rides (if you want them), the best weather, and the least crowds. Pin down any places that you have to be on a certain date (and ask yourself if it's really worth the stifle).

6. Write in the number of days you'd like to stay in each place, considering transportation time. Eurailers often use night trains (NT) to save time and money whenever possible.
Steps 5 and 6 example: Logical order and desired time in each place:

Days	
3	London
1	English Channel crossing
5	Paris (NT)
3	Alps (NT)
2	Florence
3	Rome (NT)
7	Greece (NT)
2	Venice (NT)
3	Munich/Bavaria
3	Romantic Road/Rhine Cruise
_4_	Amsterdam
36	*Notes: I have 23 days for my vacation. If I eliminate Greece, I'll still need to cut six days. Open-jaws into London and out of Amsterdam is economical. "Logical" order may be affected by night-train possibilities.*

7. Adjust by cutting, streamlining, or adding to fit or fill your time limitations. Consider economizing on car rental or Eurailpass. For instance, try to manage a 23-day trip on a 15-day train pass by doing London, Paris, and Amsterdam before or after you use the pass.

Step 7 example: Itinerary adjusted to time limitations:
Days

4	London (NT)
3	Paris (NT)
3	Alps (NT)
1	Florence
2	Rome (NT)
2	Venice (NT)
3	Munich/Bavaria
2	Romantic Road/Rhine Cruise
_3_	Amsterdam

23   Twenty-three days with a 15-day Eurailpass (valid from last day in Paris until first day in Amsterdam).

Europe's Top 23 Days

8. Fine tune. Study guidebooks. Be sure crucial sights are open the day you'll be in town. Maximize festival and market days. Ask your travel agent which flight departure days are cheapest. Write out a day-by-day itinerary.

> *Step 8 example: According to my guidebook, I must keep these points in mind as I plan my trip. London: theaters closed on Sundays, Speaker's Corner is Sunday only. Paris: most museums are closed on Tuesdays, Versailles and the Orsay Museum closed on Mondays. Florence: museums closed Mondays. Dachau: closed Mondays. Amsterdam: museums closed on Mondays and most shops closed on Monday mornings. Note that I'm choosing to pay a little extra on my flight to let my trip stretch over the weekends and minimize lost work-time. Yes, I may be a zombie on that first Monday back, but hey, what's more important?*

S	1	*Leave home. (You'll arrive the next day in Europe.)*
S	2	*Arrive in **London**. Buy train ticket to Paris and a Tuesday eve theater ticket at Victoria Station. See Speaker's Corner. Take orientation bus tour.*
M	3	*Sightsee all day London.*
T	4	*Sightsee all day London. Leave bags at station. See play. NT.*
W	5	*Arrive early in **Paris**. Find hotel. Explore Latin Quarter, Louvre, Champs-Elysées, take bus orientation tour.*
T	6	*Sightsee all day Paris, Orsay museum, Notre-Dame; Evening at Montmartre.*
F	7	*Early side trip to Versailles. Afternoon in Paris. NT.*
S	8	*Arrive early in Interlaken. All day **Alps** hike.*
S	9	*Free in Alps, Lauterbrunnen, Gimmelwald, Schilthorn.*
M	10	*Cruise Swiss lakes, afternoon and evening in Bern. NT.*
T	11	***Florence**. Check museum hours carefully. David closes at 2:00, Uffizi open all day.*
W	12	*Early train to **Rome**. Set up near station. Explore classical Rome.*
T	13	*Visit Vatican, St. Peter's, famous night spots. NT.*
F	14	*Arrive early in **Venice**. Slow boat down Grand Canal to St. Mark's. All day free.*
S	15	*All day free in Venice. NT.*
S	16	*Arrive early in **Munich**. Reserve Romantic Road bus tour at station. Sightsee all day. Evening beer hall.*
M	17	*All-day side trip to Neuschwanstein Castle.*
T	18	*Most of day in Salzburg (90-minute train from Munich).*

W   19   **Romantic Road** *bus tour from Munich to Frankfurt,*
           stopping at Rothenburg and Dinkelsbühl. Short train to
           Bacharach. Check boat schedule.
T   20   *Cruise the* **Rhine,** *Bacharach to St. Goar (one hour) for the*
           best castles. Tour Rheinfels castle.
F   21   *Early train to* **Amsterdam.** *Call to reconfirm flight home.*
           Orientation canal tour, nightlife.
S   22   *All day free in Amsterdam for museums, shopping, or bike*
           ride into countryside.
S   23   *Catch plane, Amsterdam—U.S.A.*

ITINERARY MISCELLANY

Hit as many festivals, national holidays, and arts seasons as you can. This takes some study. Ask the national tourist office of each country you'll visit for a calendar of events. An effort to hit the right places at the right time will drape your trip with festive tinsel.

Carefully consider travel time. Driving, except on super-freeways, is slower than in the United States. Borrow a Thomas Cook Continental Train Timetable from your travel agent or library and get an idea of how long various train journeys will take. Learn which trains are fast, and avoid minor lines in southern countries.

Remember that most cities close many of their major tourist attractions for one day during the week. It would be a shame to be in Milan only on a Monday, for instance, when Leonardo da Vinci's *Last Supper* is out to lunch. Mondays are closed days for major tourist sights in many cities, including Amsterdam, Brussels, Munich, Lisbon, Florence, Rome, and Naples. Paris closes the Louvre and many other sights on Tuesdays.

Minimize "mail stops." Arrange mail pickups before you leave. Most American Express offices offer a free clients' mail service for those who have an AmExCo card or traveler's checks (even just one). Have mail marked "Clients' Mail." They'll hold for 30 days unless the envelope instructs otherwise. For the "Travelers' Companion" booklet listing participating AmExCo offices, call 800/528-4800. Friends or relatives are fine for mail stops. Every city has a general delivery service. Pick a small town where there is only one post office and no crowds. Have letters sent to you in care of "Poste Restante." Tell your friends to print your surname in capitals, underline it, and omit your middle name. If possible, avoid the Italian male, I mean mail.

To avoid mail pick-up commitments on a long trip, have mail sent to a friend or relative at home. When you know where you'll be you can telephone them from Europe with instructions on where to mail or FedEx your letters. Second-day services are reliable and reasonable.

With the ease of phoning these days, I've dispensed with mail pick-ups altogether.

High Speed Town-Hopping

When I tell people that I saw three or four towns in one day, many either say or think, "That guy must be crazy! Nobody can really see several towns in a day!" Of course, it's folly to go too fast, but many stopworthy towns take only an hour or two to cover. Don't let guilt feelings tell you to slow down and stay longer if you really are finished with a town. There's so much more to see in the rest of Europe! Going too slow is as bad as going too fast.

If you're efficient and use the high-speed town-hopping method, you'll amaze yourself at what you can see in a day. Let me explain with an example.

You wake up early in Town A. Checking out of your hotel, you have one sight to cover before your 10:00 train. (You checked the train schedule the night before.) After the sightseeing and before getting to the station, you visit the open-air market and buy the ingredients for your brunch and pick up a Town B map and tourist brochure at Town A's tourist office.

From 10:00 to 11:00, you travel by train to Town B. During that hour you'll have a restful brunch, enjoy the passing scenery, and prepare for Town B by reading your literature and deciding what you want to see. Just before your arrival, you put the items you need (camera, jacket, tourist information) into your small day-pack and, on arrival, check the rest of your luggage in a locker. Virtually every station has storage lockers or a baggage check desk.

Before leaving Town B's station, write down on a scrap of paper the departure times of the next few trains to Town C. Now you can sightsee as much or as little as you want and still know when to comfortably catch your train. You're ready to go. You know what you want to see. You aren't burdened by your luggage. And you know when the trains are leaving.

Town B is great. After a snack in the park, you catch the 2:30 train. By 3:00, you're in Town C, where you repeat the same procedure you followed in Town B. Town C just isn't what it was cracked up to be, so after a walk along the waterfront and a look at the church, you catch the first train out.

By 5:30, you arrive in D, the last town on the day's agenda. The man in the station directs you to a good budget pension just two blocks down the street. You're checked in and unpacked in no time, and after a few moments of horizontal silence, it's time to find a good restaurant and eat dinner. After a meal and an evening stroll, you're ready to call it a day. Writing in your journal, it's clear: you packed a lot of travel into this day. You spent it high speed town-hopping.

The Home Base Strategy

The home base strategy is a clever way to make your trip itinerary smoother, simpler, and more efficient. Set yourself up in a central location and use that place as a base for day trips to nearby attractions.

The advantages of this approach are:

1. The home base approach minimizes set-up time (usually an hour). Searching for a good hotel can be exhausting, frustrating, and time-consuming. And hotels often give a better price, or at least more smiles, for longer stays. Many private homes don't accept those staying only one night.

2. You are freed from your luggage. Being able to leave your luggage in the hotel lets you travel frisky and with the peace of mind that you are set up for the night.

3. You feel comfortable and "at home" in your home base town. This feeling takes more than a day to get, and when you are changing locations every day or two, you may never enjoy this important rootedness. Home basing allows you to sense the rhythm of daily life.

4. The home base approach allows you to spend the evening in a city, where there is some exciting nightlife. Most small countryside towns die after 9:00 p.m. If you're not dead by 9:00, you'll enjoy more action in a larger city.

5. My *Best of Europe* and my six *Best of* Country guidebooks are made to order for this home base approach. They give you the necessary step-by-step details for all of Europe's best home bases.

Europe's generally frequent and punctual train and bus systems (which often operate out of a hub anyway) make this home base strategy very practical. With a train pass, the round-trips are free; otherwise, the transportation is reasonable, often with reductions offered for round-trip tickets. Use train time productively.

If this home base strategy really appeals to you, a handy series of books features day-trips from various major hubs. The king of the day-trippers, Earl Steinbicker, has written *Daytrips in Holland/Belgium/ Luxembourg, Daytrips in Britain, Daytrips in France, Daytrips in Italy,* and *Daytrips in Germany* (published by Hastings House).

Here are some of my favorite home base cities and some of their best day trips:

Madrid	Toledo, Segovia, El Escorial
Amsterdam	Alkmaar, the Arnhem Folk Museum, Hoge Veluwe

	Park with its Kröller-Müller Museum, Scheveningen, Delft, most of the Netherlands
Copenhagen	Lund, Malmo, Roskilde, Helsingor, Odense
Paris	Reims, Versailles, Chartres, Fontainebleau, Chantilly, Giverny
London	Oxford, Stratford, Cambridge, Salisbury (Stonehenge), Bath, and many others
Avignon	Nimes, Arles, the Rhône Valley
Florence	Pisa, Siena, San Gimignano, Arezzo, many small towns
Munich	Salzburg, Berchtesgaden, Augsburg, Neuschwanstein, Linderhof, and Herrenchiemsee (three of King Ludwig's castles), many small Bavarian towns including Oberammergau, Wies Church
Sorrento	Naples, Capri, Pompeii, Herculaneum, Amalfi Coast, Paestum

Minimizing Peak Season Crowds

Except for the crowds, summer is a great time to travel. Here are a few crowd-minimizing tips that I've learned over many peak seasons in Europe.

Get off the beaten path. So many people energetically jockey themselves into the most crowded square of the most crowded city in the most crowded month (St. Mark's Square, Venice, July) and complain about the crowds. You could be in Venice in July and walk six blocks behind St. Mark's Basilica, step into a café, and be greeted by Venetians who act as though they've never seen a tourist.

Be an early bird. Walk around Rothenburg's ancient wall before breakfast. Joggers and crack-of-dawn walkers enjoy a special look at wonderfully medieval cities as they yawn and stretch and prepare for the daily onslaught of the twentieth century.

Arrive at the most popular sights early or late in the day to avoid tour groups. Germany's fairy-tale Neuschwanstein castle is cool and easy with relaxed guides and no crowds at 8:30 or 9:00 in the morning. And very late in the day, when most tourists are long gone—exhausted in their rooms or searching for dinner—I linger alone, taking artistic liberties with Europe's greatest art in empty galleries.

See how the locals live. Residential neighborhoods rarely see a tourist, much less a crowd of them. Browse through a department store. Buy a copy of the local *Better Homes and Thatches* and use it to explore that particular culture. Dance with the locals while your pizza cooks. Play street soccer with the neighborhood gang.

Spend the night. Popular day-trip destinations near big cities and resorts like Toledo (near Madrid), San Marino (near huge Italian beach

It's Tuesday at Versailles, and these people now have time to read their guidebooks, which warn: On Tuesday, most Paris museums are closed and Versailles has very long lines.

resorts), San Gimignano (near Florence), and Rothenburg (near Frankfurt) take on a more peaceful and enjoyable atmosphere at night when the legions of day-trippers retreat to the predictable plumbing of their big-city hotels. Small towns normally lack hotels big enough for tour groups and are often inaccessible to large buses. So they will experience, at worst, midday crowds.

Know the alternatives. Keep in mind that accessibility and promotional budgets determine a place's fame and popularity just as much as its worthiness as a tourist attraction. For example, Zurich is big and famous—with nothing special to offer the visitor. The beaches of Greece's Peloponnesian Peninsula offer the same weather and water as the highly promoted isles of Mykonos and Ios but are out of the way, not promoted, and wonderfully deserted.

Develop a minimize-the-crowd mentality. Avoid museums on their weekly free days when they're most crowded. And because nearly all Parisian museums are closed on Tuesday, nearby Versailles, which is open, is predictably crowded—very crowded. And it follows that Parisian museums are especially crowded on Mondays and Wednesdays. While crowds at the Louvre can't be avoided altogether, some thought before you start your trip can help. If you're traveling by car or bike, take advantage of your mobility by leaving the well-worn tourist routes. The Europe away from the train tracks seems more peaceful and relaxed. It's one step behind the modern parade and overlooked by the Eurail mobs.

Off-Season Europe? The Pros and Cons

Each summer, Europe greets a stampede of sightseers and shoppers with cash registers cocked and ready. Before jumping into the peak season pig-pile, consider an off-season trip.

In travel industry jargon, the year is divided into peak season (late June, July, and August), shoulder season (May, early June, September, early October), and off-season (the rest of the year). Each time has its pros and cons. While shoulder season is the best mix of decent weather and minimal crowds, off-season (November through April) is worth considering.

The advantages of winter travel are many. Off-season airfares are much cheaper. With fewer crowds in Europe, you'll sleep cheaper. Many fine hotels drop their prices. Budget hotels will have plenty of vacancies. And, while many of the cheap alternatives to hotels will be closed, those still open are usually empty and therefore more comfortable.

Off-season adventurers wander all alone through Leonardo's home, sit quietly in Rome's Forum, stroll desolate beaches, and enjoy log fires and a cup of coffee with the guards in French châteaus. Lines in tourist offices and at bank exchange desks will be gone. Although many popular tourist-oriented parks, shows, and tours will be closed, the real arts seasons, such as the Vienna Opera's, will be rolling, and the people you deal with will be more relaxed.

But winter travel has its drawbacks. Because much of Europe is in Canadian latitudes, the days are very short. It's dark by 5:00. The weather can be miserable—cold, windy, and drizzly—and then turn worse. But just as summer can be wet and gray, winter can be crisp and blue, and even into mid-November, hillsides blaze with colorful leaves.

Off-season hours are limited. Some sights close down entirely, and most operate on shorter hours (such as 10:00-5:00 rather than 9:00-7:00), with darkness often determining the closing time. Winter sightseeing is fine in big cities, which bustle year-round, but it's more frustrating in small tourist towns, which often shut down entirely. In December, many beach resorts are shut up tight as canned hams. In the north, Europe's wonderful outdoor evening ambience, a fair-weather phenomenon, hibernates. English-language tours, common in the summer, are rare off-season, when most visitors are natives. Tourist information offices normally stay open year-round but with shorter hours in the winter. A final disadvantage with winter travel is loneliness. The solo traveler won't have the built-in camaraderie of other travelers that he or she would find in peak season.

To thrive in the winter, you'll need to get the most out of your limited daylight hours. Start early, eat a quick lunch. Tourist offices close early, so call ahead to double-check hours and confirm your plans. Pack for the cold and wet—layers, rainproof parka, gloves, wool hat, long johns, waterproof shoes, and an umbrella. Remember, cold weather is colder when you're outdoors trying to enjoy yourself all day long. Use undershirts to limit the washing of slow-drying heavy shirts.

Accommodations will be easy to find. I conducted an 18-day November tour of Germany, Italy, and France with 22 people and no room reservations. We'd amble into town around 5:00 p.m. and always found 22 beds with breakfast for our $20-per-bed budget. Cheap hotels are not always adequately heated in the off season.

Most hotels charge less in the winter. To save some money, arrive late, notice how many empty rooms they have (keys on the rack), let them know you're a hosteler (student, senior, honeymooner, or whatever) with a particular price limit, and bargain from there. The opposite is true of big-city business centers (especially in Scandinavia) which are busiest and most expensive outside of summer holiday time.

Italy, so crowded in peak season, is back to normal; its hill towns are brisk and glorious. The Alps are crowded with skiers. It's easy to rent gear, but the snow often comes late. Off-season hiking is disappointing. Travel north of the Alps suffers more in the winter.

A Few Itinerary Considerations

A Six-week Plan: Here's an efficient overall plan for a six-week introduction to Europe: Fly into London. Spend four days there. Rent a car for a week in England (Bath, Cotswolds, Oxford, Blenheim, Warwick, Iron Bridge Gorge, North Wales). Drop it in North Wales. Boat to Dublin, and take a look at West Ireland. Begin your 21-day Eurailpass to catch the included 20-hour boat ride from southeast Ireland to France. Spend three weeks touring central Europe (Paris, Benelux, Rhine, Romantic Road, Bavaria, Swiss Alps, Italy, boat to Athens where train pass expires). Relax in the Greek Isles before flying home from Athens.

To Greece or Not to Greece?

Many itineraries are really stressed out by people who underestimate the travel time involved and wrongly plug in Greece. It takes two days of solid travel—if all goes well—to get from Rome to Athens and two days to get back. If all you've got is a week for Greece, I question the sanity of traveling four days for a couple of days in huge, overrated, and polluted Athens and a quick trip to an island, especially when you consider that 500 years before Christ, southern Italy was called Magna Graecia

(Greater Greece). You can find excellent Greek ruins at Paestum just south of Naples. Greece is great, but it needs more time or an open-jaws plan that lets you fly out of Athens.

In the summer, Greece is the most-touristed, least-explored country in Europe. It seems that nearly all of its tourists are in a few places, while the rest of the country casually goes about its traditional business.

Getting to Greece: The Brindisi (Italy)–Patras (Greece) Boat Connection

Brindisi, the spur on the Italian boot, is a funnel where thousands of Eurailers (who get to cross for free, except taxes and supplement), back-packers, and other travelers fall out to catch the boat to Greece. Boats sail throughout the year. Three boats make the 18-hour crossing each day in the summer. Boats depart in the evening. Getting on the boat is no problem without reservations except at peak season time (Italy to Greece—late July to mid-August; Greece to Italy—about August 11 to September 3), when it's a mob scene.

Make Reservations at a Travel Agency in Italy or Greece

Prices for the Italy-Greece connection vary between the competing lines. If you don't have a Eurailpass, compare prices before you sail. Without a Eurailpass, you may find it cheaper and easier to depart from Bari. Brindisi-Patras tickets cost about $50 for basic deck class. "Deck" is taken literally and it's chilly at night, even in summer. If it rains, they open up the otherwise closed restaurant. For more comfort and a warm night inside you can pay an extra $10 for an assigned airplane-type seat, $25 for a *couchette* bed, and $40 for a bed in a four-person stateroom. During the mid-July to mid-August rush crossing prices are $20 higher. Students and those under 26 save about $10. Cars cost $40 and bikes go for free. A Eurailpass gives you a free deck-class passage but you'll have to pay a reservation fee, a port tax, and if traveling in the summer, a peak season supplement. You get a free stopover halfway on the lush and popular island of Corfu if you have "S.O. Corfu" marked on your ticket.

For a summer crossing, make a reservation at least three days in advance from an Italian (or Greek) travel agency (easy but with a small service charge). On arrival in Brindisi, follow the mob on the half-mile stampede from the train station down the city's main drag to the dock. You'll see several agencies along the way which sell tickets and handle boat-related business such as reserving staterooms, collecting port taxes and Eurail supplements, and distributing boarding passes. Expect con artists to tell you your Eurailpass doesn't work on today's boat or some similar nonsense. Then, at the port, go through another round of

customs-related bureaucracy and board your boat. The crossing from
Patras to Brindisi features similar headaches. Off-season, I'd go to the
port and bargain. Student discounts are often given to anyone who asks
for them.

The Patras-to-Athens connection is a 5-hour train ride or a frightening 3-hour bus ride. (The fear welds some special friendships on the
bus.) Buses meet the boat, and (even with a railpass) I'd buy the $10 bus
ticket with the boat ticket. Consider putting off Athens and hooking
south through the fascinating Peloponnesian Peninsula. Start with the
hour-long bus ride (leaving Patras every two hours) to Olympia.

Brindisi is well connected by night trains from Rome, Milan,
Florence (via Bologna), and Venice. If you have time to kill (boats leave
in the evening, overnight trains arrive early), do it in Lecce, a hot, noble,
but sleepy city of lovely baroque facades and Roman ruins; pick up a
town map at the three-star hotel in front of the station (a $2, 40-minute
train ride south, hourly departures) or at nearby beaches. Mobbed by
transit tourists throughout the summer, Brindisi has arranged an hourly
"Sea Bus Service" that shuttles those on their way to Greek beaches to
one last Italian beach, either Punta Penne or Apani (the better, just 30
minutes north of town on the Adriatic coast). The beaches are fair; the
water is clean. Get information in Brindisi on the bus service (when you
arrange for your boat trip).

How Much Italy?
Italy is Europe's richest cultural brew. Get out of the Venice-Florence-
Rome crush and enjoy its hill towns and Riviera ports. Italy intensifies as
you go south. If you like Italy as far south as Rome, go farther. It gets
better. If Italy is getting on your nerves by the time you get to Rome,
don't go farther south. It gets worse. For most first-timers, after a week
in Italy, Switzerland starts looking really good. The travelers I respect
most count Italy as one of their favorite countries.

By train, you might consider seeing everything except Venice on your
way south. Enjoy a last romantic late evening in Rome before catching the
midnight train north, arriving in Venice at 8:00 a.m., when it's very easy to
find a room.

Crossing the English Channel
Even with the completion of the"Chunnel" (English Channel tunnel),
there are still many channel-crossing options to sort through. From
London, consider it a train ride. Don't worry about which boat or which
harbor, just buy a train ticket that says "London-Paris" or whatever. The
boat is figured in. If the train is late, the boat will wait. Usually, the train is

Crossing the English Channel

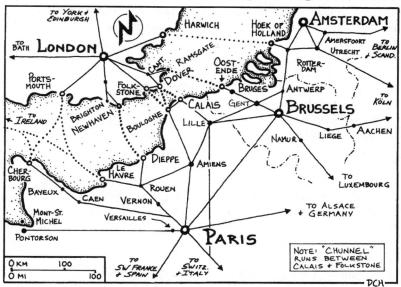

The "Chunnel" goes roughly between Folkstone and Calais

a nonstop express to the boat dock. Catch the train (the correct London station is listed on the ticket). When everyone gets out, follow them through customs and onto the boat. Stay on the boat until the first stop (that's Europe). Go through customs and find your train among the many that await the boat passengers fanning out to various points in Europe.

This train-boat-train trip is cheaper overnight but a miserable trip with the two tedious changes and border crossings. Still, this is my preferred way to arrive in Paris—inexpensively and in time to find a room. To get to Amsterdam, you can choose the longer boat ride (via the Hoek of Holland) or the longer train ride (via Oostende, Belgium). I sleep well on the longer boat ride. On any boat, you can normally buy a $25 stateroom from a staff person upon boarding. Anyone can wander downstairs and take a shower.

Many travelers get excited about the hovercraft or jet-foil crossing. This pound-pound, stay-seated-please "flight" takes 40 minutes (compared to 2½ hours on the ferry) but has none of the romance of the boat crossing and is around $10 more expensive. A little choppiness cancels the flight and you're back on the big slow-boat standing in line for a refund. I don't mess with them and just enjoy the crossing.

In London, get information and tickets at the Sealink office in

Victoria Station. If you're under 26, save money by getting a Transalpino ticket (office near Victoria Station). Reservations are rarely needed. Bus-boat connections from London to Paris, Amsterdam, and Brussels are one-third cheaper than train-boat trips (and one-third less comfortable).

Paris to Amsterdam, Not Skipping Brussels
Anyone taking the 5-hour train ride from Paris to Amsterdam will stop in Brussels, but few even consider getting out. Each train stops in Brussels. There's always another train coming in an hour or so. Leave an hour early, arrive an hour late, and give yourself two hours in one of Europe's underrated cities. Luckily for the rushed tourist, Brussels Central Station has easy money-changing and baggage storage facilities and puts you 2 blocks (just walk downhill) from the local and helpful tourist office, a colorful pedestrian-only city core, Europe's greatest city square (Grand Place), and its most overrated and tacky sight, the *Mannekin Pis* (a much-photographed statue of a little boy who thinks he's a fountain). Brussels has three stations: Nord, Midi, and Central. Ask if your train stops at Central (middle) Station. If you have to get off at Nord or Midi, there are local subway-like connecting trains every few minutes. You'll have no trouble finding English-speaking help.

The Best of Germany in a Week
The most interesting sightseeing route through Germany today follows the most prosperous trade route of medieval Germany: down the Rhine, along the "Romantic Road" from Frankfurt to Munich, and through Bavaria near the Austrian border.

While many travelers spend too much time cruising the Rhine and not enough time in castles, I'd cruise just the best hour (St. Goar to Bacharach) and get some hands-on castle experience crawling through what was the Rhine's mightiest fortress, Rheinfels. (See Back Doors.)

From the end of this most interesting section of the Rhine, it's a short train ride to Frankfurt where you can catch the Romantic Road bus tour (see Back Doors) through the medieval heartland of Germany to Munich. From there the old trading route crossed the Alps (today's Brenner Pass) and headed into Italy—which makes sense for today's travelers as well.

Itinerary Priorities, Country by Country
Use this chart to get ideas on how speedy travelers can prioritize limited sightseeing time in various countries. Add places from left to right as you build plans for the best of that country in 3, 5, 7, 10, or 14 days. In

some cases the plan assumes you'll take a night train. So according to this chart, the best week in Britain would be spread between London, Bath, the Cotswolds, and York.

Country	3 days	5 days	7 days	10 days	14 days
Europe	Forget it	London, Paris	Amsterdam	Rhineland, Swiss Alps	Munich, Venice
Britain	London, Bath	Cotswolds	York	Edinburgh	N. Wales, Cambridge
France	Paris, Versailles	Loire, Chartres	Normandy	Provence, Nice, Riviera	Chamonix, Burgundy
Germany	Rhine, Munich	Romantic Road, Rothenburg	Bavarian sights	Berlin	Black Forest, Mosel, Köln
Austria	Salzburg, Vienna	Hallstatt	Danube Valley	Prague	—
Switzerland	Bern and Berner Oberland	French Switzerland, Murten	Appenzell Luzern	Zermatt	—
Italy	Rome	Florence, Venice	Italian Riviera	Hill towns	Milan and Lake Como
Scandi-navia	Copen-hagen, Oslo, Stockholm	Bergen, "Norway in a Nutshell"	More time in capitals	Helsinki, Tallinn	Aero, more fjords
Spain/ Portugal	Madrid, Toledo	Lisbon	Barcelona	Andalusia, Sevilla	Algarve
Turkey	Istanbul, Bosphorus	Ephesus, West Coast	Konya, Pamukkale	Cappadocia	Ankara, more Istanbul

Note: See the Appendix for seven sample 22-day itineraries, destinations that are covered in the Rick Steves' Country Guides.

3

Transportation

Flying to Europe

Flying to Europe is a great travel bargain—for the well-informed. The rules and regulations are confusing and always changing, but when you make the right choice, the price is right.

Travel agents save you money. Save money and headaches by putting your energy into finding the right agent, not the cheapest flight. Rather than trying to keep up with the ever-changing world of airline tickets, I rely on the experience of my agent—who specializes in budget European travel—to come up with the best combination of economy, reliability, and convenience. These days, with so many airlines on the brink, the judgment of an experienced travel agent is more important than ever.

You cannot save money by buying directly from the airlines. Airlines won't work the rules in your favor. They won't remind you that if you left a day earlier you could get in on shoulder season and save $50. And these days, consolidators enable agencies to get their full mark-up and still beat the airline's regular ticket prices.

There is no great secret to getting to Europe for next to nothing. Basically, assuming you know your options, you get what you pay for. There's no such thing as a free lunch in the airline industry. Remember this equation:

Dollars saved = discomfort + restrictions + inflexibility

Regular fare is very expensive. You get the ultimate in flexibility, but I've never met anyone spending his own money who flew that way.

Consolidator tickets are cheapest. Consolidators buy huge numbers of tickets from airlines at deep discounts; they wholesale these tickets to your travel agent, who can then sell you a flight to Europe actually cheaper than the airline itself can sell that ticket. Consolidator tickets often waive the normal advance-purchase and minimum- and maximum-stay requirements that come with other budget tickets. But remember the "dollars saved" equation. Consolidator tickets are cheaper because they come with several disadvantages: They are "non-

endorsable," meaning no other airline will honor that ticket if your airline is unable to get you home. It won't give you frequent-flier points. And, if the airline drops its ticket prices (which often happens), you are stuck with what was, but no longer is, a cheap fare. (Generally, this last point is true even of non-consolidator tickets.)

Fly open-jaws. It's been ten years since I flew into and out of the same European city. I fly "open-jaws," into one city and out of another. The fare is figured simply by taking half of the round trip fare for each of those ports. I used to fly into Amsterdam, travel to Istanbul, and (having rejected the open-jaws plan because flying home from Istanbul cost $200 more than returning from Amsterdam) pay $200 to ride the train for two days back to Amsterdam to catch my "cheap" return flight. Now I see the real economy in spending more for open-jaws. Open-jaws is cheapest when one airline can cover each segment of the round-trip journey.

Budget airfares are restrictive. Most are nonchangeable and non-refundable. Some offer changes on the return dates for a penalty of about $100. Return dates can sometimes be changed for a fee in Europe by telephoning your airline. If that fails, I've found that airlines become more flexible if you go to their European office in person with a good reason for your need to change the return date. If you're really dying to get home early, go out to the airport. If you're standing at the airport needing to go home two days before your ticket says you will and they have seats open on that flight, regardless of the rules, they may figure that they can win a happy customer and gain two more days to try to sell that seat that's about to go empty anyway if they just let you fly. (Besides, at that point, it's the easiest way to get rid of you.)

Courier flights get some travelers to Europe for free. But for most, this is a pipe-dream. You need to be very flexible and live in the right cities (such as New York or San Francisco). *Travel Unlimited* is a good monthly newsletter which keeps flying cheapskates on top of the latest in courier and discount airfares ($25/year, Box 1058, Allston,

MA 02134). Lately, courier services have found that they can get away with charging a percent of the ticket value and the whole notion has become less exciting.

Chartered flights can save you money. A charter company offers flights on certain days in and out of the same city. In return for fitting into their limits, you can fly cheaper than on scheduled airlines. For instance, in Seattle the cheapest and only direct way to fly to Amsterdam is on the reliable Martinair charters. If their dates work for me, and I don't mind starting and finishing in Amsterdam, this is a good deal. Remember, charter companies can cancel flights that don't fill. Anyone selling charters promotes an air of confidence, but at the last minute any flight can be "rescheduled" if it won't pay off. Those who "saved" by booking onto that charter are left all packed with nowhere to go. Get an explicit answer to what happens if the flight is canceled. "It won't be canceled" is not good enough. Some charter companies are reliable. Ask about their track record. How many flights did they cancel last year?

Scheduled airlines are most reliable. If for some reason they can't fly you home, they find you a seat on another airline (unless you have a discounted ticket marked "non-endorsable"). You won't be stranded in Europe.

THOUGHTS ON THE FEAR OF FLYING

Like many people, I'm afraid to fly. But despite my fears, I still fly. It always scares me because I can't, for the life of me, imagine how a plane can take off and land safely. I always think of the little rubber wheels splashing down on a rain-soaked runway and then hydroplaning out of control. Or the spindly landing gear crumbling. Or if not that, then the plane tilting just a tad, catching a wing tip, and the whole thing flipping into a flaming trip finale.

I always remind myself that every day 60,000 planes take off and land safely in the United States alone. The pilot and crew fly daily, and they don't seem to be terrified. They let an important guy like Bill Clinton fly all over the place and nothing has happened to him.

I guess it's a matter of aerodynamics. Somehow, air has mass and the plane maneuvers itself through that mass. I can understand a boat coming into a dock—maneuvering through the water. That doesn't scare me. So I tell myself that a plane's a boat with an extra dimension to navigate, and its water is a lot thinner.

Turbulence scares me, too. A United pilot once told me that he'd have bruises from his seat belt before any turbulence really bothered him. I never met anybody who came home complaining about turbulence bruises.

Still, every time the plane comes in for a landing I say a prayer, close my eyes, and take my pen out of my shirt pocket so it won't impale me if something goes wrong. And every time I stick my pen back in my shirt pocket, I feel thankful.

Flights within Europe

Europe is a small continent notorious for its big plane fares. But with recent deregulation, there are more budget airfares than ever before. These days, before buying any long surface ticket, drop by a travel agency to check out budget airfares. A plane ticket can even be cheaper than the train. While your hometown travel agent may be able to get you a decent fare, the super-cheap fares for inter-European flights can be purchased only in Europe. Remember, extending your flight from the United States deeper into the Continent (without stopovers) can be very cheap. Explore your open-jaws possibilities before purchasing your ticket.

London, Amsterdam, Paris, and Athens have many "bucket shops"— agencies that clear out plane tickets at super-discounted prices. If your travel plans fit the tickets available and you're flexible enough to absorb delays, these can be a great deal. Any cheap flight from London must be purchased from an agency in London. (This can be done by telephone and credit card from the U.S.A.) *Let's Go: Europe* lists a few of the bigger bucket shops. Your local library should have a London newspaper. Look in the classifieds under "Travel" to see what's available. Tickets from London to the Mediterranean can be incredibly—and reliably—cheap. There are normally special deals on flights from London to Dublin, Paris, or Frankfurt which are as inexpensive as surface travel. Athens also has some great buys on tickets to London, Western Europe, and the Middle East. Aeroflot and other Eastern European airlines have some cheap flights, often on a roundabout route. On Aeroflot you may get a forced stopover in Moscow with a free hotel.

Train and Eurailpass Skills

The European train system makes life easy for the American visitor. The great trains of Europe shrink that already small continent, making the budget whirlwind or far-reaching tour an exciting possibility for anyone.

Generally, European trains go where you need them to go and are fast, frequent, and inexpensive (faster and more frequent in the north, less expensive but slower in the south). By using the train, you could easily have dinner in Paris, sleep on the train, and have breakfast in Rome, Madrid, Munich, or London.

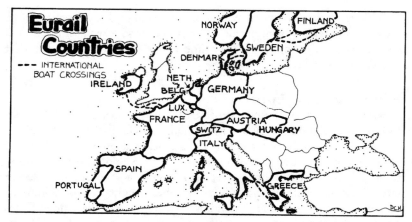

Eurail covers all countries shown on this map (not Britain)—over 100,000 miles of track!

THE EURAILPASS, COUNTRY PASSES, AND TICKET OPTIONS

The popular Eurailpass gives you unlimited first-class travel on all public railways in 17 European countries (see the map). It gives you Western Europe (except Britain) by the tail: you travel virtually anywhere, anytime without reservations. Just step on the proper train, sit in an unreserved seat, and when the uniformed conductor comes, flash your pass. For the average independent first-timer planning to see lots of Europe (from Norway to Portugal to Italy, for instance), the Eurailpass is usually the best way to go.

Eurailpasses are available in many forms: Consecutive-day first-class passes in durations ranging from 15 days to 3 months, cheaper first-class "flexipasses" giving you any 5, 10, or 15 days out of a two-month period, 15 days first-class "saverpasses" giving traveling couples a discount, and various consecutive-day and flexi second-class "youth passes" for those under 26. There are even "rail and drive" passes which let you economically mix rail travel and car rental.

In the last few years there has been a confusing explosion of different country and regional passes, giving the train traveler quite a mess to sort through for the best value. The Eurailpass is slowly pricing itself out of business. While it's still a good deal for those planning to travel widely through Europe, every year car rentals and single-country train passes are becoming better deals for more and more travelers.

In a nutshell, you need to travel from Amsterdam to Rome to Madrid and back to Amsterdam to justify the purchase of a one-month Eurailpass. Two people on a 3-week car trip (3,000 miles) and two

Europe by rail: time and cost

Connect the dots, add up the cost, and see if a railpass is right for your trip.

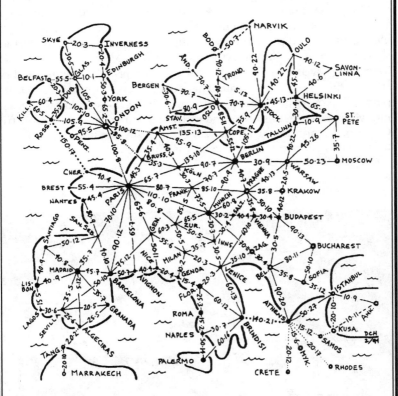

The first number between cities = cost in US$ for a one-way, second-class ticket. The second number = number of hours the trip takes.

● = Cities served by railpass.

○ = Cities **not** served by railpass. (For example, if you want to go from Munich to Prague, you'll need to pay extra for the portion through Czechoslovakia.)

••• = Boat crossings covered by Eurailpass.

•••• = Boat crossings **not** covered by Eurailpass.

Fares and times are from the 1994 Eurail Tariff and may vary slightly. For approx. first-class prices, multiply prices shown by 1½. In some cases faster trains (like the TGV in France) are available.

Travelers under age 26 can receive up to 50% off the second-class fares shown. Eurailpasses are not honored in Great Britain, Turkey, or Eastern Europe (except Hungary and former East Germany).

people each using a 3-week first-class Eurailpass will spend about the same, around $600 each. Travelers focusing on one country will save with that country's pass. If you're planning on patching together several country passes, however, you're probably better off with the Eurailpass.

This is confusing and tedious material, but if you're planning to do Europe by rail on limited money this book's "European Railpass Guide" chapter (in the Appendix) is very important. It's the only information source where you'll find everything for sale in the U.S.A. compared with everything for sale in Europe, researched and produced by me and my staff—whose goal is to create smart consumers (as well as sell a few passes). It covers everything you need to know to walk knowledgeably into your travel agent's office and order the best train pass for your trip. Or to order nothing at all and save money by buying point-to-point tickets or some train pass on sale only in Europe.

Eurail freedom. My idea of good travel is being on this platform in Hamburg. In 5 minutes, the train on track 7 is going to Berlin. In 6 minutes, a train will leave from track 8 for Copenhagen. And I've yet to decide which train I'll be on.

For a complete listing of prices and an analysis of all the various rail-passes available for European travel in 1995, see the Appendix. I'll go directly to general rail travel skills here.

GETTING ON THE RIGHT TRACK

Armed with a train pass or ticket, Europe becomes the independent traveler's playground. Most will master the system simply by diving in and learning from their mistakes. To learn quicker . . . from someone else's mistakes . . . here are a few tips:

Multistation Cities. Most large European cities and some small ones have more than one train station. Brussels has three stations. Even little Interlaken has two. Be sure you know whether your train is leaving from Interlaken East or Interlaken West, even if that means asking what might seem like a stupid question. A city's stations are easily connected by train, subway, or bus.

Pay attention. Get help. Managing on the trains is largely a matter of asking questions, letting people help you, assuming things are logical, and thinking. I always ask someone on the platform if the train is going where I think it is. (Point to the train and ask, "Roma?") Uniformed train personnel can answer any question you can communicate. Speak slowly, clearly, and with caveman simplicity. Be observant. If the loud-speaker comes on, gauge by the reaction of those around you if the announcement concerns you and if it's good or bad news. If, after the babble, everyone dashes across the station to track 15, you should assume your train is no longer arriving on track 2.

Train-splitting. Never assume the whole train is going where you are. Each car is labeled separately, because cars are usually added and dropped here and there all along the journey. I'll never forget one hot afternoon in the middle of Spain. My train stopped in the middle of nowhere. There was some mechanical rattling. Then the train pulled away leaving me all alone in my car . . . all alone in La Mancha. Ten minutes later another train came along, picked up my car, and I was on my way. To survive all of this juggling easily, just check to be sure that the city on your car's nameplate is your destination. The nameplate lists the final stop and some (but not all) of the stops in between.

The configuration of most trains is charted in little display cases on the platform next to where your train will arrive. As you wait, study the display to note where the first-class and sleeping cars are, whether there's a diner, and which cars are going where on your train. Also, some train schedules will say, in the fine print, "Munich-bound cars in the front, Vienna-bound cars in the rear." Knowing which cars you're eligible for can be especially handy if you'll be competing with a mob for a seat. If I expect a real scramble, I'll stand on a bench at the far end of the track and study each car as the train rolls by, noting where the most empty places are. If there are several departures within an hour or so and the first train looks hopeless, I'll wait for the next.

Baggage. This has never been a problem for me on the train. Every car has plenty of room for luggage. The average tourist never checks baggage. Simply carry it on and heave it up onto the racks above the seats. I've seen Turkish families moving all their worldly goods from Germany back to Turkey without checking a thing. They just packed everything into the compartment they reserved and were on their way.

People complain about the porters in the European train stations. I think they're great—I've never used one. People who travel with more luggage than they can carry deserve porters.

Photo by Andrea Hagg

Luggage is never completely safe. There is a thief on every train (union rules) planning to grab a bag (see "Theft and the Tourist" section in Chapter 11). Don't be careless. Before leaving my luggage in a compartment, I establish a relationship with everyone there. I'm safe leaving it among mutual guards.

Using Train Time Wisely. Train travelers, especially Eurailers, spend a lot of time on the train. This time can be dull and unproductive, or you can make a point of using travel time wisely. This helps pass the time and frees up more leisure time away from the train. It makes no sense to sit bored on the train and then, upon arrival, sit in the station for an hour reading your information and deciding where to go for hotels and what to do next.

Spend train time studying, reading, writing postcards or journal entries, eating, organizing, cleaning, doing anything you can so you don't have to do it after you arrive. Talk to local people or other travelers. There is so much to be learned. Europeans are often less open and forward than Americans. You could sit across from a silent but fascinating and friendly European for an entire train ride, or you could break the ice by quietly offering a cigarette or some candy; showing your Hometown, U.S.A. postcards; or asking a question. This may start the conversation flowing and the friendship growing.

Station Facilities. Europe's train stations can be one of the independent traveler's best and most helpful friends. Take advantage of the assistance they can offer. Virtually every station has storage lockers and/or a luggage-checking service where, for about $2, you can leave your luggage. People traveling light can fit two rucksacks into one storage locker, cutting their storage costs in half.

In this French train station arrivals and departures are clearly listed. Who says you can't read French? The small schedule in the middle lists trains that are about to depart. The Tabac stand sells candy, phone cards, newspapers, and often subway and bus tickets.

Most stations have comfortable waiting rooms. The bigger stations are equipped with day-hotels for those who want to shower, shave, rest, and so on. If, for one reason or another, you ever need a free, warm, and safe place to spend the night, a train station (or an airport) is my choice. Some stations boot everyone out from about midnight to 6:00 a.m. Ask before you bed down. Thieves work the stations in the wee hours. Be on guard.

Every station has a train information office eager (or, at least, able) to help you with your scheduling. I usually consult the timetables myself first and write down my plan, then confirm this with the information desk. Written communication is easiest and safest.

Tourist information and room-finding services are usually either in the station (in the case of major tourist centers) or nearby. If this is my first stop in a new city, I pick up a map with sightseeing information and, if I need it, advice on where to find budget accommodations. Often, the station's money-changing office is open long after others have closed for the night. Train stations are major bus stops, so connections from train to bus are generally no more difficult than crossing the street. Buses go from the stations to the nearby towns that lack train service. If you have a bus to catch, be quick, since many are scheduled to connect with the train and leave promptly.

Safety. Physically, I feel completely safe on trains. Women should use discretion, however, in choosing a compartment for an overnight ride. Sleeping in an empty compartment in southern Europe is an open invitation to your own private Casanova. Choose a room with a European granny or nun in it. That way you'll get a little peace, and he won't even try.

TRAIN SCHEDULES—BREAKING THE CODE

Learning to decipher train schedules will make life on Europe's rails a lot easier. These list all trains that come to and go from a particular station each day, and are clearly posted in two separate listings: departures (the ones we're concerned with, usually in yellow) and arrivals (which you'll rarely use, normally in white).

You'll also find airport-type departure schedules that flip up and list the next eight or ten departures. These often befuddle travelers who don't realize that all over the world there are four easy-to-identify columns listed, and these are always: destination, type of train, track number, and departure time. I don't care what language they're in, you can accurately guess which column is what.

Train schedules are a great help to the traveler—if you can read them. Many Eurail travelers never take the time to figure them out.

Here are a few pointers and a sample map and schedule to practice on.
Understand it. You'll be glad you did.

You'll find these confusing-looking charts and maps in the Cook
Timetable and in display cases in every station. Find the trip you want
to take on the appropriate train map. Your route will be numbered,
referring you to the proper timetable. That table is the schedule of the
trains traveling along that line, in both directions (a. = arrivals,
d. = departures).

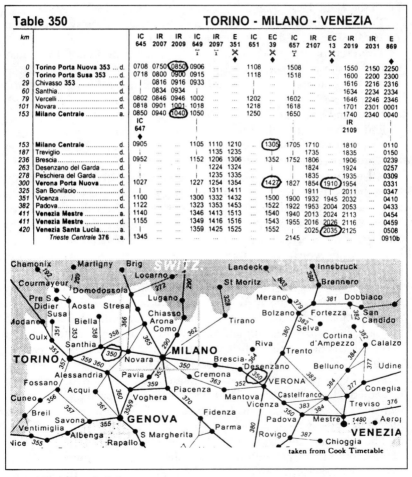

Sample train schedule

As an example, let's go from Turin to Venice (the local spellings are always used, in this case, Torino and Venezia). This is #350 on the map. So refer to table 350. Locate your starting point, Torino. Reading from left to right, you will see that trains leave Torino for Venezia at 7:08, 9:06, 15:08, 15:50, and 22:50. Those trains arrive in Venezia at 11:55, 13:59, 19:55, 21:25, and 5:08, respectively. (European schedules use the 24-hour clock.) Note that Venezia has two stations (Mestre and the more central Santa Lucia). As you can see, not all Torino departures go all the way to Venezia. For example, the 8:50 train only goes to Milan, arriving at 10:40. From there, the 10:50 train will get you to Venezia by 13:59.

This schedule shows an overnight train. You could leave Torino at 22:50 (10:50 p.m.) and arrive in Venezia by 5:08.

Train schedules are helpful in planning your stopovers. For instance, this table shows a train leaving Torino at 8:50, arriving in Milan at 10:40. You could spend two hours touring Milan's cathedral, catch the 13:05 train for Verona (arrive at 14:27, see the Roman Arena and Juliet's balcony), and hop on the 19:10 train to arrive in Venezia by 20:35.

Remember: each table shows just some of the trains that travel along that track. Other tables feed onto the same line, and the only person who knows everything is the one at the train station information window. Let that person help you. He or she can fix mistakes and save you many hours. Each table has three parts: a schedule for each direction and a section explaining the many exceptions to the rules (not shown here). You never know when one of those confusing exceptions might affect your train. Schedule symbols also indicate problem-causing exceptions, such as which trains are first-class only, sleepers only, or charge supplements. An X means you'll have to change trains, crossed hammers indicate the train goes only on workdays, a little bed means the train has sleeping compartments, an R in a box means reservations are required for that departure, and a cross means the train goes only on Sundays and holidays. Use the tables, but always confirm your plans with the person at the information window. Just show your plan on a scrap of paper (i.e., Torino-Milano, 8:50-10:40; Milano-Verona, 13:05-14:27) and ask, "OK?" If your plan is good, the information person will nod, direct you to your track, and you're on your way. If there's a problem, he or she will solve it. Uniformed train employees on the platforms or on board the trains can also confirm your plans.

The Thomas Cook Continental Timetable is a handy tool that has become my itinerary-planning bible. Published several times a year, it has nearly every European train schedule in it, complete with maps. (To order the up-to-date Cook Timetable, about $29 postpaid, and/or to get their fine free travel guide catalog, call the Forsyth Travel Library, 800-FORSYTH.) I find that the schedules vary more with the season than with the year. I don't rely on them for the actual train I'll take, but I use an old one (which your travel agent might loan or give to you) at home before I leave to familiarize myself with how to read train schedules and to learn the frequency and duration of train trips I expect to take. Every station and most trains will be equipped with the same schedule, updated. Although I don't carry the bulky "Cook Book" with me, those who do find it very handy.

New train schedule computers (in most Italian stations and spreading quickly across Europe) will save you many long waits in station information lines. Use them to understand all your options. Indicate your language, departure and arrival points, and rough time of departure, and all workable connections will flash on the screen.

HOW TO SLEEP ON THE TRAIN

The economy of night travel is tremendous. You slaughter two birds with one stone. Sleeping while rolling down the tracks saves time and money, both of which, for most travelers, are limited resources. The first concern about night travel is usually, "Aren't you missing a lot of beautiful scenery? You just slept through half of Sweden!" The real question should be "Did the missed scenery matter, since you gained an extra day for hiking the Alps, biking through tulips, or island-hopping in the Greek seas?" Maximize night trips.

To assure a safer and uninterrupted night's sleep, you can usually reserve a sleeping berth known as a *couchette* (pronounced koo-SHETT) at least a day in advance from a travel agency, at the station ticket counter, or, if there are any available, from the conductor on the train. For about the cost of a cheap hotel bed ($15), you'll get sheets, pillow, blankets, a fold-out bunk bed in a compartment with three to five other people, and, hopefully, a good night's sleep.

As you board, you'll give the attendant your *couchette* voucher, rail pass or ticket, and passport. He deals with the conductors and customs officials and keeps the thieves out so you can sleep soundly and safely. While some trains (especially in France) have cushier first-class *couchettes* (double rather than triple bunks for the same cost if you have a first-class ticket), most *couchettes* are the same for both classes. While the top bunk gives you more privacy and luggage space, it can be hotter and stuffier than lower bunks and a couple of inches shorter (a concern if you're 6'2" or taller). You can request smoking or non-smoking. Some countries offer to limit the six-bed compartment to four passengers for a small extra fee.

Shoestring travelers avoid the $15 cost of a *couchette* and just sack out for free, draping their tired bodies over as many unoccupied seats as possible. Trying to sleep on an overnight train ride without a bed can be a waking nightmare.

One night of endless headbobbing, swollen toes, and a screaming tailbone, sitting up straight in a dark eternity of steel wheels crashing along rails, trying doggedly—yet hopelessly—to get comfortable will teach you the importance of finding a spot to stretch out for the night. This is an art that vagabond night travelers cultivate. Those with the greatest skill at this game sleep. Those not so talented will spend the night gnashing their teeth and squirming for relief.

A traditional train car has about ten compartments, each with six or eight seats (three or four facing three or four). Most have seats that pull out and armrests that lift, turning your compartment into a bed on wheels. But this is possible only if you have more seats than people in your compartment. A compartment that seats six can sleep three. So if between 30 and 60 people choose your car, some will sleep and some will sit. Your fate depends on how good you are at encouraging people to sit elsewhere. There are many ways to play this game (which has few rules and encourages creativity). Here are my two favorite techniques.

The Big Sleep. Arrive 30 minutes before your train leaves. Walk most of the length of the train but not to the last car. Choose a car that is going where you want to go, and find an empty compartment. Pull two

A Typical Train Compartment

By day   *By night*

For every night you spend on the train, you gain a day for sightseeing and avoid the cost of a hotel. If your compartment is not full, you can try sleeping for free by pulling out the seats to make a bed.

For $15, you can rent a couchette *(bunk bed) on your overnight train*

seats out to make a bed, close the curtains, turn out the lights, and pretend you are sound asleep. It's amazing. At 9:00 p.m., everyone on that train is snoring away! The first 30 people to get on that car have room to sleep. Number 31 will go into any car with the lights on and people sitting up. The most convincing "sleepers" will be the last to be "woken up." (The real champs put a hand down their pants and smile peacefully.)

The Hare Krishna Approach. A more interesting way that works equally well and is more fun is to sit cross-legged on the floor and chant religious-sounding, exotically discordant harmonies, with a faraway look on your face. People will open the door, stare in for a few seconds—and leave, determined to sit in the aisle rather than share a compartment with the likes of you. You'll probably sleep alone, or end up chanting the night away with five other religious fanatics.

These tricks work not to take advantage of others but to equal out the train load. When all compartments are lightly loaded and people continue to load in, let the air out of your inflatable travel partner, and make room for your new roommates. To minimize the misery on a full train, sit opposite your partner, pull out the seats, and share a single bed (and the smell of your feet).

Another trick is to use the reservation cards to your advantage. Each compartment will have a reservation board outside the door. Never sit in a seat that is reserved, because you'll be "bumped out" just before the train leaves. Few people realize that you can determine how far the people on a train will travel by reading their reservation tags. Each tag explains which segment of the journey that seat is reserved for. Find a compartment with three or four people traveling for just an hour or two, and then for the rest of the night you will probably have that compartment all to yourself.

Remember that trains add and lose cars throughout the night. A train could be packed with tourists heading for Milan, and at 1:00 a.m. an empty Milan-bound car could be added. The difference between being packed like sardines and stretching out in your own fishbowl could be as little as one car away.

Many train travelers are ripped off while they sleep. A $15 *couchette* is safer because the car attendant monitors who comes and goes. Those sleeping for free should exercise extreme caution. Keep your valuables either in a money belt or at least securely attached to your body. For good measure, I clip and fasten my rucksack to the luggage rack. If one tug doesn't take the bag, a thief will usually leave it rather than ask, "Scusi, how is your luggage attached?" You'll hear stories of entire train cars being gassed and robbed in Italy. It happens—but I wouldn't lose sleep over it.

BUS VERSUS TRAIN

Except in Ireland, Greece, Turkey, Portugal, and Morocco, the trains are faster, more comfortable, and have more extensive schedules than buses. Bus trips are usually less expensive (especially in the British Isles) and are occasionally included on your Eurailpass (where operated by the train companies, as many are in Germany, Switzerland, and Belgium).

There are some cheap, long-haul buses (often hippie-type "magic buses") from the hub cities of London, Munich, Amsterdam, and Athens. These can save you plenty over train fares. For example, Amsterdam to London costs $100 by train, $55 by bus; Amsterdam to Paris costs $80 by train, $40 by bus; and Amsterdam to Athens costs over $300 by train and about $200 by bus.

Use buses mainly to pick up where Europe's great train system leaves off. Buses fan out from the smallest train stations to places too small for the train to cover. For towns whose train stations are far from the center (e.g., hill towns), buses are often scheduled to meet each arrival and shuttle passengers to the main square (often for no extra cost). Many bus connections to nearby towns not served by train are timed to depart just after the train arrives.

Car vs. Train— Rough Costs of Sample Trips per Person

Mode of Transportation	3 weeks 1,600 mi.	3 weeks 3,000 mi.	2 months 3,000 mi.	2 months 8,000 mi.
Eurailpass (first class)	$650	$650	$1,100	$1,100
Second-class individual train tickets	$320	$600	$600	$1,600
Subcompact car (two people)	$500	$650	$900	$1,300
Midsized car (four people)	$350	$400	$600	$800

Sample trips: Munich–Paris–Florence–Munich = 1,600 miles. Amsterdam–Munich–Rome–Barcelona–Paris = 3,000 miles. Amsterdam–Copenhagen–Stockholm–Oslo–Copenhagen– Berlin–Vienna–Athens–Rome–Nice–Madrid–Lisbon– Madrid–Paris–Amsterdam = 8,000 miles.

Train tickets cost about 18 cents per mile in the south and east, 25 cents per mile in the north. Car rates based on best rentals or leases including collision damage waiver (CDW) supplements, and figuring $4 per gallon and 30 mpg. Rates vary wildly from company to company and from country to country, and so should you.

COST OF CAR RENTAL: ABOUT $400 A WEEK

A rough estimate for weekly rental with unlimited mileage plus collision damage waiver (CDW) insurance. Two people in a car for three weeks pay around $550 each . . . about the cost of a three-week Eurail Saverpass.

Ford Fiesta:	$135–$300
Tax:	15%–25% extra
CDW:	$8–$13/day
Gas:	$130/week ($4/gallon, 30 mpg, 140 miles/day)
Parking in big cities:	$20/day
Freeway tolls (France and Italy only):	$5 per hour

Driving in Europe

DRIVING EUROPE CRAZY

Behind the wheel you're totally free. You go where you want to, when you want to. You're not limited by tracks and schedules. You can carry more luggage. (If you didn't like my Packing Light chapter, you can even tow a trailer.) And driving can be economical.

Solo car travel is expensive, but three or four people sharing a rented car travel cheaper than three or four using train passes. The super-mobility of a car saves you time in locating budget accommodations in small towns and away from the train lines. This savings helps me rationalize the "splurge" of a car rental. You can also play it riskier in peak season, arriving in a town late with no reservation. If the hotels are full, you simply drive to the next town.

Gas in Europe is expensive—$3 to $5 a gallon—but their petite puddle-jumpers get great mileage. And when compared to the high cost of train tickets, expensive gas is not a real factor. Europe's superhighways are *wunderbar*, but the smaller roads are slow and often congested. You'll make slower time in Europe than in the United States, but distances are short and you'll be impressed by how few miles you need to travel to enjoy the diversity of Europe.

CONSIDERATIONS WHEN RENTING A CAR

Every year, as train prices go up, car rental becomes a better option for budget travelers in Europe. While most travel dreams come with choo-choo noises, and most first trips are best by rail, you should at least consider driving.

Cars are economical when rented by the week with unlimited mileage through your travel agent or directly with the rental company in the U.S.A. (There are a few decent four-day deals.) The cheapest company for rental in one country might be the most expensive in the next. Use the toll-free phone numbers listed below for the latest prices and policies in the competitive and ever-changing world of European car rental. Rentals arranged from major companies in Europe are so expensive, you'd save money by having someone arrange your rental for you back in the United States.

Leasing (technically, buying the car and selling it back) gets around many tax and insurance costs and is a good deal for people needing a car for three weeks or more. Europe by Car now leases cars for as few as 16 days in France for $450, and DER offers a 21-day lease out of Frankfurt for under $600. Lease prices include all taxes and CDW

Vanning through the windmills

insurance. Germany, France, Belgium, and the Netherlands are particularly good for leasing.

Cars are ridiculously expensive to rent by the day. (That's why the various rail 'n' drive passes are a good deal. They basically rent cars one day at a time at one-seventh the cheap weekly rate). Cars are rented for a 24-hour day with a 59-minute grace period.

The model names and features of many European cars are unfamiliar to most Americans. For a little help, refer to the handy car comparison table below.

To really compare car costs with train costs, figure your weekly unlimited mileage rental rate plus:

• The tax is clear and consistent with each country, generally 18 to 25 percent (less in Spain, Germany, Ireland, and Luxembourg, and zero in Switzerland—but Swiss rental rates are that much higher);

• CDW insurance supplement (figure $90 a week);

• Gas ($130 a week, giving you about 1,000 miles);

• Tolls for super-freeways in France and Italy, and $25 for the highway permit decal as you enter Switzerland;

• Parking ($20 a day in big cities, free otherwise).

Then subtract the money you'll save by using the car to get to cheaper accommodations in the countryside and to cart your luggage around effortlessly.

The car insurance included in the rental cost comes with a very high deductible, often equal to the value of the car! For the peace of mind, if nothing more, you need to buy a collision damage waiver (CDW) supplement. This costs from $6 to $15 a day, depending on the country and the car rental company. Figure roughly $90 a week for CDW. Some credit cards cover the deductible for free for their customers, but this is getting dicey. (Read about CDW in Chapter 1 and check with your agent or credit-card company.)

Your American driver's license is all you need in most European countries. An international driver's license basically provides a translation of your American license—making it easier for the cop to write out the ticket. Exactly where you need one depends on who you talk to. The people who sell them say you should have them almost everywhere. The people who rent cars say you need them almost nowhere. Police can get mad and fine you if you don't have one. Those traveling in Portugal, Spain, Italy, Austria, Germany, Greece, and Eastern Europe probably should get an international driver's license. (They cost $10 with two passport-type photos, and are easy to get at your local AAA office.)

LEADING CAR RENTAL COMPANIES

CAR OR TRAIN?

While you should travel the way you like, consider these variables when deciding if your European experience might be better by car or train:

Concern	By Car	By Train
packing heavy?	no problem	must go light
scouring one area	best	frustrating
all over Europe	too much driving	great
big cities	expensive/worthless	ideal
camping	perfect	more like boot camp
one or two people	expensive	probably cheaper
three or more	probably cheaper	more expensive
traveling with small kids	survivable, given time	miserable

COMPARING SMALL EUROPEAN RENTAL CARS

Car	Trunk, cu ft	Engine CC	Length	MPG	Body type
Ford Fiesta	8.8	1001	12' 4"	38	hatchback
Ford Escort	12.7	1117	13' 2"	31	hatchback
Ford Sierra	14.8	1598	14' 8"	28	sedan/hatch
Fiat Panda	9.5	750	11' 2"	33	hatchback
Fiat Uno	9.5	999	12' 1"	38	hatchback
Opel Corsa	7.9	993	12' 3"	31	hatchback
Opel Astra	12.7	1398	13' 4"	27	hatchback
Peugeot 205	10.2	954	12' 2"	35	sedan
Peugeot 309	10.4	1124	13' 4"	31	hatchback
Renault 5	8.3	956	11' 10"	36	hatchback
Renault Clio	9.4	1171	12' 6"	32	hatchback
VW Polo	8.5	1043	12' 2"	34	hatchback
VW Golf III	11.6	1391	13' 2"	29	hatchback
VW Passat	20.4	1781	15' 0"	22	sedan

Big companies (toward the top of the list) offer more reliability and flexibility but consolidators and wholesalers (the lower half) can be cheaper. All can be arranged through your travel agent.

Hertz	800-654-3001
Avis	800-331-1084
Dollar	800-800-6000
Budget	800-472-3325
Kemwel	800-678-0678
Europcar	800-227-3876
Auto Europe	800-223-5555
Europe by Car	800-223-1516
DER Tours (best for German/Czech)	800-782-2424

While ages vary from country to country and company to company, those between 23 and 70 should have no trouble renting a car. If you're older or younger than that, consider leasing, which has less stringent age restrictions. Car companies advertising in *Let's Go* guide-books are seeking young renters.

Rental cars come with the necessary insurance and paperwork to cross borders effortlessly in all of Western Europe. Ask for specific limitations if driving through Eastern Europe. You are generally not allowed to take your car from England to the Continent or to Ireland. Even if you could, the high ferry costs make renting two separate cars a better deal (two single weeks of car rental usually cost the same as two weeks in a row). Take advantage of open-jaws possibilities to save you rental days and avoid big-city driving. You can normally pick up and drop off a car at any of your rental company's offices in one country. There is usually about a $100 fee to drop in another country (with some happy and some outrageous exceptions) and some companies are now charging 7 percent or so for airport pick-ups.

BEHIND THE EUROPEAN WHEEL

Horror stories about European traffic abound. They're fun to tell, but really, driving in Europe is a problem only to those who make it one. Any good American driver can cope with European traffic.

Europe is a continent of frustrated race-car drivers. You'll find highly skilled maniacal drivers in any country, but the most dangerous creature on the road is the timid American. Be aggressive, observe, fit in, avoid big-city driving when you can, wear your seat belt, and pay extra for zero-deductible insurance (CDW–collision damage waiver).

Invest in an extra key. Most rental cars come with only one. That's needlessly risky. Besides, it's more convenient for two people to have access to the locked car.

Drive European. After a few minutes on the autobahn (German freeway), you'll learn that you don't cruise in the passing lane and when going under 80 mph you should stick to the right curb. In Rome, my cabbie went through three red lights. White-knuckled, I asked, "Scusi, do you see red lights?" He said, "When I come to light, I look. If no cars come, red light stupido, I go through. If policeman sees no cars—no problem—red light is stupido." England's roundabouts work wonderfully if you take advantage of the yield system and don't stop. Stopping before a roundabout is as bothersome (and dangerous) as stopping on our freeway on-ramps.

The shortest distance between any two European points is found on the autobahn/strada/route. Although tolls can be high in Italy and France ($30 to get from Paris to the Italian border), I normally figure that the gas and time saved on European super-freeways justifies the expense. Others prefer the more scenic and free national highway systems ("route nationale" in France). Small roads can be a breeze or they can be dreadfully jammed up.

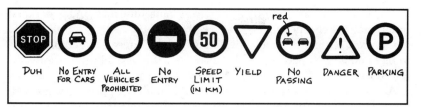

Don't even think of driving in Europe without knowing these standard signs

For drivers in Europe, the language barrier is a road turtle. All of Europe uses the same simple set of road symbols. Just take a few minutes to learn them. Autobahn rest stops have free local driving almanacs explaining such signs, roadside facilities, and exits. Don't skimp on maps.

Americans are timid about passing. In Europe, passing is essential. On winding, narrow roads, you'll notice a kind of turn-signal sign language from the slower car ahead of you indicating when it's OK to pass. This is used inconsistently and should not be relied on blindly.

I drive in and out of strange towns fairly smoothly by following a few basic signs. Most European towns will have signs directing you to the "old town" or the center (such as centrum, centro, centre ville, stadt-mitte). The tourist office, which is normally right downtown, will usually be clearly signposted ("i," "turismo," "VVV," or various abbreviations that you'll learn in each country). The tallest church spire often marks the center of the old town. To leave a city, I look for autobahn signs (distinctive green or blue, depending on the country) or "all directions" (*toutes directions*) signs. Try to avoid heavy traffic times. Big cities are great fun and nearly traffic-free for Sunday drives.

Don't use your car for city sightseeing. Park it and use public transportation. City parking is a pain. Basically, find a spot as close to the center as possible, grab it and keep it. For overnight stops, it's crucial to choose a safe, well-traveled, and well-lit spot. Vandalism to a tourist's car parked overnight in a bad urban neighborhood is as certain as death and taxes. In big cities, it's often worth parking in a garage ($10 to $30 a day and up). Ask your hotel receptionist for advice.

Pumping gas in Europe is as easy as finding a gas station ("self-service" is universal), sticking the nozzle in, and pulling the big trigger. Gas prices are listed by the liter (about a quart). Don't get confused: gas is called "petrol" or "benzine," while diesel is known as "gasoil." "Super" is super and "normal" or "essence" is normal and increasingly rare. In Eastern Europe, use the highest octane available. Unleaded gas has caught on fast and is easy to find throughout Western Europe. Freeway stations are more expensive than those in towns, but during siesta, only freeway stations are open. Giant suburban supermarkets often offer the cheapest gas.

On the Continent you'll be dealing with kilometers—to get miles, cut in half and add 10 percent (90 km/hr = 45 + 9 miles: 54 mph—not very fast in Europe).

Although Americans rarely consider this budget option, Aussies and New Zealanders routinely buy used cars for their trip and sell them when they're done. The most popular places to buy one are Amsterdam, Frankfurt, London, and U.S. military bases. Before your trip, or once in Europe, you can check the classified ads in the armed forces' *Stars and Stripes* newspaper. In London, check the used-car market on Market Road (Caladonian Road Tube). There's no reason Americans can't join the budget-minded Aussies and New Zealanders who find lots of related travel information (jobs, flats, cheap flights, travel partners, as well as used cars for sale) in London periodicals such as *TNT, Law,* and *New Zealand-UK News.* When buying or renting a vehicle, consider the advantage of a van or motor home, which gives you the flexibility to drive late and just pull over and camp for free. Campanje is a Dutch company that rents and sells new and used VW campers fully loaded for camping through Europe. Rates vary from 600 to 1,000 guilders per week including tax and insurance. (For a brochure: tel. 31-30-447070, fax 31-30-420981, Box 9332, 3506 GH Utrecht, Netherlands.) Rafco in Copenhagen (Englandsvej 380, DK-2770 Kastrup, Denmark, tel. 45-31511500, fax 45-31511089) rents fully-equipped motorhomes cheap (and gives *ETBD* readers a discount). For information on buying, renting, or leasing something to camp in, including registration and insurance issues, see *Europe by Van and Motor Home* by David Shore and Patty Campbell (1994, ISBN 0-938297-08-2, 240 pages, $15 postpaid, 1842 Santa Margarita Dr., Fallbrook, CA 92028, tel. 800/659-5222).

Savvy budget travelers offer rental companies their service to return cars to another office for them. You go now and direct but pay for only the gas.

The British Isles are good for driving—reasonable rentals, no language barrier, exciting rural areas, fine roads, not covered on Eurail, and, after one near head-on collision scares the bloody heck out of you, you'll have no trouble remembering which side of the road to drive on.

Instead of intersections with stop lights, the British have roundabouts. For many, these are high-pressure circles that require a snap decision about something you really don't completely understand—your exit. To take the stress out of roundabouts and actually make them fun, make it standard operating procedure to take a 360-degree case-out-your-options circuit, discuss the exits with your navigator, and then confidently wing off on the exit of your choice.

Other good driving areas are Scandinavia (call for free reservations to avoid long waits at ferry crossings), Belgium, Holland, and Luxembourg (yield for bikes—you're outnumbered); Germany, Switzerland, and Austria (driving down sunny Alpine valleys with yodeling on the tape deck is auto-ecstasy); and Spain and Portugal (with their exasperating public transportation system, I spell relief C-A-R). The whirlwind, see-Europe-from-top-to-bottom-type trip is best by train.

Biking in Europe

Europe on $20 a day? You don't need a time machine. What you need is a bike, local markets, and campgrounds or youth hostels. Traveling this way, you'll not only save money and keep fit, but you'll experience a quieter side of Europe that many travelers rarely see.

While bicycle touring is one of the cheapest ways to see Europe, most bikers choose to pedal for the sheer joy of it. Imagine low-gearing up a beautiful mountain road on a bike (smell the freshly mown hay), then picture an air-conditioned Mercedes with the windows closed and the stereo on (smell the upholstery). The driver might pass by and say, "Masochistic nut!" but he also might notice the biker's smiling face–the face of a traveler who can see clearly from mountain to village, smell the woods, hear the birds singing, the trees breezing, and the bugs bouncing

Europe is made for biking

gaily off her or his teeth, while anticipating a well-earned and glorious downhill run on the other side. If this is for you, bring a bike. Rich Sorensen and Edwin McCain, who for years have gotten their travel thrills crisscrossing Europe by bike, helped me assemble these tips on biking in Europe.

The most important first step is to define what part of Europe you want to experience, and then ask yourself some basic questions to see whether your bicycle will be your key to freedom or an albatross around your neck. Remember that it takes an entire day to travel the same distance by bicycle that you could cover in a single hour by train or car. Sixty miles per day is a high average. With bakery stops, Rich averages about forty. For example, if you have the entire summer free, you and your bike can cover a lot of ground through, say, France, Germany, Benelux, Switzerland, and Italy. But if you have a month or less, will you be content to focus on a single country or region? Given what you want to see in the time you have, is the slow pace of bicycling a worthwhile trade-off for the benefits? And finally, do you want to spend much more of your time in rural and small-town Europe than in cities?

Planning your trip is half the fun. Start with good maps and biking guidebooks. Michelin's Europe and individual country maps are fine for strategic planning. Once in Europe, use local maps for day-to-day navigation. Michelin and Die Generalkarte 1:200,000 maps reveal all the quiet back roads, and even the steepness of hills. Don't be obsessed with following a preplanned route. Delightful and spontaneous side-trips are part of the spirit and joy of biking.

Some recommended guidebooks are the newly-updated *Europe by Bike* by Karen and Terry Whitehill (Mountaineers); *Biking Through Europe* by Dennis and Tina Jaffe, published by Williamson (a popular guide listing 17 cycle tours); and the classic *Cycling in Europe* by Nicholas Crane (Pan Books). For regional tours, Gay and Kathlyn Hendricks have authored a series of *Bicycle Tours of . . .* books which include Great Britain and Ireland, Italy, and France (Plume Books). Adventure Cycling Association's *Cyclists Yellow Pages* and *Cyclosource* catalog contain first-rate touring information and accessories (for more info call 406-721-1776).

Before setting out, get in shape and make sure you really enjoy taking long rides weighed down with loaded panniers. If you'll be traveling with a partner, make sure your cycling paces and temperaments are compatible. Try some 60-mile-a-day rides (five hours at 12 mph) around home. If possible, take a weekend camping trip with everything you'll take to Europe. Know which tools to bring, and get good at basic repair work (like repairing flat tires, replacing broken spokes, and adjusting your brakes and shifters). Ask about classes at your local bike shop.

You might want to join one of many good organized bike tours. These usually average an easy 30 to 40 miles a day. For more information, check out the American Youth Hostels Association (Box 37613, Washington, D.C. 20013-7613), or the ads in *Bicycling* magazine. Or you can go it alone, with occasional pickup pals on the way. As a loner, you'll go where, when, and as far and fast as you want. But riding with a companion or two is more cost-effective, and more fun.

When to go depends somewhat on where you go. Ideal biking temperatures are between 50 and 70 degrees F, so May is a good time to bike in the Mediterranean countries. Edwin started in May in Greece before it got too hot and then pedaled up through the Balkans to England, where, on his arrival five weeks later, it wasn't too cold. He had good temperatures all the way, but he also had headwinds (the prevailing westerlies). Rich and his wife set out from Barcelona on a more leisurely spring-to-fall route that took them through France, England, Germany, Switzerland, Italy and Greece, and they had not only ideal temperatures but also fewer headwinds.

Expect rain, and bring good bikers' rain gear. A Gore-tex raincoat can double as a cool-weather windbreaker. But hopefully you'll be exposed to the sun a lot, so plan on using plenty of sunscreen. To guard against unsightly "road rash" (and worse), always wear a helmet and biking gloves.

Although you can buy good touring bikes in Europe, they're no cheaper than here, and you're better off bringing a bike that you're sure is the right fit for you, your racks, and your panniers. The current debate among cyclists is whether to tour on a thick-tired mountain bike or a touring bike with skinnier tires. Mountain-bike tires are much more forgiving on the occasional cobblestone street, but they are more durable than necessary for most European roads and the chunky tread design will slow you down a little. In addition, straight mountain-bike handlebars will limit your hand positions, increasing fatigue on long riding days. If you already have a mountain bike, go ahead and take it, but add some bolt-on handlebar extensions. Smaller "Presta" tire valves are standard in most of Europe, so if your bike has the automotive-type "Shraeder" valves, take along an adapter. A bell is generally required by law in Europe, so you should have one on your bike, too, for giving a multilingual "Hi!" to other bikers as well as a "Look out, here I come!" Even if you never ride at night, you should at least bring a strobe-type taillight for the many long and unavoidable tunnels.

The most difficult part about taking your bike on a plane is deter-mining the airline's policies–especially if you try to ask a travel agent. It's best to call airlines directly for this kind of information. Although some will charge a fee for your bike (more likely if there is a domestic leg to your flight), most airlines will fly it to Europe free, considering it to be one of your two allotted pieces of checked baggage. Most airlines require that bikes be partially disassembled and boxed. Get a box from your local bike shop or from Amtrak (known for their cavernous bike boxes). Reinforce your box with extra cardboard, and be sure to put a plastic spacer between your front forks (any bike shop will give you one). You can also toss in your panniers, tent, and so on for extra padding, as long as you stay under the airline's weight limit. If you're traveling with a tandem bike, some airlines will take it unboxed if you sign a "fragile" waiver. Don't forget to bring the tools you'll need to get your bike back into riding form, so you can ride straight out of your European airport.

Traffic rules in Europe apply to bikers. The closer you get to Holland, the more bike signs you'll see: a bike in a blue circle indicates a bike route; a bike in a red circle indicates bikes are not allowed. Be alert, follow the blue bike signs, and these required bike paths will get you through even some of the most complicated highway interchanges. Beware of the silent biker who might be right behind you, and use hand signals before stopping or turning. Stay off the freeways. Little roads are nicer for biking anyway.

Taking your bike on a train can greatly extend the reach of your trip, since every hour by rail saves a day that would have been spent in the saddle (and there's nothing so sweet as taking a train away from the rain and into a sunny place). But the hassle of lugging equipment through train cars, and the likelihood that your bike will often arrive a day later than you, can make frequent train-hopping a headache. To make sure you and your bike can travel on the same train, look for trains marked in timetables with little bicycle symbols, or ask at the station's information window.

Those traveling by train or car can always rent a bike for a day (about $5) and enjoy a fun and practical change of pace. Wherever its worth biking, you'll find a bike rental shop. In many countries (especially France, Germany, Austria, Belgium, and the Netherlands), the train sta-tions rent bikes (often with 50 percent discounts for those with train tickets or passes) and have easy "pick up here and drop off there" plans. For mixing train and bike travel, ask at stations for the "Fahrrad am Bahnhof" (German) or "Train + Velo" (French) booklet. Many cities (such as Amsterdam, Munich, and Copenhagen) are great by bike.

Bike thieves abound in Europe, especially at youth hostels after midnight. Precautions: use a good Kryptonite-style bike lock; never leave your pump, water bottle, or computer on your bike when you can't see it; take your bike inside whenever possible; at hostels, always ask if there is a locked bike room and, if not, ask or even plead for a place to put your bike inside overnight; and remember that hotels and many pensions don't really have rules against taking a bike up to your room. Just do it unobtrusively. You can even wheelie it into the elevator (be careful to avoid tire marks on the walls). Rich and his wife found campgrounds to be safe, but they always locked their bikes together.

Smart bikers travel very light. Unless you really love camping, staying in youth hostels makes more sense, since it frees you from lugging around a tent, sleeping bag and cooking equipment. European campgrounds tend to be more crowded but better equipped than American ones, so if you're willing to sacrifice some privacy in order to mix with Europeans, camping can add a fun dimension to your trip.

Which brings us to what may be the most rewarding aspect of bicycling in Europe: meeting people. Europeans love bicycles, and they are often genuinely impressed when they encounter that rare American who rejects the view from the tour-bus window in favor of huffing and puffing through Europe on two wheels. Your bike provides an instant conversation piece, the perfect bridge over a maze of cultural and language barriers.

Hitchhiking—Rules of Thumb

Hitching, sometimes called "auto-stop," is a popular and acceptable means of getting around in Europe. Without a doubt, hitching is the cheapest means of transportation. It's also a great way to meet people. Most people who pick you up are genuinely interested in getting to know an American. (Hitching is risky, and that coupled with the overabundance of lawyers in the U.S.A. means I cannot recommend it.)

After picking up a Rhine riverboat captain in my rental car and running him back to his home port, I realized that hitchhiking doesn't wear the same hippie hat in Europe that it does in the United States. The farther you get from the militant self-sufficiency of our culture, the more volunteerism you'll encounter. Bumming a ride is a perfect example. In the Third World—rural Europe in the extreme—anything rolling with room will let you in. You don't hitch, you just flag the vehicle down.

Hitching has two drawbacks. First, it can be time-consuming. Some places have 20 or 30 people in a chorus line of thumbs, just waiting their turns. Once I said what I thought was good-bye forever to an Irishman after breakfast. He was heading north. We had dinner together that night, and I learned a lot about wasting a day on the side of a road. Second, although hitching in Europe is safer than hitching in the United States, there is the ever-present danger involved in hitchhiking.

Crank up your good judgment. Feel good about the situation before you commit yourself to it. Keep your luggage on your lap, or at least out of the trunk, so if things turn sour you can excuse yourself quickly and easily. Women should not sit in the back seat of a two-door car. A fake wedding ring and modest dress are indications that you're interested only in transportation.

Personally, I don't hitchhike at home, and I wouldn't rely solely on my thumb to get me through Europe. But I never sit frustrated in a station for two hours because there's no bus or train to take me 15 miles down the road. I thumb my way out of train and bus schedule problems, usually getting to my destination in a friendly snap. You'll find that Germany, Ireland, and Great Britain offer generally good hitchhiking, and southern countries are much slower for hitching.

Hitchhiking at the Bulgaria-Greece border, or wherever the train and bus schedules leave you stranded

Your success as a hitchhiker will be determined by how well you follow several rules. The hitchhiking gesture is not always the outstretched thumb. In some countries, you ring an imaginary bell. In others, you make a downward wave with your hand. Observe and learn. Consider what the driver will want to let into his car. Arrange your luggage so it looks as small and desirable as possible. Those hitching with very little or no luggage enjoy a tremendous advantage.

Look like the Cracker Jack boy or his sister—happy, wholesome, and a joy to have aboard. To get the long ride, take a local bus out of town to the open country on the road to your destination and make a cardboard sign with your destination printed big and bold in the local language, followed by the local "please."

Share-a-ride organizations (Mitfahrzentralen in Germany, Allostop in France) match rides and riders. You pay a small amount to join, and you help with gas expenses, but it works well and is much cheaper than train travel. Use student Tourist Information centers or big-city phone books. Informal ride services are on school and hostel bulletin boards all over Europe.

Speed and safety are a trade-off when it comes to hitching. A single woman maximizes speed and risk. Two women travel more safely and nearly as fast. A man and a woman together are the best combination. A single man with patience will do fine. Two guys go slow, and three or more should split up and rendezvous later. Single men and women are better off traveling together; these alliances are easily made at hostels.

When I'm doing some serious hitchhiking, I work to create pity. I walk away from town and find a very lonely stretch of road. In a lot of cases, I feel that the sparser the traffic, the quicker I get a ride. On a busy road, people will assume that I'll manage without their ride. If only one car passes in five minutes, the driver senses that he may be my only chance. Look clean, safe, respectable, and a little gaunt. Establish eye contact. Charm the driver. Stand up. Smile. Don't walk and hitch. Pick a good spot on the road, giving the driver both plenty of time to see you and a safe spot to pull over.

When you're in a hurry, there are two surefire ways of getting a ride fast. Find a spot where cars stop, and you can encounter the driver face to thumb. A toll booth, border, gas station, or—best of all—a ferry ride gives you that chance to smile and convince him that he needs you in his car or truck. At borders, you might decide to choose only a ride entirely through that country. Use decals and license plates to determine where a car is from (and therefore likely heading). Every car has to have a large decal with a letter or two indicating in which country the car is registered. And in some countries (such as Germany and Italy) hometowns are indicated by the first few letters on the license plate. Although it's easy to zoom past a hitchhiker at 60 mph and not feel guilty, it's much more difficult to turn down an in-person request for a ride. A man and a woman traveling together have it easy. If the woman hitches and the guy steps out of view around the corner or into a shop, you should both have a ride in a matter of minutes. (Dirty trick, but it works.)

With the "hitch when you can't get a bus or train" approach, you'll find yourself walking down lovely mountain or rural roads out of a village, getting rides from small-town folk—fanatically friendly and super safe. I can recall some "it's great to be alive and on the road" days riding my thumb from tiny town to waterfall to desolate Celtic graveyard to coastal village and remembering each ride as much as the destinations.

Sometimes hitching almost becomes an end in itself. In the British Isles, especially Ireland, I've found so much fun in the front seat that I've driven right by my planned destination to carry on with the conversation. In rural Ireland, I'd stand on the most desolate road in Connemara and hitch whichever way the car was coming. As I hopped in, the driver would ask, "Where you goin'?" I'd say, "Ireland."

Walking (and Dodging)

You'll walk a lot in Europe. It's a great way to see cities, towns, and the countryside. Walking tours are the most intimate look at a city or town. A walker compliments the place she walks through by her interest and will be received warmly. Many areas, from the mountains to the beaches, are best seen on foot.

Be careful—walking can be dangerous. Pedestrians are run down every day. More than 300 pedestrians are run down annually on the streets of Paris. The drivers are crazy, and politeness has no place on the roads of Europe. Cross carefully, but if you wait for a break in the traffic, you may never get a chance to cross the street. Look for a pedestrian underpass or, when all else fails, find a heavy-set local person and just follow him or her like a shadow—one busy lane at a time—across that seemingly impassable street. Joggers have no problem finding good routes and enjoy a good early morning tour as well as the exercise.

Hiking

Hiking in Europe is a joy. Travelers explore entire regions on foot. The Jungfrau is an exciting sight from a hotel's terrace café. But those who hike the region enjoy nature's very own striptease as the mountain reveals herself in an endless string of powerful poses.

The Alps are especially suited to the walking tourist. The trails are well kept and carefully marked. Very precise maps (scale 1:25,000) are readily available. You're never more than a day's hike from a mountain village, where you can replenish your food supply or enjoy a hotel and a restaurant meal. By July, most trails are free of snow, and lifts take less-rugged visitors to the top in a sweat-free flash.

Throughout the Alps, trail markings are both handy and humiliating. Handy, because they show hours to hike rather than miles to walk to various destinations. Humiliating, because these times are clocked by local senior citizens. You'll know what I mean after your first hike.

Hundreds of Alpine huts exist to provide food and shelter to hikers. I know a family that hiked from France to Slovenia, spending every night along the way in a mountain hut. The huts are generally spaced 4 to 6 hours apart. Most serve hot meals and provide bunk-style lodging. If you plan to use the huts extensively, join an Alpine club. Membership in one of these European or American clubs entitles you to discounts on the cost of lodging and priority over nonmembers. The club can provide information about the trails and huts at which reservations are likely to be necessary.

Do some research before you leave. Buy the most appropriate guide-book for your hiking plans. Ask for maps and information from the National Tourist Offices.

A firsthand look at fairy-tale Alpine culture is just a $10 gondola ride away (Walderalm, above Hall in Tirol; see Back Doors)

4

The Budget:
Eating and Sleeping
on $50 a Day

Many Americans are saying, "Europe's getting expensive!" Actually, it's staying about the same, and, in relative terms, we're getting poorer. Travelers from post-Reagan America, a debtor nation with a reshuffled social deck, are no longer as affluent as their European counterparts. This becomes painfully clear when you compare buying power with new European friends. You can live well in Europe on a budget, but it will take some artistry, and if you travel like a big-shot, you better be loaded.

Overall, most of today's Europe is more expensive than the United States, and the sloppy traveler can blow a small fortune in a hurry. Still, smart travelers can thrive on $50 a day plus sightseeing and transportation—less if necessary. For 1995, figure on $25 per person in a ($50) hotel double, $5 each for breakfast and lunch, and $15 for dinner.

The key is finding budget alternatives to international-class hotels and restaurants and consuming only what you want to consume. If you want real tablecloths and black-tie waiters, your tomato salad will cost 20 times what it costs in the market. If you want a private shower, toilet, room service, TV, and chocolate on your pillow, you'll pay in a day what many travelers pay in a week for a good, quiet eight hours of sleep.

We consumers get what we order. They say it takes two incomes for the American family to make ends meet these days. And likewise, when we travel, we order and get lavish plumbing. The only thing that really changes is the material appetite of the rich and wishful. Trains are faster, cars are better, youth hostels are getting classy, and thousands of showers and toilets clutter the corners of Europe's formerly square, spacious, and cheap hotel rooms. And "budget" travel, while more comfortable, has also become more expensive.

My idea of "cheap" is simple but not sleazy. My budget morality is to never sacrifice safety, reasonable cleanliness, sleep, or nutrition to save money. I go to safe, central, friendly, local-style hotels, shunning TVs, swimming pools, people in uniforms, private plumbing, and transplanted American niceties in favor of an opportunity to travel as a temporary European. Unfortunately, simple will be subversive in the 1990s, and the system will bully even the cozy Scottish bed and breakfast into more and more facilities, more and more debt, and higher and higher prices.

I'm very cautious about sending people to Europe without enough money, skills, and reservations. The ideas in this chapter are tried and tested in the worst circumstances every year. And my feedback from Back Door travelers bolsters my confidence. It can be done—by you.

In 1995, you can travel comfortably for a month for around $3,600. That includes: $800 for a round-trip plane ticket, $700 for a one-month Eurailpass or split car rental, and $1,500 for room and board ($50 a day). Add $20 a day ($600) for souvenirs, personal incidentals, admissions, and sightseeing costs. In 1995, the student or rock-bottom budget traveler can enjoy a month of Europe at least as much for about a third less, $2,500. That includes: $700 budget round-trip airfare, $600 for transportation (a one-month youth Eurailpass), $900 for room and board ($15 for a dorm bed or a bed in a private home with breakfast, $5 for a picnic lunch, $10 for dinner—$30 a day) and $300 fun money.

Your budget is basically transportation, room and board, sightseeing, and incidentals. Transportation expenses are fixed. Flying to Europe is a bargain. Get a good agent, understand all your options, and make the best choice. This cost cannot be cut. Transportation in Europe is reasonable if you take advantage of a Eurailpass or split a car rental between three or four people. Your budget should not dictate how freely you travel in Europe. If I want to go somewhere, I will, taking advantage of whatever money-saving options I can. I came to travel.

The area that will make or break your budget—where you have the most control—is in your eating and sleeping expenses. People who spend $8,000 for their vacation spend about the same on transportation as those whose trips cost half as much. Room and board is the beaver in your bankbook. If you have extra money, it's more fun to spend it in Europe, but if your trip will last only as long as your money does and you develop and deploy a good strong SDI (spending defense initiative), figure about $50 per day plus sightseeing and transportation.

Sightseeing costs have risen faster than anything else. Admissions to major attractions are now $5 to $8, $2 to $3 for smaller sights. Your incidentals will also add up: coffee, beer, ice cream, and soft drinks cost $1 to $2, bus and subway rides $1, postcards 50 cents.

I traveled every summer for years on a part-time piano teacher's income (and, boy, was she upset). I ate and slept great by learning and using the skills that follow.

Sleeping Cheap

HOTELS

Hotels are the most expensive way to sleep and, of course, the most comfortable. With a reasonable budget, I spend most of my nights in hotels. Hotels, however, can rip through a tight budget like a grenade in a dollhouse.

I always hear people complaining about that "$160 double in Frankfurt" or the "$200-a-night room in London." They come back from their vacations with bruised and battered pocketbooks, telling stories that scare their friends out of international travel and back to Florida or Hawaii one more time. True, you can spend $200 for a double, but I never have. That's four days' accommodations budget for me.

As far as I'm concerned, spending more for your hotel just builds a bigger wall between you and what you came to see. If you spend enough, you won't know where you are. Think about it. "In-ter-con-ti-nental." That means the same everywhere—designed for people who wish they weren't traveling, people who are spending someone else's

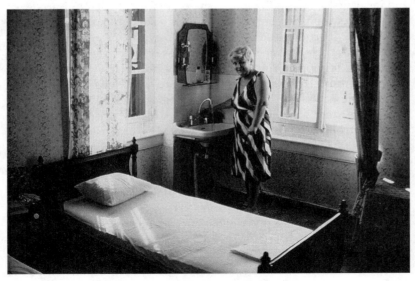

Budget hotels can be comfortable, cheery, and friendly

money. It's uniform sterility, a lobby full of stay-press Americans with wheels on their suitcases, English menus, and lamps bolted to the tables.

Europe is full of European hotels—dingy, old-fashioned, a bit rundown, central, friendly, safe, and government-regulated, offering good-enough-for-the-European-good-enough-for-me beds for $15 to $25 a night ($30-$50 doubles). No matter what your favorite newspaper travel writer or travel agent says, this is hard-core Europe: fun, cheap, and easy to find.

WHAT'S A CHEAP ROOM?

A typical cheap room in Europe (a one-star, $40 double in Paris; a $35 simple guest house-type hotel double in Germany; a $30 double for a pension in Madrid; or a $50 room in a mission-owned hotel in Oslo) is very basic. It has a simple bed (occasionally a springy cot, so always check); a rickety, pre-World War II or new plastic chair and table; a freestanding closet; a small window; old wallpaper; a good sink under a neon light; a mysterious bidet; a view of another similar room across a tall, thin courtyard; peeling plaster; and a tiled or wood floor. Rooms often come with a continental breakfast (usually served from about 7:30 to 10:00 in the breakfast room near the front desk), which includes coffee, tea or hot chocolate, and a roll (that's firmer than your mattress). The light fixtures are very simple, often with a weak and sometimes even bare and dangling ceiling light bulb. Some travelers BYOB when they travel. A higher wattage kills a lot of dinginess. Naked neon is common in the south. You won't have a TV or telephone, and, while more and more European hotels are squeezing boat-type prefab showers and toilets into their rooms, the cheapest rooms give you only a WC and shower or tub down the hall, which you share with a half-dozen other rooms.

Although the rooms themselves lack *en suite* facilities, in the lobby there is nearly always a living room with a good TV, a couple of phone booths, and a person at the desk who is at your service and a good information source. You'll climb lots of stairs, as a hotel's lack of an elevator is often the only reason it can't raise its prices. You'll be given a front-door key because the desk is not staffed all night.

The bottom-of-the-line European hotel ($50 doubles in the north, $30 in the south) usually has clean enough but depressing shower rooms with hot water normally free and constant (but occasionally available only through a coin-op meter or at certain hours). The WC, or toilet, is reliably clean and has toilet paper but is often missing its lid or has a cracked or broken plastic lid. In some hotels, you pay $2 to $5 for a towel and a key to the shower room. The cheapest hotels are run by and filled with people from the Two-thirds World.

In a Back Door-style hotel, you get more by spending less. Here, the shower's down the hall and the Alps are in your lap.

I want to stress that there are places I find unacceptable. I don't mind dingy wallpaper, climbing stairs, and "going down the hall," but the place must be clean, central, friendly, safe, quiet enough for me to sleep well, and provide good beds. The hotel described above is appalling to many Americans; it's colorful, charming, or funky to others. ("Funky" means spirited, with character, a caged bird in the TV room, the grand-children in the backyard, a dog sleeping in the hall, no uniforms on the help, singing maids, the night-shift man tearing breakfast napkins in two so they'll go farther, a handwritten neighborhood history lesson on the wall, furniture different in each room, a little key for the side door after hours, willingness to buck the system when the local tourist board starts requiring shoeshine machines in the hallways.) An extra $15 or $20 per night will buy you into cheerier wallpaper and less funkiness.

There is a real trend toward materialism throughout Europe. Land in big cities is so expensive that cheap hotels can't survive and are bought out, gutted, and turned into modern hotels. More and more Europeans are expecting what, until lately, have been considered American standards of plumbing and comfort. A great value is often a hardworking family-run place that structurally can't fit an elevator up its spiral staircase and showers in each room. Prices are regulated and, regardless of how good it is, with no elevator and a lousy shower-to-room ratio, it's a cheap hotel.

RESERVING HOTELS

I used to travel with absolutely no reservations. A daily chore was checking out several hotels or pensions and choosing one. Europe was ramshackle, things were cheap, hotel listings were unreliable and unnecessary. Now, like hobos in a Jetson world, budget travelers need to travel with information and think one step ahead. My standard operating procedure when it comes to room-finding is to travel with a good-hotel list and make telephone reservations six hours to four days in advance— basically as soon as I'm ready to commit myself to being somewhere on a certain date.

Travel with a good list of hotels (from a guidebook whose travel philosophy matches yours). These days, those who rely on the tourist office or go potluck are likely to spend $30 more than necessary and get a lousy room. That's why I give hotel listings a very high priority in researching and writing my seven "Best of" country guidebooks (formerly 2 to 22 Days guidebooks). If I know when I'll be somewhere and where I want to stay (as I normally do these days), a simple phone call a little in advance assures me a good value room. Lately, I've been getting aced out by my own readers. So when I want to be certain to get my first choice, I call two or three days in advance.

Making reservations long in advance through your travel agent or a room booking agency is a needless and expensive security blanket. You won't know what you're getting. You'll destroy your itinerary flexibility. And you'll pay top dollar.

Generally you should not make reservations from the U.S.A. I reserve only my first night's accommodations and places where I know for certain where I want to stay and exactly when I'll be there.

Try to fax your long-distance reservations. Fax machines are standard now in European hotels, most pensions, and many B&Bs. A typed fax in simple English communicates clearly, minimizes the language barrier, and gives your hotel a quick and easy way to respond. You can also make a reservation by telephone (about $1 a minute from the U.S.A.).

Always list your dates (with date and expected time of arrival, number of nights you'll stay, and date of departure), your rooms needs (number of people, what facilities you require), and your budget concerns (of course, a trade-off with facilities), and ask for mercy on their deposit requirements (either by promising to telephone a day in advance to reconfirm or giving them your credit card number as security). If you include your credit-card information you may avoid the extra cost of an extra volley of faxes. Request a written confirmation with price quoted.

Try to avoid having to send a bank draft. It's a costly headache for all involved. Ideally they'll accept your credit-card number or have you mail a signed $50 travelers check. (They can hold the check until you arrive and you can pay with local cash if you leave the "pay to" line blank.) Mail can be slow. Allow a month for round-trip correspondence.

If, after several tries, it seems that every hotel in town is full, don't panic. Hotels take only so many long-distance advance reservations. They never know how long guests will stay and like to keep a few beds for their regulars. A good time to make a telephone reservation is from 8:00 to 10:00 on the morning you plan to arrive. This is when the receptionist knows exactly who's leaving and which rooms he needs to fill and is eager to get a name on every available room. Those who are there in person are also likelier to land a room. Some very cheap hotels take no reservations at all. Just show up and sleep with your money belt on.

Remember, a hotel prefers a cash deposit with a reservation unless there's not enough time to mail it in. In this case, most hotels will hold a room if you promise to arrive early. The earlier you promise, the better your chances of being trusted. If you'll be a little late, call again to assure them you're coming. Also, cancel if you won't make it. If someone cancels after 5:00 p.m. and the room-finding service is closed, the room will probably go unfilled that night. When that happens too often, hotel managers start to get really surly and insist on cash deposits. On recent trips, my standard peak season room-finding tactic (assuming I knew where I wanted to be) has been to telephone in the morning to reserve my room for the night and travel relaxed, knowing a good place was holding a room for me until late afternoon.

BASIC BED-FINDING

In more than a thousand unreserved nights in Europe, I've been shut out three times. That's a 99.7 percent bedding average earned in peak season and very often in crowded, touristy, or festive places. What's so traumatic about a night without a bed anyway? My survey shows those who have the opportunity to be a refugee for a night have their perspectives broadened and actually enjoy the experience—in retrospect.

The cost of a wonderfully reservation-free trip is the remote chance you'll end up spending the night on a bench in the train station waiting room. Knowing the basic skills of bed-finding is much more valuable than having the best hotel list. Every year, I travel peak season (lately, with my wife and toddler or a television film crew), arrive early or call a day or so in advance, and manage fine by using the few tricks listed here.

1. Use a guidebook for hotel lists. I spend more time in Europe finding and checking hotels than anything else. I can spend a day in Amsterdam, scaling the stairs and checking out the rooms of 20 different hotels, all offering double rooms from $50 to $100 a night. After doing the grand analysis, what's striking to me is how little correlation there is between what you pay and what you get. You are just as likely to spend $90 for a big impersonal place on a noisy highway as you are to spend $60 for a charming family-run guesthouse on a pedestrian-only stretch of canal.

These days, to sleep well and inexpensively in a big-city bed, you need a good guidebook's basic listing of hotels and budget alternatives. These lists, whose recommendations are often crowded with people using the same book, are reliable and work well. Don't expect the prices to be the same. Few guidebooks have the guts to list the very least expensive options. In the last few years, I've expanded my 102Country Guides to include all the room listings you'll need for the parts of Europe I cover.

2. Use room-finding services. Popular tourist cities usually have a room-finding service at the train station or tourist information office. For a few dollars, they'll get you a room in the price range and neighborhood of your choice. They have a listing of that town's "acceptable" available accommodations, and, especially in a big city (if you don't have a guidebook's listings), their service can be worth the price when you consider the time and money saved by avoiding the search on foot. Because of several problems, I use room-finding services only when I have no listings or information of my own. Their hotel lists normally make no quality judgments. So what you get is potluck. The stakes are too high for this to be acceptable (especially when you consider how readily available good hotel listings are in other guidebooks). Also, since many room-finding services profit from taking a "deposit" which they pocket, many of the best budget places tell the room-finding service they're full when they aren't. They know they'll fill up with travelers coming direct, allowing them to keep 100 percent of the room cost. Some room-finding services are in the private service of a group of supporting hotels. Room-finding services are not above pushing you into their "favored" hotels, and kickbacks are powerful motivators. Room-finding services give dormitory, hostel, and "sleep-in" (circus tents, gyms with mattresses on the floor, and other $5-a-night alternatives to the park or station) information only if you insist. Remember, many popular towns open up hostels for the summer which are not listed in your guidebook. (If the line at the room-finding service is too long, ask someone who just got a room where they're going.)

3. Use the telephone. If you're looking on your own, telephone the places in your guidebook that sound best. Not only will it save the time and money involved in chasing down these places with the risk of finding them full, but you're beating all the other tourists—with the same guidebook—who may be hoofing it as you dial. It's rewarding to arrive at a hotel when people are being turned away and see your name on the reservation list because you called first. If the room or price isn't what you were led to believe, you have every right to say, "No, thank you." (See "Telephoning in Europe" in Chapter 11.) If you like and trust the values of your guidebook's author, track down his or her recommendations by phone and use the tourist office only as a last resort.

4. Consider hotel runners. Sometimes you'll be met by hotel runners as you step off the bus or train. My gut reaction is to steer clear, but these people are usually just hardworking entrepreneurs who lack the location or write-up in a popular guidebook that can make life easy for a small hotel owner. If you like the guy and what he promises, and the hotel isn't too far away, follow him to his hotel. You are obliged only to inspect the hotel. If it's good, take it. If it's not, leave. You're probably near other budget hotels anyway. Establish the location very clearly, as many of these people have good places miserably located way out of town.

5. The early bird gets the room. If you anticipate crowds, go to great lengths to arrive in the morning when the most (and best) rooms are available. If the rooms aren't ready until noon, take one anyway; leave your luggage behind the desk; they'll move you in later and you're set up—free to relax and enjoy the city. I would leave Florence at 7:00 a.m. to arrive in Venice (a crowded city) early enough to get a decent choice of rooms. One of the beauties of overnight train rides is that you arrive, if not bright, at least early.

Your approach to room finding will be determined by the market situation—if it's a "buyer's market" or a "seller's market." Sometimes you'll grab anything with a pillow and a blanket. Other times you can arrive late, be selective, and even talk down the price.

When going door-to-door, rarely is the first place you check the best. It's worth ten minutes of shopping around to find the going rate before you accept a room. You'll be surprised how prices vary as you walk farther from the station or down a street strewn with B&Bs. Never judge a hotel by its exterior or lobby. Lavish interiors with shabby exteriors (blame the landlord, not the hotel) are a cultural trait of Europe. (If there are two of you, let one watch the bags over a cup of coffee while the other runs around.)

6. Leave the trouble zone. If the room situation is impossible, don't struggle—just leave. An hour by car, train, or bus from the most miserable hotel situation anywhere in Europe is a town—Dullsdorf or

Nothingston—that has the Dullsdorf Inn or the Nothingston Gasthaus just across the street from the station or right on the main square. It's not full—never has been, never will be. There's a guy sleeping behind the reception desk. Drop in at 11:00 p.m., ask for 14 beds, and he'll say, "Take the second and third floors, the keys are in the doors." It always works. Oktoberfest, Cannes Film Festival, St. Tropez Running of the Girls, Easter at Lourdes—your bed awaits you in nearby Dullsdorf. If you anticipate trouble, stay at the last train stop before the crowded city.

7. Follow taxi tips. A great way to find a place in a tough situation is to let a cabbie take you to his favorite hotel. They are experts. Cabs are also handy when you're driving lost in a big city. Many times I've hired a cab, showed him that elusive address, and followed him in my car to my hotel.

8. Let hotel managers help. Have your current manager call ahead to make a reservation at your next destination. If you're in a town and having trouble finding a room, remember that nobody knows the hotel scene better than local hotel managers do. If one hotel is full, ask for help there. Often the manager has a list of neighborhood accommodations or will even telephone a friend's place that rarely fills up and is just around the corner. If the hotel is too expensive, there's nothing wrong with asking where you could find a "not so good place." I've always found hotel receptionists understanding and helpful.

The most expensive hotels have the best city maps (free, often with other hotels listed) and an English-speaking staff that can give advice to the polite traveler in search of a cheap room.

A person staying only one night is bad news to a hotel. If, before telling you whether there's a vacancy, they ask you how long you're staying, be ambiguous.

Remember, my experience is based on budget European-style situations. People who specialize in accommodating soft, rich Americans are more interested in your money than your happiness. Europe's small hotels, guest houses, and bed and breakfast places may have no room service and offer only a shower down the hall, but their staffs are more interested in seeing pictures of your children and helping you have a great time than in thinning out your wallet.

TO SAVE MONEY, REMEMBER . . .

Large hotels, international chains, big-city hotels, and hotels in the north are more expensive. Prices usually rise with demand during festivals and in July and August. Off-season, try haggling. If the place is too expensive, tell them your limit; they might meet it. In Scandinavia, fancy "business hotels" are desperate in the summer and on weekends when their business customers stay away. They offer some amazing deals through the local tourist offices. The later your arrival, the better the deals.

Many national governments regulate hotel prices according to class or rating. To overcome this price ceiling (especially in peak season when demand exceeds supply), hotels often require that you buy dinner there. Breakfast normally comes with the room, but in some countries, it is an expensive, kind-of-optional, tack-on. One more meal (demi- or half-pension) or all three meals (full-pension) is usually uneconomical, since the hotel is skirting the governmental hotel price ceilings to maximize profit. I prefer the freedom to explore, experiment, and sample the atmosphere of restaurants in other neighborhoods.

Consume smart. Know the government ratings and don't stray above your needs. A three-star hotel is not necessarily a bad value. But if I stay in a three-star hotel, I've spent $50 extra for things I don't need. You can get air conditioning, elevators, private showers, room service, 24-hour reception desk, and people in uniforms to carry your bags. But each of those services adds $10 to the cost of your room and before you know it the simple $50 room is up to $100.

Room prices vary tremendously within a hotel according to facilities provided. Most hotels have a room list clearly displayed, showing each room, its bed configuration, facilities, and price for one and for two. Also read the breakfast, tax, and extra bed policies. By studying this list, you'll see that, in many places, a shower is cheaper than a bath and a double bed is cheaper than twins. In other words, a sloppy couple who prefer a shower and a double bed can pay $20 more for a bath and twins. In some cases, if you want any room for two and you say "double," they'll think you'll only take a double bed. To keep all my options open (twin and double) I ask for "a room for two people." Be snoopy. Hotels downplay their cheap rooms.

Some hotels offer a special price for a long stay. It doesn't hurt to ask for this discount. If you came direct and point out that the Tourist Office didn't get their 10 percent, you have a better chance of talking the price down.

Family rooms are common and putting four in a quad is much cheaper than two doubles. Many doubles come with a small double bed and a sliver single. A third person pays very little. A family with two small children can ask for triples and bring a sleeping bag for the stowaway.

Avoid doing outside business through your hotel. It's better style to go to the bullring and get the ticket yourself. You'll learn more and save money, and you won't sit with other tourists who drown your Spanish fire with Yankee-pankee. So often, tourists are herded together by a

Formule 1 is a European-style Motel 6. Fully automated, no character, $25 triples at nearly every freeway off-ramp.

conspiracy of hotel managers and tour organizers and driven through gimmicky folk evenings featuring a medley of cheesy cultural clichés kept alive only for the tourists. You can't relive your precious Madrid nights; do them right—on your own.

CHECK-IN PROCEDURE

Ask to see the room before accepting. Then the receptionist knows the room must pass your inspection. He'll have to earn your business. Notice the boy is given two keys. You asked for only one room. He's instructed to show the hard-to-sell room first. If you insist on seeing both rooms, you'll get the best. Check out the rooms, and snarl at anything that deserves displeasure. The price will come down or they'll show you a better room. Think about heat and noise. I'll climb a few stairs to reach cheaper rooms higher off the noisy road. Some towns never quiet down. A room in back may lack a view, but it will also lack night noise. It's only natural for the hotel receptionist to try to unload the most difficult-to-sell room on the easiest-to-please traveler. Somebody has to sleep in it.

When checking in, pick up the hotel's business card. In the most confusing cities, the cards come with a little map. Even the best pathfinders get lost in a big city, and not knowing where your hotel is can be scary. With the card, you can hop into a cab and be home in minutes.

Establish the complete and final price of a room before accepting. Know what's included and what taxes and services will be added on. More than once I've been given a bill that was double what I expected. Dinners were required, and I was billed whether I ate them or not; so I was told—in very clear Italian.

When you pay is up to the hotel and you. Normally I pay upon departure. If they want prepayment, that's fine, but unless I'm absolutely certain I'll be staying on, I pay one night at a time. Don't assume your room is yours once you're in. Make it clear when you check in how long you intend to stay or you may get the boot.

If you didn't get the kind of room you wanted, ask to switch when possible. Although you don't want to be a pest, remember, hotels are in the business of accommodating people. If you need a different pillow, another blanket, mosquito netting, an electrical adapter, advice on a good restaurant or show, driving instructions for your departure, help telephoning your next hotel, and so on, be sure to ask.

SHOWERS

Showers are a Yankee fetish. A morning without a shower is traumatic to many of us: it can ruin a day. Here are some tips on survival in a world that doesn't start and end with squeaky hair.

First of all, get used to the idea that you won't have a shower every night. The real winners are those who manage with four showers a week and a few sponge baths tossed in when needed.

Many times, you'll have a shower—but no pressure or hot water. When you check in, ask when is the best time to take a hot shower. Many have water pressure or hot water only during certain times. Heating water 24 hours a day is a luxury many of us take for granted.

Americans are notorious (and embarrassing) energy gluttons—wasting hot water and leaving lights on as if electricity is cheap. Who besides us sings in the shower or would even dream of using a special nozzle to take a hot water massage? European electric rates are shocking, and some hotels have had to put meters in their showers to survive. Fifty cents buys about five minutes of hot water. It's a good idea to have an extra token handy to avoid that lathered look. A "navy shower," using the water only to soap up and rinse off, is a wonderfully conservative method, and those who follow you will more likely enjoy some *warm wasser*. (Although starting and stopping the water doesn't start and stop the meter.)

Bathrooms in small pensions and family-run hotels make you feel like part of the family

Half of all the cold showers Americans take in Europe are cold only because they don't know how to turn the hot on. Study the particular system, and before you shiver, ask the receptionist for help. There are some very peculiar tricks. (In Italy and Spain, "C" is *caldo*, or hot. In many British places there's a "hot" switch at the base of the showerbox or even in the hallway.) You'll find showers and baths of all kinds. Occasionally, the red knob is hot and the blue one is cold.

Nearly every hotel room in Europe comes with a sink and a bidet. Sponge baths are fast, easy, and European. A bidet is that mysterious porcelain (or rickety plastic) thing that looks like an oversized bedpan. Tourists use them as anything from a laundromat to a vomitorium to a watermelon rind receptacle to a urinal. They are used by locals to clean the parts of the body that rub together when they walk—in lieu of a shower. Give it the old four S's—straddle, squat, soap up, and swish off.

The cheapest hotels rarely provide a shower or toilet in your room. Each floor shares a toilet and a shower "down the hall." To such a bathoholic people, this sounds terrible. Imagine the congestion in the morning when the entire floor tries to pile into that bathtub! Remember, only Americans "need" a shower every morning. Few Americans stay in these "local" hotels; therefore, you've got a private bath—down the hall. I spend 100 nights a year in Europe—probably

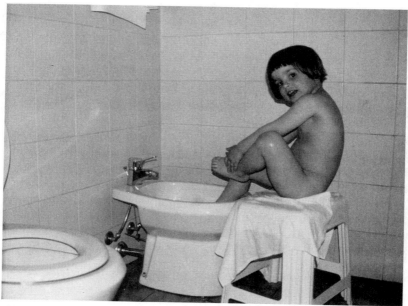

Throughout southern Europe, even the cheapest hotel rooms come with a bidet. Europeans use them to stay clean without a daily shower.

shower 80 times—and I have to wait four or five times. That's the price I pay to take advantage of Europe's simple hotels.

Many budget hotels and most dorm-style accommodations don't provide towels or soap. BYOS. Towels, like breakfast and people, get smaller as you go south. In simple places, you'll get no face towel and bath towels are not replaced every day. Hang them up to dry.

I have a theory that after four days without a shower, you don't get any worse, but that's another book. If you are vagabonding or sleeping several nights in transit and would like a shower, you can buy one in train station "day hotels," at many freeway rest stops, in public baths or swimming pools, or even, if you don't mind asking, from hostels or small hotels. Most Mediterranean beaches have free, freshwater showers all the time. Otherwise, if you bunch the sheet around your neck, it's easier to get to sleep.

THE KEY TO KEYS

Tourists spend hours fumbling with old skeleton keys in rickety hotel doors. The haphazard, nothing-square construction of old hotels means the keys need babying. Don't push them in all the way. Pull the door in or up. Try a little in, quarter turn, and farther in for full turn. Always turn the top of the key away from the door to open it. Leave the key at the desk before leaving for the day. I've never had my room ripped off in Europe. Confirm closing time. Some hotels lock up after their restaurant closes or after midnight and expect you to keep the key to the outside door with you in the evenings.

PENSIONS, ZIMMER, BED AND BREAKFASTS, AND THE LIKE
Between hotels and youth hostels or campgrounds in price and style are a special class of accommodations. These are small, warm, and family-run and offer a personal touch at a budget price. They are the next best thing to staying with a local family, and even if hotels weren't more expensive, I'd choose this budget alternative.

Each country has these friendly accommodations in varying degrees of abundance. They have different names and offer slightly different facilities from country to country, but all have one thing in common: they satisfy the need for a place to stay that gives you the privacy of a hotel and the comforts of home at a price you can afford.

While information on some of the more established places is available in many budget travel guidebooks, the best information is often found locally, through tourist information offices, room-finding services, or even from the local man waiting for his bus or selling apples. Especially in the British Isles, each B&B host has a network of favorites and can happily set you up in a good B&B in your next stop.

Many times, the information is brought to you. I'll never forget struggling off the plane on my arrival in Santorini. Fifteen women were begging me to spend the night. Thrilled, I made a snap decision and followed the most attractive offer to a very nice, budget, *Zimmer*-type accommodation.

Don't confuse European bed-and-breakfasts with their rich cousins in America. B&Bs in the United States are usually doily-pretentious places, very cozy and colorful, but as expensive as hotels.

Britain's bed-and-breakfast places are the best of all. Very common throughout the British Isles, they are a boon to anyone touring England, Scotland, Wales, or Ireland. As the name indicates, a breakfast comes with the bed, and (except in London) this is no ordinary breakfast. Most B&B owners take pride in their breakfasts. Their guests sit down to an elegant and very British table setting and feast on cereal, juice, bacon, sausages, eggs, broiled tomatoes, mushrooms, toast, marmalade, and coffee or tea. While you are finishing your coffee, the landlady (who by this time is probably on very friendly terms with you) will often present

Never judge a B&B by its name. Like many in Britain, this one is smoke-free and comes with numerous pleasant extras.

you with her guest book, pointing out the other guests from your state who have stayed in her house and inviting you to make an entry. Your hostess will sometimes cook you a simple dinner for a good price, and, if you have time to chat, you may get in on an evening social hour with tea and biscuits. When you bid her farewell and thank her for the good sleep and full stomach, it's often difficult to get away. Determined to fill you with as much information as food, she wants you to have the best day of sightseeing possible.

If you're going to the normal tourist stops, your guidebook will list some good B&Bs. If you're venturing off the beaten British path, you don't need (or want) a listing. The small towns and countryside are littered with places whose quality varies only in degrees of wonderful. I try not to take a B&B until I've checked out three. Styles and atmosphere vary from house to house, and besides, I enjoy looking through European homes.

Big-city B&Bs are much less personal. Many have recently turned their breakfast room into another room or two and serve shrink-wrapped continental breakfasts in your room. Another sad trend is the British tourist board's crown system, which rates, prices, and recommends places solely on their plumbing and appliances. Many small-time, easygoing proprietors have no choice but to go heavily into debt, gear up, and charge more. Mavericks don't play by the rules, don't get listed,

---

and rely solely on their own followings. To try to measure coziness and friendliness, the British Tourist Board has added "commended" or "highly commended" to the otherwise-sterile crown system. Germany, Austria, and Switzerland call their B&Bs *Zimmer Frei* or *Privat Zimmer*. They are very common in areas popular with travelers (such as Austria's Salzkammergut Lakes District and Germany's Rhine, Romantic Road, and southern Bavaria). You'll see signs posted clearly indicating whether they have rooms (green) or not (orange). Some (especially in Austria) discourage one-night stays. Most charge around $15 per person with a hearty continental breakfast. *Pensionen* and *Gasthäuser* are similarly priced, small, family-run hotels. Switzerland has very few *Zimmer*.

France has a growing network of *Chambre d'Hôte* (CH) accommodations where locals, mainly in the countryside and in small towns, rent double rooms for about the price of a cheap hotel ($40) but include breakfast. Some CHs post *Chambre* signs in their windows, but most are listed only through local tourist offices. While your hosts will rarely speak English, they will almost always be enthusiastic and a delight to share a home with. For longer stays in the countryside, look into France's popular network of *Gites*. Pick up regional listings at local tourist offices.

In Greece and Slovenia, you'll find many $10-per-bed *dhomatia* and *sobe*, respectively. Especially in touristy coastal and island towns, hard-

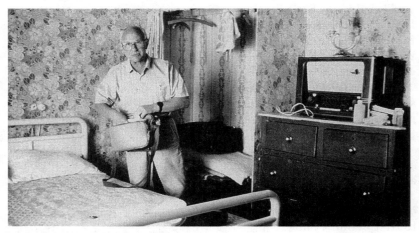

All over Europe, people rent spare bedrooms to budget travelers. Bed and breakfasts give you double the cultural experience for half the price of a hotel. In Scotland, you may get a hot-water bottle. This Portuguese B&B came with a beach view and a bedpan.

A special bonus when enjoying Britain's great bed and breakfasts: you get your own temporary local mother

working entrepreneurs will meet boats and buses as they come into town. In Greek villages with no hotels, ask for *dhomatia* at the town *taverna*.

Eastern Europe has always had brave entrepreneurs running underground bed-and-breakfasts. Now, with the hard economic times, the freer atmosphere, and the overcrowded, overpriced, official hotels, you'll find more B&Bs in Eastern Europe than ever before. Look for hustling housewives with rooms to rent at train stations and around tourist offices. Many cities now have services that efficiently connect travelers with locals renting rooms. If you pay in hard Western currency, you'll get a very cheap room and make your new friend's day.

Spain and Portugal give budget travelers an intimate peek into their small-town, whitewashed worlds by renting out *quartos, camas*, and *casas particular*. In rural Iberia, where there's tourism, you'll find private B&B accommodations.

Italy has a number of important alternatives to its expensive hotels. *Albergo, locanda*, and *pensione* all mean simple budget beds. (While these are technically all bunched together now in a hotel system with star ratings, these traditional names are still found.) Private rooms, called *camere libere* or *camere affita*, are fairly common in the small towns and touristy countryside. Small-town bars are plugged into Italy's B&B grapevine.

Scandinavia's normally luxurious B&Bs are called *rom, hus rum*, or, in Denmark, *Vaerelser*. At $20 per bed, these are incredibly cheap (well, not so incredibly, when you figure it's a common way for the most heavily taxed people in Europe to make a little money under the table). Unfortunately, many Scandinavian B&Bs are advertised only through the local tourist offices, which very often keep them a secret until all the hotels are full. Frommer's *Scandinavia on $60 a Day* and my *Best of Scandinavia* guidebook have some leads that can save you plenty. An evening with a Scandinavian family offers a fascinating look at contemporary Nordic life. If they're serving breakfast, eat it. Some places leave a roll of foil on the table, so you can pack out a sandwich for lunch.

Country	Term for Private Rooms to Rent	Rough Cost per Bed, No Breakfast
Great Britain	Bed and Breakfast	$15
Norway/Sweden	Rom or Rum	$20
Denmark	Vaerelser	$20
Germany/Austria/ Switzerland	Zimmer	$15
France	Chambre d'Hôte	$15
Italy	Camere Affita	$15
Slovenia	Sobe	$10
Greece	Dhomatia	$10
Spain	Casas Particulares	$15
Portugal	Quartos	$10
Eastern Europe	All of the above	$10

EUROPE'S 2,000 HOSTELS

Europe's cheapest beds are in hostels. Two thousand youth hostels provide beds throughout Europe for $5 to $20 per night.

As Europe has grown more affluent, hostels have been remodeled to provide more plumbing and smaller rooms. Still, hostels are not hotels—not by a long shot. Many people hate hostels. Others love them and will be hostelers all their lives, regardless of their budgets. Hosteling is a philosophy. A hosteler trades service and privacy for a chance to live simply and communally with people from around the world.

A youth hostel is not limited to young people. You may be ready to jump to the next chapter because, by every other standard, you're older than young. Well, many countries have dropped the word "youth" from their name, and a few years ago the Youth Hostel Association came out with a new card giving "youths" over the age of 54 a discount. People of any age can youth hostel if they have a membership card ($25

One of Europe's 2,000 hostels—$5 a night, your own kitchen, a million-dollar view of the Jungfrau, and lots of friends. Note the worldwide triangular hostel symbol.

a year, less for people under 18 and over 54) available through *Europe Through the Back Door*, your local student travel office, or youth hostel office. (Bavaria is the only exception, with a strictly enforced 26-year-old age limit.)

A hostel provides "no frills" accommodations in clean dormitories. The average hosteler is 18 to 26, but every year there are more oldsters and families hosteling. The sexes are segregated, with four to 20 people packed in a room full of bunk beds. Pillows and blankets, but no sheets, are provided. You can bring a regular single bedsheet (sewn into a sack if you like), rent one for about $4, or buy a regulation hostel sheet-sack at the first hostel you hit (lightweight, ideal design at a bargain price). Many hostels have a few doubles for couples and rooms for families. The buildings are usually in a good, easily accessible location and come in all shapes and sizes. There are castles (Bacharach, Germany), cutter ships (Stockholm), Alpine chalets (Gimmelwald, Switzerland), huge modern buildings (Frankfurt), medieval manor houses (Wilderhope Manor, England), former choirboys' dorms (St. Paul's, London), and former royal residences (Holland Park, London).

The facilities vary, but most provide more than you would expect. Hearty, super-cheap meals are served, often in family-style settings. A typical dinner is fish fingers and mashed potatoes seasoned by conversation with new friends from Norway to New Zealand. The self-service kitchen, complete with utensils, pots, and pans, is a great budget aid that comes with most hostels. Larger hostels even have a small grocery store. Many international friendships rise with the bread in hostel kitchens. Very good hot showers (often with coin-op meters) are the norm, but simpler hostels have cold showers or even none at all. The hostel's recreation and living rooms are my favorite. People gather, play games, tell stories, share information, marvel at American foreign policy, read, write, and team up for future travels. Solo travelers find a family in every hostel. Hostels are ideal meeting places for those in search of a travel partner (or spouse). And those with partners do well to occasionally stay in a hostel to meet some new travelers.

Hostels do have drawbacks. Many have strict rules. They often lock up during the day (usually from 10:00 to 5:00), and they have a curfew at night (10:00, 11:00, or midnight) when the doors are locked and those outside stay there. These curfews are for the greater good—not to make you miserable. In the mountains, the curfew is early because most people are early-rising hikers. In London, the curfew is 11:45, giving you ample time to return from the theater. Amsterdam, where the sun shines at night, has a 1:45 a.m. curfew.

Many school groups (especially German) turn hostels upside down (typically weekends during the school year and weekdays in the summer). Try to be understanding (many groups are disadvantaged kids); we were all noisy kids at one time. Get to know the teacher and make a "cultural experience" out of it.

Hostel rooms can be large and packed. The first half-hour after "lights out" reminds me of summer camp—giggles, burps, jokes, and strange noises in many languages. Snoring is permitted and practiced openly.

Theft is a problem in hostels, but the answer is simple: don't leave valuables lying around (no one's going to steal your tennis shoes or journal). Use the storage lockers that are available in most hostels.

Hostels were originally for hikers and bikers, but that isn't the case these days. Still, give your car a low profile; arriving by taxi is just plain bad taste. It used to be that every hosteler did a chore before his card was returned to him. These duties are a thing of the past except in Britain. Even in Britain they are becoming rare, and most that remain are token duties, never taking more than a few minutes.

Hostels are run by "wardens" or "house parents." They do their best to strictly enforce no-drinking rules, quiet hours, and other regulations. Some are loose and laid-back, others are like Marine drill sergeants, but all are hostel wardens for the noble purpose of enabling travelers to better appreciate and enjoy that town or region. While they are often overworked and harried, most wardens are great people who enjoy a quiet cup of coffee with an American and are happy to give you some local travel tips or recommend a special nearby hostel. Be sensitive to the many demands on their time, and never treat them like hotel servants.

SELECTING A HOSTEL

Hostel selectively; some hostels are sightseeing ends in themselves. Survey other hostelers and hostel wardens for suggestions. I hostel much more in the north, where hostels are generally more comfortable and the savings over hotels more exciting. I rarely hostel in the south, where hostels are less common and two or three people can sleep just as cheaply in a budget hotel.

Big-city hostels are the most crowded and institutional. Rural hostels, far from train lines and famous sights, are usually quiet and frequented by a more mature crowd. If you have a car, use that mobility to leave the Eurail zone and enjoy some of Europe's overlooked hostels.

Getting a hostel bed in peak season can be tricky. The most popular hostels fill up every day. Written reservations are possible, but I've never bothered. Telephone reservations work wonderfully where the warden will take them—about 50 percent of the time. I always call ahead to try to reserve and at least check on the availability of beds. Don't rely solely on the phone, because hostels are required to hold some beds for drop-ins. If you just show up, you have a much better chance of landing a bed or at least being sent to their recommended cheap alternative. Try to arrive in the morning before the hostel closes. Otherwise, line up with the scruffy gang for the 5:00 opening of the office, when any remaining beds are doled out.

Thankfully, many hostels are putting out envelopes for each available bed, so you can drop by any time of day, pop your card into the reservation envelope and through the slot, and show up sometime that evening. Also, many German and American hostels have a new telex reservation system where, for a small fee, you can firmly reserve and pay for your next hostel bed before you leave the last one. (If you live in a big American city, call your hostel for more specifics.)

Hostel bed availability is unpredictable. Some obscure hostels are booked out on certain days two months in advance. But I stumbled into Oberammergau one night during the jam-packed Passion Play festival and found beds for a group of eight.

Hostelling International publishes *Budget Accommodations: Europe and the Mediterranean*. This directory, available where you get your card or at any European hostel, lists each of Europe's 2,000 hostels with which

In a youth hostel, you'll have bunk beds and roommates

day or season (if any) the hostel is closed, what bus goes there, distance from the station, how many beds, its altitude, phone number with area code, and a handy map of Europe locating all the hostels. Individual countries have a more accurate and informative directory or handbook (never expensive, usually free). England's is especially worthwhile. If you're sticking to the more popular destinations, the *Let's Go* guidebook (Europe, or individual countries) lists hostels well enough to make the *Budget Accommodations* hostel directory unnecessary.

UNOFFICIAL HOSTELS

There seem to be nearly as many unofficial or independent hostels as there are official (International Youth Hostel Federation [IYHF]) ones. Many wardens and student groups prefer to run their own show and avoid the occasionally heavy-handed bureaucracy of the IYHF. These hostels are looser and more casual but not as clean or organized.

Ireland's Independent Hostel Owners (IHO) Association is a less institutional (fewer rules, no membership required) network of these maverick independent hostels. Pick up their booklet at any IHO hostel.

Many large cities have wild and cheap student-run hostels that are popular with wild and cheap student travelers. If these sound right for you, *Let's Go: Europe* has great listings. In the Alps, look for the word *lager*, which means they have a coed loft full of $5-a-night mattresses. As in IYHF hostels, you'll usually save money if you provide your own sheets. Many Alpine huts require no linen and wash their blankets annually. I'll never forget getting cozy in my top bunk while a German with a "Rat Patrol" accent in the bottom bunk said, "You're climbing into the germs of centuries." Hut-hoppers hike with their own sheets.

CAMPING EUROPEAN-STYLE
Relatively few Americans take advantage of Europe's 10,000-plus campgrounds. Camping is the cheapest way to see Europe, the middle-class European family way to travel. And campers give it rave reviews.

"Camping" is the international word for campground. Every town has a camping with enough ground to pitch a tent or park a "caravan" (trailer), good showers and washing facilities, often a grocery store and restaurant, and a handy location on the edge of town (or a bus connection into town), all for just a few dollars per person per night.

Unlike the picturesque, rustic American campground near a lake or forest, European camping is more functional, like spending the night in a Park-and-Ride. Campings forbid open fires, and you won't find a picturesque riverfront lot with a stove, table, and privacy. Sites normally don't even have a picnic table. A camping is usually near or in the town—a place to sleep, eat, wash, and catch a bus downtown. They rarely fill up, and if they do, the Full sign usually refers to trailers (most Europeans are trailer campers). A small tent can almost always be squeezed in somewhere.

Campings are well posted, and local tourist information offices have guides and maps listing nearby campgrounds. Every country has good and bad campgrounds. Campgrounds mirror their surroundings. If the region is overcrowded, dusty, dirty, unkempt, and generally chaotic, you're unlikely to find an oasis behind the campground's gates. A sleepy Austrian valley will most likely offer a sleepy Austrian campground.

Camping with kids has many advantages. A family sleeps in a tent a lot cheaper than in a hotel. There's plenty to occupy children's attention, including playgrounds that come fully equipped with European kids. As your kids make European friends, your campground social circle will widen.

European campgrounds have great, if sometimes crowded, showers and washing facilities. Hot water, as in many hostels and hotels, is metered, and you'll learn to carry coins and "douche" quickly.

European tenters appreciate the in-camp grocery store, café, and restaurant. The store, while high-priced, stays open longer than most, offering latecomers a budget alternative to the restaurant. The restaurant or café is a likely camp hangout, and Americans enjoy mixing in this easygoing European social scene. I've scuttled many nights on the town so I wouldn't miss the fun with new friends right in the camp. Camping, like hosteling, is a great way to meet Europeans. If the campground doesn't have a place to eat, you'll find one nearby.

Silence reigns in European campgrounds after the 10:00 or 11:00 p.m. curfew. Noisemakers are strictly dealt with. Many places close the gates to cars after 10:00. If you do arrive after the office closes, set up quietly and register in the morning.

Campgrounds, unlike youth hostels, are remarkably theft-free. Campings are full of basically honest middle-class European families, and someone's at the gate all day. Most people just leave their gear zipped inside their tents.

Prices vary from country to country and within countries according to facilities and style. Expect to spend around $5 per night per person. You'll often pay by the tent, so four people in one tent sleep cheaper than four individual campers. (Beware: Italian campgrounds can be shockingly expensive.)

Camp registration is easy. As with most hotels, you show your passport, fill out a short form, and learn the rules. Checkout time is usually noon. English is the second language of campings throughout Europe, and most managers will understand the monoglot American.

The International Camping Carnet, a kind of international campground membership card, is required at some sites, handy at others. It is

Many campgrounds offer "bungalows" with kitchenettes and four to six beds. Comfortable and cheaper than hotels, these are particularly popular in Scandinavia.

available for $30 through the National Campers and Hikers Association, Inc. (4804 Transit Road, Bldg. 2, Depew, NY 14043, tel. 716-668-6242; purchase includes membership in NCHA, a handy resource for campers) or at many European campgrounds. The carnet will get you an occasional discount or preferential treatment in a very crowded situation. Sometimes you are required to leave either your passport or your camping carnet at the office.

European sites called weekend campings are rented out on a yearly basis to local urbanites. Too often, weekend sites are full or don't allow what they call "stop-and-go" campers (you). Camping guidebooks indicate which places are the "weekend" types.

Even if you don't have a car or trailer but are a camper at heart, camping may still be the way to go. Europe's campgrounds mix well with just about any mode of transportation. And very light modern camp gear makes camping without a car easier than ever. Tent and train is a winning combination for many. Nearly every train station has a tourist office nearby. Stop by and pick up a map with campgrounds marked, local camping leaflets, and bus directions. In most cases, buses shuttle campers from station to campground with ease. Every station has lockers, in which those with limited energy can leave unneeded baggage.

Hitchhikers find camping just right for their tender budget. Many campgrounds are located near the major road out of town, where long rides are best snared. Any hitching camper with average social skills can find a friend driving his way with an empty seat. A note on the camp bulletin board can be very effective.

Tents and bikes also mix well. Bikers enjoy the same we-can-squeeze-one-more-in status as hikers and are rarely turned away.

Camping by car is my favorite combination. A car carries all your camp gear and gets you to any campground fast and easy. Good road maps always pinpoint "campings," and when you're within a few blocks, the road signs take over. In big cities, the money you save on parking alone will pay for your camping. I usually take the bus downtown, leaving the car next to my tent.

Commit yourself to a camping trip or to a no-camping trip and pack accordingly. Don't carry a sleeping bag and a tent just in case.

Your camping trip deserves first-class equipment. Spend some time and money outfitting yourself before your trip. There are plenty of stores with exciting new gear and expert salespeople to get you up to date in a hurry. European campers prefer a very lightweight "three season" sleeping bag (consult a climate chart for your probable bedroom temperature) and a closed-cell ensolite pad to insulate and soften your bed. A camp stove is right for American-style camping but probably not your cup of tea in Europe. Start without a stove. If you figure you need one, buy one there. In Europe, it's much easier to find fuel for a European camp stove than for its Yankee counterpart. (If you take one from home, it should be the butane *gaz* variety.) I kept it simple, picnicking and enjoying food and fun in the campground restaurant. (For a good catalog full of camping gear, call the REI cooperative at 800-426-4840.)

Informal camping ("camping wild" or "free camping") is legal in most of Europe. Low-profile, pitch-the-tent-after-dark-and-move-on-first-thing-in-the-morning free camping is usually allowed even in countries where it is technically illegal. Use good judgment, and don't pitch your tent informally in carefully controlled areas such as cities and resorts.

It's a good idea to ask permission when possible. In the countryside, a landowner will rarely refuse a polite request to borrow a patch of land for the night.

Formal camping is safer than free camping. Never leave your gear and tent unattended without the gates of a formal campground to discourage thieves.

There are several good camping guidebooks out. Lenore Baken's *How to Camp Europe by Train* is a popular guide on this subject. The *Let's Go* guide gives good instructions on getting to and from the campgrounds. Each country's national tourist office in the United States can send you information on camping in its country.

Sleeping Free

There are still people traveling in Europe on $10 a day. The one thing they have in common (apart from B.O.) is that they sleep free. If even cheap pensions and youth hostels are too expensive for your budget, you too can sleep free. I once went 29 out of 30 nights without paying for a bed. It's neither difficult nor dangerous, but it's not always comfortable, convenient, or legal, either. This is not a vagabonding guide, but any traveler may have an occasional free night. Faking it until the sun returns can become, at least in the long run, a good memory.

Europe has plenty of places to roll out your sleeping bag. Some large cities, such as Amsterdam and Athens, are flooded with tourists during peak season, and many of them spend their nights dangerously in a city park. Some cities enforce their "no sleeping in the parks" laws only selectively. Many now offer a free, safe, and legal "sleep-in." Away from the cities, in forests or on beaches, you can pretty well sleep where you like. I have found that summer nights in the Mediterranean part of

Europe are mild enough that I am comfortable with just my jeans, sweater, and hostel sheet. I no longer lug a sleeping bag around Europe, but if you'll be vagabonding a lot, bring a light bag.

Trains and stations are great for sleeping free. On the trains, success hinges on getting enough room to stretch out, and that can be quite a trick. See the section on sleeping on trains in Chapter 3.

When you have no place to go for the night in a city, you can always retreat to the station for a free, warm, safe, and uncomfortable place to spend the night (assuming the station stays open all night). Most popular tourist cities in Europe have stations whose concrete floors are painted nightly with a long rainbow of sleepy campers. This is allowed, but everyone is cleared out at dawn before the normal rush of travelers converges on the station. In some cases, you'll be asked to show a ticket. Any ticket or your Eurailpass entitles you to a free night in a station's waiting room: you are simply waiting for your early train. Whenever possible, avoid the second-class lounges; sleep with a better breed of hobo in first-class lounges.

It's tempting but quite risky to sleep in a train car that's just sitting there going nowhere. No awakening is ruder than having your bedroom jolt into motion and roll toward God-knows-where, although many would argue it's more pleasant to sleep on a train to God-knows-where than to be stuck in the station all night. If you do find a parked train car to sleep in, check to see when it's scheduled to leave. Some Eurailers get a free if disjointed night by riding a train out for four hours and catching one back in for another four hours. Scandinavia, with Europe's most expensive hotels, offers couchettes for a reasonable $15.

An airport is a large, posh version of a train station, offering a great opportunity to sleep free. After a late landing, I crash on a comfortable sofa rather than waste sleeping time looking for a place that will sell me a bed for the remainder of the night. Many cut-rate inter-European flights leave or arrive at ungodly hours. Frankfurt airport is served conveniently by the train and is great for sleeping free—even if you aren't flying anywhere. Most large airports have "rest cabins" which rent out cheaper than hotels (often for only eight hours at a time).

Imaginative vagabonds see Europe as one big free hotel (barns, churches, buildings under construction, ruins, college dorms, etc.). Just carry your passport with you, attach your belongings to you so they don't get stolen, and use good judgment in your choice of a free bed.

FRIENDS AND RELATIVES

There is no better way to really enjoy a strange country than as the guest of a local family. And, of course, a night with a friend or relative is very easy on the budget. I've had nothing but good experiences (and good sleep) at my "addresses" in Europe. There are two kinds of addresses: European addresses brought from home and those you pick up while traveling.

Before you leave, do some research. Dig up some European relatives. No matter how far out on the family tree they are, unless you are a real jerk, they're tickled to have an American visitor in their nest. I send mine a card announcing my visit to their town and telling them when I'll arrive. They answer with "Please come visit us" or "Have a good trip." It is obvious from their letter (or lack of one) if I'm invited to stop by.

Follow the same procedure with indirect contacts. I have dear "parents away from home" in Austria and London. My Austrian "parents" are really the parents of my sister's ski instructor. In London, they are the parents of a friend of my uncle. Neither relationship was terribly close—until I visited. Now we are friends for life.

This is not cultural freeloading. Both parties benefit from such a visit. Never forget that a Greek family is just as curious and interested in you

The Europeans you visit don't need to be next-of-kin. This Tirolean is the father of my sister's ski teacher. That's close enough.

as you are in them (and the same old nightly family meals are probably pretty boring). Equipped with hometown postcards and pictures of my family, I make a point of giving as much from my culture as I am taking from the culture of my host. I insist on no special treatment, telling my host that I am most comfortable when no fuss is made over me. I try to help with the chores, I don't wear out my welcome, and I follow up each visit with postcards to share the rest of my trip with my friends. I pay or reimburse my hosts for their hospitality only with a thank-you letter from home, possibly with color prints of me with their family.

The other kind of address is one you pick up during your travels. Exchanging addresses is almost as common as a handshake in Europe. If you have a business or personal card, bring a pile. When people meet, they invite each other to visit. I warn my friend that I may very well show up some day at his house, whether it's in Osaka, New Zealand, New Mexico, or Dublin. When I have, it's been a good experience.

A wonderful new book offers an extensive listing of people interested in meeting English-speaking travelers. *People to People: Czech-Slovakia, Hungary, and Bulgaria* (by Jim Haynes, ISBN: 0-86241-398-2, Zephyr Press) lists a lifetime of potential friends with each of their special interests, addresses and just what sort of hospitality they'd like to offer. New editions introducing you to Poland, Romania, and the Baltic States are on the way.

SERVAS

Servas is a worldwide organization that sets up travelers with host families with the noble goal of building world peace through international understanding. Travelers pay $55 to join. They can stay for two nights (more only if invited; arrangements are made after an exchange of letters—no money changes hands) in homes of other members around the world. This is not a crash-pad exchange. It's cultural sightseeing through a real live-in experience, a cultural exchange, so plan to hang around to talk and share and learn. Many travelers swear by Servas as the only way to really travel and build a truly global list of friends. Opening your own home to visitors is not required. For more information, write to Servas at 11 John St., #407, New York, NY 10038, tel. 212/267-0252.

HOUSE SWAPPING

Many families enjoy a great budget option year after year. They trade houses (sometimes cars, too, but draw the line at pets) with someone at the destination of their choice. Ask your travel agent for information or contact Intervac Home Exchange (Box 590504, San Francisco, CA

94159, tel. 800/756-HOME). *Trading Places: The Wonderful World of Home Exchange* (Rutledge Hill Press) is a good resource.

Eating Cheap

Many vacations revolve around great restaurant meals, and for good reason. Europe serves some of the world's top cuisine—at some of the world's top prices.

I'm no gourmet, so most of my experience lies in eating well cheaply. Galloping gluttons thrive on $10 a day—by picnicking. Those with a more refined palate and a little more money can mix picnics with satisfying, atmospheric, and enjoyable restaurant meals and eat just fine for $25 a day.

This $25-a-day budget includes a $5 continental breakfast (usually figured into your hotel bill), a $5 picnic midday feast, and a $15 good and filling restaurant dinner (more with wine or dessert). If your budget requires, you can find a satisfying dinner for $10 anywhere in Europe.

European restaurant meals are about as expensive as those in the United States. The cost of eating is determined not by the local standard but by your personal standard. Many Americans can't find an edible meal for less than $20 in their hometown. Their neighbors enjoy eating out for half that. If you can enjoy a $10 meal in Boston, Detroit, or Seattle, you'll eat well in London, Rome, or Helsinki for the same price. Last year I ate 100 dinners in Europe. My budget target was: $5 to $10 for a simple, fill-the-tank meal, $15 for a memorable restaurant dinner, and $20 for a splurge meal.

Forget the scare stories. People who spend $50 for a dinner in Dublin and then complain either enjoy complaining or are fools. Let me fill you in on filling up in Europe.

RESTAURANTS

Restaurants are the most expensive way to eat. They can pillage and plunder a tight budget, but it would be criminal to pass through Europe without sampling the local specialties served in good restaurants. A country's high cuisine is just as important culturally as its museums. Experience it.

When I splurge on a restaurant meal (about once a day), I want good value. Average tourists are attracted—like flies to cow pies—to the biggest neon sign that boasts, "We speak English and accept credit cards." Wrong! The key to finding a good meal is to find a restaurant filled with loyal, local customers enjoying themselves. After a few days in Europe, you'll have no trouble telling a local hangout from a tourist trap. Take advantage of local favorites.

Restaurants listed in your guidebook are usually fine, but too often when a place becomes famous this way it goes downhill. You don't need those listings to find your own good restaurant. Leave the tourist center and stroll around until you find a happy crowd of locals eating. Ask your hotel receptionist, or even someone on the street, for a good place—not a good place for tourists but a place they'd take a local guest.

European restaurants post their menus outside. Check the price and selection before entering. If the menu's not posted, ask to see one.

DECIPHERING THE MENU

Finding the right restaurant is half the battle. Then you need to order a good meal. Ordering in a foreign language can be fun, or it can be an ordeal. Ask for an English menu—if nothing else, you might get the waiter who speaks the goodest English. Most waiters can give at least a very basic translation—cheekin, bunny, zuppa, green salat, and so on. A pocket phrase book or menu reader (especially one of the handy little Marling Menu Masters) is very helpful for those who want to avoid ordering sheep stomach when all they want is a lamb chop.

If you don't know what to order, go with the waiter's recommendation or look for your dream meal on another table and order by pointing. You can't go wrong. People are usually helpful and understanding to the poor and hungry monoglot tourist. If they aren't, you probably

A fun neighborhood restaurant; no English menus, no credit cards, but good food, good prices, and a friendly chef

picked a place that sees too many of them. Europeans with the most patience with tourists are the ones who rarely deal with them.

People who agonize over each word on the menu season the whole experience with stress. Get a basic idea of what's cooking, have some fun with the waiter, be loose and adventurous, and just order something.

To max out culturally, I never order the same meal as my partner. We share, sampling twice as many dishes. My groups cut every dish into bits and our table becomes a lazy Susan. If anything, the waiters are impressed by our interest in their food, and very often they'll run over with a special treat for all of us to sample—like squid eggs.

I like to order a high-risk and a low-risk meal with my partner. At worst, we learn what we don't like and split the veal and fries. Meals don't always come simultaneously, and in Europe, it's fine to eat when served. If you're eating alone, fight the loneliness by bringing something to read.

The *menu turistico* (tourist menu), *prix fixe* menu, or *menu du jour* is very popular and normally a good value. For a set price, you get the "special of the day" multicourse meal complete with bread, service, and sometimes wine. Often you can choose from several appetizers and entrées. When I'm lazy and the price is right, I go for it, and it usually turns out OK. But you'll notice that people in the know (locals) order à la carte. Be careful—asking for the *menu* in France may get you the fixed price meal of the day. Asking for the *carte* is a better way to get a listing of what's cooking.

The best values in European entrées are usually fish, veal, and chicken. Drinks (except for wine in France and Italy, which is very reasonable) and desserts are the worst value. Skipping those, I can enjoy some surprisingly classy meals for $10 to $15.

Although fast food has gained a foothold in Europe, a real Continental meal is a leisurely experience, the focus of the evening. In a good restaurant, service will be slower, and you won't get your bill until you ask for it. A European meal is an end in itself. Europeans will spend at least two hours enjoying a good dinner, and, for the full experience, so should you. Fast service is rude service.

To get the bill, you'll have to ask for it (catch the waiter's eye and, with raised hands, scribble with an imaginary pencil on your palm). Before it comes, make a mental tally of roughly how much your meal should cost. The bill should vaguely resemble the figure you expected. It should have the same number of digits. If the total is a surprise, ask to have it itemized and explained. Some waiters make the same "innocent" mistakes repeatedly, knowing most tourists are so befuddled by the money and menu that they'll pay whatever number lies at the bottom of the bill.

Fast-food places are everywhere. Yes, the Hamburgerization of the world is a shame, but face it—the busiest and biggest McDonald's in the world are in Tokyo, Rome, and Moscow. The burger has become a global thing. You'll find Big Macs in every language—not exciting (and more than the American price), but at least at McDonald's you know exactly what you're getting, and it's fast. A hamburger, fries, and shake are fun halfway through your trip. Each country has its equivalent of the hamburger or hot dog stand. Whatever their origin, they're a hit with the young locals and a handy place for a quick, cheap bite.

American fast-food joints are kid-friendly and satisfy the need for a cheap salad bar and a tall orange juice. They've grabbed prime bits of real estate in every big European city. Since there's no cover, this is an opportunity to savor a low-class paper cup of coffee while enjoying some high-class people watching.

Self-service is an international word. You'll find self-service restaurants in big cities everywhere offering low-price, low-risk, low-stress, what-you-see-is-what-you-get meals. A sure value for your dollar, franc, or shilling is a department store cafeteria. These places are designed for the shopping housewife who has a sharp eye for a good value. At a salad bar, grab the small (cheap) plate and stack it like the locals—high.

TIPPING

Tipping is a minuscule concern of mine during a European trip. Front-door travel agents advise going to Europe armed with dollar bills for tipping. They'll advise putting five bucks under your pillow to get extra towels from the maids. Traveling through the Back Door, the only tipping you'll do is in the rare restaurant where service isn't included, rounding the taxi bill up, or when someone assists you in seeing some sight and is paid no other way (such as the man who shows people an Etruscan tomb that just happens to be in his backyard).

In restaurants, a service charge of about 15 percent is almost always included in the menu price or added automatically to your bill. If service is not included the menu will say so explicitly (e.g., *service non compris*). Tipping is another matter and never expected. Leaving the coins or rounding up the bill is a nice touch for especially good service. Overtipping is Ugly American. Americans in the days of the big buck shaped an image that Yankees in the days of the smaller dollar are having a hard time living down. If your bucks talk at home, muzzle them in Europe. As a matter of principle, if not economy, the local price should prevail.

LOCAL SPECIALTIES, ONE COUNTRY AT A TIME
Greece
The menus are all Greek to me. It is common and acceptable for you to go into the kitchen and physically point to the dish you want. This is a good way to make some friends, sample from each kettle, get what you want (or at least know what you're getting), and have a very memorable meal. (The same is true in Turkey.) Be brave; try the local food. My favorite Greek snack is a tasty *shish kebab* wrapped in flat bread—called a *souvlaki pita*. *Souvlaki* stands, offering $1 take-out pita sandwiches, are all over Athens. On the islands, dunk bread into *tzatziki*, a refreshing cucumber and yogurt dip, and eat fresh seafood. Don't miss the creamy yogurt with honey. The *feta* (goat) cheese salads and the flaky nut 'n honey dessert called *baklava* are two other taste treats. If possible, go to a wine festival. *Retsina* is a pine resin-flavored wine that is a dangerous taste to acquire. Eat when the locals do—late. For American-style coffee, order "Nescafe."

Turkey
Bring an appetite and order high on the menu in nice restaurants. Eating's cheap in Turkey. The typical eatery is a user-friendly cafeteria with giant bins of lots of delicacies you always thought were Greek. *Kebabs* are a standard meaty snack. *Pide*, fresh out of the oven, is the ready-to-go flat-football-shaped Turkish pizza. The rice pudding (*sutlac*, pronounced: soot-lach), *baklava*, and pockets full of pistachios will handle your sweet tooth and munchies. Tea in tiny hourglass-shaped glasses is served constantly everywhere (and often appears as a freebie). This and a refreshing milky yogurt drink called *ayran*, cheap boxes of cherry juice, and fresh-squeezed orange juice make quenching your Turkish thirst fun. For breakfast get ready for cucumbers, olives, tomatoes and lots of goat cheese.

Italy
Italy is no longer so cheap. In fact, it's caught up with and passed much of Europe in price. And the most popular cities—Florence, Venice, and Rome—are most expensive.

Italians eat huge meals consisting of a first course of pasta, a second plate of meat, plus a salad, fruit, and wine. The pasta course alone is enough to fill the average tourist. While some restaurants won't serve just pasta, for a cheap meal I find one that will and enjoy reasonably priced lasagna or minestrone and a salad. Anytime you eat or drink at a table, you'll be charged a cover (*coperto*) of a dollar or two. That, plus service, makes even a cheap, one-course restaurant meal cost $10.

For inexpensive Italian eateries, look for the term *osteria, tavola calda, rosticceria, trattoria, pizzeria,* or "self-service." A big pizza (everywhere for under $7) and a cold beer is my idea of a good, fast, cheap Italian meal. Look for a Pizza Rustica (which serves pizza by the slice sold by weight) for a stand-up super bargain meal. Just point to the best-looking pizza and tell them how much you want (200 grams is a meal); they heat it up and it's yours.

Piatti del giorno (plate of the day, usually a good deal), *pane e coperto* (charge for bread and cover), and *servizio compreso* (service included) are three important phrases to know. But the most important word in your Italian vocabulary is *gelato*—probably the best ice cream you'll ever taste. A big cone or cup with a variety of flavors costs about $2.

Cappuccino—rich coffee with a frothy head of steamed milk—is very popular, and it should be. Tiny coffee shops are tucked away on just about every street. All have a price list, and most require you to pay the cashier first and take the receipt to the man with the drinks. Experiment; try coffee or tea *freddo* (cold) or a *frappe*. Discover a new specialty each day. Bars sell large bottles of cold mineral water, with or without gas, for about $1. *Panini* (sandwiches) are widely available and cheap.

Bar-hopping is fun. A bottle of wine serves four or five people for four dollars. Many bars have delicious *cicheti* (pronounced cheh-KAY-tee), local toothpick munchies. A *cicheteria* is a great place for an entire meal of these pint-sized taste treats.

Spain

The greatest pleasure in Spanish eating is the price tag. Take advantage of the house wine. Fit the local schedule—lunch late (1:00–3:00) and dinner later (8:30–11:30). Restaurants are generally closed except at mealtimes. *Platos combinados* (combination plates of three or more items) are a reasonable way to sample Spanish cuisine. At other times, bars and coffee spots serve snacks of *bocadillos* (sandwiches) and *tortillas* (omelets, great in a bar for a cheap and hearty breakfast) along with *tapas* (hors d'oeuvres). On my last trip, I ate at least one easy, quick, and very cheap *tapas* meal a day. Restaurants associated with bars are often excellent as well as inexpensive.

Portugal

Portugal has some of the best and cheapest food I've found in Europe. Find a local sailors' hangout and fill up on fresh seafood, especially clams and cockles. While Portuguese restaurants are not expensive, food stands in the fairs and amusement parks are even cheaper. The young *vinho verde* is an addictive local specialty and a favorite of visiting wine buffoons.

Switzerland

Rösti (a sort of hash-browns-with-onions dish) is a good, hearty budget standby. *Raclette* (melted cheese, potatoes and pickles) is another popular dish. Split a cheese fondue with your hiking partner before filling up on Swiss chocolate. The Migros and Co-op grocery stores sell groceries for about the same price as you'd find in American stores—cheap by European standards. Youth hostels usually serve large family-style dinners at a low, low price. Expensive Swiss restaurant prices make these budget food alternatives especially attractive. The remote mountain huts offer more than shelter. Many have provisions helicoptered in, are reasonably priced, and bubble with Alpine atmosphere. Swiss wine (*Fendant*) is expensive but worth every franc. Local beer is cheap and good.

The Netherlands

My favorite Dutch food is Indonesian. Indonesia, a former colony of the Netherlands, fled the nest, leaving behind plenty of great Indonesian restaurants. The cheapest meals, as well as some of the best splurges, are found in Holland's many Indonesian (or "Chinese-Indisch") restaurants. The famous *rijstafel* (rice table) is the ultimate Indonesian meal, with as many as 36 delightfully exotic courses, all eaten with rice. One meal is plenty for two, so order carefully.

In a small town restaurant a *rijstafel* can be a great bargain—12 exotic courses with rice for $10. *Bami* or *nasi goring* are smaller, cheaper, but still filling versions of *rijstafel*.

Other Dutch treats include *nieuwe haring* (raw herrings), and *siroopwafels*—a syrup-filled cookie that's best eaten warm.

Scandinavia

Most Scandinavians avoid their highly taxed and very expensive restaurants. The key to budget eating in Nordic Europe is to take advantage of the smorgasbord. For about $8 (cheap in Scandinavia), the breakfast smorgasbords of Denmark, Norway, and Sweden will fill you with plenty of hearty food. Smorgasbords do not provide doggie bags, but I have noticed many empty rucksacks (or zip-lock baggies) filling out as fast as their owners. Since my stomach is the same size all day long and both meals are, by definition, all-you-can-eat, I opt for the budget breakfast meal over the fancier and more expensive ($20) *middag*, or midday, smorgasbord. Many train stations and boats serve smorgasbords.

For a budget lunch in Denmark, find a *Smorrebrod* (open-face sandwich) shop. A delightful alternative to a fast-food joint, these places make artistic and delicious sandwich picnics to go.

All over Scandinavia, keep your eyes peeled for daily lunch specials called *dagens ratt*. And you can normally have all the vegetables (usually potatoes) you want when you order a restaurant's entrée. Just ask for seconds. Many Scandinavian pizzerias offer amazing all-you-can-eat deals and hearty salad bars. The cheapest cafeterias often close at 5:00 or 6:00 p.m. Fresh produce, colorful markets, and efficient supermarkets abound in Europe's most expensive corner. Picnic.

Germany

Germany is ideal for the "meat-and-potatoes" person. With straightforward, no-nonsense food at budget prices, I eat very well in Deutschland. Small-town restaurants serve up wonderful plates of hearty local specialties for around $7. The *würst* is the best anywhere, and *kraut* is not as *sauer* as the stuff you hate at home. Eat ugly things whenever possible. So many tasty European specialties come in gross packages.

Drink beer in Bavaria and wine on the Rhine, choosing the most atmospheric *bräuhaus* or *weinstube* possible.

Browse through supermarkets and see what Germany eats when there's no more beer and pretzels. Try Gummi Bears, a bear-shaped jelly bean with a cult following, and Nutella, a sensuous choco-nut spread that turns anything into a first-class dessert. Fast-food stands are called *Schnell Imbiss*. For budget relief in big-city Germany, find a Greek, Turkish, or Italian restaurant.

France

France is famous for its cuisine—and rightly so. Dining in France can be surprisingly easy on a budget, especially in the countryside. Small restaurants throughout the country love their local specialties and take great pride in serving them. The cheese boards that come with four-course meals offer the average American a new adventure in eating. When it comes, ask for a little of each cheese. Wine is the cheapest drink, and every region has its own wine and cheese. Order the house wine (*vin du patron*). Bars serve reasonable omelettes, salads, and the *croque monsieur*—your standard grilled cheese and ham sandwich. The *plat du jour* is a good value, and to afford a classy restaurant, remember, at lunch you'll eat the same food at substantially reduced prices. In France, the "menu" refers to a fixed price, three-to-six-course meal—often a good deal.

Degustation gratuite is not a laxative but an invitation to sample the wine. You'll find D/G signs throughout France's wine-growing regions.

When buying cheese, be sure to ask for samples of the local specialties. Croissants are served warm with breakfast, and *baguettes* (long, skinny loaves of French bread) are great for budget munching.

Regardless of your budget, picnic for a royal tour of French delicacies. Make a point of visiting the small specialty shops and picking up the finest (most expensive) pâtés, cheeses, and hors d'oeuvres. As you spread out your tablecloth, every passerby will wish you a cheery *"Bon appetit!"*

MENSAS

When you're in a European university town, with a wallet as empty as your stomach, find a "mensa." Mensa is the pan-European word for a government-subsidized institutional (university, fire station, union of gondoliers, etc.) cafeteria. If the place welcomes tourists, you can fill yourself with a plate of dull but nourishing food for an unbeatable price in the company of local students or workers.

University cafeterias (often closed during summer holidays) offer a surefire way to meet educated English-speaking young locals with open and stimulating minds. They're often anxious to practice their politics and economics as well as their English on a foreign friend. This is especially handy as you travel beyond Europe.

THE CONTINENTAL BREAKFAST

In Europe (except for Britain, Holland, and Scandinavia), breakfast is a roll with marmalade or jam, occasionally a slice of ham or cheese, and coffee and tea. Even the finest hotels serve the same thing—on better plates. It's the European way to start the day. (Sorry, no Mueslix.) I supplement my CBs with a piece of fruit and a separately wrapped chunk of cheese from my rucksack stash. If you're a coffee drinker, remember this is the only cheap time to caffeinate yourself. Some hotels will serve you a bottomless cup of a rich brew only with breakfast. After that, the cups acquire bottoms. Juice is often available, but you have to ask and you might be charged. Buffets are becoming more common. Smart food thieves come to breakfast with an empty zip-lock baggie in their day-bag.

I'm a big-breakfast person at home. When I feel the urge for a typical American breakfast in Europe, I beat it to death with a hard roll. You can find bacon, eggs, and orange juice, but it's nearly always overpriced and a disappointment. Breakfast, normally "included" in your hotel bill, can sometimes be skipped and deducted from the price of your room. Ask what it includes and costs. You can usually save money and gain atmosphere by buying coffee and a roll or croissant at the café down the street or by brunching picnic-style in the park. Never buy breakfast in a restaurant. You'll get the same meal with a better price and more atmosphere in a bar or café. I can't think of a hotel breakfast worth waiting around for. If you need to get an early start, skip it. Many places will fill your thermos with coffee cheaply.

DRINKS

As I'll discuss in Chapter 7, Health, European water has a different bacterial content than our systems are accustomed to. Many people will have some problem adjusting—not because European water is dirty but because our systems are weak.

For me, the trouble involved in avoiding European water outweighs the benefits. I drink the water throughout Europe and generally avoid water in North Africa and east of Bulgaria.

In restaurants, however, even the Europeans drink bottled water (for taste, not health). Tap water is not normally served (except in France). You can get free tap water, but you'll need to be polite, patient, and inventive and know the correct phrase. There's nothing wrong with ordering tap water, and waiters are accustomed to this American request. But it is a special favor, and while your glass or carafe of tap water is often served politely, occasionally it just isn't worth the trouble and it's best to just put up with the bottle of Perrier or order a drink from the menu. (The tap water along the Rhine River is chalky and local beverage salespeople swear it should not be drunk.)

Bottled water is usually quite cheap, served crisp and cold, either with or without carbonation, and usually by happier waiters. Most tourists don't like the bubbly stuff. Learn the phrase–*con/avec/mit*/with gas or *senza/sans/ohne*/without gas (in Italian/Spanish, French, German, and English, respectively), and you will get the message across. Acquire a taste for *acqua con gas*. It's a lot more fun (and read on the label what it'll do for your rheumatism).

If your budget is tight and you want to save $5 a day, never buy a restaurant drink. Scoff if you have the money, but remember—the drink is, along with the dessert, the worst value on any menu. Water is jokingly called "the American champagne" by the waiters of Europe.

Drink like a European. Cold milk, coffee with rather than after your meal, orange juice, and ice cubes are American habits, either overpriced or nonexistent in European restaurants. Insisting on cold milk, tap water, or ice cubes will get you nothing but strange looks and a reputation as the ugly—if not downright crazy—American. Order local drinks, not just to save money but to experience that part of the culture and to

---

Tap Water in Five Languages

Italian–*acqua del rubinetto*
French–*l'eau du robinet*
German–*Leitungswasser*
Spanish–*agua del grifo*
Portuguese–*agua a torneira*

In all other languages, just do the international charade: hold imaginary glass in left hand; turn on tap with right; make sound of faucet. Stop it with a click and drink it with a smile.

---

get the best quality and service. The "American waters" (Coke, Fanta, and 7-Up) are sold everywhere. Orange juice fans pick up the liter ($2) boxes in the grocery store and start the day with a glass in their hotel room.

Buying local alcohol is much cheaper than insisting on your favorite import. A shot of the local hard drink in Portugal should cost a dollar, while an American drink would cost at least the American price. Drink the local stuff with the local people in the local bars; a better experience altogether than a gin and tonic in your hotel with a guy from Los Angeles. Drink wine in wine countries and beer in beer countries. Sample the local specialties. Let a local person order you her favorite. You may hate it, but you'll never forget it.

Seek out and eat or drink, at least once, the notorious "gross" specialties—ouzo, horse meat, snails, raw herring, and so on (but not lutefisk). All your life you'll hear references to them, and you'll have actually experienced what everyone's talking about.

PICNIC—SPEND LIKE A PAUPER, EAT LIKE A PRINCE

There is only one way left to feast for $4 or $5 anywhere in Europe—picnic. I am a picnic connoisseur. (After four months in Europe, the first thing I do when I get home is put some cheese on a hard roll.) I think I eat better while spending $15 to $20 a day less than those who eat exclusively in restaurants.

While I am the first to admit that restaurant meals are an important aspect of any culture, I picnic almost daily. This is not solely for budgetary reasons. I love to dive into a marketplace and actually get a chance to do business. I can't get enough of Europe's varied cheeses, meats, fresh fruits, vegetables, and still-warm-out-of-the-bakery-oven bread. Many of my favorite foods made their debut in a European picnic. I pride myself on my ability to create unbeatable atmosphere for a meal by choosing just the right picnic spot.

I don't like to spend a lot of time looking for a decent restaurant, then waiting around to get served. And nothing frustrates me more than to tangle with a budget-threatening menu, finally order a meal, then walk away feeling unsatisfied, knowing my money could have done much more for my stomach if I had invested it in a marketplace. So, let me talk a bit about picnicking.

Every town, large or small, has at least one very colorful outdoor or indoor marketplace. Assemble your picnic here. The unit of measure throughout the Continent is a kilo, which is 2.2 pounds. A kilo has 1,000 grams. One hundred grams (a common unit of sale, in Italy called *un etto*) of cheese or meat tucked into a chunk of French bread gives you about a quarter-pounder. Make an effort to communicate with the merchants in the markets. Know what you are buying and what you are spending.

Most markets are not self-service. Point to what you want, and let the merchant bag it up and weigh it for you. But you may want only one or two pieces of fruit, and many merchants refuse to deal in such small quantities. The way to get what you want and no more is to estimate about what it would cost if he were to weigh it and then just hold out a coin worth about that much in one hand and the apple, or whatever, in the other. Have a look on your face that says, "If you take this coin, I'll go away." Rarely will he refuse the deal.

If no prices are posted, be wary. I've seen terrible cases of tourists getting ripped off by market merchants in tourist centers. Find places that print the prices. I suspect that any market with no printed prices has a double price-standard—one for locals and a more expensive one for tourists. Watch the scale when your food is being weighed (it'll show grams, which are thousandths of a kilo). The produce is priced per kilo. So if the cost is "25 francs," that means 25 francs per kilo (about $5, or $2.25 per pound), and the scale says 400, that means 4/10 of 25 francs (or 10F), which is about $2. Whether you understand the numbers or not, act as though you do. In supermarkets, buying a tiny amount of fruit or vegetables is no problem because most now have an easy push-button pricing system: put the banana on the scale, push the picture of a banana (or the banana bin number), and a sticky price tag prints out. You could weigh and sticker a single grape.

I'll never forget a friend of mine who bought two bananas for our London picnic. He grabbed the fruit, held out a handful of change, and said, "How much?" The merchant took three 50-pence coins (worth over $2). My friend turned to me and said, "Wow, London really is expensive." People like this go home and spread wild, misleading rumors:

"Bananas sell for a buck apiece in London!" Anytime you hold out a handful of money to a banana salesman, you're just asking for trouble.

To save your budget, picnic dinners must be a several-night-a-week routine. Save time and money by raiding the refrigerator for dinner, which, in Europe, is the corner deli or grocery store. There are plenty of tasty alternatives to sandwiches. These days grocery stores are getting very yuppie, with salads, quiche, fried chicken, and fish, all "to go." "Microwave" is a universal word. Some of my all-time favorite picnics have been accompanied by medieval fantasies in the quiet of after-hours Europe, or just taking it very easy, sprawled out with dinner in my hotel room. Hotels hate any hint of eating in the room, so do it like a mouse.

Picnic Drinks

There are plenty of cheap ways to wash down a picnic. Milk is always cheap, available in quarter, half, or whole liters. Be sure it's normal drinking milk. More than once I've been stuck with buttermilk or some even stranger white liquid dairy product. Look for local words for whole or light, such as *voll* or *lett*. Nutritionally, half a liter provides about 25 percent of your daily protein needs. Get refrigerated, fresh milk. You will often find a "longlife" kind of milk that needs no refrigeration. This milk will never go bad—or taste good.

Liter bottles of Coke are cheap, as is wine in most countries. The local wine gives your picnic a very nice touch. Fruit juice (look for "100% juice, no sugar" to avoid stuff that's closer to Kool-Aid) comes in handy boxes costing about $2 per quart. Use a reusable half-liter plastic mineral-water bottle (sold next to the Coke all over) to store what you can't comfortably drink in one sitting. Any place that serves coffee has free boiling water. Those who have more nerve than pride get their plastic water bottle (a sturdy plastic bottle will not melt) filled with free boiling water at a café, then add their own instant coffee or tea bag later. Many hotels or cafes will fill a thermos with coffee for about the price of two cups.

Picnic Atmosphere

There is nothing second-class about a picnic. A few special touches will even make your budget meal a first-class affair.

Proper site selection can make the difference between just another meal and *le picnic extraordinaire*. Since you've decided to skip the restaurant, it's up to you to create the atmosphere. I try to incorporate a picnic brunch, lunch, or dinner into the day's sightseeing plans. For example, I'll start the day by scouring the thriving market with my senses and my camera. Then I fill up my shopping bag and have brunch on a riverbank. I combine lunch and a siesta in a cool park to fill my stomach, rest my body, and escape the early afternoon heat. It's fun to eat dinner on a castle wall enjoying a commanding view and the setting sun.

To pleasantly pass time normally wasted in transit, plan a picnic meal to coincide with a train or boat ride. When you arrive, you are nourished, fat, happy, rested, and ready to go, rather than weak and in search of food. Mountain hikes are punctuated nicely by picnics. Food tastes even better on top of a mountain. Europeans are great picnickers, and I've had many a picnic become a potluck, resulting in a new friend as well as a full stomach.

Nutritionally, a picnic is unbeatable. Consider this example: 100 grams (about ¼-pound) of cheese, 100 grams of thin-sliced salami or ham, fresh bread, peaches, carrots, a cucumber, a half-liter of milk, and fruit yogurt for dessert. For variety, a pizza to go is fun. Cold cereal is a fun switch. Cornflakes can be found in any small grocery store. European yogurt is delicious and can usually be drunk right out of its container.

"Table Scraps" and Miscellaneous Tips
Bring zip-lock baggies (large and small) and a good knife with a can opener; a dishtowel serves as a small tablecloth and comes in handy. In addition to being a handy plate, fan, and a lousy Frisbee, a plastic coffee can lid makes an easy-to-clean cutting board with a juice-containing lip. And a fancy hotel shower cap contains messy food nicely on your picnic

Picnic on the train—cheap, hearty, scenic

A quick dashboard picnic halfway through a busy day of sightseeing

cloth. Bring an airline-type coffee cup and spoon for cereal, and a fork for take-out salad and chicken. Bread has always been cheap in Europe. (Leaders have learned from history that when stomachs rumble, so do the mobs in the streets.) Cheese is a specialty nearly everywhere and is, along with milk, one of Europe's cheapest sources of protein. The standard low-risk option anywhere in Europe is Emmentaler cheese (the kind with holes that we call "Swiss"). Supermarkets hide out in the basements of big city department stores.

In many countries outside of Europe, eating can be hazardous to your health. In these cases, peel fruits and vegetables. A travelers' guidebook to health or your doctor can tell you where you'll have to be careful. I don't worry in Western Europe. Tourists who have been in a country for a while usually know how to stay healthy and are excellent information sources.

Know where certain foods are good and reasonably priced by doing quick market surveys. For instance, in season, tomatoes, cucumbers, and watermelons are good deals in Italy. Citrus fruits are expensive (and not very good) in Eastern Europe, while the Eastern countries have some of the best and cheapest ice cream anywhere. Ice cream is costly in Scandinavia (what isn't?), and wine is a best buy in France. Anything American is usually expensive and rarely satisfying. Europeans have not yet mastered the fine art of the American hamburger, although each has its own variation on McDonald's: I saw a "McCheaper" in Switzerland.

My big meal of the day is often a picnic lunch or dinner. Only a glutton can spend more than $5 for a picnic feast. In a park in Paris, on a Norwegian ferry, high in the Alps, on your dashboard at an autobahn rest stop, on your convent rooftop, or in your hotel room, picnicking is the budget traveler's key to cheap and good eating.

Serious snackers artfully equip their hotel rooms with local drinks, munchies, even immersion heaters for hot drinks to go with the fancy pastry they picked up to eat before calling it a day.

VEGETARIANS

Vegetarians find life a little frustrating in Europe. Very often, Europeans think "vegetarian" means "no red meat" or "not much meat." If you are a strict vegetarian, you'll have to make things very clear. Write the appropriate phrase below, keep it handy, and show it to each waiter before ordering:

German: *Wir sind (Ich bin) Vegetarier. Wir essen (Ich esse) kein Fleisch, Fisch oder Geflügel. Eier und Käse OK.*

French: *Nous sommes (Je suis) vegetarien. Nous ne mangons (Je ne mange) pas de viandes, poissons, ou poulets. Oeufs et fromage OK.*

Italian: *Noi siamo (Io sono) vegetariani. Non mangiamo (mangio) ne carne, ne pesce, ne polli. Uova e formaggio OK.*

Dutch: We are (I am) vegetarian. We (I) do not eat meat, fish, or chicken. Eggs and cheese are OK. (Most Dutch speak English.)

Vegetarians have no problem with continental breakfasts, which are normally meatless anyway. Meat-free picnic lunches are delicious: bread, cheese, and yogurt are wonderful throughout Europe. It's in restaurants that your patience may be minced. Big-city tourist offices list restaurants by category. Look under "V." Italy seems to sprinkle a little meat in just about everything. German cooking normally keeps the meat separate from the vegetables. Hearty German salads, with beets, cheese, and eggs, are a vegetarian's delight. Vegetarians enjoy Third World cuisine and ethnic restaurants throughout Europe. Salad bars are becoming more popular. (See the guidebook *Europe on Ten Salads a Day*, from Mustang Publishing.)

EATING AND SLEEPING ON A BUDGET—
THE SIX COMMANDMENTS

You could get eight good, safe hours of sleep and three square meals in Europe for $20 a day if your budget required it. If your budget is tight, keep the following rules of thumb in your wallet.

1. Minimize the use of hotels and restaurants. Enjoying the sights and culture of Europe has nothing to do with how much you're spending to eat and sleep. Learn about and take advantage of each country's many alternatives to hotels and restaurants.

If your budget dictated, you could have a great trip without hotels and restaurants—and probably learn, experience, and enjoy more than the tourist who spends in a day what you spend in a week.

2. Budget for price variances. Prices as much as double from south to north. Budget more for the north and get by on less than your daily allowance in Spain, Portugal, and Greece. Exercise those budget alternatives where they'll save you the most money. A hostel saves $3 in Crete and $30 in Finland. I walk, sleep on trains, and picnic in Sweden and live like a king in the south, where my splurge dollars go the farthest. And if your trip will last only as long as your money does, travel fast in the north and hang out in the south.

3. Adapt to European tastes. Most unhappy people I meet in my travels could find the source of their problems in their own stubborn desire to find the United States in Europe. If you accept and at least try doing things the European way, besides saving money you'll be happier and learn more on your trip. You cannot expect the local people to accept you warmly if you don't accept them. Things are different in Europe—that's why you go. European travel is a package deal, and you have no choice but to accept the good with the "bad." If you require the comforts of home, that's where you'll be happiest.

4. Avoid the tourist centers. The best values are not in the places that boast, in neon signs, "We Speak English." Find local restaurants and hotels. You'll get more for your money. If you do follow the tourists, follow the savvy Germans, not the Japanese and never tour groups.

5. Swallow pride and save money. This is a personal matter, depending largely on how important pride is to you and how much money you have. Many people cringe every time I use the word "cheap"; others appreciate the directness. I'm not talking about begging and groveling around Europe. I'm talking about insisting on the room with no shower ($15 saved), drinking tap water ($3 saved), finding out the complete price before ordering anything, and saying "no thanks" if the price isn't right. Expect equal and fair treatment as a tourist; when appropriate, fight the price, set a limit, and search on. Remember, even if the same thing would cost much more at home, the local rate should prevail. If you act like a rich fool, you're likely to be treated like one.

6. Be a good guest. You need to be liked. Americans occasionally seem to Europeans like we "just got off the boat" (shoes on the train seats, grapes chilling in the bidet, talking loudly in restaurants, flash attachments and camcorders during Mass, wet clothes hanging out the window, treating energy like it's cheap and ours to waste, messing up faraway countries). The Europeans you'll deal with can dim or light up your trip, depending on how they react to you. When I'm in good favor with the receptionist or whoever, I can make things happen that people whose bucks talk can't.

As I update my books, I hear over and over how *Back Door* readers are the most considerate and fun-to-have-as-guests travelers my recommended hotels and private homes deal with. Thank you for traveling sensitive to the culture and as temporary locals. It's fun to follow you in my travels.

5

Finances and Money

Changing Money

Cut your losses: You'd be appalled if you knew how much money you'll lose in banks over the course of your trip. You can't avoid these losses but you can minimize them by understanding how the banks make their money. People change money only to make money.

Fees and Rates: Banks make money changing money in two ways: from fees and rates. Banks with great rates have high fees. Others have lousy rates and no fees. Any place advertising "no fees" should complete the equation with "and lousy rates." For a small exchange you don't care what the rate is, you want no fee. For a large exchange, the fee doesn't matter. You want a good rate. When I change several thousand dollars

RATES OF EXCHANGE		WE BUY AT	WE SELL AT	TRAV. CHEQUES
ADDITIONAL CHARGE PER TRANSACTION FOR NON BARCLAYS CUSTOMERS WILL BE £1.00				
AUSTRIA	SCH	27.35	25.95	
BELGIUM	FR	79.00	75.20	
CANADA	$	2.04	1.95	1.98
DENMARK	KR	14.06		
FRANCE	FR	11.80	11.26	11.478
GREECE	DR	270.00	240.00	
IRELAND	£	1.26	1.20	
ITALY	LIR	2615.	2485.	
NETHERLANDS	FL	4.36	4.16	4.249
NORWAY	KR	11.67	11.12	
PORTUGAL	ESC	242.00	230.00	
SPAIN	PTA	237.00	225.00	
SWEDEN	KR	11.67	11.12	
SWITZERLAND	FR	3.19	3.03	
U.S.A.	$	1.50	1.43	3.097
WEST GERMANY	DM	3.88	3.70	1.441
YUGOSLAVIA	DIN	620.00	500.00	3.768

RATES FOR SOME LARGE DENOMINATION NOTES MAY VARY FROM THE ABOVE
ALL RATES MAY CHANGE WITHOUT NOTICE.

for one of my tours, I can save $50 in a few minutes by checking three banks and choosing the one whose strategy is to profit from its fees rather than its rates.

Change only at places showing both rates: Every decent place to change money displays both their buying and selling rates. The English bank in the photo is selling British pounds for $1.43 and buying them for $1.50 (third line up from bottom). After all the traveling I've done, I still can't conceptualize what's what here. Who's getting pounds? Who's giving dollars? It doesn't matter. We lose.

Here, all the cards are clearly on the table. This money changer is a pro and you can see what he buys for and what he sells for. You don't need to shop around for the real rate. The true value of the local currency is halfway between what the pros buy and sell it for. In this case, a pound would be worth about $1.46. If I can establish a split of five percent (1.43 to 1.50 is the same as 95 to 100), and the fee is reasonable, it's fair. What you want to avoid is a place that shows only one rate. "One-rate exchange bureaus" are hiding something . . . and that's an obscene profit margin. Check it out. Every rip-off exchange desk at every border crossing, casino, and night club in Europe shows only one rate . . . and it's a lousy one.

Minimize trips to the bank: It's expensive and time-consuming to change money. Bring your passport, find a decent bank, estimate carefully what you'll need, and get it all at once when you enter a new country. Rather than risk having to endure another round of bank hassles and expenses on my last day in a country, I usually change a little more than I think I'll need. If I leave the country with some extra local money, I can change that over later.

Most banks, especially in touristy places, levy a service fee for each transaction. This added charge is usually higher for checks than cash, but many banks give a slightly better exchange rate for checks than cash. (They prefer traveler's checks to cash for the same reason we do.) Have the extra-charge policy explained before you start signing checks.

Dollars are not sacred: Paper money of any Western country is good at banks anywhere. If you leave Italy with paper money, that 10,000-lire note is just as convertible as dollars at any European bank or exchange office. Many people change excess local money back to dollars before they leave a country. Then they change those dollars into the next country's money. This double changing makes no sense and is expensive. It can be handy, however, to change your remaining local currency into the next country's currency before leaving a country. But changing dollars into, say, francs in Germany will send you through the bank expense wringer twice, since you'll actually be changing twice: from dollars to marks, and from marks to francs. Getting American cash from dollar traveler's checks is also expensive, involving going through that same wringer twice.

There are 24-hour money munchers in big cities all over Europe. At midnight in Florence, you can push in a $20 bill (or any major European currency) and, assuming the president (or royalty) is on the right side, the correct value of local currency will tumble out. Rates are good, there are no fees, and they're always open.

Carry Your Money in Traveler's Checks

Yes, in ten years ATMs and credit cards will have driven traveler's checks into extinction. But, for now, smart travelers still use traveler's checks. These checks function almost like cash but are replaceable if lost or stolen. Before you buy your checks, choose the best company, currency, and mix of denominations.

The company doesn't matter. Choose whichever big, well-known company (American Express, Cooks, Barclays, Visa) you can get for no fee. Ask around. There are plenty of ways to avoid that extra charge. Any legitimate check is good at banks, but it's nice to have a well-known check that private parties and small shops will recognize and honor. Remember, in many cases traveler's checks get a better exchange rate than cash, so they even save you money.

Understand the refund policies and services provided. The American Express Company is popular for its centrally located "landmark" offices, travel service, and clients' mail service. And AmExCo checks (which normally come with a 1½% charge) are free through AAA. AmExCo has two helpful services for people planning long-term trips or carrying lots of money. You can keep your money belt thin by using their $500 or $1,000 checks, which can be broken at no charge into smaller checks (in dollars) at most of their foreign offices. And those with AmExCo cards can travel anywhere, buying traveler's checks as they go from AmExCo offices abroad, writing personal checks on their personal bank accounts (up to $10,000 per 21 days with a platinum card, $5,000 with a gold card, and $1,000 with their regular peasants' card).

A traveler's check is a traveler's check. You'll hear many stories about slow or fast refunds. None of them matter. Extenuating circumstances—not the company—dictate the refund speed. If you keep your money belt tied around your waist and your brain tied to your head, you won't lose your checks. Choose whichever well-known company's checks your savings bank or automobile club offers without the 1 to 2 percent charge.

If you're traveling only in England, go with Barclays—a British bank with a branch in every town. They waive the $2-to-$5-per-transaction service charge if you have their checks. While AmExCo offices offer mediocre exchange rates, they usually change their checks without the customary $2 to $5 fee. This fee relief can make up for their bad rates if you're exchanging less than several hundred dollars.

Buy checks in U.S. dollars. Traveler's checks come in U.S. dollars, Swiss francs, British pounds, Deutsche marks, and even Japanese yen. When the dollar is shaky and unpredictable, many travelers consider bailing out early and buying traveler's checks in another, more stable, currency. You lose a couple of percent with this transaction, and then you lose 2 or 3 percent more when you change your "strong currency" into the local currency you need. The dollar does not drop drastically or predictably enough to merit this double loss. I get my traveler's checks in U.S. dollars for this reason and because merchants around the world generally know what their currency is worth in dollars. Besides, it's simpler for me—I think in dollars.

If your trip is mostly in one country, however, and the dollar is on a downward trend, you might buy checks in the currency of that country. But if you over-buy and have to trade them back to dollars, you've double changed with a double loss—expensive. If you bring home extra travelers checks in dollars and have to change back, you lose nothing.

Get a mix of denominations. Large bills and small bills each have advantages and disadvantages. Large checks ($100, $500) save on signing and bulk. Small checks ($20, $50) are more exact and, in some cases, easier to cash. If you're only passing through a country, you may want just $20. If you have only $100 checks, you'll have to change back $80. (You'll change $180 at that uniform 2% or 3% loss with two bank fees to spend $20. Ouch.) If you're out of cash and the banks are closed, it's easy to find a merchant or another traveler who will change a $20 traveler's check. Changing a large check in such a situation would be tough. Since more and more banks (especially in Scandinavia) are charging their $2–$4 fee per check rather than per transaction, checks in large denominations can save money.

For $2,000 in checks, I would choose thirteen $100, ten $50, and ten $20 checks.

Traveler's checks are replaceable if lost or stolen only if you keep track of the serial numbers and know exactly which checks you've cashed and lost. Leave a photocopy of all your check numbers (along with photocopies of your passport, plane ticket, and any other vital statistics) with someone at home, in your luggage, and in your wallet. I update one list regularly as I cash checks. If I lose my checks, I'll know exactly which ones to claim. Do a complete inventory each week.

Thieves commonly steal checks from the middle of your wad in the hope that the missing checks will go unnoticed.

The Credit Card and ATM Alternatives to Traveler's Checks

Lately, many fund their travels by relying solely on credit-card cash advances. This works all over Europe, letting you change quickly, easily, and at a good rate. The problem is that you are immediately into the 18 percent interest category with your new credit-card debt. (There's no one-month grace period on cash advances.) You can avoid this by over-paying on your credit card before leaving home or by using a "debit card" which lets you draw money (at the same preferred rate of exchange but without the un-preferred interest rate) from an existing bank account.

Automatic teller machines (ATMs), common in most of Europe, are also widely used. Know your personal identification number (PIN) and confirm with your home bank that it will work in Europe. Ask exactly where, with which systems, and on what machines. (Tellers say "It works everywhere: Bermuda, Canada, Virgin Islands, even Britain." But there's more to "Europe" than that.) You'll want a PIN with numbers and no letters. Those relying on ATM cash advances to fund their travels will avoid a little running around if they bring both a VISA and a MasterCard, since many banks accept only one or the other's PINs.

Many do fine with their credit cards, ATMs, and all this exciting new banking technology. But to save time and avoid hassles, I still go with the universally accepted standby: traveler's checks. It'll be a few years until cash advances are as widely available. Those relying solely on credit cards and ATMs will needlessly waste time looking for a bank or branch that speaks their electronic language. Bring at least some traveler's checks.

Buying on Plastic

Credit cards are widely accepted (at hotels, gas stations, shops, fancy restaurants, travel agencies, and so on) throughout Europe. Plastic fans gloat that you get a better exchange rate by using your card. While it is true that credit-card transactions are processed at the highest possible exchange rate, credit-card users are buying from businesses that have enough slack in their prices to absorb the bank's charge for the credit-card service. Those who travel on their plastic may be getting a better rate, but on a worse price. (As more and more consumers believe they are getting "free use of the bank's money," we're all absorbing the 4%

the banks are making in higher purchase prices.) Credit cards work fine in Europe. But Pedro's Pension, the guide at the cathedral, and the merchants in the market take only cash. Going through the back door requires hard local cash. I use my credit card mostly when I'm about finished with a country and I'm low on local cash.

VISA and MasterCard are most widely accepted. VISA is best for cash advances. AmExCo is much less widely accepted but popular for its extra services (for specifics, call for the free *AmExCo Traveler's Companion*, 800/528-4800). Your credit card is useful for cash advances (good rates, easier and cheaper than wiring money), making hotel reservations over the telephone, major purchases (such as car rentals and plane tickets), and car-rental security. Credit-card scams are commonplace and many travelers are ripped off big-time. Take all the precautions.

Cash

Carry plenty of cash. Cash in your money belt comes in handy for emergencies, such as when banks go on strike. I've been in Greece and Ireland when every bank went on strike—shutting down without warning. Some places (such as Russia and the Baltic states) make life with traveler's checks very difficult. But hard cash is cash. People always know roughly what a dollar, mark, or pound is worth, and you can always sell it.

You'll save time and money by bringing one day's budget in each country's currency with you from home. Your bank can sell you one bill worth $30 to $50 from each country for a fair price. With six bills—for six countries—hidden safely in your money belt, you'll have enough money to get settled in each new country without worrying about banking. Arriving at night or when the banks are closed with $2,000 in your money belt but not enough local cash to catch a subway or make a phone call is maddening. After-hours exchange places come with long lines and lousy rates.

Coins are generally worthless outside their country. Since $3 coins are common in Europe, exporting a pocketful of change can be an expensive mistake. Spend them (postcards, newspaper, a quick phone call home, food or drink for the train ride), change them into paper before you cross the border, or give them away. Otherwise, you've just bought a bunch of souvenirs.

Most border towns accept both currencies. For instance, waiters in Salzburg keep German money in one side of their coin bags, Austrian in the other.

While paper money from any Western country is good at banks in every other country, some Eastern European currencies are still "soft"—kept at unrealistically high rates. You can't avoid buying this money when you're in Bulgaria, Romania, the Baltics, or Poland. But this money is worthless in Western Europe, so until Eastern currency becomes hard, exchange it, spend it, buy candles in churches, ice-cream cones for strangers, give it away if you have to—but don't take it out of its country.

Many Americans exclaim gleefully, "Gee, they accept dollars! There's no need ever to change money." Without knowing it, they're changing money—at a lousy rate—every time they buy something with their dollars. Use the local money.

Many Americans refuse to understand the "funny money" of Europe. It's all logical. Each system is decimalized just like ours. There are a hundred "little ones" (cents, pence, centimes, pfennig, stotinki) in every "big one" (dollar, pound, franc, mark, leva). Only the names have been changed—to confuse the tourist. Get a good sampling of coins after you arrive and in two minutes you'll be comfortable with the "nickels, dimes, and quarters" of each new currency. A currency-converting calculator isn't worth the trouble. Upon arrival, make it a point to figure out the money.

Very roughly, figure out what the unit of currency (franc, mark, krona, or whatever) is worth in American cents. For example, if there are 1.5 deutsche marks in a dollar, each DM is a 70-cent piece. If a hot dog costs 5 marks, then it costs five 70-cent pieces or $3.50. Fifty little ones (pfennig) equals half a mark (35 cents). If mustard costs 10 pfennig (a tenth of a 70-cent piece), it costs the equivalent of 7 cents. Ten marks is $7, and 250 DM = $175 (250 x .7 or 250 less one third). Quiz yourself. Soon it'll be second nature. Survival on a budget is more likely when you're comfortable with the local currency.

In banks, restaurants, at ticket booths, everywhere . . . assume you'll be short-changed if you don't do your own figuring. People who spend their lives sitting in booths for eight hours a day taking money from strangers often have no problem stealing from dumb tourists who don't know the local currency. For ten minutes I observed a man in the Rome metro shortchanging half of the tourists who went through his turnstile. Half of those shortchanged caught him and got their correct change with apologies. Overall, about 25 percent didn't even notice his simple scam. They probably found Italy to be an expensive country. And I don't blame the dishonest ticket-taker.

6

Hurdling the Language Barrier

Communicating in a Language You Don't Speak

That notorious language barrier is about two feet tall. It keeps many people out of Europe, but with a few communication tricks and a polite approach you can step right over it.

While it's nothing to brag about, I speak only English. Of course, if I spoke more languages, I could enjoy a much deeper understanding of the people and cultures I visit, but even with English only I have no problems getting transportation, rooms, eating, and seeing the sights. While you can manage fine with the blunt weapon of English only, you'll get along with Europe better if you learn and use a few basic phrases and polite words.

Having an interest in the local language wins the respect of those you'll meet. Get an English-German (or whatever) dictionary and start your practical vocabulary growing right off the bat. You're surrounded by expert, native-speaking tutors in every country. Let them teach you. Spend bus and train rides learning. Start learning the language when you arrive. Psychologically, it's hard to start later because you'll be leaving so soon. I try to learn five new words a day. You'd be surprised how handy a working vocabulary of 50 words is. A two-language dictionary is cheap and easy to buy locally and can be as helpful as a phrase book.

We English-speakers are the one linguistic group that can afford to be lazy. English is the world's linguistic common denominator. When a Greek meets a Norwegian, they speak English. What Greek speaks Norwegian?

Europe is multilingual where necessary. At Croatian truck stops, the packet says "sugar" in five languages.

While Americans are notorious monoglots, Europeans are very good with languages. Most young North Europeans speak several languages. Scandinavian students of our language actually decide between English and "American." My Norwegian cousin speaks with a touch of Texas and knows more slang than I do! Most Swiss grow up trilingual, like their country. People speaking minor languages (Dutch, Belgians, Scandinavians) have more reason to learn German, French, or English, since their linguistic world is so small.

Imagine if each of our states spoke its own language. That's the European situation. They've done a great job of minimizing the communication problems you'd expect to find in a small continent with such a Babel of tongues. Not only are most educated people multilingual but most signs that the traveler must understand (such as road signs, menus, telephone instructions, and safety warnings) are printed either in several languages or in universal symbols. Europe's uniform road sign system enables drivers to roll right over the language barrier. And rest assured that any place trying to separate tourists from their money will explain how to spend it in whatever languages are necessary. English always makes it.

English may be Europe's *lingua franca*, but communicating does require some skill. If you have a trip coming up and you don't speak French yet, forget it. It's hopeless. Rather than learning a few more

French verbs, the best way to increase your ability to communicate is to master what the Voice of America calls "simple English." That's how the rest of this chapter will help you hurdle the language barrier.

Always start out by politely asking, *"Parlez-vous anglais?, Sprechen Sie Englisch?"* or whatever. If they say "No," then I do the best I can in their language. Normally, after a few sentences they'll say, "Actually I do speak some English." One thing Americans do well linguistically is put others at ease with their linguistic shortcomings. Your European friend is doing you a favor by speaking your language. The least we can do is make our English simple and clear.

Speak slowly, clearly, and with carefully chosen words. You're dealing with someone who learned English out of a book, reading British words, not hearing American ones. They are reading your lips, wishing it was written down, hoping to see every letter as it tumbles out of your mouth. Choose easy words and clearly pronounce each letter. (Cris-py po-ta-to chips.) Use no contractions. When they aren't understood, many Americans speak louder and toss in a few extra words. Listen to other tourists and you'll hear your own shortcomings.

Can the slang. Our American dialect has become a super-deluxe slang pizza not found on any European menu. The sentence "Cut out all slang," for example, would baffle the average European. "Use easy words" would be better understood. If you learned English in school for two years, how would you respond to the American who exclaims, "What a day!" or asks, "Howzit goin'?" Listen to yourself. If you want to be understood, talk like a Dick and Jane primer. For several months out of every year, I speak with simple words, pronouncing every letter. When I return home my friends say (very deliberately), "Rick, you can relax now, we speak English."

Keep your messages and sentences grunt simple. Make single nouns work as entire sentences. When asking for something, a one-word question ("Photo?") is more effective than an attempt at something more grammatically correct. ("May I take your picture, sir?") Be a Neanderthal. Strip your message naked and drag it by the hair into the other person's mind.

Use internationally understood words. Some spend an entire trip telling people they're on vacation, draw only blank stares, and slowly find themselves in a soundproof, culture-resistant cell. The sensitive communicator notices that Europeans understand the word "holiday" (probably because that's what the English say), plugs that word into her simple English vocabulary, is understood, and enjoys a much closer contact with Europe. If my car is broken in Portugal, I don't say "Excuse me, my car is broken." I point to the vehicle and say clearly, "Auto kaput."

Hurdle the language barrier by thinking of things as multiple-choice questions and making educated guesses. This is a sign on a shop in Germany. It lists open times. Hours can only be open or closed. I'd guess it lists hours open, from (vom = from, if it rhymes, I go for it) the 4th of July. Those six words on the left, most of which end in tag, must be days of the week. Things are open from 9:00 to 11:00 and from 16:00 to 18:00 (24-hour clock). On Mittwoch (midweek) afternoon, something different happens. Since it can only be open or closed, and everything else is open, you can guess that on Wednesdays, nach mittag this shop is geschlossen!

Find creative ways to communicate, at the risk of looking goofy. Even with no common language, rudimentary communication is easy. Butcher the language if you must, but communicate. I'll never forget the lady in the French post office who flapped her arms and asked, "Tweet, tweet, tweet?" I understood immediately, answered with a nod, and she gave me the airmail stamps I needed. At the risk of getting birdseed, I communicated successfully. If you're hungry, clutch your stomach and growl. If you want milk, "moo" and pull two imaginary udders. If the liquor was too strong, simulate an atomic explosion starting from your stomach and mushrooming to your head. If you're attracted to someone, pant.

Figure things out. Most major European languages are related, coming from Latin. With that awareness and an effort to make some sense of the puzzle, lots of words become meaningful. The French word for Monday (our "day of the moon") is *Lundi* (lunar day). The Germans say the same thing—*Montag*. *Sonn* is sun, so *Sonntag* is Sunday. If *buon giorno* means good day, *zuppa del giorno* must mean soup of the day. If *tiergarten* is zoo (literally "animal garden") in German, then *stinktier* is skunk and *kindergarten* is children's garden. Think of *vater, mutter, trink, gross, gut, nacht, rapide, grand, economico, delicioso*, and you can *comprende mucho*.

Many letters travel predictable courses (determined by the physical way a sound is made) as related languages drift apart over the centuries. For instance, *p* often becomes *v* or *b* in the next language. Italian menus always have a charge for *coperto*—a "cover" charge.

Practice your understanding. Read time schedules, concert posters, multilingual signs in bathrooms, and newspaper headlines. Develop your ear for foreign languages by tuning into the other languages on a multilingual tour. It's a puzzle. The more you play, the better you get.

Be melodramatic. Exaggerate the local accent. In France, communicate more effectively (and have more fun) by sounding like Maurice Chevalier or Inspector Clousseau. The locals won't be insulted; they'll be impressed. Use whatever French you know. But even English, spoken with a sexy French accent, makes more sense to the French ear. In Italy, be melodic, exuberant, and wave those hands. Go ahead, try it: *Mama mia*! No. Do it again. *MAMA MIA*! You've got to be uninhibited. Self-consciousness kills communication.

Make your communicating job easier by choosing a multilingual person to begin communicating with. Business people, urbanites, young well-dressed people, and anyone in the tourist trade are most likely to speak English.

A small notepad works wonders in a tough spot. The written word or number is understood much easier than when it's spoken—and mispronounced. (My back-pocket notepad is my constant travel buddy.) To repeatedly communicate something difficult and important (such as medical instructions, "I'm a strict vegetarian," "boiled water," "well-done meat," "your finest ice cream," or "Yes, I am rich and single"), have it written in the local language on your notepad.

EUROPEAN GESTURES

In your travels gestures can contribute to the language barrier. While you may recognize a gesture, pointing to your head can mean smart in one country and crazy in another. Gesture boundaries often follow linguistic ones, but not always. Occasionally a gesture that is very popular in one town or region will be meaningless or have another meaning in the next. Here are a few common gestures, their meaning and where you are likely to see them:

Fingertips kiss—gently bring the fingers and thumb of your right hand together, raise to your lips, kiss lightly and joyfully toss your fingers and thumb into the air. Be careful, tourists look silly when they overemphasize this subtle action.

This is used commonly in France, Spain, Greece, and Germany as a form of praise. It can mean sexy, delicious, divine, or wonderful.

Hand purse—straighten the fingers and thumb of one hand, bringing them all together making an upward point about a foot in front of your face. Your hand can be held still or moved a little up and down at the wrist.

This is a common and very Italian gesture for a query. It is used to say "what do you want?" or "what are you doing?" or "what is it?" or "what's new?" It can also be used as an insult to say "You fool." The hand purse can also mean "fear" (France), "a lot" (Spain), and "good" (Greece and Turkey).

Cheek screw—make a fist, stick out your forefinger and (without piercing the skin) screw it into your cheek.

The cheek screw is used widely and almost exclusively in Italy to mean good, lovely, beautiful. Many Italians also use it to mean clever. Be careful—in Southern Spain the cheek screw is used to call a man effeminate.

Eyelid pull—place your extended forefinger below the center of your eye and pull the skin downward.

In France and Greece this means "I am alert. I'm looking. You can't fool me." In Italy and Spain it is a friendlier warning meaning "Be alert, that guy is clever."

Forearm jerk—clench your right fist and jerk your forearm up as you slap your right bicep with your left palm.

This is a rude phallic gesture that men throughout southern Europe often use the way many Americans "give someone the finger." This jumbo version of "flipping the bird" says "I'm superior" (it's an action some monkeys do with their penises to insult their peers). This "get lost" or "up yours" gesture is occasionally used in Britain and Germany as an "I want you" gesture about (but never to) a sexy woman.

Chin flick—tilt your head back slightly and flick the back of your fingers forward in an arc from under your chin.

In Italy and France this means "I'm not interested, you bore me," or "you bother me." In Southern Italy it can mean "no."

The **"thumbs up"** sign popular in the U.S.A. is used widely in France and Germany to say "Okay". The **"V for victory"** sign is used in most of Europe as in the U.S.A. (Beware, the V with your palm toward you is the rudest of gestures in England.) In Greece and Turkey, you signal "no" by jerking your eyebrows and head upward. In Bulgaria, "yes" is indicated by happily bouncing your head back and forth as if you were one of those Asian dolls with a spring neck and someone slapped you. "Expensive" is often shown by shaking your hand and sucking in like you just burned yourself. To beckon someone, remember that in northern Europe you bring your palm up and in the south you wave it down. While most people greet each other by waving with their palm out, you'll find many Italians wave "at themselves" as infants do, with their palm towards their face. Ciao-ciao.

CONFESSIONS OF A MONOGLOT
Even if you have no real language in common, you can have some fun communicating. Consider this profound conversation I had with a cobbler in Sicily:

"Spaghetti," I said, with a very saucy Italian accent.

"Beel Cleenton," was the old man's reply.

"Mama mia!" I said, tossing my hands and head into the air.

"Yes, no, one, two, tree," he returned, slowly and proudly. By now we'd grown fond of each other and I whispered, secretively, "Molto buono, ravioli."

He spit, "Be sexy, drink Pepsi!"

And I waved good-bye saying, "Arrivederci."

"Ciao," he said, smiling.

Assume you understand and go with your educated guess. My master key to communication is to see most communication problems as multiple choice questions, make an educated guess at the meaning of a message (verbal or written), and proceed confidently as if I understood it correctly. This applies to rudimentary things like instructions on customs forms, museum hours, menus, questions the hotel maid asks you, and so on. With this approach, I find that 80 percent of the time I'm correct. Half the time I'm wrong I never know it, so it doesn't really matter. So 10 percent of the time I really blow it. My trip becomes easier—and occasionally much more interesting.

Let's take a border crossing as an example. I speak no Bulgarian. At the border, a uniformed guard struts up to my car and asks a question. Not understanding a word he said, but guessing what the average border guard would ask the average tourist, I look at him and answer with a solid "Nyet." He steps back, swings his arm open like a gate and says, "OK." I'm on my way, quick and easy. I could have gotten out of the car, struggled with the phrase book, and made a big deal out of it, but I'd rather fake it, assuming he was asking if I'm smuggling anything in, and keep things simple. It works.

TRAIN PHRASES

English	French	German	Italian	Spanish	Danish
National Railway	SNCF	DB/DBB	FS	RENFE	DSB
station	gare	Bahnof	stazione ferroviario	estación	banegaard
information	resignements	Auskunft	informazioni	información	oplysning
Tourist Office	Syndicat D'Initiative	Auskunft	(EPT)	información turistica	turistbureau
currency exchange	change	Wechsel	cambio	cambio	veksling/valuta
lockers	consigne-automatique	Spinde	armadietto	casilleros	opbevaring-box
check room	consignee	Garderobe	deposito	la consigna	opbevaring
toilets	toilettes	Toiletten	gabinetto	servicios	toilet
men	messieurs	Herren	uomini	caballero	sherrer
women	dames	Damen	donne	señoras	damer
waiting room	salle d'attente	Wartesaal	sala d'espetto	sala de espera	ventesalen
entrance	entre	Eingang	entrata	entrada	indgang
exit	sortie	Ausgang	uscita	salida	udgang
timetable	horaire	Fahrplan	orario	horarios	timeplan
arrival	arrivee	Ankunf t	arrivi	llegada	ankomst
departure	depart	Abfahrt	partenze	partida	afgang
train	train	Zug	treno	tren	tog
tickets	billet	Fahrkarten	biglietto	billetes	billet
reservation	reservation	Platzkarte	prenotazione	reserva	pladsbestillingen
one way/round-trip	aller/retour	Einfach/Zurück	andata/andata e ritorno	ida/ida y vuelta	enkelt/retur
1st/2nd	premiere/deuxieme	erster/zweiter	prima/seconda	primera/segunda	forte/anden
change	change	Umsteigen	cambio	cambio	skifte
ferry	bateau	Schiff	traghetto	balsadero	faerge
track	quai	Gleis	binario	via	perron/spor
car	wagon	Wagen	carrozza	vagon	vogn
seat	place	Platz	posto	plaza/asiento	saede
smoking	fumeurs	Raucher	fumatori	coche-fumador	ryger
couchette	couchette	Liegewagen	cuccetta	coche-litera	liggevogn
sleeping	wagon-lit	Schlafwagen	vagone letto	coche-cama	sovevogn
restaurant	wagon-restaurant	Speisewagen	ristorante	coche-restaurante	spisvogn

The insults that follow are taken from *The Insult Dictionary—How to Snarl Back in Five Languages*. (To be used in jest.)

English	German	French	Italian	Spanish
Hairy creep	Oller Leisetreter (*oller hyserrayter*)	Troglodyte (*Troglodeet*)	Stupido scrimmione (*Stoo-peedob scheemee-obneh*)	Espantapajaros (*Spantahpahharos*)
Moron	Nackter Wilder (*Naackter veelder*)	Cretin (*Craytan*)	Deficiente (*Deh-fee-chenteh*)	Carcamal (*Carcamahll*)
Ass	Narr (*Naarr*)	Ane bate (*Ann battay*)	Somaro (*Sob-mah-rob*)	Asno (*Asnob*)
Donkey	Esel (*Ayzel*)	Bourricot (*Boorreeko*)	Asino (*Ah-zeenob*)	Burro (*Boorob*)
Crazy in the head	Schwach Kopf (*Shvaach kopf*)	Dingue (*Dang*)	Pazzoide (*Pab-tzo-ee-deb*)	Majareta (*Mahharetah*)
Ugly	Haesslich (*Hasslick*)	Laideron (*Laidrom*)	Brutto (*Broot-tob*)	Asqueroso (*Askebrosob*)
Useless vampire	Blutsaugendes Gespenst (*Blootsaogendes geshpenst*)	Vampire a la gomme (*Vampeer a la gom*)	vampiro innutile (*Vam-peerob in-ootee leb*)	Vampiro caduco (*Bahm-peerob cadookob*)
Blood-sucking leech	Shmarotzer (*Shmaarotser*)	Sangsue (*Sansi*)	Sanguisuga (*Sangoo-ee-sooga*)	Tacaño (*Tahkanyoh*)
Repulsive, evil-smelling dog	Widerlicher Lump (*Veederlicher loomp*)	Repugnant voyou (*Raipünian vvuahyoo*)	Repulsivo vagabondo puzzolent (*Ree-pulsee-vo vagabond-ob poot-zolehnteh*)	Roñoso (*Ronyoso*)
Dribbling, senile fool	Bloder Sabberer (*Blowder zaabberer*)	Vieux baveux (*Vyer bavehr*)	Stupido vecchio rincitrullito (*Stoopeedob veh-keeob rreen-chee-trrool-leeto*)	Viejo baboso (*Beeyehho bahhosob*)

International Words

As our world shrinks, more and more words leap their linguistic boundaries and become international. Sensitive travelers develop a knack for choosing words most likely to be universally understood ("auto" instead of "car," "kaput" rather than "broken," "photo," not "picture"). They also internationalize their pronunciation. "University," if you play around with its sound (oo-nee-vehr-see-tay) can be understood anywhere. The average American is a real flunky in this area. Be creative.

Analogy communication is effective. Anywhere in Europe, "Attila" means "the crude bully." When a bulky Italian crowds in front of you, say, "Scuzi, Ah-tee-la" and retake your place. If you like your haircut and want to compliment your Venetian barber, put your hand sensually on your hair and say "Casanova." Nickname the hairstylist "Michelangelo," or "Rambo."

Here are a few internationally understood words. Remember, cut out the Yankee accent and give each word a pan-European sound.

Stop	Kaput	Vino
Restaurant	Ciao	Bank
Hotel	Bye-bye	Rock 'n' roll
Post	Camping	OK
Auto	Picnic	Amigo
Autobus (booos)	Nuclear	English (Engleesh)
Yankee, Americano	Tourist	Mama mia
Michelangelo (artistic)	Beer	Oo la la
Casanova (romantic)	Coffee	Moment
Disneyland (wonderland)	Tea	Hercules (strong)
Coke, Coca-Cola	No problem	Attila (mean, crude)
Sexy	Europa	Self-service
Toilet	Police	Super
Taxi	Telephone	Photo
Photocopy	Central	Information
Mañana	University	Passport
Chocolate	Pardon	Fascist
Rambo	Communist	Hello
America's favorite four-letter words		No
Elephante (a big clod)		Bon voyage

A Yankee-English Phrase Book

Oscar Wilde said, "The English have everything in common with the Americans—except, of course, language."

On your first trip to England, you'll find plenty of linguistic surprises. I'll never forget checking into a small-town bed and breakfast, a teenager on my first solo European adventure. The landlady cheerily asked me, "And what time would you like to be knocked up in the morning?" I looked over at her husband, who winked, "Would a fry at eight be suitable?" The next morning, I got a rap on the door at 7:30 and a huge British breakfast a half-hour later.

Traveling through England is an adventure in accents and idioms. Every day you'll see babies in "prams," sucking "dummies" as mothers change wet "nappies." Soon the kids can trade in their "nappies" for "smalls" and "spend a penny" on their own. "Spend a penny" is British for a visit to the "loo" (bathroom). Older British kids enjoy "candy floss" (cotton candy), "naughts and crosses" (tic-tac-toe), "big dippers" (roller coasters), and "iced lollies" (popsicles), and are constantly in need of an "elastoplast" (Band-Aid).

If you're just "muckin' about," it's fun to browse through an "ironmonger's" (hardware store), "chemist's shop" (pharmacy), or Woolworths and notice the many familiar items with unfamiliar names. The school supplies section includes "sticking plaster" (adhesive tape), "rubbers" (erasers), and "scribbling blocks" (scratch pads). Those with "green fingers" (a green thumb) might pick up some "courgette" (zucchini), "swede" (rutabaga), or "aubergine" (eggplant) seeds.

In England, "chips" are fries and "crisps" are potato chips. A hamburger is best on a toasted "bap." You wipe your fingers with a serviette—never a napkin.

The English have a great way with names. You'll find towns with names like Upper and Lower Piddle, Once Brewed, and Itching Field. This cute coziness comes through in their language as well. Your car is built with a "bonnet" and a "boot" rather than a hood and trunk. You drive it on "motorways," and when the freeway divides, it becomes a "dual carriageway." Gas is "petrol," a truck is a "lorry," and when you hit a traffic jam, don't "get your knickers in a twist" (make a fuss), just "queue up" (line up) and study your American-English phrase book.

A two-week vacation in England is unheard of, but many locals "holiday for a fortnight" in a "homely" (pleasant) rural cottage, possibly on the "Continent" (continental Europe). They'll pack a "face flannel" (washcloth), "torch" (flashlight), "hoover" (vacuum cleaner), and "hair grips" (bobby pins) before leaving their "flat" (apartment). You can

This is Danish for "tour bus." These days most come with air-conditioning.

"post" letters in the "pillar box" and give your "bird" (girlfriend) a "trunk" (long distance) call, "reversing the charges" (collect), of course. On a cold evening it's best to pick up a "pimp" (bundle of kindling) and make a fire or take a walk wearing the warmest "mackintosh" (raincoat) you can find or an "anorak" (parka) with "press studs" (snaps). After "washing up" (doing the dishes), you can go up to the first floor (second floor) with a "neat" (straight) Scotch and a plate of "biscuits" (sweet cookies) and just enjoy the view. It's a "smashing" view, guaranteed to give you "goose pimples" (goose bumps).

All across the British Isles, you'll find new words, crazy local humor, and colorful accents. Pubs are colloquial treasure chests. Church services, sporting events, the House of Parliament, live plays featuring local comedy, the streets of Liverpool, the docks of London, and children in parks are playgrounds for the American ear. One of the beauties of touring the British Isles is the illusion of hearing a foreign language and actually understanding it—most of the time.

7

Health

Before Your Trip

CHECKUP

Just as you'd give your car a good checkup before a long journey, it's smart to meet with your doctor before your trip. Get a general checkup. Tell the doctor about every place you plan to visit and any place you may go. Then you can have the flexibility to take that impulsive swing through Turkey or Morocco knowing that you're prepared medically and have the required shots. At the time of this printing, no shots are required for basic European travel, although some shots are recommended. It's always best to check (keeping in mind that a government "requires" shots to protect its people and "recommends" shots to protect those who visit). Get advice on maintaining your health and about drinking the water. Obtain recommended immunizations and discuss proper care for any preexisting medical conditions while on the road. Bring along a letter from your doctor describing any special health problems and a copy of any pertinent prescriptions. If you plan to travel beyond Europe, ask your doctor about gamma globulin, antidiarrheal medicines, and any extra precautions necessary.

Remember, only travel medicine specialists keep entirely up to date on health conditions for travelers around the world. While I consider Europe as safe as the United States, those traveling to more exotic destinations should consult one of these specialists. Many travelers join the International Association for Medical Assistance to Travelers (free, but donation requested, 417 Center St., Lewiston, NY 14092, tel. 716/ 754-4883) for a list of English or American-trained doctors in member countries to whom you'll have access at special rates and from whom you can get travel medicine advice and updates.

Have a dental checkup before you go. Emergency dental care during your trip is time and money-consuming, and it can be hazardous and painful.

Give yourself a psychological pep talk. Europe can do to certain travelers what south France did to van Gogh. Romantics can get the sensory bends, patriots can get their flags burned, and anyone can suffer from culture shock. Europe is intense, and travel can be an emotional spin-cycle for dainties that have always hung in the sun. Europe is crowded, smoky, and not particularly impressed by Americans or America. It will challenge givens that you always assumed were above the test of reason, and most of Europe on the street doesn't really care that much about what you, the historical and cultural pilgrim, have waited so long to see. If you need a break: a long, dark, air-conditioned trip back to California in a movie theater; a pleasant sit in an American embassy reading room surrounded by eagles, photos of presidents, *Time* magazines, and other Yankees; or a break in the lobby of a world-class hotel, where any hint of the local culture has been lost under a big business bucket of intercontinental whitewash, can do wonders for the struggling traveler's spirit.

TRAVELER'S FIRST-AID KIT
My kit contains soap, supplemental vitamins, aspirin, cold capsules, bandages, and medications—antibiotic, antidiarrheal, and motion-sickness. Tweezers and a thermometer in a hard case are also recommended.

Soap prevents and controls infections. Young travelers concerned about acne (which can be especially troublesome when traveling) should wash with soap five times a day, six if you're touring the Swiss chocolate factories. Supplemental vitamins (with iron, for women) are most effective when taken with the day's largest meal. Aspirin is a great general pain reliever for headaches, sore feet, sprains, bruises, Italian traffic, hangovers, and many other minor problems.

Swelling, which often accompanies a physical injury, is painful and retards healing. Ice and elevate any sprain or bruise periodically for 48 hours. An Ace bandage is useful to immobilize and to stop swelling and, later, to provide support. It is not helpful to "work out" a sprain.

A high fever merits medical help. (To convert from Celsius to Fahrenheit, use the formula $F = [(C \times 9/5) + 32]$.) A temperature of 101 degrees Fahrenheit equals 38.3 degrees Celsius. To be effective, medication for motion sickness (Dramamine) should be taken several hours before you think you'll need it. This medication can also serve as a mild sleeping pill. Ask your doctor to recommend an antidiarrheal medication.

If you have any serious dietary restrictions, have a multilingual friend write it in the local language on the back of a business card and use it to order in restaurants.

Bandages help keep wounds clean but are not a substitute for thorough cleaning. A piece of clean cloth can be sterilized by boiling for ten minutes or by scorching with a match. Bandages, tape, moleskin, or two pairs of socks can prevent or retard problems with the feet. Cover any irritated area before it blisters.

Those with corrected vision should bring extra glasses in a solid protective case as well as the lens prescription. Contact lenses are used all over Europe, and the required solutions for their care are easy to find. Soft lenses can be boiled like eggs. (Remind your helpful landlady to leave them in their case.) If you have the money, you can avoid all the cleaning headaches and enjoy the comfort of home wear with a trip's worth of disposable-once-a-week contacts. Do not assume that you can wear your contacts as comfortably in Europe as you can at home. I find that the hot, dusty cities and my style of travel make contacts impossible, and every summer I end up wearing my glasses and carrying my contacts.

Jet Lag and the First Day of Your Trip

Flying halfway around the world is stressful. If you leave frazzled after a hectic last night and a wild bon-voyage party, there's a good chance you won't be healthy for the first part of your trip. Just a hint of a cold coupled with the stress of a long flight through eight time zones will mean a sniffly first week. Once you're on the road, it's pretty hard to slow down enough to fight that cold properly.

Leave home well rested. An early trip cold used to be a regular part of my vacation until I learned a very important trick. Plan from the start as if you're leaving two days before you really are. Keep that last 48-hour period sacred, even if it means being hectic before your false departure date. Then (even though you'll still be going to work) you have two orderly, peaceful days after you've packed so that you are physically ready to fly. Mentally, you'll be comfortable about leaving home and starting this adventure. You'll fly away well-rested and 100 percent capable of enjoying the bombardment of your senses that will follow.

Anyone who flies through time zones has to grapple with the biorhythmic confusion known as jet lag. When you switch your wristwatch eight hours forward, your body says, "Hey, what's going on?" Body clocks don't reset so easily. All your life, you've done things on a 24-hour cycle. Now, after crossing the Atlantic, your body wants to eat when you tell it to sleep and sleep when you tell it to enjoy a museum. You can't avoid jet lag, but with a few tips, you can minimize the symptoms.

You dehydrate during a long flight, so drink plenty of liquids. I ask for "two orange juices with no ice" every chance I get. And you can usually help yourself to the juice pitchers in the gallery area. Eat light and have no coffee and only minimal sugar until the flight's almost over. Alcohol is stressful to your body and will aggravate jet lag. The in-flight movie is

Jet lag hits even the very young

good for one thing—nap time. With three hours of sleep during the transatlantic flight, you will be functional the day you land.

When the pilot announces the local European time, reset your mind along with your wristwatch. Don't prolong jet lag by reminding yourself what time it is back home. Be in Europe.

On arrival, make yourself stay awake until an early local bedtime. If you doze off at 4:00 p.m. and wake up at midnight, you've accomplished nothing. Plan a good walk until early evening. Jet lag hates fresh air, strong daylight, and exercise. Your body may beg for sleep, but stand firm: refuse. Force your body's transition to the local time. Then, after a solid eight hours of sleep, you should wake up feeling like super-tourist.

Too many people assume their first day will be made worthless by jet lag. Don't prematurely condemn yourself to zombiedom. Most people I've traveled with, of all ages, have enjoyed productive—even hyper—first days. Many people awaken very early on their first morning. Trying to sleep later is normally futile.

Get out and enjoy a "pinch me, I'm in Europe" walk as merchants set up in the marketplace and the town slowly comes to life. This will probably be the only sunrise you'll see in Europe.

Jet lag is a joke to some and a major problem to others. It's hard to predict just how serious your jet lag will be. Those who keep strict 24-hour schedules will probably feel more jet lag than those who work the swing shift or keep crazy hours.

You'll read about many jet lag "cures." Most are worse than the disease. Just leave unfrazzled, minimize jet lag's symptoms, force yourself into European time, and give yourself a chance to enjoy your trip from the moment you step off the plane.

Health in Europe

Europe is generally safe. All the talk of gamma globulin, doxycycline, and treating water with purification tablets is applicable only south and east of Europe.

Many may disagree with me but, with discretion and common sense, I eat and drink whatever I like in Europe. If any area deserves a little extra caution, it is rural areas in the southern countries of Spain, Portugal, Italy, and Greece. As our world becomes more chemical, reasons for concern and caution will increase on both sides of the Atlantic.

I was able to stay healthy throughout a six-week trip traveling from Europe to India. By following these basic guidelines, I never once suffered from Tehran Tummy, Delhi Belly, or the Tegucigallop.

Outside of Europe, use good judgment when eating. Avoid unhealthy-looking restaurants. Peel all fruit. When in serious doubt, eat only thick-skinned fruit (peeled). Even in the worst places, anything well cooked and still hot is safe. Meat should be well cooked and in some places avoided altogether. Have "well done" written on a piece of paper in the local language and use it when ordering. Avoid possibly spoiled foods, and remember, pre-prepared foods gather germs.

Honor your diet. Eat nutritiously and hearty. The longer your trip, the more you'll be affected by an inadequate diet. Budget travelers often eat more carbohydrates and less protein to stretch their travel dollar. This is the root of many nutritional problems encountered by travelers. Protein helps you resist infection and rebuilds muscles. Get the most nutritional mileage from your protein by eating it with the day's largest meal (in the presence of all those "essential" amino acids). Supplemental super-vitamins, taken regularly, help me to at least feel healthy.

A basic hygiene hint is to wash your hands often, keep your nails clean, and never touch your fingers to your mouth. In 20 years of walking barefoot in the cheap hotel showers of Europe, surrounded by countless moldy shower curtains, I've never picked up a fungus.

Venereal disease is widespread. Obviously, the best way to prevent VD is to avoid exposure. Condoms (readily available in rest room vending machines) are fairly effective in preventing transmission for those unable to avoid exposure. Cleaning with soap and water before and after exposure is also helpful if not downright pleasurable. AIDS is also a risk; according to CNN, over 60 percent of the prostitutes in Amsterdam are HIV-positive.

Physically, travel is great living—healthy food, lots of activity, fresh air, and all those stairs! Still, you may want to work out during your trip. Jogging, while not as widespread in Europe, is nothing weird. Traveling joggers enjoy Europe from a special perspective—at dawn. Swimmers will find that Europe has plenty of good, inexpensive public swimming pools. Whatever your racket, if you want to badly enough, you'll find ways to keep in practice as you travel. Most big-city private tennis and swim clubs welcome foreign guests for a small fee. This is a good way to make friends as well as stay fit.

I DRINK THE WATER

I drink European water. Read signs carefully, however, because some taps, like those on trains, are not for drinking. If there's any hint of nonpotability—a decal showing a glass with a red "X" over it or a skull and crossbones—don't drink it. I drink any water served in restaurants.

East of Bulgaria and south of the Mediterranean, do not drink untreated water. Water can be treated by boiling it for ten minutes or by using purifying tablets or a porcelain filter.

Bottled water, beer, wine, boiled coffee and tea, and bottled soft drinks are safe. Coca-Cola products (if the top is on and the carbonation is still present) are as safe in Syria as they are at home.

YOU WILL GET SICK—LOOSEN UP

Travel is a package deal. You will probably get sick in Europe. Get used to the fact that you'll have diarrhea for a day. (Practice that thought in front of the mirror tonight.) When you get the runs, take it in stride. If you stay healthy, you'll feel lucky.

It's simply not worth taking eight Pepto Bismol tablets a day or brushing your teeth in Coca-Cola all summer long to avoid a day of the runs. I take my health seriously, and for me, traveling in India or Mexico is a major health concern. But I find Europe very mild.

The water (or, just as likely, the general stress of travel on your immune system) may, sooner or later, make you sick. The water is not necessarily dirty. The bacteria in European water is different from that in American water. Our bodily systems—raised proudly on bread that rips in a straight line—are the most pampered on earth. We are capable of handling American bacteria with no problem at all, but some people can go to London and get sick. Some French people visit Boston and get sick. Some Americans travel around the world, eating and drinking everything in sight, and don't get sick, while others spend weeks on the toilet. It all depends on the person.

Every year I take a group of 24 Americans through Turkey for two weeks. With adequate discretion, we eat everything in sight. At the end of the trip, my loose-stool survey typically shows that five or six travelers coped with a day of the Big D and one person was stuck with an extended week-long bout.

If (or when) you get diarrhea, it will run its course. Revise your diet, don't panic, and take it easy for a day. When I get diarrhea, I make my diet as bland and boring as possible for a day or so (bread, rice, baked potatoes, clear soup, weak tea). Keep telling yourself that tomorrow you'll feel much better. You will. Most conditions are self-limiting. For me, the bland diet is the best remedy. If your loose stools persist, replenish lost liquids and minerals. (Bananas are effective in replacing potassium, which is lost during a bout with diarrhea.) If you have a prolonged case of diarrhea (especially dangerous for an infant), a temperature greater than 101 degrees F (38.3 degrees C), or if you notice blood in your stools, get a doctor's help. Europeans use a pill called Enterovioform to get solid. American doctors warn that it can harm your eyesight. Don't use it.

I visited the Red Cross in Athens after a miserable three-week tour of the toilets of Syria and Jordan. My intestinal commotion was finally stilled by its recommended strict diet of boiled rice and plain tea. As a matter of fact, after five days on that dull diet, I was constipated.

With all the bread you'll be eating, constipation, the other side of the intestinal pendulum, is (according to my surveys) as prevalent as diarrhea. Get exercise, eat lots of roughage—raw fruits, leafy vegetables, prunes, or bran tablets from home—and everything will come out all right in the end.

Throughout Europe, people with a health problem go first to the local pharmacy, not to their doctor. European pharmacists diagnose and prescribe remedies for most simple problems. They are usually friendly and English-speaking. If necessary, they'll send you to a doctor.

Serious medical treatment in Europe is generally of high quality. To facilitate smooth communication, it's best to find an English-speaking doctor. Information leading you to these doctors can be obtained through agencies that deal with Americans, such as embassies, consulates, American Express companies, tourist information offices, and large hotels.

8

The Woman Traveling Alone

In my classes, women often ask, "Is it safe for a woman to travel alone in Europe?" This is a question best answered by a woman. Europe Through the Back Door tour guide Risa Laib wrote this chapter, based on her solo experience and tips gleaned from other travelers: Gail Morse, Peggy Roberts, Suzanne Hogsett, Bharti Kirchner, Kendra Roth, and Claire McIntyre. Collectively, these women have more than three years of solo travel experience in over 30 countries.

Every year, thousands of women, young and old, travel to Europe on their own. You're part of a grand group of adventurers. Traveling alone, you'll have the chance to make your own discoveries and the freedom to do what you like. It becomes habit-forming.

As a solo woman, you're more approachable than a couple or a solo man. You'll make friends from all over the world, and you'll have experiences that others can only envy. When you travel with a partner, your focus narrows and doors close. When you're on your own, you're utterly open to the moment.

Solo travel is fun, challenging, vivid, and exhilarating. It's a gift from you to you. Prepared with good information and a positive attitude, you'll dance through Europe. And you'll come home stronger and more confident than ever before.

Here's how to make it happen.

Getting Inspired

Read exciting books written by solo women travelers about their experiences (try Dervla Murphy's outrageous adventures). For practical advice, read "how to" travel guidebooks written by and for women.

Seek out other women travelers. Invite them out for dinner, and warn them you'll be asking a lot of questions.

Take classes. A foreign language course is ideal. Consider a class in European history, art history, travel skills, and for peace of mind, self-defense.

Keep up on international news so you can discuss local politics. Study a map of Europe—get to know your neighbors.

Pretend you're traveling alone before you ever leave America. Practice reaching out. Strike up conversations with people in the grocery line. Consciously become more adaptable. If it rains, marvel at the miracle.

Think hard about what you want to see and do. Create the trip of your dreams.

Facing the Challenges

These are probably your biggest fears: vulnerability to theft, harassment, and loneliness. Take heart. You can tackle each of these concerns head-on.

If you've traveled alone in America, you're more than prepared for Europe. In America, theft and harassment are especially scary because of their connection with violence. In Europe, you'll rarely, if ever, hear of violence. Theft is past tense (as in, "Where did my wallet go?"). Experiencing harassment, you're far more likely to think, "I'm going to ditch this guy A.S.A.P.," rather than "This guy is going to hurt me."

Loneliness is often the most common fear. But remember, if you get lonely, you can do something about it.

Traveling Alone Without Feeling Lonely

Here are some tips on meeting people, eating out, and enjoying your nights.

Meeting people: Stay in hostels and you'll have a built-in family (hostels are open to all ages, except in Bavaria where the age limit is 26). Or choose small pensions and B&Bs, where the owners have time to talk with you. Join Servas (see Chapter 4) and stay with local families. Camping is also a good, safe way to meet Europeans.

At most tourist sites, you'll meet more people in an hour than you would at home in a day. If you're feeling shy, cameras are good ice-breakers; offer to take someone's picture with their camera.

Talk to other solo women travelers and share advice.

Go to a laundromat. You'll end up with a stack of clean clothes and conversations.

Stop by any American Express office.

Take a walking tour of a city (ask at the tourist information office). You'll learn about the town and meet other travelers, too.

It's easy to meet local people on buses and trains. You're always welcome at a local church service (dress conservatively in small towns); stay for the coffee hour. Play with kids. If you play peek-a-boo with a baby or fold an origami bird for a kid, you'll make friends with the parents. When you meet locals who speak English, find out what they think—about anything.

Call the English department at a university. See if they have an English conversation club you can visit. Or ask if you can hire a student to be your guide (you'll see the city from a local's perspective, give a student a job, and possibly make a friend).

Try pairing up with another solo traveler. Or return to a city you enjoyed. The locals will remember you, you'll know the neighborhood, and it'll feel like home.

Eating out: Consider quick cheap alternatives to formal dining. Try a self-service café, a local fast-food restaurant, or a small ethnic eatery. Visit a supermarket deli and get a picnic to eat in the square or a park (local families often frequent parks). Get a slice of pizza from a take-out shop and munch it as you walk along, people-watching and window-shopping. Eat in the member's kitchen of a hostel; you'll always have companions. Make it a potluck.

A restaurant feels cheerier at noon than at night. Have lunch as your main meal. If you like company, eat in places so crowded and popular that you have to share a table. Or ask other single travelers if they'd like to join you.

If you eat alone, be busy. Use the time to learn more of the language. Practice with the waiter or waitress (when I asked a French waiter if he had kids, he proudly showed me a picture of his twin girls). Read your mail, a guidebook, a juicy novel, or the *International Herald Tribune*. Do trip planning, write or draw in your journal, or scrawl a few postcards.

Most countries have a type of dish or restaurant that's fun to experience with a group. When you run into tourists during the day, make plans for dinner. Invite them to join you for, say, a *rijstafel* dinner in the Netherlands, a *smorgasbord* in Scandinavia, a *fondue* in Switzerland, a *paella* feast in Spain, or a spaghetti feed in an Italian *trattoria*.

At night: Experience the magic of European cities at night. Go for a walk along well-lit streets. With gelato in hand, enjoy the parade of people, busy shops, and illuminated monuments. Night or day, you're invariably safe when lots of people are around. Take advantage of the wealth of evening entertainment: concerts, movies, puppet shows, and folk-dancing. Some cities offer tours after dark; you can see Paris by night on a river cruise.

If you like to stay in at night, get a room with a balcony overlooking a square. You'll have a front-row seat to the best show in town. Bring along a radio to brighten your room; pull in local music, a friendly voice, maybe even the BBC. Call home, a friend, your family. With a USA-Direct type of calling card, it's easier than ever. Read novels set in the country you're visiting. Learn to treasure solitude. Go early to bed, be early to rise . . . explore the city as it opens its eyes. Shop at a lively morning market for fresh rolls and fruit.

Protecting Yourself from Theft

As a woman, you're often perceived as being more vulnerable to theft than a man. Change that misperception. Here are tips that'll help keep you safe:

Carry a day-pack instead of a purse. Leave expensive-looking jewelry at home. Keep your valuables in your money belt, and your wallet (containing only a day's worth of cash) in your front pocket. Keep your camera zipped up in your day-pack. In crowded places (buses, subways, street markets), carry your day-pack over your chest, held close to you, straps looped over one shoulder. Ask at your hotel or the tourist office if there's a neighborhood you should avoid, and mark it on your map.

Avoid tempting people into theft. Wear your money belt when you sleep in hostels. Make sure any valuables in your hotel room are kept out of sight. When you're sightseeing, never set down anything of value (such as a camera or wallet). Either have it in your hand or keep it hidden. If you're sitting and resting, loop a strap of your day-pack around your arm, leg, or chair leg. Remember, you're unlikely ever to be hurt by thieves. They want to separate you from your valuables painlessly.

In Europe, sometimes blondes have more trouble

Dealing with Men

In small towns in continental Europe, men are often more likely to speak English than women. If you never talk to men, you could miss out on a chance to learn about the country. So by all means, talk to men. Just choose the men and choose the setting.

In northern and central Europe, you won't draw any more attention from men than you do in America. In southern Europe, particularly in Italy, you'll get more attention than you're used to, but it's nothing you can't handle.

Be aware of cultural differences. In Italy, when you smile and look a man in the eyes, it's considered an invitation. If you wear dark sunglasses, no one can see your eyes. And you can stare all you want.

Dress modestly to minimize attention from men. Take your cue from what the local women wear. In Italy, slacks and skirts (even short ones) are considered more proper than shorts.

Wear a real or fake wedding ring and carry a picture of a real or fake husband. There's no need to tell men that you're traveling alone. Lie unhesitatingly. You're traveling with your husband. He's waiting for you at the hotel. He's a professional wrestler who retired from the sport for psychological reasons.

If you'd like to date a local man, meet him at a public place. Tell him you're staying at a hostel—you have a 10:00 p.m. curfew and 29 roommates. Better yet, bring a couple of your roommates along to meet him. After the introductions, let everyone know where you're going and when you'll return.

Handling Harassment

The way you handle harassment at home works in Europe, too.

In southern Europe, men may think that if you're alone, you're available. If a man sits close to you or walks right next to you, say "no" firmly in the local language. That's usually all it takes. Tell slow learners that you want to be alone. Or say that you're meeting friends.

If men are paying too much attention to you, solicit the help of others. Ask people at a café or on the beach if you can join them for a while.

If a man is well-meaning but too persistent, talk openly to him. Turn him into an ally. If he's a northern Italian, ask him about southern Italian men. Get advice from him on how you can avoid harassment when you travel farther south. After you elicit his "help," he'll be more like a brother than a bother.

Usually men are just seeing if you're interested. Only a few are obnoxious. If a man makes a lewd gesture, simply ignore him and leave the scene.

Harassers don't want public attention drawn to their behavior. Shout if you need to. I went out for a walk in Madrid one evening, and a man came up much too close to me, scaring me. I shouted, "Get!" And he was gone. I think I scared him as much as he scared me. Ask a local woman for just the right thing to say to embarrass jerks. Learn how to say it, loudly.

I've never needed a weapon such as Mace. If you feel the need to carry Mace, take a self-defense class instead. Mace can be confiscated at the airport, but knowledge and confidence are yours to keep. And remember, the best self-defense is common sense.

Traveling Smart

Create conditions that are likely to turn out in your favor. By following these tips, you'll have a safer, smoother, more enjoyable trip.

Have a little local cash with you when you enter a country, and change money before you run low. Bank holidays strike without warning throughout Europe.

Be self-reliant, so that you don't need to depend on anybody unless you want to. I always carry food, water, a map, a guidebook, and a phrase book. When I need help, I ask another woman or a family.

Walk purposefully. Look like you know where you're going. Use landmarks (such as church steeples) to navigate. If you get lost in an unfriendly neighborhood, go into a restaurant or store to ask for directions or to look at your map.

Learn enough of the language to get by. With a few hours' work, you'll know more than most tourists and be better prepared to deal with whatever situation arises. At a bus station in Turkey, I witnessed a female tourist repeatedly asking in English, louder and louder, "When does the bus leave?" The frustrated ticket clerk kept answering her in Turkish, "Now, now, now!" If you know even just a little of the language, you'll make it much easier on yourself and those around you.

Before you leave a city, visit the train or bus station you're going to leave from, so you can learn where it is, how long it takes to reach it, and what services it has. Reconfirm your departure time.

On a bus, if you're faced with a choice between an empty double seat and a seat next to a woman, sit with the woman. You've selected your seat partner. Ask her (or the driver) for help if you need it. They will make sure you get off at the right stop.

If you have to hitchhike, choose people to ask, instead of being chosen. Try your luck at a gas station, restaurant, or the parking lot of a tourist attraction. If possible, pair up with another traveler. (Though I wouldn't recommend hitchhiking alone, I've found it necessary on rare occasions and have hitched without hassles.)

On a train, avoid empty compartments. Share a compartment with women, a couple, a mixed group, or a family. Rent a *couchette* for overnight trains. For about $15, you'll stay with like-minded roommates in a compartment you can lock, in a car monitored by an attendant. You'll wake reasonably rested, belongings intact, ready to tackle your next adventure.

Try to arrive at your destination during the day. Daylight feels safer than night. For peace of mind, consider reserving a room. If you can't avoid a late-night arrival or departure, use the waiting room of the train station or airport as your hotel for the night.

The same good judgment you use at home applies to Europe. If anything, I've suggested being more cautious than Europe warrants. Start out cautious, and figure out as you travel what feels safe to you.

Resources

Visit a travel bookstore and browse through the books. Here are a few you'll find: *A Journey of One's Own: Uncommon Advice for the Independent Woman Traveler*, by Thalia Zepatos; *The Independent Woman's Guide to Europe*, by Linda White; *The Virago Woman's Travel Guide* (four books: for Rome, Paris, Amsterdam, and London); and *Women Travel: Adventures, Advice, and Experience*, Rough Guide. To get a listing of 50 books by and about women travelers, call Globe Corner Bookstore at 800/358-6013 and ask for a free copy of "Women & Travel."

A Few Final Tips

Ask lots of questions, but if you're not fluent in the language, accept the fact that you won't always know what's going on. There's a reason why the Greek bus driver drops you off in the middle of nowhere. It's a transfer point, and another bus will come along in a few minutes. Often the locals are looking out for you.

Treat yourself right—get enough rest, food, and exercise. Walking is a great way to combine exercise and sightseeing. I've jogged alone in cities and parks throughout Europe without any problems. If a neighborhood looks seedy, head off in an another direction.

Relax. There are other trains, other buses, other cities, other people. If one thing doesn't work out, something else will. Thrive on optimism.

Have a grand adventure!

9
Travel Photography

If my hotel were burning down and I could just grab one thing, it would be my exposed film. Every year I ask myself whether it's worth the worry and expense of mixing photography with my travels. After my film is developed and I relive my trip through those pictures, the answer is always, "Yes!" Here are some tips and lessons that I've learned from the photographic school of hard knocks.

The Camera

Good shots are made by the photographer, not the camera. For most people, a very expensive camera is a bad idea. Your camera is more likely to be lost, broken, or stolen than anything else you'll travel with. A very expensive model may not be worth the risks and headaches that accompany it.

A good basic 35mm point-and-shoot or single-lens reflex (SLR) can provide most people everything they need. When buying a camera, get one that will do what you want and a little bit more. You're buying a camera not only for the trip but also for use later. Don't buy a camera a day or two before you fly. Not every camera works perfectly right out of the box. Shoot a roll of 24-exposure film, indoors with flash and outdoors, before you leave. Check your pictures for a good exposure and sharp focus. If they're not right, take it back. Do the same checks with the replacement camera.

The simple choice for an amateur photographer is a disposable or "single-use" camera. These disposables cost as little as $8 ($13 with flash) for an ISO of 400 and 24 exposures. There's a new camera out with a very wide-angle lens for 180-degree panoramic shots. This is a fun supplement to your regular camera.

Next, the compact little "focus-free" cameras ($25 to $50) give you

A good eye is more important than an extra lens

very little creative control but are almost foolproof in getting a good picture. They're fragile and when broken usually just tossed out.

Moving up the cost line, the "point and shoot" cameras ($50 to $100) are auto-focus but have just a wide-angle 38mm lens. Models over $100 come with small zoom lenses of 38 to 70 mm plus some other things to play with. The best units have a zoom lens from about 28 to 105mm. These can cost more than a low-end single-lens reflex. If you don't spend at least $100 you are getting a cheap camera and it might not hold up much longer than the trip. The point-and-shoot cameras should be used only with color-print film. Their shutters are set to overexpose about a half-stop, which gives the best prints from negative film (but not for slides). Some of the very latest point-and-shoot cameras let you reprogram them for use with slide film.

Those shooting slides should stick with a good SLR. Regardless of advertising claims, there's no real difference between the mind of Minolta and the mind of Pentax, Nikon, or Canon. The trend in SLR's is auto-focus (AF) lenses but most of these units have a manual focus override switch. There aren't many non-auto-focus SLR's still being made. For traveling, the quick and accurate auto-focus is handy, but creative photographers will want the manual capabilities also.

Your best all-around lens is an f 3.5 28-70 or 80mm "mid-range" zoom lens. Yes, it's not as fast as an f 1.7 but with the fine grain ISO 400 films on the market today it's almost like having an f 1.7 lens. Visit your local camera shops and look things over, ask questions, ask your friends and neighbors what they use. Be careful of what the salesperson tries to sell. They make more money if they can sell you the camera that is being promoted for the month, but it may not be what you need. Get a camera built by a well-known company.

Make sure all your lenses have a haze or UV filter on them. It's better to bang and smudge up your filter than your lens. The only other filter you might use is a polarizer which eliminates reflections and enhances color separation, but you can lose up to two stops in speed with it. Never use more than one filter at a time.

When choosing film, I go with 400 film in 36-exposure rolls. Print films are all about the same. You'll see more difference between print processors than the films themselves. With slide film, stick with the films that are known as E-6 developing (Ektachrome, Fujichrome, and so on). They can be developed overnight in most large cities and usually cost less, too.

A GALAXY OF GADGETS

Like many hobbies, photography is one that allows you to spend endless amounts of money on accessories. I have some favorites that are particularly useful to the traveling photographer.

First of all, you need a gadget bag. The most functional and economical one is simply a small nylon stuff bag made for hikers. When I'm in a market or somewhere taking a lot of pictures, I like to wear a nylon belt pouch (designed to carry a canteen). This is a handy way to have your different lenses and filters readily accessible, allowing you to make necessary changes quickly and easily. A formal camera bag is unnecessary and attracts thieves.

A mini C-clamp/tripod is a great gadget. About five inches high, this tool screws into most any camera, sprouts three legs, and holds the camera perfectly still for slow shutter speeds and time exposure shots. (It looks like a small lunar landing module.) The C-clamp works where the tripod won't, such as on a fence or a handrail. A conventional tripod is too large to lug around Europe. Those without a mini-tripod use a tiny beanbag (or sock filled with rice) or get good at balancing their camera on anything solid, adjusting the tilt with the lens cap or strap and still getting good timed exposures and automatic shutter release shots.

A lens-cleaning tissue and a small bottle of cleaning solution are wise additions to any gadget bag. A lead-lined bag is unnecessary since airport X-rays these days are "film safe." I leave my protective camera case at home and protect my lens with a cap that dangles on its string when I'm shooting.

Tricks for a Good Shot

Most people are limited by their skills, not by their camera. Understand your camera. Devour the manual. Shoot experimental shots, take notes and see what happens. You may put a lot of expense and energy into your travel photography. If you don't understand "f-stops" or "depth of field," find a photography class or book and learn. Camera stores sell good books on photography in general and travel photography in particular. I shutter to think how many people are underexposed and lacking depth in this field.

A sharp eye connected to a wild imagination will be your most valuable piece of equipment. Develop an eye for what will look good and be interesting after the trip. The skilled photographer's eye sees interesting light, shade, form, lines, patterns, and colors. Weed out dull shots before you take them, not after you get them home. It's cheaper.

Postcard-type shots are boring. Everyone knows what the Eiffel Tower looks like. Find a unique or different approach to sights that everyone has seen. Shoot the bell tower through the horse's legs or lay your camera on the floor to shoot the Gothic ceiling.

Buildings, in general, are not interesting. It doesn't matter if Karl Marx or Beethoven was born there, a house is as dead as its former resident. As travel photographers gain experience, they take more people shots and fewer buildings or general landscapes. Show the personal and intimate details of your trip: how you lived, who you met, what made each day an adventure (a close-up of the remains of a picnic, your leech bite, laundry day, or a local schoolboy playing games with his nose).

Vary the perspective of your camera—close, far, low, high, day, night, etc. Don't fall into the rut of always centering a shot. Use foregrounds to add color, depth, and interest to landscapes. Grab bright colors.

Be bold and break rules. For instance, we are told never to shoot into the sun. But some into-the-sun shots bring surprising results. Try to use bad weather to your advantage. Experiment with strange or difficult light situations. Buy a handbook on photographing in existing light.

Real photographers get single-minded at the magic hours—early morning and late afternoon when the sun is very low and the colors glow. Plan for these times.

Get close and notice details. Get closer, real close. Eliminate distractions. Get so close that you show only one thing. Don't try to show it all in one shot. Take several shots.

People are the most interesting subjects. It takes nerve to walk up to people and take their picture. It can be difficult, but if you want some great shots, be nervy. Ask for permission. The way to do this in any language is to point at your camera and ask, "Photo?" Your subject will probably be delighted. You most likely just made his day, as well as a good picture. Try to show action. A candid is better than a posed shot. Even a posed candid is better than a posed shot. Give your subject something to do. Many photographers take a second shot immediately after the first portrait to capture a looser, warmer subject. If the portrait isn't good, you probably weren't close enough. My best portraits are so close that the entire head can't fit into the frame.

It's very important to be able to take a quick shot. Know your camera, practice setting it, understand depth of field and metering. In a marketplace situation, where speed is crucial, I preset my camera. I set the meter on the sunlit ground and focus at, let's say, 12 feet. Now I know that, with my depth of field, anything from about 10 to 15 feet will be in focus and, if it's in the sunshine, properly exposed. I can take a perfect picture in an instant, provided my subject meets these preset requirements. It's possible to get some good shots by presetting the camera and shooting from the waist. Ideally, I get eye contact while I shoot from the hip.

Be sure you expose for your subject. Even if your camera is automatic, your subject can turn out a silhouette. Meter without the sky. Get those faces in the sun, ideally lit from the side. For slides, you'll get richer tones if you underexpose just a bit. Expose for the highlights.

You'll hear that the focal length of your lens dictates the slowest safe hand-held shutter speed you can use. For instance, a 50mm lens should shoot no slower than 1/50th of a second. That rule is too conservative. I get decent shots out of my 50mm lens at 1/30th of a second, even 1/15th. Don't be afraid to hand-hold a slow shot, but do what you can to make it steady. If you can lean against a wall, for instance, you become a tripod instead of a bipod. If you have a self-timer, it can click the shutter more smoothly than your finger can. Using these tricks, I can get good-looking pictures inside a museum at 1/15th of a second. With ISO 400 film, I manage indoors without a flash. Most museums allow photography without a flash or tripod. (A flash ages a painting the equivalent of three days of sunshine.) A tripod gives you professional (profitable) quality. Nearly every important museum will have a good selection of top quality slides, cards, and prints at reasonable prices.

A lot of time-exposure photography is guesswork. The best way to get good shots of difficult lighting situations is to "bracket" your shots by trying several different exposures of the same scene. You'll have to throw out a few slides that way, but one good shot is worth several in the garbage can. Automatic cameras usually meter properly up to eight or ten seconds, making night shots easy, but bracketing may still be necessary.

Contrary to what you may think, you won't be able to remember the name of every monastery, fellow hosteler, or mountain that you take a picture of. A running list of shots is unnecessary, but I record the name of anything I want to be sure to remember.

When you assemble your slide show, remember to limit its length. Nothing is worse than sitting through an endless parade of lackluster and look-alike shots. Set a limit (maximum two carousels of 140 slides each) and prune your show down until it bleeds. Keep it tight. Keep it moving. Leave the audience crying for more . . . or at least awake.

Traveling with a Video Camera

With video cameras getting better, smaller, and more affordable, more and more Americans are compromising a potentially footloose and fancy-free vacation to get a memory of what's left on videotape. To me, a still camera is trouble enough. But thousands of amateur videographers happily seeing Europe through their viewfinders can't all be wrong. I've had a lot of experience with a lap-top computer in Europe, and charging its batteries (same as a video camera) has always been easy. If your camera doesn't have a built-in converter, you'll have to get one. And remember, European sockets are different (usually two round holes rather than two flat ones). Adapters, which can be tough to find in Europe, are available at your hometown travel accessories store. Cheap hotel rooms generally have only one or two outlets. You can buy a two-socket adapter at any European hardware store so you can charge your battery without having to unplug your lamp.

10

Museums

Culture Beyond the Petri Dish

Europe is a treasure chest of great art. Many of the world's greatest museums will be a part of your trip. Here are a few hints on how to get the most out of them.

I've found that some studying before the trip makes the art I see in Europe more exciting. It's criminal to visit Rome or Greece with no background in those civilizations' art. I remember touring the National Museum of Archaeology in Athens as an obligation. My mom said it would be a crime to miss it. It was boring. I was convinced that those who looked like they were enjoying it were actually just faking it—trying to look sophisticated. Two years later, after a class in ancient art history, that same museum was a fascinating trip into the world of Pericles and Socrates, all because of some background knowledge.

A common misconception is that a great museum has only great art. A museum like the Louvre in Paris is so big (the building itself was, at one time, the largest in Europe), you can't possibly cover everything—so don't try. Be selective. Only a fraction of a museum's pieces are really "greats" anyway. It's generally best, with the help of a guide or guide-book, to focus on just the museum's best two hours. Some of Europe's great museums provide brief guide pamphlets recommending the best basic visit. With this selective strategy, you'll appreciate the highlights when you're fresh. If you still have any energy left, you can explore other areas of specific interest to you. For me, museum-going is the hardest work I do in Europe, and I'm rarely good for more than two or three hours at a time. If you're determined to cover a large museum thoroughly, try to tackle one section a day for several days.

If you are especially interested in one piece of art, spend half an hour studying it and listening to each passing tour guide tell his or her story about *David* or the *Mona Lisa* or whatever. They each do their own research and come up with different information to share. Much of it is true. There's nothing wrong with this sort of tour freeloading. Just don't stand in the front and ask a lot of questions.

A victim of the Louvre

On arrival, I thumb through a museum guidebook index or look through the postcards to make sure I won't miss anything of importance to me. For instance, I love Salvador Dali's work. One time I thought I was finished with a museum, but as I browsed through the postcards— Hello, Dali. A museum guide was happy to show me where this Dali painting was hiding. I saved myself the disappointment of discovering after my trip was over that I was there but didn't see it.

Readable English guidebooks are rare. To get the most out of your trip, consider getting my art guidebook, *Mona Winks: Self-Guided Tours of Europe's Top Museums* (Santa Fe, N.M.: John Muir Publications). This book is a collection of fun and easy-to-follow take-you-by-the-hand two-hour tours of Europe's 20 most important (and difficult) museums and sights. It's just me and you together with the greatest art of our civilization. Of the 12 travel guidebooks I've written, *Mona Winks* sells the least and has the most devoted following. If you decide to travel without *Mona*, try to make friends and tag along with someone in the big museums who's got it. (See the back of this book for ordering instructions.)

Remember, most museums are closed one day during the week (usu- ally Monday or Tuesday). Your guidebook or a tourist information office has that information. Many museums also stop selling tickets and start closing down rooms 30 to 60 minutes before closing. Free admission days are usually the most crowded. In many cases, it's worth the entrance fee to avoid the crowds. My favorite time in museums is the cool, lazy, last hour. But I'm careful to get to the far end early, see the rooms that are first to shut down, and work toward the entry.

Try to get a tour. If it's French or German only, let the guide know politely, persistently, at the beginning that there are several English-speaking people in the group who'd love some information. Occasionally, if you telephone ahead, you can meet a scheduled English group and tag along.

Open-Air Folk Museums

Many people travel in search of the old life and traditional culture in action. While we book a round-trip ticket into the romantic past, those we photograph with the Old World balanced on their heads are struggling to dump that load and climb into our world. In Europe, most are succeeding.

The easiest way and, more than ever, the only way to see the "real culture" is by exploring an open-air folk museum. True, it's culture on a lazy Susan, but the future is becoming the past faster and faster, and in many places it's the only "Old World" you're going to find.

An open-air folk museum is a collection of traditional buildings from every corner of a country or region carefully reassembled in a park, usually near the capital or major city. These sprawling museums are the best bet for the hurried (or tired) tourist craving a magic carpet ride through that country's past. Log cabins, thatched cottages, mills, old school-houses, shops, and farms come complete with original furnishings and usually a local person dressed in the traditional costume who's happy to answer any of your questions about life then and there.

In the summer, folk museums buzz with colorful folk dances, live music performances, and young craftspeople specializing in old crafts. Many traditional arts and crafts are dying, and these artisans do what they can to keep the cuckoo clock from going the way of the dodo bird. Some of my favorite souvenirs are those I watched being dyed, woven, or carved by folk-museum artists.

To get the most out of your visit, start by picking up a list of that day's special exhibits, events, and activities at the information center, and take advantage of any walking tours.

Popularized in Scandinavia, these sightseeing centers of the future are now found all over the world. The best folk museums are still in the Nordic capitals. Oslo's, with 150 historic buildings and a twelfth-century stave church, is just a boat ride across the harbor from the city hall.

Traditional culture is kept alive in Europe's Open-Air Folk Museums. At Stockholm's you may be entertained by this rare band of left-handed fiddlers.

Skansen, in Stockholm, gets my first-place ribbon for its guided tours, feisty folk entertainment, and Lapp camp complete with reindeer.

Switzerland's Ballenberg Open-Air Museum near Interlaken is a good alternative when the Alps hide behind clouds.

The British Isles have no shortage of folk museums. For an unrivaled look at the Industrial Revolution, spend a day at the Blists Hill Open-Air Museum in the Ironbridge Gorge, northwest of Stratford. You can cross the world's first iron bridge to see the factories that lit the fuse of our modern age.

Every year, new folk museums open. Travel with a current guide and use tourist information centers abroad. Before your trip, send a card to each country's National Tourist Office (addresses are listed in Chapter 1, Planning) requesting, among other things, lists of open-air folk museums.

Folk museums teach traditional lifestyles better than any other kind of museum. As the world plunges toward 100 billion McDonald's hamburgers served, these museums will become even more important. Of course, they're as realistic as Santa's Village, but how else will you see the elves?

Some of Europe's best open-air folk museums

Norway

Norwegian Folk Museum, at Bygdoy near Oslo. *Norway's first, with 150 old buildings from all over Norway and a twelfth-century stave church.*

Maihaugen Folk Museum, at Lillehammer. *Folk culture of the Gubrandsdalen. Norway's best.*

Trondheim and Trondelag Folk Museum at Sverresborg fortress near Trondheim. *60 buildings showing old Trondheim, Lapp village, and farm life.*

Sweden

Skansen, Stockholm. *One of the best museums, with over 100 buildings from all over Sweden, craftspeople at work, live entertainment, and a Lapp camp with reindeer.*

Kulteren, Lund. *Features Southern Sweden and Viking exhibits.*

Finland

Seurasaari Island, near Helsinki. *Reconstructed buildings from all over Finland.*

Handicraft Museum, Turku. *The life and work of nineteenth-century crafts-people.*

Denmark

Funen Village (Den Fynske Landsby), just south of Odense.

Old Town, Arhus. *60 houses and shops show Danish town life from 1580 to 1850.*

Lyngby Park, north of Copenhagen.

Hjerle Hede Iron Age Village, 10 miles south of Skive in northern Jutland. *Lifestyles of prehistoric times.*

Oldtidsbyen Iron Age Village, in Lejre near Roskilde.

Germany

Cloppenburg Open-Air Museum, southwest of Bremen. *Traditional life in Lower Saxony, seventeenth and eighteenth centuries.*

Switzerland

Ballenberg Swiss Open-Air Museum, just northeast of Lake Brienz. *A fine collection of old Swiss buildings with furnished interiors.*

Benelux

Zaanse Schaans near Zaandijk, 30 miles north of Amsterdam. *Windmills, wooden shoes, etc.*

De Zeven Marken Open-Air Museum, in Schoonoord.

Netherlands Open-Air Museum at Arnhem. *70 old Dutch buildings; the Netherlands' first, biggest, and best museum of its kind.*

Bokrijk Open-Air Museum, between Hasselt and Genk, in Belgium. *Old Flemish buildings and culture in a natural setting.*

Great Britain

Blists Hill Open-Air Museum, near Coalport. *Shows life from the early days of the Industrial Revolution.*

Beamish Open-Air Museum, north-west of Durham. *Life in northeast England in 1900.*

Welsh Folk Museum, at St. Fagan's near Cardiff. *Old buildings and crafts-people illustrate traditional Welsh ways.*

Ireland

Bunratty Folk Park, near Limerick.
*Buildings from the Shannon area and
artisans at work.*

Irish Open-Air Folk Museum, at
Cultra near Belfast. *Traditional Irish
lifestyles and buildings from all over
Ireland.*

Glencolumbcille Folk Museum,
Donegal. *Thatched cottages show life
from 1700-1900. A Gaelic-speaking
cooperative runs the folk village and a
traditional crafts industry.*

Bulgaria

Gabrovo Folk Museum, Gabrovo.
Old buildings and skilled craftspeople.

Spain

Pueblo Español, Barcelona. *Buildings
from all over Spain depict regional
architecture, costumes, and folk craft.*

11

Coping Abroad:
Everyday Survival Skills

City Survival

Many Americans are overwhelmed by European big-city shock. Struggling with the Chicagos, New Yorks and L.A.s of Europe is easier if you follow three rules: (1) get and use information; (2) orient yourself; (3) take advantage of the public transportation systems.

GETTING INFORMATION OUT OF LOCAL TOURIST OFFICES

You can't Magoo Europe's large cities. Get information and plan. Have a directory-type guidebook for wherever you're traveling. Spend the last hour as you approach by train or bus reading and planning. Know what you want to see. Your sightseeing strategy should cover the city systematically, arranged efficiently, one neighborhood at a time. Check for closed days and free days.

No matter how well I know a town, my first stop is the tourist office. Any place with a tourist industry has an information service for visitors located on the central square, in the city hall building, at the train station, or at the freeway entrance. You don't need the address—just follow the signs. An often-hectic but normally friendly and multilingual staff will equip you with a map and general sightseeing and tour information, reserve a room for you, sell you concert or play tickets, and answer your questions. I always prepare a list of needs and questions so I'm well organized and get the most out of my visit.

A checklist of concerns includes a written-out proposed sightseeing schedule for the information person to check (is it workable, efficient, anything missing, or changes recommended); what's going on in the way of special events (pick up any local periodical entertainment guide); a map of the town with public transit information; list of sights with current hours; ideas on where to eat and sleep (remember, they don't volunteer information on cheap alternatives to hotels and they pocket any "deposits" collected); walking tours available or self-guided walking tour brochures; and any miscellaneous needs (such as safety, laundry, bike rental, parking, regional camping guide, transportation tips for your departure, map of the next town you'll be visiting, and book-a-room-ahead help). If you'll be arriving late, call ahead before the TI closes. Good information (in English) is worth a long-distance phone call. (Guidebooks list the phone numbers.) If the TI is closed, youth hostel wardens, big-hotel information desks, other travelers, and guidebooks are alternative information sources.

All big cities have English bookstores. Large bookstores and university bookstores have English sections. Most kiosks and newsstands sell local guides in English.

Find a good map. The best and cheapest map is often the public transit map. Try to get one that shows bus lines, subway stops, and major sights. Many hotels can give you a free city map. In Paris and Rome, grab a fine free city map at any McDonald's.

If you find yourself in a town with no information and the tourist office is closed, a glance through a postcard rack will quickly show you the town's most visit-worthy sights.

Big European cities bubble with entertainment, festivities, and nightlife. But they won't come to you. New in town and unable to speak the local language, it's easy to be oblivious to a once-in-a-lifetime event erupting just across the bridge. In this case, a periodical entertainment guide is the ticket. Every big city has one, either in English (such as London's *What's On* or *This Week in Oslo*) or in the local language but easy to decipher (such as the *Pariscope* guide). In Venice, Florence, and Rome, the best ones are published monthly by the big, fancy hotels and are available for free at their desks. (Leave your rucksack outside.)

Ask at your hotel and at the tourist office about entertainment. Read posters. Events are posted on city walls everywhere. They are in a foreign language, but that really doesn't matter when it reads: Weinfest, Musica Folklorico, 9 Juni, 21:00, Piazza Major, Entre Libre, and so on. Figure out the signs—or miss the party.

ORIENTATION

Get the feel of the city. Once oriented, you're more at ease. The city warms up and sightseeing is more enjoyable. Study the map to understand the city's layout. Relate the location of landmarks—your hotel, major sights, the river, main streets, and station—to each other. Use any viewpoint—such as a church spire, tower, top story of a skyscraper, or hilltop—to look over the city. Retrace where you've been, see where you're going. Back on the ground, you won't be in such constant need of your map.

Many cities have fast-orientation bus tours like London's famous "Round London" tour. These show you the major sights and give you a feel for the urban lay of the land. Some cities have inexpensive public transit buses designed to orient visitors and move them conveniently from one major sight to the next, often with printed or recorded narrations. Tourist office-organized walking tours offer a fine orientation to the old town center.

Many cities, especially in the north, have industrious youth travel-aid offices. The Scandinavian capitals have Interpoint centers for traveling students, offering comfortable lounges, showers, free luggage storage, discounts at local restaurants, and city information. Copenhagen has a great youth center called Use It, and several cities publish very practical youth-oriented budget travel magazines (available at the tourist office).

PUBLIC TRANSPORTATION

When you master a city's subway or bus system, you've got it by the tail. Europe's public transit systems are so good that many Europeans choose not to own a car. Their wheels are trains, buses, and subways.

The buses and subways all work logically and are run by people who are happy to help lost tourists locate themselves. Anyone can decipher the code to cheap and easy urban transportation. Too many timid tourists never venture into the subways or buses and use up their energy on walking or their money on taxis.

Paris and London have the most extensive—and the most needed—subway systems. Both cities are covered with subway maps and expert subway tutors. Paris even has maps that plan your route for you. Just push your destination's button and the proper route lights up! Subways are speedy and comfortable, never slowed by traffic jams. While they feel safe, be constantly on guard. Wear your money belt. Thieves thrive underground.

Make it a point to get adequate transit information. Pick up a map. Find out about any specials—like packets of subway tickets sold at a discount (in Paris) or tourist tickets allowing unlimited travel on all public transport for a day or several days (in London). These "go as you please" passes may seem expensive, but if you do any amount of running around, they can be a convenient money-saver. And remember, they are more than economical. With a transit pass, you'll avoid the often-long ticket lines.

Have a local person explain your ticket to you. Two dollars may seem expensive for the bus ride until you learn that your ticket is good for round-trip, two hours, or several transfers. And if you tell them where you're going, bus drivers and local people sitting around you will gladly tell you where to get off.

Taxis are often a reasonable option. In southern countries they are cheap and, while expensive for the lone budget traveler, a group of three or four people can often travel cheaper by taxi than by buying three or four bus tickets. (You can go anywhere in downtown Athens for $2.) Don't be bullied by cabbie con-men (common only in the south). Insist on the meter, agree on a rate, or know the going rate. Taxi drivers intimidate too many tourists. If I'm charged a ridiculous price for a ride, I put a reasonable sum on the seat and say good-bye. But don't be too mistrusting. Many tourists wrongly accuse their cabbies of taking the long way around or adding unfair extras. Cabbies are generally honest. There are lots of legitimate supplements (nights, weekends, baggage, extra person, ride out of town, etc.), and winding through medieval street plans is rarely even close to direct.

You can always call for a cab, but the meter will be well under way by the time you get in. It's cheaper and easy to just flag one down or walk to the nearest taxi stand. If it seems unusually frustrating to hail a cab, ask a shopkeeper to direct you to the nearest taxi stand.

Bus Tour Self-Defense

Average American tourists see Europe on an organized bus tour and don't even consider using a guidebook. They pay a guide to show them around.

Independent-minded travelers can do very well on a big bus tour. If you understand the tour business you can take advantage of the tour and it won't take advantage of you. Keep in mind that many savvy travelers take escorted coach tours year after year only for the hotels, meals, and transportation provided. Every day they do their own sightseeing, simply applying the skills of independent travel to the efficient, economical structure an organized coach tour provides. You can take a tour and, to a limited degree, still go "on your own."

A typical big bus tour has a professional multilingual European guide and 40 to 50 people on board. The tour company is probably very big, booking rooms by the thousand and often even owning the hotels it uses. Typically, the bus is a luxurious, fairly new 48-seater with a high, quiet ride, comfy seats, air-conditioning, and a toilet on board. The hotels will be fit for American standards—large, not too personal, and offering mass-produced comfort (but normally no air-conditioning), good plumbing, and all double rooms. The location of your hotel can make the difference between a fair trip and a great trip. Central hotels are much more interesting than a place listed in the brochure as "Florence area." If this is important to you, get explicit locations in writing before your trip. Most meals are included, generally in unmemorable hotel restaurants that can serve large groups at prices driven to almost inedible lows by the tour company. A common complaint among tourists is that hotel meals don't match the local cuisine.

As long as people on board don't think too much or try to deviate from the plan, things go smoothly and reliably and you really do see a lot of Europe. Note I said "see" rather than "experience." If you like the itinerary, guide, and people on your bus, it's a good, easy, and inexpensive way to go.

Having escorted several large European coach tours and now owning and operating a tour company of my own, I've learned that you must

Most bus tours come with a ready-made circle of friends

understand tour guides and their position. Leading a tour is a demanding job with lots of responsibility, paperwork, baby-sitting, and miserable hours. Very often, guides are tired. They're away from homes and families, often for months on end, and are surrounded by foreigners having an extended party that they're probably not in the mood for. Most guides treasure their time alone and, except for romantic adventures, keep their distance from the group socially. Each tourist has personal demands, and a group of 50 can often amount to one big pain in the bus for the guide.

To most guides, the best group is one that lets him or her do the thinking, is happy to be herded around, and enjoys being spoon-fed Europe. The guide's base salary is normally low (about $30 a day from most companies), but an experienced guide makes $250 to $350 a day when the wage is supplemented by a percentage of the optional excursions, kick-backs from merchants that the group patronizes, and the trip-end tips from the busload.

The best guides are happy guides. It's very important to be independent without alienating them. Independent-type tourists tend to threaten guides. Don't insist on individual attention when the guide is hounded by 49 others. Wait for the quiet moment to ask for advice. If the guides want to, they can give the entire group a lot of unrequired

Many who take an organized bus tour could have managed fine on their own

extras that will add greatly to your tour—but only if they want to. Your objective, which requires some artistry, is to keep the guides on your side without letting them take advantage of you.

Most tours don't include the daily sightseeing programs. Each day, one or two special excursions or evening activities, called "options," are offered for $20 to $50 apiece. Each person decides which options to take and pay for. Since budget tours are so competitive, the profit margin on their base price is very thin. The tour company assesses the work of a guide not by how much fun the trip was but by how many options were sold. Guides sell these options aggressively (discouraging people from going off on their own and even withholding information from them). Dishonest tour guides pad their income by cleverly cutting out excursions that the tour company includes (e.g., pocketing $90 by showing his group the windmills but not taking them inside) or by doing "black excursions" where he'll charge for a visit which is suppose to be free (such as to Dachau) and not report the income to the tour company.

Discriminate among options. Some are great, others are not worth the time or money. In general, the half-day city sightseeing tours are a good value. A local guide will usually show you his or her city much more thoroughly than you could do on your own, given your time limitations. Illuminated night tours of Rome and Paris can be marvelous. I'd skip most other illuminated tours and "nights on the town." On a typical big bus tour evening, several bus tours come together for the "evening of local color." Two hundred tourists having a glass of *sangria* and watching flamenco dancing on-stage to the rhythm of their automatic rewinds isn't exactly local. I'd rather save the money and take a cab or a bus downtown to just poke around.

A major problem with tours is that the groups see only a thin slice of people—not real locals but hardened businesspeople who know how to make money off tour groups. Only one kind of Italian is attracted to an umbrella-following group of 48 Americans. Make a point to break away and meet locals who never deal with tourist groups. One summer night in Regensburg, I skipped out. While the tour waited to get off the bus, the great-great-great-grandson of the astronomer Johannes Kepler bought me a beer and we drank it under shooting stars, overlooking the Danube.

Your guide may pressure you into taking the "options." Stand firm. In spite of what you may be told, you are capable of doing plenty on your own. Maintain your independence. Get maps and tourist information from your hotel desk (or another hotel desk) or a tourist information office. Tour hotels are often located outside the city, where they cost the tour company less and where they figure you are more likely to

A well-chosen tour can be a fine value, giving you a great trip and a busload of new friends

book the options just to get into town. Some tours promise to take you downtown if the hotel is outside the city limits. Ask the person behind the desk how to get downtown using public transportation. Taxis are always a possibility, and with three or four people sharing, they're affordable.

Team up with others on your tour to explore on your own. No city is dead after the shops are closed. Go downtown and stroll.

Tour guides call the dreaded tourists with a guidebook "informed passengers." But a guidebook is *your* key to travel freedom. Do your own research. Know what you want to see. Don't just sit back and count on your guide to give you the Europe you're looking for. The guide will be happy to spoon-feed you Europe, but it will be from his or her menu. This often distorts the importance of the sights you'll see. Many tours seem to make a big deal out of a statue in Lucerne called the *Dying Lion* and most tourists are impressed on command. The guide declares that this mediocre-at-best sight is great, and that's how it's perceived. What makes it "great" for the guide is that Lucerne (which has a hotel the tour company owns but not a lot of interesting sights) was given too much time in the itinerary and it's easy for the bus to park and wait. Leonardo da Vinci's *The Last Supper*, however, is often passed over as bus tours skirt Milan. It's an inconvenient sight.

Remember, you can't take 40 people into a cozy pub and enjoy a cozy pub. A good stop for a guide is one with great freeway accessibility where the bus can easily be parked; where guides and drivers are buttered up with free coffee and cakes; where they serve bottomless cups of American-style coffee, speak English, accept bank cards, and will mail souvenirs home; and where 30 people can go to the bathroom at the same time. *Arrivederci, Roma.*

Many people make their European holiday one long shopping spree. This suits your guide and the local tourist industry just fine. In Venice and Florence, guides bringing in a busload of tourists get a standard 15 percent commission. In Turkey, guides (with visions of carpet sales dancing in their heads) actually bid for the opportunity to lead cruise-ship groups around. Every tour guide in Europe knows just where to park the bus in Lucerne for Swiss clocks. You get $40 and a bottle of champagne as soon as you park, and 45 minutes later, when all the tourists are back on the bus, the guide steps into the back room and gets 15 percent of whatever went into the till. That's good business. And any tour guide in Europe knows that if she's got Americans on board, she's carting around a busload of stark raving shoppers.

Don't necessarily reject your guide's shopping tips; just keep in mind that the prices you see often include a 15 percent kickback. Shop around and never swallow the line, "This is a special price available only to your tour, but you must buy now." The sellers who prey on tour buses are smooth. They zero right in on the timid and gullible group member who has no idea what a good buy is. If you buy, buy carefully.

When you're traveling with a group, it's fun, as well as economical, to create a kitty for communal "niceties." If each person contributes $10, the "kitty-keeper" can augment dry continental breakfasts with fresh fruit, provide snacks and drinks at rest stops for a fraction of the exorbitant prices you'll find in the freeway restaurants, get stamps for postcards so each person doesn't have to find the post office individually, and so on.

Remember that the best-selling tours are the ones that promise you the most in the time you have available. No tour can give you more than 24 hours in a day or seven days in a week. What the "blitz" tour can do is give you more hours on the bus. Choose carefully among the itineraries available, and don't assume more is better.

The groups I have escorted on typical European big-bus tours have been almost universally happy and satisfied with their vacations. They got the most out of their tour—and their tour didn't get the most out of them—because they traveled with their own information and exercised a measure of independence.

ORGANIZED HALF-DAY CITY BUS TOURS

Throughout your trip—whether on a group tour or on your own— you'll encounter hour-long, half-day, and all-day sightseeing excursions or tours. There are several kinds. Orientation bus tours are fast, inexpensive, and superficial. Rarely do you even get out of the bus. They cost around $25 and, if you've got the money and not much time, they provide a good orientation. If I had only one day in a big city, I might spend half of it on one of these bus tours.

There are also cases when a bus tour is worthwhile for the transportation it provides. For instance, the châteaus of France's Loire, the sights of southern Bavaria (Ludwig's castles), and the stave church and Grieg's home outside Bergen, Norway, are all awkward to get to on your own; an organized tour not only whisks you effortlessly from one hard-to-reach-without-a-car sight to the next but gives you lots of information as you go.

If you're about to spend $40 anyway for a train ticket, let's say, from London to Bath, why not take a $40 one-day tour from London that visits Stonehenge and Bath. You can leave it in Bath before it returns to London and enjoy a day of transportation, admissions, and information for the price of a 2-hour train ticket.

Walking tours are my favorite. They are thorough, since they focus on just a small part of a city. They are usually conducted by well-trained local people who are sharing their town for the noble purpose of giving you an appreciation of the city's history, people, and culture—not to make a lot of money. Walking tours are personal, inexpensive, and a valuable education. I can't recall a bad one. Many local tourist offices organize the tours or provide a do-it-yourself walking tour leaflet. The avid walking tourist should consider purchasing one of the many guidebooks (such as *Turn Right at the Fountain*) which are carefully written collections of self-guided walks through major cities.

Fancy coach tours—the kinds that leave from the big international hotels—are expensive. Some are great. Others are boring and so depersonalized, sometimes to the point of multilingual taped messages, that you may find the Chinese sound track more interesting than the English. These tours can, however, be of value to the budget-minded do-it-yourselfer. Pick up the brochure for a well-thought-out tour itinerary and do it on your own. Take local buses at your own pace and tour every sight for a fraction of the cost. A popular trend in Europe these days is a bus or boat route that connects all the major sightseeing attractions. Tourists buy the one-day pass and make the circuit at their leisure.

The best guides are often those whose tours you can pick up at the specific sight. These guides usually really know their museum, castle, or whatever.

Telephoning in Europe

Smart travelers use the telephone. Call tourist offices to check sightseeing plans, train stations to check travel plans, restaurants to see if they're open, and so on.

The only way to travel smoothly is to telephone ahead and double-check things. I get earnest letters from readers asking me to drop a hotel from my listings because they made a reservation, got a written confirmation, and still arrived to find no room available. Hotels make mistakes. Smart travelers need to call a day in advance to double-check things. Last year as we were filming my PBS TV show in Ireland I took a minute to call Avis in England to confirm our car pickup the next day at the ferry dock in North Wales. The man at Avis said, "Right-tee-o, Mr. Steves, we'll have your car waiting for you, noon tomorrow, at Heathrow airport." No, at North Wales! "Oh, sorry, Mr. Steves. It's good you called ahead." That call saved us five hours tomorrow. It's not an issue of who makes a mistake. The more I travel, the more I use the telephone.

European phone booths use phone cards rather than coins

Desperate Telephone Communication

Let me illustrate with a hypothetical telephone conversation. I'm calling a hotel in Barcelona from a phone booth in the train station. I just arrived, read my guidebook's list of budget hotels, and I like Pedro's Hotel. Here's what happens:

Pedro answers, "Hotel Pedro, grabdaboodogalaysk."

I ask, "Hotel Pedro?" (Question marks are created melodically.)

He affirms, already a bit impatient, "Si, Hotel Pedro."

I ask, "Habla Eng-leesh?"

He says, "No, dees ees Ehspain." (Actually, he probably would speak a little English or would say "moment" and get someone who did. But we'll make this particularly challenging. Not only does he not speak English—he doesn't want to . . . for patriotic reasons.)

Remembering not to overcommunicate, you don't need to tell him you're a tourist looking for a bed. Who else calls a hotel speaking in a foreign language? Also, you can assume he's got a room available. If he's full, he's very busy and he'd say "complete" or "no hotel" and hang up. If he's still talking to you, he wants your business. Now you must communicate just a few things, like how many beds you need and who you are.

I say, "OK, hotel." (OK is international for, "Roger, prepare for the next transmission.") "Two people"—he doesn't understand. I get fancy, "Dos people"—he still doesn't get it. Internationalize, "Dos pehr-son"—no comprende. "Dos hombre"—nope. Digging deep into my bag of international linguistic tricks, I say, "Dos Yankees."

"OK!" he understands, you want beds for two Americans. He says, "Si," and I say, "Very good" or "Muy bueno."

Now I need to tell him who I am. If I say, "My name is Mr. Steves and I'll be over promptly," I'll lose him. I say, "My name Ricardo (Ree-KAR-do)." In Italy, I say, "My name Luigi." Your name really doesn't matter; you're communicating just a password so you can identify yourself when you walk through the door. Say anything to be understood.

He says, "OK."

You repeat slowly, "Hotel, dos Yankees, Ricardo, coming pronto, OK?"

He says, "OK."

You say, "Gracias, ciao!"

Twenty minutes later you walk up to the reception desk, and Pedro greets you with a robust, "Eh, Ricardo!"

Each country's phone system is different, but each one works—logically. The key to figuring out a foreign phone is to approach it without comparing it to yours back home. It works for the locals, and it can work for you. Many people flee in terror when a British phone starts its infamous "rapid pips." They go home telling tales of the impossibility of using England's phones.

Each country has phone booths with multilingual instructions. If you follow these step by step, the phone will work—usually. Operators generally speak English and are helpful. International codes, instructions, and international assistance numbers are usually on the wall or in the front of the phone book. If I can't manage in a strange phone booth, I ask a nearby local person for help.

The first step is to find the right phone. The increasingly rare coin-op phones are being replaced by more convenient and vandal-resistant phones that accept only the phone cards that you buy at post offices or tobacco shops. For coin-op phones, have enough small coins to complete your call. The instructions may say the local minimum, your credit total is generally shown, and only entirely unused coins will be returned. Many phones allow run-on calls, so you won't lose your big-coin credit (if you have one and need to make another call). Look for this (usually black) button and push it rather than hanging up. In some countries, your voice won't be heard until you push a button to engage the call.

European telephone cards (not to be confused with American phone credit cards) are common throughout Europe. They're easy to use and sold conveniently at newsstands, street kiosks, and post offices. You just slide your card into a slot and dial. The phone reads your card's magnetic strip and a readout tells you how much money is remaining on your card. The only drawback is that the cheapest cards can cost $5, more phone time than you may need in that country. If you're as frugal as me, you'll lay awake at night wondering how to productively use it up before you cross the next border—a worthwhile exercise. (You can always blow the remaining telephone time by calling home.) Still, you can't travel smart without using the phone. So use these cards.

Prefixes are a common source of phone booth frustration. They are usually listed by city on the wall or in the phone book. There are three prefixes: the international access number, the country code (1 for U.S.A.), and the city or area code. "Areas" are much smaller in Europe than in the United States, and nearly any call out of town will require one. When calling long distance in Europe, you must dial the area code first. Area codes start with a zero, which is used only when calling with-

Country	International access code*	Country code**	Emergency # for much of country
Austria	00	43	144
Belgium	00	32	900
Denmark	009	45	100
Finland	990	358	002
France	19	33	17
Germany	00	49	110
Great Britain	010	44	999
Ireland	16	353	999
Italy	00	39	113
Netherlands	09	31	222222
Norway	095	47	000
Spain	07	34	091
Sweden	009	46	90000
Switzerland	00	41	117
U.S.A.	011	1	911

*Dial these digits first, to get out of the country you are calling from.
**Dial these digits next, for the country you are calling to.

in the country. Calling internationally, drop the zero and replace it with the country code. Local numbers vary in length from three to eight digits. (Note that France, Denmark, and Norway have recently gone to eight-digit local numbers and have dropped area codes. You dial direct throughout the country.)

Here's an example: France's international access code is 19. Germany's country code is 49, Munich's area code is 089. My favorite Munich hotel's telephone number is 260-3107. To call that hotel within Munich, dial 260-3107. To call it from Frankfurt, dial 089/260-3107. To call it from France, dial 19-49-89-260-3107. From the U.S.A., dial 011-49-89-260-3107.

Once you've made the connection, the real challenge begins—communication. With no visual aids, getting the message across in a language you don't speak requires some artistry.

Some key rules are: speak slowly and clearly, pronouncing every letter; keep it very simple—don't clutter your message with anything less than essential; don't overcommunicate—many things are already understood and don't need to be said (those last six words didn't need to be written); and use international or carefully chosen English words. When all else fails, let a local person on your end (such as a hotel receptionist) do the talking after you explain to him, with visual help, the message. My

Rick Steves' Phrase Books predict conversations you'll need to make on the phone and provide the necessary foreign language templates with all the various options you may need to fill in the blanks.

CALLING HOME

Most European countries have direct connections to the United States now, and you can get through for as little as 50 cents—about the cost of a postcard stamp. Rather than write postcards, I just call in my "scenery's here, wish you were beautiful" messages.

You can call home from your hotel's phone, the post office phone, or a public phone booth. Telephoning through your hotel's phone system is fine for local calls but an almost-criminal rip-off for long distance. I do this only when I'm feeling flush and lazy for a quick "Call me in Stockholm at this number" message. Post offices are much cheaper, with metered international phone booths. The person who sells stamps will plug you in, assign you a booth, and help you with your long-distance prefixes. You sit in your private sweat-box, make the call, and pay the bill when you're done. I normally just get a local phone card or a pile of coins, find a public phone booth (same price as the post office), dial direct, and keep it short and sweet. Beware: a popular new rip-off is small businesses on main tourist streets which look like telephone company long-distance services but actually charge like hotels. Ask the price per minute before you take a metered phone booth.

Nearly all European countries have "dial direct to anywhere" phone booths. Calls to the United States cost $2 to $4 per minute. There is no minimum. First get a pile of coins. Put in a coin and dial: (1) international access code, wait for tone; (2) country code; (3) area code; and (4) the seven-digit number. Try calling me from France: put in two francs (40 cents), dial 19-1-206-771-8303, and talk fast. Every country has its quirks. Try pausing between codes if you're having trouble, or dial the English-speaking international operator for help. Off-hours calls are cheaper per minute.

I start with a small coin worth 25 to 50 cents to be sure I get the person I need or can say, "I'm calling back in five minutes, so wake him up." (Remember, it's about six hours earlier in New York and nine hours earlier in California.) Then I plug in the larger coins. I keep one last sign-off coin ready. When my time is done, I pop it in and say good-bye. The digital meter warns you when you're about to be cut off.

Calling collect is sometimes more complicated and always more expensive. It's cheaper (about $1 a minute—and the other end pays) and easier (coin-free) if you have your friend call you back, dialing direct from the states. Tell them to dial 011 (the U.S. international access code), your country code, your area code without the zero, and your number.

If you'll be calling home a lot, take advantage of the handy USA Direct service offered by SPRINT, AT&T, and MCI. Each company has a toll-free access number in nearly every European country. Cardholders can dial this operator, give their card number, and be put through immediately. It's a snap, and your home account is billed at the cheap (about $2 for the first minute and $1 per minute after that) American long-distance rate plus a $2.50 service fee for the call. (In three minutes, you save enough on the rate to cover the service fee.) With USA Direct, you can call cheap from your hotel room or from a phone booth. Calling an answering machine can be expensive. As soon as you connect you're billed for the full first minute—$4.50). To see if the record-a-call is off or if the right person's at home for less than 25 cents, call first with a coin or local phone card.

Theft and the Tourist

Europe is safe when it comes to violent crime. But it's a very dangerous place—if you're an American—from a petty purse-snatching, pick-pocketing point of view. We are targets. If I were a European street thief, I'd specialize in Americans. Yanking only Yankees, I'd do fine because Americans are the ones with all the good stuff in their bags and wallets. Only American women keep money belts in their purses. And that juicy little tip is in every street-thief newsletter.

If you're not constantly on guard, you'll have something stolen. One summer, four out of five friends I traveled with lost cameras in one way or another. (Don't look at me.) In 22 summers of travel I've been mugged once (in a part of London where only fools and thieves tread), had my car broken into six times (broken locks and shattered wing windows, lots of nonessential stuff taken), and had my car hot-wired once (it was abandoned a few blocks away when the thief found nothing to take). But I've never had my room rifled and never had any money-belt-worthy valuables stolen. In Europe, I'm on guard and wary.

A tourist is an easy and logical target. Loaded down with valuables in a strange new environment, we stick out like jeweled thumbs. Nearly all crimes suffered by tourists are nonviolent and avoidable. Many of the most successful scams require a naïve and trusting tourist. If you exercise the proper caution and aren't overly trusting, you should have no problem. Here are some tips given to me by a Gypsy who won the lotto.

Everything crucial should fit into your money belt or be left home.

Purses and wallets are handy for odds and ends and a day's spending money, but plan on losing them. A Velcro strip sewn into your front or back pocket slows down fast fingers. Luxurious luggage lures thieves. The thief chooses the most impressive suitcase in the pile—never mine. Those with nothing worth stealing (cars, video cameras, jewelry, and so on) except what's in their money belt travel virtually invulnerable.

My money belt is my key to peace of mind. I never travel without one. The money belt is a small, nylon-zippered pouch that ties around the waist under your pants or skirt. You wear it completely hidden from sight, tucked in like a shirttail (over your shirt and under your pants). It costs only $8 (see Back Door Catalog) to protect your fortune. In my money belt I keep my passport, cash, traveler's checks (or their receipt), train pass, airline ticket (without the needless paper), American driver's license, credit card (bring no more than two), and any very important documents, vouchers, and identity cards. Wear it slim. Sweep out all non-essential papers. Even traveler's checks are replaceable and can be stored elsewhere if you keep the original receipt in your money belt.

With a money belt, all your essential documents are on you as securely and thoughtlessly as your underpants. Have you ever thought

These are not beggars. They are thieves. Using babies or newspapers to distract you, Gypsies target tourists at major sights in Italy, especially around Rome's Forum and the Florence train station.

about that? Every morning you put on your underpants. You don't even think about them all day long. And every night when you undress, sure enough, there they are, exactly where you put them. When I travel, my valuables are just as securely out of sight and out of mind, around my waist in a money belt. It's luxurious peace of mind.

You don't get at your money belt for every nickle, dime, and quarter. You operate with a day's spending money in your pocket. Your money belt is your deep storage . . . for select deposits and withdrawals. Lately, I haven't even worn a wallet. A few bills in my shirt pocket—no keys, no wallet . . . I'm on vacation! I keep bulky or replaceable documents in a second money belt or small zipper pouch tied or sewn to the inside of my rucksack or suitcase.

I'm uncomfortable only when I'm not wearing my money belt. Never leave a money belt "hidden" on the beach while you swim. It's safer left in your hotel room. You can shower with your money belt (hang it—maybe in a plastic bag—from the nozzle) in sleazy or dorm situations where it shouldn't be left alone in your room.

I keep the contents of my money belt dry and unsweaty with a zip-lock baggie. Damp traveler's checks can be hard to cash.

Cameras tempt thieves. Never leave yours lying around where hotel workers and others can see it and be tempted. Keep it either around your neck or zipped safely out of sight.

When sleeping on a train (at an airport, or anywhere in public), clip

or fasten your pack (or suitcase) to the chair, luggage rack, or to yourself. Even the slight inconvenience of undoing a clip foils most thieves. Women probably shouldn't sleep in an empty train compartment. You're safer sharing a compartment with a family or a couple of nuns.

Imaginative artful-dodger thief teams create a fight or commotion to distract their curious or helpful victims. Crowding through the Paris metro turnstiles is a popular way to rip off the unsuspecting tourist. Crowded flea markets and city buses that cover the tourist sights (like Rome's notorious #64) are also happy hunting grounds. Thieves posing as concerned locals will warn you to store your wallet safely—and then steal it, since they now know where it is. Thieves assume that anyone leaving a bank with their luggage just changed money. Thieves wait for distracted mothers to change diapers. If you check your luggage at the station, keep the claim ticket or key in your money belt. Thieves know just where to go if they get one of these.

Groups of kids with big eyes and colorful dresses play a game where they politely mob the unsuspecting tourist, beggar-style. As their pleading eyes grab yours and they hold up their sad message scrawled on cardboard, you're fooled into thinking that they're beggars. All the while, your purse, fanny-bag, or rucksack is being expertly rifled. This is particularly common in touristed areas of Florence and Rome. If you're wearing a money belt and you understand what's going on here, there's nothing to fear. In fact, having a street thief's hand in your pocket becomes just one more interesting cultural experience.

Your hotel is a relative haven from thieves. Bags are much safer in your room than with you on the streets. Hotels are a good resource for advice on personal and parking safety.

Thieves target tourists' cars—especially at night. Don't leave anything even hinting of value in view in your parked car. Put anything worth stealing in the trunk. Leave your glove compartment open so the thief can look in without breaking in. Choose your parking place carefully. (Your hotel receptionist knows what's safe and what precautions are necessary.)

Make your car look local. Take off or cover the rental company decals. Leave no tourist information laying around. Leave a local newspaper in the back. Over half of the work that European automobile glass shops get is repairing wings broken by thieves. Before I choose where to park my car, I notice how many shattered wing windows glitter on the parking lot's asphalt. If you have a hatchback, leave the trunk covered during the day, and at night take the cover off the trunk and lay it on the back seat so the thief thinks you're savvy and can see there's nothing stored in the back of your car. Many police advise leaving your car unlocked at night. Worthless but irreplaceable things are stolen only if left in a bag. Lay these things loose in the trunk. In Spain these days, crude thieves reach into windows or even smash the windows of occupied cars at stop lights to grab a purse or camera. In Rome, my favorite pension is next to a large police station—a safe place to park, if you're legal.

Photocopy your valuable documents and tickets. It's easier to replace a lost or stolen plane ticket, passport, Eurailpass, or rental voucher if you have a picture proving that you really owned what you are claiming is lost.

American embassies or consulates are located in major European cities. They're there to help American citizens in trouble but don't fancy themselves as travelers' aid offices. Things they'll do happily are help find medical or legal assistance (unless drug-related), inform those at home that you need help, assist in replacing lost or stolen passports, arrange for emergency funds to be sent from home (or, in rare cases, loan it to you directly), give travel advisories, supply tax forms, help with absentee voting, and party with the local aristocracy.

Even the most careful traveler can get ripped off. If it happens, don't let it ruin your trip. Many trips start with a major rip-off, recover, and with the right attitude and very light bags, finish wonderfully.

Be aware of the pitfalls of traveling, but relax and have fun. Limit your vulnerability rather than your travels. Most people in every country are on your side. If you exercise adequate discretion, aren't overly trusting, and don't put yourself into risky situations, your travels should be about as dangerous as hometown grocery shopping. Don't travel afraid—travel carefully.

Traveler's Toilet Trauma

Every traveler has one or two great toilet stories. Foreign toilets can be traumatic. And they can be hard to find. But, when all is said and done, they are one of those little things that make travel so much more interesting than staying home. Before you dive into that world of memorable porcelain experiences, let me prepare you for toilet-shock, and pass on a few tips on finding a WC quickly when you need one.

First, about toilet trauma. While most European toilets are reasonably similar to our own, be prepared for some toilets that are dirtier than and different from what you're used to. Only Americans need disposable bibs to sit on and a paper strip draped over their toilet, assuring them that no one has sat there yet. In fact, those of us who need a throne to sit on are in the minority. Most humans sit on their haunches

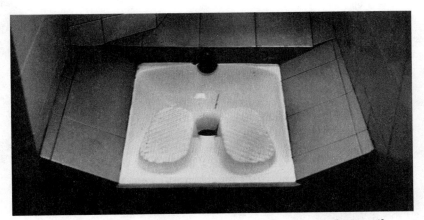

One of Europe's many unforgettable experiences, the squat-and-aim toilet

and nothing more. When many Asian refugees are de-Oriented in the United States, they have to be taught not to stand on our rims.

So if you plan to venture away from the international-style hotels in your Mediterranean travels and become a temporary local person, "going local" may take on a very real meaning. Experienced travelers enjoy recalling the shock they got the first time they opened the door and found only porcelain footprints and a squat-and-aim hole in the ground—complete with flies in a holding pattern. When confronted by the "nontoilet," remind yourself that if a Western-style toilet were there, it would be so filthy you wouldn't want to get near it.

Toilet paper (like a spoon or a fork) is another Western "essential" that most people on our planet do not use. What they use varies. I won't get too graphic here, but remember that a billion people in south Asia never eat with their left hand. Some countries, such as Turkey, have very frail plumbing, and toilet paper will jam up the WCs. If wastebaskets are full of dirty paper, leave yours there, too.

The TP scene has improved markedly in the last few years, and while you'll still find some strange stuff worth taking home to show your friends, there is no longer any need to BYOTP.

FINDING A TOILET

Finding a decent public toilet can be frustrating. I once dropped a group off in a town for a potty stop, and when I picked them up 20 minutes later, none had found relief. Most countries have few public restrooms. You'll need to develop a knack for finding a private WC.

I can sniff out a biffy in a jiffy. Any place that serves food or drinks has a rest room. No restaurateur would label his WC so those on the street can see, but you can walk into nearly any café or restaurant, politely and confidently, and find a bathroom. Assume it's somewhere in the back, upstairs or downstairs. It's easiest in large places that have outdoor seating, because waiters will think you're a customer just making a quick trip inside. Some call it rude—I call it survival. If you feel like it, ask permission. Just smile, "Toilet?" I'm rarely turned down. Timid people buy a drink they don't want in order to leave one. That's unnecessary. American-type fast-food places are very common these days and always have a decent and fairly "public" rest room. When nature beckons and there's no restaurant or bar handy, look in parks, train stations, museums, hotel lobbies, and government buildings, and on trains or upper floors of department stores.

Large, classy old hotels are as impressive as many palaces you'll pay to see. You can always find a royal retreat here and plenty of very soft TP. These are oases in Third World countries, where a pleasant Western sit-down toilet experience is a rare treat.

Many cities (Paris, London, Amsterdam) are dotted with coin-op telephone-booth-type WCs on street corners. You insert a coin, the door opens, and you have 15 minutes of toilet accompanied by Sinatra Muzak. When you leave, it disinfects itself.

After you've found and used a toilet, you're down to your last challenge—flushing it. Rarely will you find a familiar handle. Find some protuberance and push, pull, twist, squeeze, step on, or pray to it until the waterfall starts. Electric-eye sinks and urinals are increasingly common.

In many countries, you'll need to be selective to avoid the gag-a-maggot variety of toilets. Public toilets like those in parks are often repulsive. I never leave a museum without taking advantage of its restrooms—free, clean, and decorated with artistic graffiti. Use the toilets on the train rather than in the station to save time and money. Toilets on first-class cars are a cut above second-class toilets. I go first class even with a second-class ticket. Train toilets are located on the ends of cars, where it's most jiggly. A trip to the train's john always reminds me of the rodeo. Never use a train WC while stopped in a station (unless you didn't like that particular town). Train WC cleanliness deteriorates as the journey progresses.

Tipping or paying to use a public WC is a European custom that irks many Americans. But isn't it really worth a quarter, considering the cost of water, maintenance, and cleanliness? And you're probably in no state to argue, anyway. Many times, the toilet is free but the woman in the corner sells sheets of toilet paper. Most common is the tip dish by the entry. The local equivalent of about 25 cents is plenty. Caution: many attendant-ladies leave only bills and too-big coins in the tray to bewilder the full-bladdered tourist. The keepers of Europe's public toilets have earned a reputation for crabbiness. You'd be crabby, too, if you lived under the street in a room full of public toilets. Humor them, understand them, and leave them a coin.

Men: The women who seem to inhabit Europe's WCs are a popular topic of conversation among Yankee travelers. Sooner or later, you'll be minding your own business at the urinal and the lady will bring you your change or sweep under your feet. Yes, it is distracting, but you'll just have to get used to it—she has.

Getting comfortable in foreign rest rooms takes a little adjusting, but that's travel. When in Rome, do as the Romans do—and before you know it . . . Euro-peein'.

Counting and Other Bugaboos

Europeans do many things different from the way we do. Simple as these things are, they can be frustrating and cause needless, occasionally serious problems. Enjoy the differences.

Their numbers 7 and 1 look slightly different from ours. European ones have an upswing: *1*. To make the seven more distinctive, add a cross: *7*. If you don't cross your 7 it may be mistaken as a sloppy 1 and you may miss your train (and be mad at the French for refusing to speak English). Fours often look like short lightning bolts: *4*.

Europeans reverse the day and month in numbered dates. Therefore, Christmas is 25-12-95 instead of 12-25-95, as we would write it. Commas are decimal points and decimals commas, so a dollar and a half is 1,50 and there are 5.280 feet in a mile.

Floors are numbered differently. The bottom floor is called the ground floor. What we would call the second floor is a European's first floor. So if your room is on the second floor (European), bad news— you're on the third floor (American). On the elevator, push whatever's below "1" to get to the ground floor.

Just like when they're driving, Europeans keep the left lane open for passing on moving sidewalks and escalators. Stand to the right.

When counting with your fingers, start with your thumb. If you hold up your first finger, you'll probably get two, and making a "peace" sign to indicate the number 2 may get you a punch in the nose in parts of Britain, where that is an obscene gesture.

The 24-hour clock is used in any official timetable. This includes bus, train, and tour schedules. Learn to use it quickly and easily. Everything is the same until 12:00 noon. Then, instead of starting over again at 1:00 p.m., the Europeans keep on going—13:00, 14:00, and so on. 18:00 is 6:00 p.m. (subtract 12 and add p.m.).

Europeans measure temperatures in degrees Celsius. Zero degrees C = 32 degrees Fahrenheit (C x 9/5 + 32 = F); or, easier and nearly as accurate, double the Celsius temperature and add 30. A memory aid: 28°C = 82°F—darn hot.

European countries (except Great Britain) use kilometers instead of miles. A kilometer is six-tenths of a mile. To translate kilometers to miles quickly, I cut the kilometer figure in half and add 10 percent of the original figure (e.g., 420 km = 210 + 42 = 252 miles). Quick, what's 360 km? (180 + 36 = 216 miles.) "36-26-36" means nothing to a European (or metric) girl-watcher. But a "90-60-90" is a real pistachio.

Italian lire, with 1,500 to the dollar, drive visiting Yankees crazy. To translate, just cover the last three digits with your finger and cut what's left by about a third (e.g., 18,000 lire for dinner equals about $12; 45,000 lire for a hotel is about $30; 620,000 lire for a taxi ride is about . . . uh-oh . . .).

House numbers often have no correlation to what's across the street. While odd is normally on one side and even is on the other, #27 may be directly across from #2.

Geriatric Globe-Trotting

More people than ever are hocking their rockers and buying plane tickets. Many senior adventurers are proclaiming, "Age matters only if you're a cheese." Travel is their fountain of youth. I spent three weeks last summer in Europe with a group of people who made my parents look young. They taught me many things, including the fact that it's never too late to have a happy childhood. Special discounts in much of the world encourage many older travelers.

I spend a lot of time meeting with retired couples who fly off to Europe with Eurailpasses, carry-on suitcases (9 x 22 x 14 inches) that convert into rucksacks, and $50 a day. Most of them are on their second or third retirement trip, and each time as they walk out my door, I think, "Wow, I've got a good 30 years of travel ahead of me."

Gertrude and Vernon Johnson, both 68, are in Europe now. Nobody knows where. Before they left, I quizzed them on geriatric globe-trotting.

Was this your first major trip abroad? "Last year's trip was our first trip anywhere! We spent six weeks with a train pass and $120 a day for the both of us. Out of that $120, we spent $80 on room and board, going the B&B way, and $40 a day covered everything else, including

Their fountain of youth is Europe!

miscellaneous transportation, admissions, little souvenirs, and even a weekly phone call home to the kids."

Were you hesitant at first? "Yes, indeed. I remember climbing into that airplane thinking I might be making a big mistake. But when we got over there and tackled problem after problem successfully, our confidence soared. Friendly people were always coming out of the woodwork to help us when we needed it."

What about theft and physical safety for a couple of retired people like yourselves running around Europe independently? "As far as retired people go, we never felt like we were 'retired.' I never felt any different from anyone else, and people accepted us as just two more travelers."

Gertrude added, "Later on, as we remembered our trip, we thought maybe people treated us 'gray-haired rucksackers' a little kinder because of our age. We never had a bit of a problem with theft or safety. Of course, we'd wear our money belts every day and choose our neighborhoods carefully. It's pretty obvious when you're getting into a bad neighborhood. We never felt that Ugly American problem. People treated us very well. If anything, there was more help for seniors in public in Europe than we find at home."

Were the Europeans impressed by a retired couple with such an independent travel style? "I'd say they were. In fact, at one place, Rick, we were sitting down and—"

Then the table jolted as Gertrude grabbed Vernon's knee, saying, "Nothin' doing! That's too good a story." She plans, at 68, on becoming a travel writer some day—so we'll just have to wait for the rest of that story.

Do you speak any languages? "No, but we worked on a Berlitz French record for three weeks and that was helpful. We found that the best way to get along with the locals was to try to speak their language. They'd laugh a lot, but they appreciated our effort and would bend over backward to help us. They could usually speak enough English to help us out."

Did you have trouble finding rooms? "No. We traveled from May 1 to June 15 without reservations. Arthur Frommer's guide was handy, and, of course, we got help from the tourist offices and people in the towns. We had no problems. Decent budget hotels are close to the station, and that made setting up a snap.

"We always planned to arrive early. The overnight trains were ideal because they arrived first thing in the morning. We took our Frommer's guide into the tourist office, which was always in or near the station, and they'd call the hotel for us. A few times they charged extra for their service, but it was always very convenient. For older people, I would insist on arriving early in the day, using Frommer's, and having local money with you when you arrive."

How much did you pack? "Our luggage weighed a total of 25 pounds. Gertrude carried 11, and I packed 14. We just packed a few easy-wash and fast-dry clothes. Before our first trip you told us to bring nothing electrical. We didn't listen, and we almost burned down our hotel in Paris." (The table jolted again.) "So this time we're bringing nothing electrical."

What was the most important lesson you learned on your first trip? "Pack even less. When you pack light you're younger—footloose and fancy-free. And that's the way we like to be."

Organizations that arrange discounts and provide information and special help to the growing legions of senior globe-trotters include AARP (tel. 800/927-0111) for those over 50; Elderhostel (tel. 617/426-7788), with Boston-based study programs around the world for those over 60, will send you a free catalog listing their three-week liberal arts programs (usually one week per course and location). There are also more guidebooks on the subject, including a guide to Elderhostel programs, *Elderhostels: The Students' Choice* (Santa Fe, NM.: John Muir Publications).

Travels with Baby Andy—Leashes and Valium?

My wife (Anne), 7-year-old (Andy), and VW van (Vinnie) have spent seven one-month trips with me traveling from Norway to Naples and Dublin to Dubrovnik. It's not hell, but it's not terrific travel, either. Still, we'd rather change diapers in Paris than in Seattle.

Young European families, like their Yuppie American counterparts, are traveling, babies and all. You'll find more and more kids' menus, hotel playrooms, and kids-go-crazy zones at freeway rest stops all over Europe. And people, especially southern Europeans, love babies. Babies are great icebreakers—socially and in the Arctic.

An international adventure is a great foundation for a mountain of family memories. Here are some of the lessons we've learned whining and giggling through Europe with baby, toddler, and now little boy, Andy.

BABY GEAR

Since a happy baby on the road requires a lot of gear, a key to survival with a baby in Europe is to have a rental car or stay in one place. Of course, you'll pack as light as you can, but if Mom figures you'll need it, trust her judgement.

Bring a car seat, buy one in Europe, or see if your car rental company can provide one. If you're visiting friends, with enough notice they can often borrow a car seat and a stroller for you. If you'll be driving long hours while the baby sleeps, try to get one that reclines.

A stroller is essential. Umbrella models are lightest, but we found a heavy-duty model with reclining back worth bringing for the baby. Andy could nap in it, and it served as a luggage cart for the Bataan Death March parts of our trip when we had to use public transportation. Carry the stroller onto the plane—you'll need it in the airport. Big wheels handle cobblestones best.

A small travel crib was a godsend. No matter what kind of hotel, pension, or hostel we ended up in, as long as we could clear a 4-by-4-foot space on the floor, we'd have a safe, clean, and familiar home for Andy to sleep and play in. During the day, we'd salvage a little room by flipping it up on its side and shoving it against the wall.

If a baby backpack works for you at home, bring it to Europe. (I just used my shoulders.) Rucksacks in general are great for parents who wish they had the hands of an octopus. Prepare to tote more than a tot. A combo purse/diaper bag with shoulder straps is ideal. Be on guard: purse-snatchers target mothers (especially while busy and off guard, as when changing diapers).

There's lots more to pack. Encourage bonding to a blanket or stuffed critter and take it along. We used a lot of Heinz dehydrated food dumped into zip-lock baggies. Tiny Tupperware containers with lids were great for crackers, raisins, and snacks. You'll find plenty of disposable diapers, wipes, baby food, and so on, in Europe, so don't take the whole works from home. Before you fly away, be sure you've packed ipecac, a decongestant, Acetaminophen, and a thermometer. For a toddler, bring a few favorite books and a soft (easy on hotel rooms) ball, and buy little European toys as you go. As Andy got older, activity and puzzle books and a Sega Game Gear kept him occupied for what might have been countless boring hours. Also, a healthy daily holiday allowance as a reward for assembling a first-class daily picture journal gave our 6-year-old reasons to be enthusiastic about every travel day.

Common sense and lessons learned from day-trips at home are your best sources of information. *Take Your Kids To Europe* (by Cynthia Harriman, Mason-Grant Publications, 1994, 276 pages, $16 postpaid, Box 6547, Portsmouth, NH 03802, tel. 603/436-1608) is full of practical, concrete lessons from firsthand family travel experience and the only good book I've seen for those traveling with kids aged 6 to 16. The best book we found on traveling with infants was Maureen Wheeler's *Travel with Children* (Lonely Planet Publications). Though designed for Asian travel, it's good advice for Europe-bound parents. (For a catalog full of fam-

Siena? Dad and I love Siena!

ily travel guides, send $1 to Carousel Press, Box 6061, Albany, CA
94706, tel. 510/527-5849. John Muir publishes a series called the
Kidding Around guides; see the back of this book for titles.)

PARENTING AT 32,000 FEET

Gurgling junior might become an airborne Antichrist as soon as the seat
belt light goes off. You'll pay 10 percent of the ticket cost to take your
under-2-year-old on an international flight. The child doesn't get a seat,
but many airlines have flying baby perks for moms and dads who ask for
them in advance—roomier bulkhead seats, hang-from-the-ceiling
bassinets, and baby meals. After age 2, a toddler's ticket costs 67 percent
of the adult fare—a major financial owie. (From age 12 on, they pay full
fare.)

Ask your pediatrician about sedating your baby for a 10-hour intercontinental flight. We think it's the only merciful (for the entire family)
thing to do. (Dimetapp, Tylenol, or Pediacare worked well for us.)
Prepare to be 100 percent self-sufficient throughout the flight. Expect
cramped seating and busy attendants. Bring extra clothes for you and
the baby. Bring special toys. Those colored links are handy for attaching
toys to the seat, crib, high chairs, jail cells, and so on. The in-flight
headphones are great entertainment for flying toddlers.

Landings and takeoffs can be painful for ears of all ages. A bottle, a
pacifier, or anything to suck helps equalize the baby's middle-ear

Two kids whizzing through Europe

pressure. For this reason, nursing moms will be glad they do when it comes to flying. If your kid cries, remember: crying, too, is a great pressure equalizer.

Once on foreign soil, remember that your footloose and see-it-all days of travel are over for a while. Go easy. Traveling with a tyke is tiring, wet, sticky, and smelly. Your mobility plummets.

Be warned—jet lag is nursery purgatory. On his first night in Europe, baby Andy was furious that darkness had bullied daylight out of his up-till-then reliable 24-hour body clock cycle. Luckily, we were settled in a good hotel with thick walls, and most of the guests were able to find accommodations elsewhere.

SHELTER

We slept in rooms of all kinds, from youth hostels (many have family rooms) to hotels. Until he was 5, we were never charged for Andy, and while we always use our own bedding, many doubles have a sofa or extra bed we can barricade with chairs and use instead of the crib.

Childproof the room immediately on arrival. A roll of masking tape makes quick work of electrical outlets. Anything breakable goes on top of the free-standing closet. Proprietors are generally helpful to considerate and undemanding parents. We'd often store our bottles and milk cartons in their fridge, ask (and pay) for baby-sitting, and so on.

Every room had a sink where baby Andy could pose for cute pictures, have a little fun, make smelly bubbles, and get clean. With a toddler, budget extra to get a bath in your room—a practical need and a fun diversion. Toddlers and campgrounds—with swings, slides, and plenty of friends—mix wonderfully.

FOOD

We found European restaurants and their customers cool to noisy babies. High chairs are rare. We learned to eat at places with outdoor seating; at the many McDonald's-type, baby-friendly fast-food places; or to picnic. In restaurants (or anywhere), if your infant is making a disruptive fuss, apologetically say the local word for "teeth," and previously annoyed locals will become sympathetic.

Nursing babies are easiest to feed and travel with. Remember, some cultures are uncomfortable with public breast-feeding. Be sensitive.

We stocked up on munchies (fruit, pretzels, tiny boxes of juice—which double as squirt guns). A 7:00 a.m. banana worked wonders, and a 5:00 p.m. snack made late European dinners workable. In restaurants, we ordered an extra plate for Andy, who just nibbled off of our meals. We'd order "fizzy" (but not sticky) mineral water, call it "pop," and the many spills were no problem. With all the candy and sweet temptations at toddler eye level in Europe, you can forget a low-sugar diet. While gelati and pastries are expensive, Andy's favorite suckers and Popsicles were very cheap and available everywhere.

Plan to spend more money. You'll travel in taxis rather than buses and subways. Hotels can get baby-sitters, usually from professional agencies. The service is expensive but well worth the splurge when you crave a leisurely, peaceful evening *sans* bibs and cribs.

With a baby, we arranged our schedule around naps and sleep time. A well-rested baby (and child) is worth the limitation. Driving while Andy siestaed worked well. As a toddler, however, Andy was up very late, playing soccer with his new Italian friends on the piazza or eating huge ice creams in the hotel kitchen with the manager's kids. We gave up keeping any rigid naptime or bedtime, and we enjoyed Europe's evening ambience as a family.

OK, you're there, watered, fed, and only a little bleary. Europe is your cultural playpen, a living fairy-tale, a sandbox of family fun and adventure. Grab your kid and dive in.

Family update and warning: now, with little sister Jackie, our family travels mean double the dribbles. While our 7-year-old is more fun and less trouble than ever, traveling with two small kids is much more complicated and limiting than with one. This chapter will grow with our family.

The Disabled Traveler

Disabled travelers have been heading off to Europe in ever-increasing numbers. If you're planning a trip, don't let your disability limit your destinations. Plan to go to whatever countries your heart desires. Then find good information to get over any hurdles.

Write to the tourist offices of every country you'll be visiting, and request information on travel for the disabled. The Netherlands Board of Tourism, for example, offers a fine pamphlet entitled *The Handicapped in the Netherlands*, which lists handicapped-accessible hotels, hostels, camping sites, tourist attractions, museums, and restaurants.

Recently published by the Rough Guide, *Able to Travel: True Stories by and for People with Disabilities* is the most up-to-date guidebook available for disabled travelers.

Mobility International, a non-profit organization with branches around the world, publishes a quarterly newsletter (available on audio cassette), runs a travel information and referral service, and sponsors international exchange programs for the disabled. They've put together a handy book entitled *A World of Options For the 90's: A Guide to International Educational Exchange, Community Service, and Travel for Persons with Disabilities* (1994, 360 pages, $18 ppd, contact the U.S.A. branch at 503/343-1284, P.O. Box 10767, Eugene, OR 97440).

Travelin' Talk, a newsletter for disabled travelers, focuses on America, but is gradually going global (615/552-6670, P.O. Box 3534, Clarksville, TN 37043).

If you're interested in a tour, here are three reputable companies that offer international travel for the disabled: *Accessible Journeys* (800/846-4537, 35 W. Sellers Ave., Ridley Park, PA 19078), Evergreen Travel Service (206/776-1184 in the Seattle area), and Flying Wheels Travel (800/535-6790, P.O. Box 382, Owatonna, MN 55060).

Servas, an organization that enables travelers to stay with families in other countries, has recently become more accommodating to the needs of the disabled. Its listings note which homestays are handicapped-accessible and which hosts know sign language (212/267-0252, 11 John St., #407, New York, NY 10038).

Travel Laundry

I met a woman in Italy who wore her T-shirt frontward, backward, inside-out frontward, and inside-out backward to delay the laundry day. A guy in Germany showed me his take-it-into-the-tub-with-you-and-make-waves method of washing his troublesome jeans. Some travelers just ignore their laundry needs and stink.

Anybody traveling anywhere has to wash clothes. My washer and dryer won't fit under the airplane seat, so I've learned to do without. Here are some tips.

Choose a quick-dry and no-wrinkle travel wardrobe. Your self-service laundry kit should include a stretchable "travel clothesline." These are twisted so clothespins are unnecessary. Stretch it over your bathtub or across the back of your car, and you're on the road to dry clothes. Pack a concentrated liquid detergent in a small, sturdy, plastic squeeze bottle, wrapped in a zip-lock baggie for safety. A large plastic bag with a drawstring is handy for dirty laundry.

Every real hotel room in Europe has a sink, usually equipped with a multilingual "no washing clothes in the room" sign. This may be the most ignored rule on earth after "eat your peas." Interpret this as an "I-have-lots-of-good-furniture-and-a-fine-carpet-in-this-room-and-I-don't-want-your-drippy-laundry-ruining-things" order. In other words, you can wash clothes very carefully, wring them nearly dry, and hang them in an non-destructive way. Occasionally, a hotel will keep the stoppers in an attempt to discourage in-room washing. You can line the sink with your laundry bag and wash in it.

Your laundry should keep a low profile. Don't hang it out the window. The maid hardly notices my laundry. It's hanging quietly in the bathroom or shuffled among my dry clothes in the closet.

Whistler's laundry

Some hotels will let your laundry join theirs on the lines out back or on the rooftop. Many youth hostels have coin-op washers and dryers or heated drying rooms to ease your laundry hassles.

Wring your wet laundry as dry as possible. Rolling it in a towel (putting it on the floor and stomping on it) can be helpful, but most places don't provide new towels everyday. Always separate the back and front of hanging clothes to speed drying. Some travelers pack an inflatable hanger. Smooth out your wet clothes, button shirts, set collars, and "hand iron" to encourage wrinkle-free drying. If your shirt or dress dries wrinkled, hang it in a steamy bathroom. (I test-hand-wash and wring dry my shirts at home before I let them come to Europe with me.) A piece of tape is a good ad-lib lint brush. In very hot climates, I wash my shirt several times a day, wring it, and put it on wet. It's clean and refreshing, and in 15 minutes it's dry.

For a thorough washing, ask your hotel to direct you to the nearest laundromat. Nearly every neighborhood has one. It takes about $6 and an hour if there's no line. Better laundromats have coin-op soap dispensers, change machines, and helpful attendants. Others can be very frustrating. Use the time to catch up on postcards and your journal or chat with the local crowd. Laundromats throughout the world seem to give people the gift of gab. Full-service places are quicker—just drop it off and come back in the afternoon—but much more expensive. Still, every time I slip into a fresh pair of jeans, I figure it was worth the hassle and expense.

Souvenir Strategy

Gift shopping is getting very expensive. I remember buying a cuckoo clock 15 years ago for $5. Now a "Happy Meal" at the Munich McDonald's will cost that much.

I try to do my souvenir and gift shopping in countries where my dollar stretches farthest, like Turkey, Morocco, Portugal, Spain, and Greece. Prices vary tremendously. For the price of a four-inch pewter Viking ship in Norway, you can buy a real boat in Turkey.

In the interest of packing light, try to put off shopping until the end of the trip. Ideally, you should end your trip in a cheap country, do all of your shopping, then fly home. One summer, I had a 16-pound rucksack and nothing more until the last week of my trip when, in Spain and Morocco, I managed to accumulate two medieval chairs, two sets of bongos, a camel-hair coat, swords, a mace, and a lace tablecloth.

Large department stores often have a souvenir section with prices much less than those you would pay in the cute little tourist shops nearby. Shop around and remember that in the southern countries, most things sold on the streets or in markets have soft prices. When appropriate, bargain like mad. Flea markets anywhere have soft prices.

Shopping is an important part of the average person's trip, but be careful not to lose control. All too often, slick marketing and cutesy, romantic window displays can succeed in shifting the entire focus of your trip toward things in the tourist shops. (It's a lucrative business. Many souvenir merchants in Italy work through the tourist season, then retire for the rest of the year.) This sort of tourist brainwashing can turn you into one of the many people who set out to see and experience Europe but find themselves wandering in a trancelike search for signs announcing Duty-Free Shopping. I've seen half the members of a British-Halls-of-Parliament guided tour skip out to survey an enticing display of plastic "bobby" hats and Union Jack panties. Even if the sign says, "Keep Italy green, spend dollars," don't let your trip degenerate into a glorified shopping spree.

I think it's wise to restrict your shopping to a stipulated time during the trip. Most people have an idea of what they want to buy in each country. Set aside one day to shop in each country, and stick to it. This way you avoid drifting through your trip thinking only of souvenirs.

Boxloads of Davids *await busloads of tourists*

Some of the most colorful shopping in Europe is at its flea markets. Among the best are Amsterdam (Waterlooplein, Saturdays), London (Bermondsey early Fridays, bus #1 from Trafalgar and Portobello Market on Saturdays, and many others), Madrid (El Rastro, Sundays), and Paris (Porte de Clignancourt, best on Sundays, also on Saturdays and Mondays, go by taxi).

When you are shopping, ask yourself if your enthusiasm is merited. More often than not, you can pick up a very similar item of better quality and for a cheaper price at home. Unless you're a real romantic, the thrill of where you bought something fades long before the item's usefulness. My life has more room for a functional souvenir than for a useless symbol of a place I visited. Even thoughtful shoppers go over-board. I have several large boxes in my attic labeled "great souvenirs."

My favorite souvenirs are books (a great value all over Europe, and many impossible-to-find-in-the-U.S. editions), local crafts (well explained in guidebooks, such as hand-knit sweaters in Portugal or Ireland, glass in Sweden, lace in Belgium), strange stuffed animals (at flea markets), cassettes of music I experienced live, posters (one sturdy tube stores eight or ten posters safely), clothing, photographs I've taken, and memories whittled carefully into my journal.

VALUE ADDED TAX (VAT) REFUNDS

Local European sales taxes vary from 15 to 25 percent. Tourists who buy something new and don't use it until it's out of the country can often get this tax refunded. And each year over half a billion dollars of refundable taxes are left unclaimed. Yes, that is exciting. But value added tax (VAT) refunds are generally not worth the trouble.

If you're buying something worth over $100 in a country with high taxes (Britain and most of northern Europe), ask about the possibility of a refund. Normally, you buy the item, collect and save the receipt, process this at the border as you leave the country, go home, and wait for your refund check, which usually comes in the foreign currency. Considering all the hoops you went through to get it, and the bank charges to change the foreign check into dollars, your final refund is often a joke. Ideally, you'll talk your merchants into deducting the VAT from your purchase price and let them process the refund. In Scandinavia, you normally get a cash refund at the border. When VAT refunds are worthwhile, merchants use them in their sales pitch. Local merchants know the VAT ropes and are the best VAT information source for their country.

CUSTOMS AND POSTAGE FOR AMERICAN SHOPPERS

You are allowed to take $400 of souvenirs home duty-free. The next $1,000 is dutied at a flat 10 percent. After that, you pay the individual-items duty rate. You can also bring in a liter of alcohol and more cigarettes than you'd ever want to bring home duty-free.

You can mail one package per person per day worth up to $50 duty-free from Europe to the U.S.A. Mark it "Unsolicited Gift." You can mail home all the "American Goods Returned" you like with no customs concerns.

If you do some shopping, it's easy to lighten your load by sending packages home by surface mail. Postage is getting expensive. A box the size of a fruit crate costs about $40 by slow boat, a small price to pay to substantially lighten your load. Books are much cheaper if they are sent separately. Customs regulations amount to 10 or 15 frustrating minutes filling out forms with the normally unhelpful postal clerk's semi-assistance. Remember, the postal clerks you'll deal with in Europe are every bit as friendly, speedy, and multilingual as those back home.

I've never shopped enough to owe any duty. Keep it simple (contents: clothing, carving, gifts, a poster, value $50). Post offices usually provide boxes and string or tape for about $2. Service is best from the Alps north and in France. Small-town post offices can be less crowded and more user-friendly. Every box I've ever mailed has arrived—bruised and battered, but all there—within six weeks.

Keys to Successful Bargaining

In much of the world, the price tag is only an excuse to argue. Bargaining is the accepted and expected method of finding a compromise between the wishful thinking of the merchant and the tourist.

Prices are "soft" in much of the Mediterranean world. In Europe, bargaining is common only in the south. But you can fight the price in flea markets and with people selling handicrafts and tourist items on the streets anywhere.

While bargaining is important from a budgetary standpoint (if you're traveling beyond Europe), it can also become an enjoyable game. Many travelers are addicted hagglers who would gladly skip a tour of a Portuguese palace to get the price down on the black-clad lady's handmade sweater.

Here are the Ten Commandments of the successful haggler:

1. Determine whether bargaining is appropriate. It's bad shopping etiquette to "make an offer" for a tweed hat in a London department store. It's foolish not to at a Greek outdoor market. To learn if the price is fixed, fall in love with that item right in front of the merchant. Look longingly into the eyes of that porcelain Buddha, then decide that "it's just too much money." You've put him in a position to make the first offer. If he comes down even 2 percent, there's nothing sacred about the price tag. Haggle away.

2. Determine the merchant's cost. Many merchants will settle for a nickel profit rather than lose the sale entirely. Promise yourself that no matter how exciting the price becomes, you won't buy. Then work the cost down to rock bottom. When it seems to have fallen to a record low, walk away. That last price he hollers out as you turn the corner is often the best price you'll get. Armed with this knowledge, you can confidently demand a fair price for the same item at the next souvenir stand—and probably get it. (Bid carefully, though. If a merchant accepts your price, the rules say you must buy it.)

3. Find out what the locals pay. If the price is not posted, assume there's a double price-standard—one for locals and one for you. If only tourists buy the item you're pricing, see what an Arab, Spanish, or Italian tourist would be charged. I remember thinking I did well in Istanbul's Grand Bazaar until I learned my Spanish friend bought the same shirt for 30 percent less. Merchants assume American tourists are rich. And they know what we pay for things at home.

4. Preprice each item. What's it really worth to you? Remember that price tags are meaningless and serve to distort your idea of an item's true worth. The merchant is playing a psychological game. Many tourists think that if they can cut the price by 50 percent, they are doing great. So the merchant quadruples his prices and the tourist happily pays double the fair value. The best way to deal with crazy price tags is to ignore them. Before you even see the price tag, determine what it's worth to you, considering the hassles involved in packing it or shipping it home.

5. Don't hurry. Get to know the shopkeeper. Accept his offer for tea, talk with him. Leave him to shop around and get a feel for the market. Then return. He'll know you are serious. Dealing with the owner (no salesman's commission) lowers your best possible price.

6. Be indifferent; never look impressed. As soon as the merchant perceives the "I gotta have that!" in you, you'll never get the best price. He knows you have the money to buy what you really want. He knows about U.S. prices. (Sorry, commandments 1 and 6 are contradictory.)

7. Impress him with your knowledge—real or otherwise. This way he respects you, and you are more likely to get good quality. Istanbul has very good leather coats for a fraction of the U.S. cost. I wanted one. Before my trip, I talked to some leather-coat sellers and was much better prepared to confidently pick out a good coat in Istanbul for $100.

8. Employ a third person. Use your friend who is worried about the ever-dwindling budget or who doesn't like the price or who is bored and wants to return to the hotel. This trick may work to bring the price down faster.

9. Show the merchant your money. Physically hold out your money and offer him "all you have" to pay for whatever you are bickering over. He'll be tempted to just to grab your money and say, "Oh, all right."

10. If the price is too much, leave. Never worry about having taken too much of the merchant's time and tea. They are experts at making the tourist feel guilty for not buying. It's all part of the game. Most merchants, by local standards, are financially well off.

A final point for the no-nonsense budget shopper: you can generally find the same souvenirs in large department stores at fair and firm, often government-regulated prices. Department store shopping is quicker, easier, often cheaper—but not nearly as much fun.

12

Attitude Adjustment for a Better Trip

The Ugly American

Europe sees two kinds of travelers: those who view Europe through air-conditioned bus windows, socializing with their noisy American friends, and those who are taking a vacation from America, immersing themselves in different cultures, experiencing different people and life-styles, broadening their perspective.

Europeans judge you as an individual, not by your government. A Greek fisherman once told me, "For me, Reagan is big problem—but I like you." I have never been treated like the Ugly American. I've been proud to wear our flag on my lapel. My Americanness in Europe, if anything, has been an asset. (In the wake of the Gulf War, however, many Americans can relate to Germans who, because of their recent past, have been reluctant to wave flags as vigorously as their Belgian and Danish neighbors.)

You'll see plenty of Ugly Americans. Europeans recognize them and treat them accordingly, often souring their vacation. Ugly Americanism is a disease cured by a change in attitude. The best over-the-counter medicine is a mirror.

Here are the symptoms and the cure. The Ugly American:
• does not try to understand or respect strange customs and cultural differences. Only a Hindu can understand the value of India's sacred cows. Only a devout Spanish Catholic can appreciate the true worth of his town's patron saint. No American has the right, as a visitor, to show disrespect for these customs.
• demands the niceties of American life in Europe—orange juice and eggs (sunny-side up) for breakfast, long beds, English menus, punctu-

ality in Italy, or cold beer in England. He should remember that he invited himself to a land that enjoys its continental breakfasts, that doesn't grow six-foot four-inch men, that speaks its own language, that lacks the "fast-food efficiency" of the United States, and that drinks beer at room temperature. Live as a European for a few weeks; it's cheaper, you'll make more friends, you'll have a better trip, and you'll enjoy a great chance to learn something about good living.

• is ethnocentric, traveling in packs, more or less invading each country while making no effort to communicate with "the natives." He talks at Europeans and about them in a condescending manner. He finds satisfaction in flaunting his relative affluence and measures well-being by material consumption. He sees the world as a pyramid with the United States on top and the "less developed" world trying to get there. It's important to remember that the average European likes but does not envy and is not impressed by the average American.

You can be a "Beautiful American." Your fate as a tourist lies in your own hands. A graduate of the Back Door School of Touristic Beauty:

• maintains a moderate sense of humility, not flashing signs of affluence, such as over-tipping or joking about the local money. Her money does not talk.

• not only accepts but also seeks out European styles of living. She forgets her discomfort if she's the only one in a group who feels it. The customer is not "always right" in Europe.

• is genuinely interested in the people and cultures she visits. She wants to learn by trying things.

• accepts that there's more than one way to skin cats. Paying for your Italian coffee at one counter, then picking it up at another may seem inefficient, until you realize it's more sanitary: the person handling the food handles no money.

• is observant and sensitive. If sixty people are eating quietly with hushed personal conversation in a candle-lit Belgian restaurant and all can hear a table of Americans yukking it up, something is wrong.

• makes an effort to bridge that flimsy language barrier. Rudimentary communication in any language is fun and simple with a few basic words. While a debate over the merits of *Perestroika* on the train to Budapest (with a common vocabulary of 20 words) is frustrating, she surprises herself at how well she communicates—by just breaking the ice and trying. Don't worry about making mistakes—communicate! (See Chapter 6, Hurdling the Language Barrier.)

• is positive and optimistic in the extreme. Discipline yourself to focus on the good points of each country. Don't dwell on problems or compare things to "back home." With a positive attitude, things go great.

Thank You

Arabic	*shukran*	French	*merci*
Bulgarian	*blagodarya*	German	*danke*
Danish	*tak*	Greek	*efharisto*
Dutch	*dank u wel*	Russian	*spasibo*
English	*thank you*	Serbo-Croatian	*hvala*
Italian	*grazie*	Spanish	*gracias*
Portuguese	*obrigado*	Turkish	*tesekkur*
Finnish	*kiitos*	Iraqi	*shukran*

I've been accepted as an American friend throughout Europe, Russia, the Middle East, and North Africa. I've been hugged by Bulgarian workers on a Balkan mountaintop; discussed Contra-gate and the Olympics over dinner in the home of a Greek family; explained to a young, frustrated Irishman that California girls take their pants off one leg at a time, just like the rest of us; and hiked through the Alps with a Swiss schoolteacher, learning German and teaching English.

There is no excuse for being an Ugly American. Go as a guest; act like one, and you'll be treated like one. In travel, too, you reap what you sow.

Responsible Tourism

As we learn more about the problems that confront the earth and humankind, more and more people are recognizing the need for the world's industries, such as tourism, to function as tools for peace. Tourism is a $2 trillion industry that employs more than 60 million people. As travelers become more sophisticated and gain a global perspective, the demand for socially, environmentally, and economically responsible means of traveling will grow. Peace is more than the absence of war, and if we are to enjoy the good things of life—such as travel—into the next century, the serious issues that confront humankind must be addressed now.

A couple of years ago, more than 500 leaders from the tourist industry and academia (including executives from airlines and hotel chains, tour organizers, professors, futurists, and scholars), travel writers, journalists, environmental leaders, and politicians representing 65 countries met in Vancouver, Canada, at a conference called "Tourism—A Vital Force for Peace." At the end of the conference, they concluded that a healthy tourist industry requires peace.

The delegates drafted the Columbia Charter, which, among other things, calls for the tourist industry to help "build a world in which tourism promotes mutual understanding, trust, and goodwill; reduces economic inequities; develops in an integrated manner with the full participation of local host communities; improves the quality of life; protects and preserves the environment; and contributes to the world conservation strategy of sustainable development."

Well, these are high-and-mighty-sounding ideals. But the concrete news is: (1) that mainstream super-corporate industry big-shots said these things and acknowledged the need for change, and (2) that there are now more and more ways for travelers to make travel a constructive rather than a destructive activity in a cultural, environmental, and economic sense.

Although the most obvious problems relate specifically to travel in the Third World, European travel also offers some exciting socially responsible opportunities. Below are a few sources of information for the budding "green" traveler.

Co-op America is a great source of general information on responsible tourism, and its Travel-Links service can book you into the best-value socially responsible travel options (14 Arrow St., Harvard Sq., Cambridge, MA 02138, tel. 800/648-2667). The Lost Valley Educational Center (81868 Lost Valley Lane, Dexter, OR 97431, tel. 503/937-3351) is creative at connecting concerned travelers with good information and resource people. Travelers' Earth Repair Network (by the Friends of the Trees Society, tel. 509/485-2705) is a handy publication for travelers interested in restoration ecology. They have contacts throughout Europe and the world.

If you'd like to help the homeless, watch whales, or dig up old bones, send $15 (ppd) to *Chicago Review* (814 N. Franklin, Chicago, IL 60610, 312/337-0747) for "Volunteer Vacations," which lists 500 options for one- to six-week domestic and foreign volunteer programs. *Environmental Vacations: Volunteer Projects to Save the Planet*, by Stephanie Ocko, is another great source of information (John Muir Publications; see back of this book). Or get in touch with Servas (see Chapter 4, The Budget), which puts travelers in touch with host families.

The Green Travel Source Book (John Wiley Publications, ISBN-0471539112) is a good resource, as is Diane Merlino's *Going Green, An Eco-Tourism Resource for Travel Agents* (tel. 415-905-4923). For all the latest green travel guidebooks get the free catalog from Book Passage (a fine San Francisco Bay Area travel bookstore, 800/321-9785).

Understanding my power to shape the marketplace by what I decide to buy (whether in the grocery store, in the movie theater, or in my choice of hotels), I like to consume responsibly in my travels. Consuming responsibly means buying as if my choice is a vote for the kind of world we could have. In my travels (and in my writing), whenever possible, I patronize and support small, family-run, locally owned businesses (hotels, restaurants, tour guides, shops). I choose people who invest their creativity and resources in giving me simple, friendly, sustainable, and honest travel experiences—people with ideals. Back Door places don't rely on slick advertising and marketing gimmicks, and they don't target the created needs of people whose values are shaped by capitalism gone wild.

Making the Most of Your Trip

BE OPEN-MINDED

Among the palaces, quaint folk dancers, and museums, you'll find a living civilization—grasping for the future while we romantic tourists grope for its past. This presents us with a sometimes painful dose of truth.

Today's Europe is a complex, mixed bag of tricks. It can rudely slap you in the face if you aren't prepared to accept it with open eyes and an open mind. Europe is getting crowded, tense, seedy, polluted, industrialized, hamburgerized, and far from the everything-in-its-place fairy-tale land I'm sure it used to be.

If you're not mentally braced for some shocks, local trends can tinge your travels. Hans Christian Andersen's statue has four-letter words scrawled across its base. Whites are now the minority in major parts of London. Amsterdam's sex shops and McDonald's share the same street-lamp. In Paris, a Sudanese salesman accosts tourists at Notre-Dame with ivory bracelets and crocodile purses. Many a Mediterranean hotel-keeper would consider himself a disgrace to his sex if he didn't follow a single woman to her room. Drunk punks do their best to repulse you as you climb to St. Patrick's grave in Ireland, and Greek ferryboats dump mountains of trash into their dying Aegean Sea. An 8-year-old boy in Denmark smokes a cigarette like he was born with it in his mouth, and in a Munich beer hall, an old drunk spits "*Sieg heils*" all over you. The Barcelona shoeshine man will triple-charge you, and people everywhere eat strange and wondrous things.

They eat next to nothing for breakfast, mud for coffee, mussels in Brussels, and snails in Paris, and dinner's at 10:00 p.m. in Spain. Beer is warm here, flat there, coffee isn't served with dinner, and ice cubes can only be dreamed of. Roman cars stay in their lanes like rocks in an avalanche, and beermaids with huge pretzels pull mustard packets from their cleavage.

Contemporary Europe is alive and groping. Today's problems will fill tomorrow's museums. Feel privileged to walk the vibrant streets of Europe as a sponge—not a judge. Be open-minded. Absorb, accept, and learn.

DON'T BE A CREATIVE WORRIER

Travelers tend to be creative worriers. Many sit at home before their trip, all alone, just thinking of things to be stressed by. Travel problems are always there; you just notice them when they're yours. (Like people only notice the continual newspaper ads for tire sales when they're shopping for tires.) Every year, there are air controller strikes, train wrecks, terrorist attacks, new problems, and deciduous problems sprouting new leaves.

Travel is ad-libbing, incurring and conquering surprise problems. Make an art out of taking the unexpected in stride. Relax; you're on the other side of the world, playing games in a continental backyard. Be a good sport, enjoy the uncertainty, frolic in the pits.

Many of my readers' richest travel experiences were the result of seemingly terrible mishaps: the lost passport in Slovenia, having to find a doctor in Ireland, the blowout in Portugal, and the moped accident on Corfu.

Expect problems, tackle them creatively. You'll miss a museum or two and maybe blow your budget for the week. But you'll make some local friends and stack up some memories. And this is the essence of travel that you'll enjoy long after the journal is shelved and your trip is stored neatly in the slide carousel of your mind.

THE KISS RULE—"KEEP IT SIMPLE, STUPID!"

Don't complicate your trip. Simplify! Travelers get stressed and cluttered over the silliest things. Here are some common complexities that in their nibbly way can suffocate a happy holiday: Registering your camera with customs before leaving home, spending too much time trying to phone home on a sunny day in the Alps, worrying about the correct answers to meaningless bureaucratic forms, making a long-distance hotel reservation in a strange language and then trying to settle on what's served for breakfast, having a picnic in pants that worry about grass stains, sending away for Swedish hotel vouchers.

People can complicate their trips with video cameras, lead-lined film bags, special tickets for free entry to all the sights they won't see in England, inflatable hangers, immersion heaters, instant coffee, 65 Handi-wipes, and a special calculator that figures the value of the franc out to the third decimal. They ask for a toilet in 17 words or more, steal Sweet 'n' Low and plastic silverware off the plane, and take notes on facts that don't matter.

Travel more like Gandhi—with simple clothes, open eyes, and an uncluttered mind.

BE MILITANTLY HUMBLE—ATTILA HAD A LOUSY TRIP

As one of the world's elite who are rich and free enough to travel, you are leaving home to experience a different culture. If things aren't to your liking, don't change the things, change your liking.

Legions of tourists tramp through Europe like they're at the zoo—throwing a crust to the monkey, asking the guy in lederhosen to yodel, begging the peacock to spread his tail again, and bellowing Italian arias out Florentine hotel windows. If a culture misperforms or doesn't perform, they feel gypped. Easygoing travelers leave the Attila-type tourists mired in a swamp of complaints.

All summer long I'm pushing a bargain, often for groups. It's the hottest, toughest time of year. Tourists and locals clash. Many tourists leave soured.

When I catch a Spanish merchant shortchanging me, I correct the bill and smile, "*Adios.*" A French hotel owner can blow up at me for no legitimate reason. Rather than return the fire, I wait, smile, and sheepishly ask again–asking for action, innocently assertive, but never demanding "justice," I usually see the irate ranter come to his senses, forget the problem, and work things out.

"Turn the other cheek" applies perfectly to those riding Europe's magic carousel. If you fight the slaps, the ride is over. The militantly humble can spin forever.

SWALLOW PRIDE, ASK QUESTIONS, BE CRAZY

If you're too proud to ask questions and be crazy, your trip will certainly be dignified—but dull. Make yourself an extrovert, even if you aren't one. Be a catalyst for adventure and excitement. Make things happen, or often they won't.

I'm not naturally a wild-and-crazy kind of guy. But when I'm shy and quiet, things don't happen, and that's a bad rut to travel in. It's not easy, but this special awareness can really pay off. Let me describe the same

Put yourself where you become the oddity. If people stare, sing to them.

evening twice—first, with the mild and lazy me, and then, with the wild and crazy me.

The traffic held me up, so by the time I got to that great historical building I've always wanted to see, it was six minutes before closing. No one was allowed to enter. Disappointed, I walked over to a restaurant and couldn't make heads or tails out of the menu. I recognized "steak-frites" and settled for the typical meat patty and french fries. On the way home, I looked into a very colorful local tavern, but tourists didn't seem welcome, so I walked on. A couple waved at me from their balcony, but I didn't know what to say, so I ignored them. I returned to my room and did some laundry.

That's not a night to be proud of. A better traveler's journal entry would read like this:

I was late and got to the museum only six minutes before closing. The guard said no one could go in now, but I begged, joked, and pleaded with him. I had traveled all the way to see this place and I would be leaving early in the morning. I assured him that I'd be out by six o'clock, and he gave me a glorious six minutes in that building. You can do a lot in six minutes when that's all you've got. Across the street at a restaurant that the same guard recommended, I couldn't make heads or tails out of the menu. Inviting myself into the kitchen, I met the cooks and got a firsthand look at "what's cookin'." Now I could order an exciting local dish and know just what I was getting. It was delicious! On the way home, I passed a classic local bar, and while it was dark and sort of uninviting to a foreigner, I stepped in and was met by the only guy in the place who spoke any English. He proudly befriended me and told me, in very broken English, of his salty past and his six kids, while treating me to his favorite local drink. As I headed home, a couple waved at me from their balcony and I waved back, saying "Buon giorno!" I knew it didn't mean "Good evening" but they understood. They invited me up to their apartment. We joked around—not understanding a lot of what we were saying to each other—and they invited me to their summer cottage tomorrow. What a lucky break! There's no better way to learn about this country than to spend an afternoon with a local family. And to think that I could be back in my room doing the laundry.

Many tourists are actually afraid or too timid to ask a local person a question. The meek may inherit the earth, but they make lousy travelers. Local sources are a wealth of information. People are happy to help a traveler. Hurdle the language barrier. Use a paper and pencil, charades, or whatever it takes to be understood. Don't be afraid to butcher the language.

Ask questions—or be lost. If you're lost, get out a map and look lost. You'll get help. If lonely or in need of contact with a local person, get out a map and look lost again. Pledge every morning to do something entirely different today. Perceive friendliness, and you'll find it. Create adventure—or bring home a boring journal.

Becoming a Temporary European

Most travelers see Europe as if they're visiting the cultural zoo. "Ooo, that guy in lederhosen yodeled!" "Excuse me, could you do that again in the sunshine with my wife next to you so I can take a snapshot?" This is fun. It's a part of travel. But a camera bouncing on your belly tells locals you're hunting cultural peacocks.

I'm on the road for a hundred days a year. I don't get homesick. Don't get me wrong—I have plenty to get homesick for, and the happiest day of the year is the day I fly home. But when I'm there, I make Europe my home. I'm a temporary European. Here are a few ideas about how you can take Europe out of your viewfinder and put it into your lap.

Psychologically, many people shut themselves off from Europe. For instance, many regular churchgoers never even consider a European worship service. Any church would welcome a traveling American. And an hour in a small-town church provides an unbeatable peek into the local community, especially if you join them for coffee and cookies afterwards. I'll never forget going to a small church on the south coast of Portugal one Easter. A tourist stood at the door videoing the "colorful natives" (including me) shaking hands with the priest after the service. You can experience St. Peter's by taking photographs . . . or taking communion (daily 5:00 p.m. Mass).

For many Europeans, the top religion is soccer. Getting caught up in a sporting event is going local. Whether enjoying soccer in small-town Italy, greyhound racing in Scotland, or hurling in Ireland, you'll be surrounded by a stadium crammed with devout locals and be without a hint of tourism.

Extroverts have more fun. If you see four cute men on a bench, ask them to scoot over.

Play where the locals play. A city's popular fairgrounds and parks are filled with local families, lovers, and old-timers enjoying a cheap afternoon or evening out. European communities provide their heavily taxed citizens with wonderful athletic facilities. Check out a swimming center, called a "leisure center" in Britain. While tourists outnumber locals five to one at the world-famous Tivoli Gardens, Copenhagen's other amusement park, Bakken, is enjoyed purely by Danes. EuroDisney is great. But Paris' Asterix Park is much more French.

Some cafés in the Netherlands (those with plants in the windows or Rastafarian colors on the wall) have menus that look like a drug bust. Marijuana is less controversial in Holland than tobacco is these days in the U.S.A. For a casual toke of local life without the risk that comes with smoking in the U.S.A., drop into one of these cafes and roll a joint. If you have no political aspirations, inhale.

Across southern Europe, communities paseo or stroll in the early evening. Stroll along. Join a Volksmarch in Bavaria to spend a day on the trails with people singing "I love to go a-wandering" in its original language. Choose destinations busy with local holiday-goers but not on the international tourist map. Remember, youth hostels are the American target, while mountain huts and "nature's friends huts" across Europe are filled mostly with local hikers. Most hiking centers have Alpine clubs which welcome foreigners and offer organized hikes.

A caress or a stranglehold? Europe can puzzle even itself.

Campgrounds are filled with Europeans in the mood for a frisbee to toss with a new American friend. Be accessible. Accept invitations.

In Greece or Turkey, drop into a local teahouse or taverna and challenge a local to a game of backgammon. You're instantly a part (even a star) of the local cafe or bar scene. Normally, the gang will gather around and what starts out as a simple game becomes a fun duel of international significance.

Pick up a copy of the local *Better Homes and Gardens*-type magazine. Wander through a residential neighborhood to see how the locals live when they're not wearing lederhosen and yodeling. Ride a city bus or subway into the suburbs. Visit a supermarket. Make friends at the laundromat. Mill around a university and check out the announcement boards. Eat at the school cafeteria. Ask at the English language department if there's a student learning English whom you could hire to be your private guide. Be alert and even a little bit snoopy. You may stumble onto a grade-school talent show.

When you visit the town market in the morning you're just another local, picking up your daily produce. Traveling through the wine country of France during harvest time, you can be a tourist taking photos— or a you can pitch in and become a local grape-picker. Get more than a photo op. Get dirty. That night at the festival it's just grape-pickers dancing (and some of them are tourists too). You can take photos of the pilgrims at Lourdes—or volunteer to help wheel the chairs of those who've come in hope of a cure.

If you're a member of a service club, bridge club, professional association, or international organization, make a point to connect with your foreign mates.

Unless you're using it, stow your camera. If you're hunting cultural peacocks, remember they spread their tails best for people . . . not for little black boxes.

POLITE PARIS

The "mean Parisian" problem is a holdover from DeGaulle days. It's definitely fading, but France's lingering reputation of rudeness creates a self-fullfilling expectation. You can enjoy the French and that should be your goal. Here are some ideas to help. The French, as a culture, are pouting. They used to be the "crème de la crème," the definition of high class. Their language was the *lingua franca*—everyone wanted to speak French. There was a time when the czar of Russia and his family actually spoke better French than Russian. Your passport even has French on it—leftovers from those French glory days.

Modern French culture is reeling—humiliated by two world wars, lashed by Levi's, and crushed by the Big Mac of American culture. And our two cultures aren't natural buddies. The French enjoy subtleties and sophistication. American culture sneers at these fine points. We're proud, brash, and like to think we're rugged individualists. We are a smiley-face culture whose bank tellers are fined if they forget to say, "Have a nice day." The French don't find slap-on-the-back niceness terribly sincere. And too often, we judge a people on their "niceness."

Typically, Americans judge the French by the Parisians they meet. That's as fair as judging American friendliness by New Yorkers. And remember, most of us see Paris at the height of hot, busy summer when those Parisians who can't escape for the summer see their hometown flooded with insensitive foreigners who butcher their language and put ketchup on their meat. That's tough to take smiling, and, if you're looking for coldness, this is a good place to start.

To make the Parisians suddenly 40 percent friendlier, learn and liberally use these four phrases: *bonjour, s'il vous plaît, merçi,* and *pardon.* And to really revel in French friendliness, visit an untouristy part of the countryside and use those four phrases. Oh, and *vive la différence.*

Political Unrest and Tourism

An awareness of current social and political problems is as vital to smart travel as a listing of top sights. While some popular tourist destinations are entertaining tourists with "sound and light" shows in the old town, they're quelling terrorist and separatist movements in the new. Countries from England to Italy are dealing with serious or potentially serious internal threats.

Newspaper headlines shape many trips. Many people skip Northern Ireland because of "the troubles," avoid Spain in fear of the militant Basques, and refuse to fly out of Athens or Frankfurt because of a bomb attack years ago. This is like avoiding a particular stretch of highway at home because there was an accident there. Don't let these problems dictate your itinerary. I stay up on the news and exercise good common sense (don't sing Catholic songs in Ulster pubs) and travel safely, enjoying a firsthand look at the demographic chaos that explains much of what fills the front pages of our newspapers.

Travel broadens your perspective, enabling you to rise above the six o'clock entertainment we call news and see things as a citizen of our world. While monuments from the past are worthy of your sightseeing energy, travel can also plug you directly into the present.

There are many peoples fighting the same thrilling battles we Americans won 200 years ago, and while your globe may paint Turkey orange and Iran green, no political boundaries can divide racial, linguistic, or religious groups that simply.

Look beyond the beaches and hotels in your tourist brochures for background on how your vacation target's cultural, racial, and religious makeup is causing problems today or may bring grief tomorrow. With this foundation and awareness you can enjoy the nearly unavoidable opportunities to talk with involved locals about complex current situations. If you're looking to talk politics you must be approachable—on your own, or away from your tour.

Like it or not, people around the world look at "capitalist Americans" as the kingpins of a global game of Monopoly. Young, well-dressed people are most likely to speak (and want to speak) English. Universities are the perfect place to solve the world's problems in English with a liberal, open-minded foreigner over a government-subsidized budget cafeteria lunch.

Understand a country's linguistic divisions. It's next to impossible to keep everyone in a multilingual country happy. Switzerland has four languages, but *Deutsche ist über alles.* In Belgium, there's tension between the Dutch- and French-speaking halves. Like many French-Canadians, Europe's linguistic underdogs will tell you their language receives equal treatment only on Corn Flakes boxes, and many are scheming up ways to correct the situation.

In Ireland, "the troubles" are kept at least simmering. Hitchhiking through the Emerald Isle, I always get an earful of someone's passionate feelings. In "post-Cold War" Russia and Eastern Europe, whenever I want some political or economic gossip, I sit alone in a café. After a few minutes and some eye contact, I have company and a thrilling chat with a resident malcontent.

After your smashingly successful European adventure, you'll graduate to more distant cultural nooks and geographic crannies. If you mistakenly refer to a Persian or Iranian as Arabic, you'll get a stern education on the distinction, and in eastern Turkey, you'll learn more about that fiercely nationalistic group of people called Kurds who won't rest until that orange and green on the globe is divided by a hunk of land called Kurdistan.

Terrorism and Tourism

It's refreshing to be so out-of-touch while traveling that you forget what day it is. But even in areas that aren't "hot spots," it's wise to be up on the news. American and English newspapers are available in most of the world, as are English radio broadcasts. Other tourists can be valuable links with the outside world as well. Most important, the

nearest American or British consulate can advise you on problems that merit concern.

Take your government's travel advice seriously but not blindly. I try to weed through State Department travel advisories. While I travel right through advisories designed to stoke domestic hysteria to build support for a presidential adventure (generally terrorist-related), others (such as warnings about civil unrest in a country that's falling apart) are grounds to scrub my mission. Compuserve has all the latest U.S. Department of State travel advisories on-line and available free for subscribers.

Talking to people about local problems is fine. Dodging bullets isn't. I can't remember ever hearing a gun or a bomb in my Mediterranean travels. Many times, however, I've had the thrill of a firsthand experience merely by talking with people who were personally involved.

Your tour memories can include lunch with a group of Palestinian college students, an evening walk through Moscow with a Russian dissident, listening to the Voice of America with curious Bulgarians in a Black Sea coast campground, and learning why the French are worried about the reunification of Germany. Or your travel memories can be built on the blare of your tour guide's bullhorn in empty Gothic cathedrals and polished palaces learning who did the stucco.

Terrorism in Europe has been a hot topic in recent years. Since things are relatively quiet now, I hesitate to even bring up the subject.

Calming Loved Ones with Statistics as You Travel in an Age of Terror

From 1980 to 1990, Americans made about 130 million trips overseas. During that time (according to Bruce Hoffman, a specialist in international security at the Rand Corporation), less than 300 Americans were killed by terrorists. Most of those were victims of the Lockerbie crash in 1988.

Chance of an American overseas or in the air being killed by a terrorist: 1 in 650,000.

Chance of being hit by lightning this year in the U.S.A.: 1 in 600,000.

Chance you'll be killed by a fire in your home this year: 1 in 50,000.

Chance you'll be murdered this year if you live in a small American town: 1 in 12,000; in a city of over 250,000 people: 1 in 2,000.

Deaths per year in the U.S.A.:
50,000 in car accidents

8,000 by handguns (vs. less than 100 a year in Britain, France, or Germany)

2,500 choking on food

28 Americans killed by terrorists in 1985 (the scariest year yet).

300 pedestrians a year killed by drivers on the streets of Paris.

(Most of these statistics are from *What Are the Chances: Risks and Odds in Everyday Life* by Bernard Siskin, 1989.)

But there's always been terrorism, and I'm afraid there always will be terrorism. I'm concerned that people are planning their trips thinking they can slip over there and back while there's a lull in the action. It's in your best interest, psychologically, to plan your trip assuming there will be a terrorist event sometime between now and your departure date—most likely in the city you're flying into. Understand the risk of terrorism. And travel in a way that minimizes that tiny threat. Let me explain.

First of all, terrorism is nothing new. There have always been terrorists—Basque separatists, the Red Brigade in Italy, and so on. What's new is that Americans are being targeted, and our media and government reward the terrorists royally by bringing its horrors into our homes in living color and by treating it as a matter of foreign policy rather than as a common crime.

The news media profit from terrorism. Terror sells ads. TV has a sliding pay-scale for its advertising time, determined by how many of us tune in. There's a terrible temptation for the media to sensationalize terrorism. It's tailor-made for TV—quick, emotional, and gruesome 90-second spots. Consider the emotional style in which terrorism is covered and how expertly terrorists are milking that, even providing TV news broadcasts with video footage.

Understand that loved ones often take TV news to heart, lack a broad understanding of the world, and may stand between us and our travel dreams—begging and even bribing us not to go. If I'm in Europe and there's a boat hijacked or a train wreck in Italy, I always call to let my mother know I survived. Assure those who'll worry about you that you'll call home every few days. If you're a teenager with worrying parents, hit them up for a $1-per-30-second "I'm doing fine" call, and call home regularly.

Certainly we need to consider the real risk of terrorism, evaluate that risk, and if we decide to travel, travel in a way that minimizes the risk. It's either accept the risk or settle for a lifetime of *National Geographic* specials.

Travel is accelerated living. It comes with many risks—statistically, the risk of terrorism is much smaller than the ones tourists have always taken without a second thought. Let's look at it in cold unemotional statistics. 1985 was a year we let terrorism change our way of looking at the world; 28 Americans, out of 25 million who traveled, were killed by terrorists. Sure, that's a risk, but in the same year, 8,000 Americans were killed by handguns on our own streets. Europeans laugh out loud when they read of Americans choosing to stay home so they won't be murdered. Statistically, even in the worst times of terrorism, you're much safer in Europe.

Flying is also risky. I know people die in planes, but I also know that in the United States alone over 60,000 planes take off and land safely every day. There's a one-in-six-million chance that the plane I board will crash and someone will die. I take the risk, and travel. Every year, several hundred pedestrians are run down on the streets of Paris—not glamorous enough for headlines, but dead is dead. By the way, according to our State Department, more Americans were killed by terrorists in 1974 than in 1985, but the media didn't pick up on it and we tourists didn't notice.

Terrorist targets are predictable. They lash out at the high-profile symbols of our powerful and wealthy society—airplanes, luxury cruise ships, elegant high-rise hotels, posh restaurants, military and diplomatic locations. These have been the targets of nearly every terrorist incident to date. Traveling through the back door, you're melting into Europe, keeping the lowest possible profile. You're staying in simple, local-style places—like Pedro's Pension. Terrorists don't bomb Pedro's Pension. That's where they sleep. And if you just really hate terrorism, the most effective way for you to fight it is to travel a lot, learn about the world, come home, and help our country fit better into this ever-smaller planet.

13

The Whirlwind Tour: Europe's Best Two-Month Trip

Let's assume that you have two months, plenty of energy, and a desire to see as much of Europe as is reasonable. It's most economical to fly to London and travel around Europe with a two-month Eurailpass. You'll spend two months on the Continent and use any remaining time in England, before or after you start your train pass. Budgeting for a $700 round-trip ticket to London, a $1,100 two-month first-class Eurailpass, and $70 a day for room, board, and sightseeing, the entire trip will cost about $6,000. It can be done. Rookies on a budget do it all the time—often for less.

If I could relive my first two months in Europe, this is the trip I'd take. I'll have to admit, I itch just thinking about this itinerary. Fasten your seat belts, raise your travel dreams to their upright and locked position, and prepare to take off.

London is Europe's great entertainer; it's wonderfully historic. Mild compared to anything but the United States, it's the best starting point for a European adventure. The English speak English, but their accents will give you the sensation of understanding a foreign language. Every day will be busy and each night filled with a play and a pub. But the Continent beckons.

Paris is a quick overnight train ride away. Ascend the Eiffel Tower to survey a Paris studded with architectural gems and historical one-of-a-kinds. You'll recognize Notre-Dame, Sacré-Coeur, the Louvre, and much more. A busy three days await you back on the ground—especially with a visit to Europe's greatest palace, Louis XIV's Versailles.

On the way to Spain, explore the dreamy châteaus of the Loire Valley. Take the train to Madrid, where bullfights, shopping, the Prado

museum, and nearby Toledo fill your sunny days. Then sleep on the train to Lisbon, Portugal's friendly capital.

Lisbon can keep a visitor busy for days. Its highlight is the Alfama. This salty old sailors' quarter is a photographer's delight. You'll feel rich here in Europe's bargain basement, where a taxi ride is cheaper than a London bus ticket.

Circle south for a stop on Portugal's south coast, the Algarve. Cross into Andalusia for flamenco, hill towns, and a day in Sevilla.

Break the long train ride to the French Riviera with a day or two in Madrid and Barcelona. A rest on a south France beach is in order before diving into intense Italy.

Italy, steeped in history and art, is a bright spot in any itinerary. An entire trip could be spent climbing through the classical monuments of Rome, absorbing the art treasures of Florence, and cruising the canals of colorful Venice. These cities, the leaning tower of Pisa, the hill towns of Tuscany, and so much more, just might kidnap your itinerary.

Your favorite place in Italy may be the Cinque Terre. You'll find pure Italy in these five sleepy, traffic-free villages between Genoa and

Pisa. Your friends will believe it only after they see your pictures. Unknown to most tourists, it's the ultimate Italian coastal paradise.

Savor the Old World elegance of Habsburg Vienna for a few days. Side-trip east for a look at Prague. Then enjoy Salzburg's unrivaled music festival. Classical music sounds so right in its birthplace.

Tour "Mad" King Ludwig's fairy-tale castle at Neuschwanstein before visiting the Tirolean town of Reutte and its forgotten—yet unforgettable—hill-crowning, ruined castle. This is the Ehrenberg Ruins. Running along the overgrown ramparts, your imagination works itself loose and suddenly you're notching up your crossbow and ducking flaming arrows.

Europe's most scenic train ride is across southern Switzerland from Chur to Martigny. Be careful: mixing sunshine and a full dose of Alpine beauty can be intoxicating.

For the best of the Swiss Alps, establish a home base in the rugged Berner Oberland, south of Interlaken. The traffic-free village of Gimmelwald in Lauterbrunnen Valley is everything an Alp-lover could possibly want.

Munich, the capital of Bavaria, has the world's greatest street singers. But they probably won't be good enough to keep you out of the beer halls. Huge mugs of beer, bigger pretzels, and even bigger beermaids!

The Romantic Road bus tour (included on the Eurailpass) is the best way to get from Munich to Frankfurt. The bus rolls through the heart of medieval Germany, stopping at Dinkelsbühl and the always-popular queen of quaint German towns, Rothenburg.

After the bus tour, take the Rhine cruise (also covered by Eurail) from Bingen to Koblenz to enjoy a parade of old castles. Sleep in Bacharach's classic castle youth hostel with a panoramic view of the Rhine for $10.

From Köln, catch the night-train to Germany's capital, ever-vibrant Berlin. Another night train lands you in Copenhagen

Finish your Continental experience with a blitz tour of the capitals of Scandinavia: Copenhagen, Stockholm, and Oslo. Smorgasbords, Viking ships, and healthy, smiling blondes are the memories you'll pack on the train south to Amsterdam.

After a few days in crazy Amsterdam and a bike ride through the tulips, sail for England. Any remaining time is happily spent in the English countryside.

This trip is just a sampler. There's plenty more to see, but I can't imagine a better first two months in Europe. See Part Two: Back Doors and my various Country Guides for details.

The Itinerary—Some Specifics

If I were planning my first European trip and wanted to see as much as I could comfortably in two months (and I had the experience I now have to help me plan), this is the trip I'd take. (NT = overnight train, ST = side-trip from a home base)

Days/Place

3 London—Cheapest place in Europe to fly to, easiest place to adjust to. From airport (easy train or subway access from Gatwick or Heathrow), go to Victoria Station. Get ticket to Continent (Paris, overnight crossing or youth under 26 is cheapest) at Sealink Office. Great tourist information office in Victoria Station. Round London orientation bus tour from park in front of station departs every half-hour. Lay groundwork for your return to London (if ending trip there)—reserve good B&B, get tickets to a hot play. Hotel Holland Park (hotelesque, tel. 071/727-5815), Hotel Ravna Gora (funky, tel. 071/727-7725), Abbey House Bed and Breakfast (charming, tel. 071/727-2594). Night train (NT) and boat to Paris (22:00-8:45) or the day trip (9:00-17:02).

3 Paris—Arrive early—easy to find budget one- or two-star hotel room. Near Eiffel Tower on Rue Cler: Hotel Leveque (tel. 47-05-49-15), Hotel du Centre (tel. 47-05-52-33). In the Marais: Hotel Jeanne-d'Arc (elegant, tel. 48-87-62-11) or Castex Hotel (cheap, friendly, 42-72-31-52). Use Paris subway. It's fast, easy, and cheap. Walk—Latin Quarter, Notre-Dame, monument to victims of the Nazis (open 10:00), St. Chapelle, Pont-Neuf, self-serve lunch in Samaritaine department store, Louvre, Tuileries Gardens, Champs-Elysées to the Arc de Triomphe. Ask hotel to recommend small family-owned restaurant for dinner. Evening on Montmartre, soak in the spiritual waters of the Sacré-Coeur, browse among the shops and artists of the Place du Tertre. Be sure to visit Napoleon's Tomb, Les Invalides (Europe's best military museum), the Rodin Museum (*The Thinker* and *The Kiss*), the great Orsay Museum (impressionism), Pompidou Modern Art Gallery, a jazz club, and Latin Quarter nightlife. Pick up the *Pariscope* entertainment guide. Most museums are closed on Tuesdays. Side trip (ST) #1—Versailles, a must. Europe's grandest palace (take the RER train to end of line, Versailles R.G.). ST #2—Chartres, great Gothic cathedral, lectures by Malcom Miller at 12:00 and 2:45. Start your Eurailpass when you leave Paris.

2 Loire Valley—Make Amboise or Tours your headquarters. Good all-day bus tours of châteaus. If not into châteaus, skip Loire. Consider 30-minute ST from Paris to the epitome of a French château, Chantilly. NT direct Paris to Madrid, 20:00-8:32.

2   Madrid—On arrival, reserve train out. Reservations on long trains are required in Spain (and Norway) even with Eurail. Taxi to Puerto del Sol for central budget room. Try Plaza Santa Anna (#15, Hostel Fila, tel. 522-4056). On Gran Via: Hostel Miami (cheap, at #44, tel. 521-1464) or Residencia Valencia (hotelesque, #44 also, tel. 522-1115). Prado Museum (Bosch, Goya, El Greco, Velázquez), *Guernica*, and Royal Palace (Europe's most lavish interior) are musts. Bullfights on Sundays through the summer, ask at hotel, buy tickets at arena. El Rastro (flea market) for great shopping on Sundays.

1   Toledo—Perfectly preserved historic capital, best at night, El Greco's home and masterpieces. NT, Madrid-Lisbon, 23:00-8:45.

2   Lisbon—Europe's bargain basement capital. See Back Doors. ST—Sintra (ruined Moorish castle), Estoril (casino nightlife). NT—Lagos, 23:10-6:43.

2   Algarve—Settle down in Salema, the best little beach village on the south coast of Portugal

3   Sevilla and Andalusia—After rafting the river of Spain in Sevilla, the city of flamenco, head for the hills and explore Andalusia's Route of the Whitewashed Hill Towns. Arcos de la Frontera is a good home base.

1   Madrid—On arrival, reserve NT to Barcelona (23:10-8:00). Spend the day here or side-trip to El Escorial and/or Segovia. Night travel is best in Iberia— long distances, boring, hot, crowded, slow day trains. Beds *(couchettes)* are cheap on these trains.

2   Barcelona—Picasso's house (excellent), relax, shop, Gothic Quarter. NT— 19:40-7:05. Hotel Toledano (top of Ramblas #138, tel. 301-0872).

2   Rhône Valley or French Riviera—Avignon (Papal Palace), Nimes, and Arles (Roman ruins). Nice (where the jet set lies on rocks, great Chagall Museum), Riviera (crowded, expensive, stressful, good modern art). Best overnights in Arles (Hotel Regence, tel. 90-96-39-85) and Nice (Hotel Star, tel. 93-85-19-03).

2   Cinque Terre—Great villages, coastal Italy at its best. See Back Doors.

1   Florence—Europe's Renaissance art capital, packed in the summer, worth the headaches. Sleep at Hotel La Scaletta (warm, friendly, tel. 283028), Casa Rabatti (cheap, homey, near station, tel. 212393).

2 Hill Towns of Tuscany and Umbria—See Back Doors. Most neglected and underrated side of Italy. Visit Siena and Città di Bagnoregio. Accommodations easy, leave Florence late, arrive Rome early.

3 Rome—Day #1—Classical: Colosseum, Forum, Capitoline Hill (both museums), Pantheon. Evening—Piazza Navona (buy Tartufo ice cream).
Day #2—Vatican, St. Peter's, climb the dome, Sistine (see *Mona Winks* or rent headphone guide) and Vatican Museum (great market 100 yards in front of museum entry, picnic). Take advantage of the Vatican's Post Office, much better than Italy's.
Day #3—Ostia Antica, Ancient Rome's seaport (like Pompeii, but just a subway ride away from Rome). Piazza Barberini, Bernini fountain, Capuchin crypt, thousands of bones in first church on Via Veneto, do the Dolce Vita stroll from Piazza del Popolo to Spanish Steps at 6:00 p.m., dinner on Campo di Fiori. Explore Trastevere, old Rome alive today, dinner at Campo di Fiori. Sleep near Vatican Museum at Pension Alimandi, tel. 39726300, or near the station at Pension Nardizzi, tel. 4880368. Or sleep cheaply, near the station at Hotel Magic (Via Milazzo 20, 3rd floor, 00185 Roma, tel. 4959880). NT—Venice, 23:10-6:28.

2 Venice—Best introduction—boat #82 down Canale Grande. Sit in front and soak it in. Sleep at Albergo Guerrato (near Rialto Market on Ruga dei Spezieri, tel. 041/522-7131) or near the station at Hotel Marin (San Croce 6706, tel. 041/718022). Academy Gallery—best Venetian art. Doges Palace, St. Mark's, and view from Campanile are musts, then wander, leave the tourists, get as lost as possible. Don't worry, you're on an island and you can't get off. NT—Vienna, 20:50-6:51.

2 Vienna—Paris's eastern rival. Grand capital of the mighty Habsburg Empire. Lots of art history and more Old World charm and elegance than anywhere. Great tourist information behind Opera. Good half-day tours from Opera. Tour Opera. Sleep in the cheery and central home of friendly Tina and Fred Kaled (Lindengasse 42, tel. 939013).

2 Prague—Prague, a magnificently preserved baroque city, is a happening place (visas no longer required, three hours from Vienna). NT—Switzerland.

3 Switzerland—Pray for sun. Most scenic train—Chur-Martigny (two non-Eurail segments). Best region—Berner Oberland, south of Interlaken. See Back Doors. Best big city: Bern. Best small town in West: Murten.

2 Tirol and Bavaria—Reutte, Innsbruck, with its great Tirolean folk museum. Sleep in tiny medieval town of Hall, 3 miles from Innsbruck (Gasthof Badl, tel. 05223/56784). Füssen, Mad Ludwig's castles, Wies Church, villages. See Back Doors (Medieval Castle Experiences).

2 Munich—Cultural capital, great palace, museums, Mathäuser's Beer Hall (best, halfway between station and old town on right). Tourist information and room-finding service in station (open late, tel. 089/239-1256). Hotel Utzelmann (elegant, near station, tel. 594889) and Pension Diana (simple, in old center, tel. 260-3107) are good places to sleep. Lay groundwork for departure on Romantic Road bus tour on arrival (make reservation, if necessary, confirm place and time of departure). ST—Salzburg, only 90-minute train ride away.

1 Romantic Road—Bus tour, free with Eurailpass (see Back Doors). Munich-Frankfurt 9:00-20:15 with stops in Dinkelsbühl and Rothenburg. Eve on the Rhine (Hotel Kranenturm in Bacharach, tel. 06743/1308). Consider overnight in Rothenburg (Hotel Goldener Rose, tel. 09861/4638).

2 Rhine/Mosel River Valleys and Köln
Cruise from Bacharach to St. Goar, best castles, free with train pass, hike from St. Goar to Rheinfels castle, great castle youth hostel in Bacharach (tel. 06743/1266). Mosel Valley, including cruises, Cochem town and castle, Trier-Roman town, Burg Eltz—long walk, great castle. NT—Köln to Berlin, 22:51–6:47.

2 Berlin—Berlin, capital of a united Germany, with its great art and Cold War remnants, is worth two busy days. Sleep at Pension Heide am Zoo (tel. 310496). NT—Copenhagen, 0:09-8:31.

1 Copenhagen—Leave bags at station, evening at Tivoli just across the street. If you spend the night, sleep in Annette and Rudy Hollender's home (tel. 32-95-96-22). NT—22:35-7:05.

2 Stockholm—See Back Doors. Sleep on trains in Scandinavia—long, boring rides, capitals ten hours apart, hotels expensive. NT—Oslo, 23:07-7:35.

1 Oslo—Arrive in the morning, see the sights, sleep cozy near the palace at Ellingsen's Pensjonat (Holtegt 25, tel. 22-600359) or right downtown with the retired seamen at Sjomannshjem (Tollbugt 4, tel. 22-412005).

2 Scenic Train, Fjord Country, and Bergen—Catch the morning train across Norway. Do "Norway in a Nutshell" by train, boat, and bus for the best look at the interior and fjord country of West Norway. Spend the night on the fjord near Flam in Aurland (funky Aabelheim Pension, tel. 57 63-34-49, or basic Vangen Motel, tel. 57 63-35-80). After a day in Bergen (the Heskja home offers good budget beds right downtown at 17 Skivebakken, tel. 55 31-59-55), catch the night train back to Oslo, 22:45-7:00.

1 Oslo—A second day in Oslo, plenty to see. (See Back Doors.) NT— 22:40-8:20.

1 Copenhagen—Another day in Copenhagen. NT—22:05-9:52. Train goes right onto Puttgarten ferry.

2 Amsterdam—Many great side trips. Consider headquarters in small town nearby (Haarlem, Hotel Amadeus, tel. 023/32 45 30), as Amsterdam is getting awfully sleazy and seedy for many visiting Americans' tastes. Consider open-jaws flight into London, out of Amsterdam, to avoid surface return to London ($60 and 13 hours). NT—20:03-9:00.

2 London—Spend remaining time in English countryside, Bath, Cotswolds, Cambridge. Call to reconfirm flight home.

Sixty-one days scheduled. Use train times only as a rough guide. Eurailpass is good for two calendar months (e.g., the 15th through midnight on the 14th). If you validate when you leave Paris and expire (the Eurailpass, not you) on arrival in Amsterdam, you spend 53 days, leaving 8 days of train-pass time (if you can extend your trip) to slow down or add options.

The Whirlwind Tour includes 18 nights on the train, saving about $400 in hotel costs, and 18 days for doing more interesting things than sitting on a train.

Books recommended for this tour: *Let's Go: Europe; Mona Winks*; and *Rick Steves' Best of Europe* (latter two published by John Muir Publications).

EXCURSIONS YOU MAY WANT TO ADD

England—Oxford, Stratford, the Cotswold villages, Bath
French Alps—Geneva, Chamonix, Aiguille du Midi, Aosta
Morocco and South Spain
South Italy or Greece
Finland or the Arctic
Eastern Europe or Russia
A day for showers and laundry
Visiting, resting, and a little necessary slack
Travel days to avoid sleeping on the train

People of all ages are letting their hair down in Europe

PART TWO
Back Doors
of Europe

Europe, here you come

Contents

Europe's Back Doors

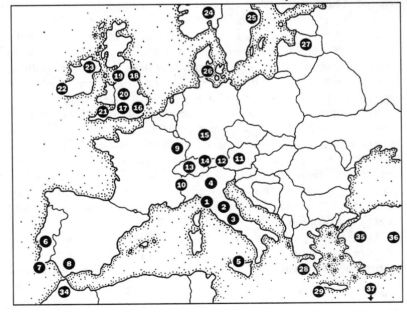

What Is a Back Door, and How Can I Find One of My Own?

The travel skills covered in the first half of this book enable you to open doors most travelers don't even know exist. Now I'd like you to meet my "Back Doors." This is a chance for you and the travel bug to get intimate. By traveling vicariously with me through these chapters you'll get a peek at my favorite places. And just as important, by internalizing the lifetime of little travel moments that I've enjoyed and compiled here, you'll develop a knack for finding your own.

Europe is a bubbling multicultural fondue. A Back Door is a steaming fork-full. It could be an all-day Alpine ridge walk, a friendly swing with a church spire bell-ringer, a sword-fern fantasy in a ruined castle, uncovering the village warmth of a big cold city, or jamming your camera with Turkish delights. By learning where to jab your fork, you'll put together a travel feast exceeding your wildest dreams.

Some of my back doors are undiscovered towns that have, for various reasons, missed the modern parade. With no promotional budgets to attract travelers, they're ignored as they quietly make their traditional way through just another century. Many of these places won't hit you with their cultural razzle-dazzle. Their charms are too subtle to be enjoyed by the tour-bus crowd. But, learning from the experiences described in the last half of this book, Back Door travelers will make their own fun.

We'll also explore natural nooks and undeveloped crannies. These are rare opportunities to enjoy Europe's sun, beaches, mountains, and natural wonders without the glitz. While Europeans love nature and

are fanatic sun-worshipers, they have an impressive knack for enjoying themselves in hellish crowds. Our goal is to experience Europe's quiet alternatives: forgotten stone circles, desolate castles, breezy bike rides, and snippets of the Riviera not snapped up by entrepreneurs.

With a Back Door angle on a big city, you can slip your fingers under its staged culture and actually find a pulse. Even London has a warm underbelly where you'll rumble with a heart that's been beating for over 2,000 years.

And finally, for maximum thrills per mile, minute, and dollar, it's important to look beyond Europe. Europe is exciting, but a dip into Turkey, Morocco, or Egypt is well worth the diarrhea.

The promotion of a tender place that has so far avoided the tourist industry reminds me of the whaler who screams, "Quick, harpoon it before it's extinct!" These places are this Europhile's cupids. Publicizing them gnaws at what makes them so great. But what kind of a travel writer can keep his favorite discoveries under wraps? Great finds are too hard to come by to just sit on. I keep no secrets.

With ever-more-sophisticated travelers armed with ever-better guidebooks, places I "discovered" eight or ten years ago are undeveloped and uncommercial only in a relative sense. And certain places that I really rave about suffer from Back Door congestion. At least from my experience, Back Door readers are pleasant people to share Europe with.

People recommended in this book tell me that Back Door readers are good guests who undo the "ugly" image created by the more demanding and ethnocentric American tourists. By traveling sensitively, you're doing yourself a favor as well as those you'll deal with, travelers who'll follow . . . and me. Thank you.

These Back Doors combine to give you a Whitman's sampler of travel thrills. While the Appendix lists nitty-gritty information and the best accommodations for each Back Door, I've written these chapters to give you the flavor of the place, not to navigate by. An appropriate directory-type guidebook (like one of my eight country guidebooks) will give you the details necessary to splice your chosen back doors into a smooth trip.

Now raise your travel dreams to their upright and locked positions and travel with me through my favorite Back Doors.

Note: In most cases more detailed information about the following places can be found in the appropriate Rick Steves' Country Guides and in this book's Appendix.

Italy

1. Cinque Terre: Italy's Traffic-free Riviera

"A sleepy, romantic, and inexpensive town on the Riviera without a tourist in sight." That's the mirage travelers chase in busy Nice and Cannes. Pssst! Paradise sleeps just across the border in Italy's Cinque Terre.

The Cinque Terre, meaning "five lands," is five pastel villages clinging to the most inaccessible bit of coast on the Italian Riviera. Put there centuries ago by pirates hiding out, today the train brings visitors into towns virtually inaccessible by car. The Cinque Terre, between Pisa and Genova, was too rugged to develop. And now, as locals sense a possible tourist boom, the government protects these well-preserved villages and new building is not allowed. The villagers have almost no choice but to go about their business as if the surrounding vineyards were the very edges of the earth.

Each town is a character. Monterosso al Mare, happy to be appreciated, boasts the area's only sandy beach, plenty of fine hotels, restaurants, and rentable paddle boats. Its four little sisters frolic

Vernazza, on Italy's Riviera

overlooked—forgotten behind battered breakwaters. (Since my mind usually goes on vacation with the rest of me when I'm here, I think of the towns by number for easy orientation. They go—east to west— from one to five. Number five is the resort.)

The first town of the Cinque Terre, Riomaggiore (#1) is a beauty that has seduced famed artists into becoming residents. The most substantial non-resort town of the group, Riomaggiore is a disappointment from the station. But walk through the tunnel next to the train tracks and you land in a fascinating tangle of pastel homes leaning on each other as if someone stole their crutches. There's homemade gelati at the Bar Central. Mama Rosa's ramshackle hostel, a block from the train station, offers the looniest budget beds in the area and an instant family of fellow backpackers.

The Via dell' Amore (walkway of love) leads from Riomaggiore to Manarola. This is a film-gobbling 15-minute promenade wide enough for baby strollers. There's no beach here, but stairways lead to remote rocks for sunbathing. Uppity little Manarola (town #2) rules its ravine and drinks its wine while its sun-bleached walls slumber on.

Corniglia (town #3) sits smug on its hilltop, a proudly victorious king of the mountain. Most visitors—lured to Corniglia by its scrawny, stony beach and the Cinque Terre's best swimming—never tackle the winding stairs to the actual town. Those who make the Corniglian climb are rewarded by the Cinque Terre's finest wine and most staggering view. Corniglia has a windy belvedere, a few restaurants, and a handful of often-empty private rooms for rent. (Ask for Sra. Silvani.) With each visit I find myself ducking into a cellar with a grape-stained local, dipping long straws into dark kegs.

As I step off the train in Vernazza (town #4), I know my race is run. With the closest thing to a natural harbor, overseen by a ruined castle and an old church, Vernazza is my 5-Terre home base. Its one street connects the harbor with the train station and meanders farther inland, melting into the vineyards. Like veins on a maple leaf, paths and stairways connect this watercolor huddle of houses with Main Street. Every day is a rerun in this hive of lazy human activity. A rainbow of laundry flaps as if to keep the flies off the old men who man the bench. Like fat barnacles filling ancient doorways, local grandmothers watch life drift by. Little varnished boats are everywhere in peely piles, and sailors suckle at salty taverns while the Old World marches on to the steady beat of the crashing waves. The sun sets unnoticed—except by tourists. About once an hour the express train screams over Main Street, reminding barnacles and visitors alike that there is a faster world.

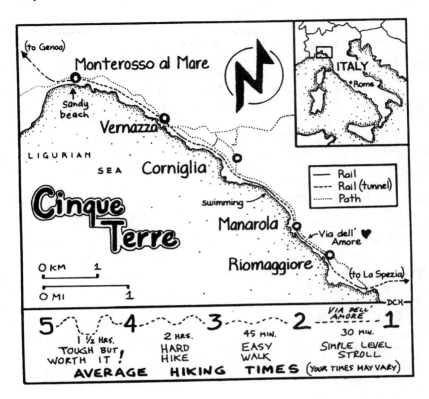

The Cinque Terre is best seen on foot. A scenic trail leads you through sunny vistas from towns one through five (Riomaggiore to Monterosso). The Vernazza-Monterosso trail is as rugged as the people who've worked the terraced vineyards that blanket the region. Flowers and an ever-changing view entertain you at every step. As you make your sweaty way high above the glistening beaches and approach each time-steeped village, you'll ponder paying for your trip with the photos you've shot.

When you run out of time or energy, simply catch a train back to your home base. While these towns are barely accessible by car, a tunnel-train blinks open at each village and provides a quick and easy way to explore the region. Milk-run trains connect all five towns for $1. A boat ferries people scenically from Vernazza to Monterosso al Mare. And those in search of private coves, refreshing waterfalls, and natural high dives find them tucked away along the coast between these two towns.

For a great day in the Cinque Terre, start by walking the Via dell' Amore from Riomaggiore to Manarola. Buy a picnic in Manarola and walk to the Corniglia beach. Swim, enjoy the shady bar, shower, picnic, and take the train to Monterosso al Mare for a look at the local big town. Enjoy its sandy beach before hiking home to Vernazza. Vernazza's best bar is the umbrella-shaded balcony halfway between the castle and the surf. Climb its rope railing for a glass of *vino de la Cinque Terre*. For extra drama, peek inside (above the door) at the photo of giant winter waves crashing over Vernazza's harbor. If you like sweet sherry-like wine, the local *Sciachetra* wine is expensive, but delicious.

While the Cinque Terre is unknown to the international mobs that ravage the Spanish and French coasts, plenty of Italians and my readers come here, so getting a room can be tough. August and weekends are bad. Weekends in August are worst. (For rooms, see the Appendix.)

Paint a dream in vineyard greens and Mediterranean blues. Italy's Cinque Terre—five towns and a rocky surf—can make it come true.

2. The Hill Towns of Tuscany and Umbria

Too many people connect Venice, Florence, and Rome with straight lines. Break out of this syndrome and you'll lick a little Italy that the splash of Venice, the finesse of Florence, and the grandeur of Rome were built on.

San Marino, just another magic Italian hill town (only this one's an independent country)

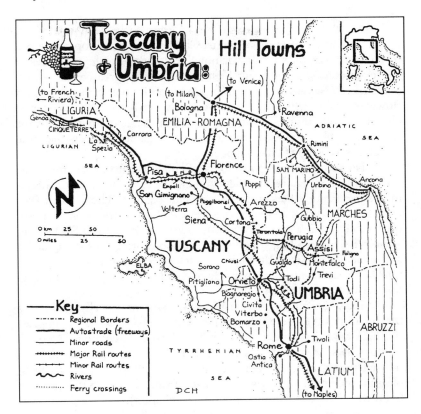

The hill towns of Tuscany and Umbria hold their crumbling heads proudly above the noisy flood of the twentieth century and offer a peaceful taste of what eludes so many tourists. Sitting on a timeless rampart high above the traffic and trains, hearing only children in the market and the rustling wind aging the weary red-tile patchwork that surrounds me, I find the essence of Italy in this small-town package.

Hill towns, like Greek islands, come in two basic varieties—touristy and untouristy. There are a dozen great touristed towns and countless ignored communities casually doing time and drinking wine. See some of each.

San Gimignano bristles with towers and bustles with tourists. A thrilling silhouette from a distance, Italy's best-preserved medieval skyline gets better as you approach. Sunset's the right time to conquer the castle. Climb high above the crowds, sit on the castle's summit, and imagine the battles Tuscany's armadillo has endured.

Siena, unlike its rival, Florence, is a city to be seen as a whole rather than as a collection of sights. Climb to the dizzy top of the bell tower and reign over urban harmony at its best. While memories of Florence consist of dodging Vespas between oppressive museums, Siena has an easy-to-enjoy, well-pickled Gothic soul: courtyards sport flower-decked wells, alleys dead-end into red-tiled rooftop views, churches modestly hoard their art, and that magic moment when the sky is a rich blue dome no brighter than the medieval towers that hold it high is savored by first-time poets.

Assisi, a worthy hometown for St. Francis, is battling a commercial cancer of tourist clutter. In the summer, the town bursts with splash-in-the-pan Francis fans and monastic knickknacks. Those able to see past the tacky monk mementos can actually have a "travel on purpose" experience. With a quiet hour in the awesome Basilica of St. Francis, some reflective reading (there's a great bookstore below the church), and a meditative stroll through the back streets, you can dissolve the tour buses and melt into the magic of Assisi. St. Francis would recognize Assisi best after dark.

Orvieto, the tourist's token hill town, sits majestically on its tufa throne, offering those on the train or autostrada to Rome its impressive hill-capping profile. Its cathedral, with some fascinating Signorelli frescoes, is surrounded by an excellent tourist information office, a fine Etruscan museum, a world-class gelati shop, and Italy's most pleasant public toilet. Buses go regularly from Orvieto to the queen of hill towns, Civ
à di Bagnoregio (see next chapter).

Any guidebook lists these popular hill towns. But if you want to dance at noon with a toothless lady while your pizza cooks, press a good luck coin into the moldy ceiling of an Etruscan wine cellar, or be introduced to a mediocre altarpiece as proudly as if it were a Michelangelo, you must stow your guidebook, buy the best local map you can find, and explore.

Perfect Back Door villages, like hidden pharaohs' tombs, await discovery. Photographers delight in Italian hill towns. Their pictorial collections (such as *Italian Hill Towns* by Norman Carver) are a fine source of information. Study these, circling the most intriguing towns on your map. Talk to travelers who have studied or lived in Italy. Ask locals for their favorites. Scan the horizon for fortified towers. Drive down dead-end roads.

Gubbio, Volterra, Cortona, and Arezzo are discovered but rarely visited. Civ
à di Bagnoregio, Sorano, Pitigliano, Trevi, Poppi, Orte (just north of Rome off the freeway), and Bagnaia (near Viterbo) are virgin hill towns. The difference between "discovered" and "virgin,"

touristically speaking, is that "discovered" towns know what tourism is and have an appetite for the money that comes with it. "Virgin" towns are simply pleased that you dropped in.

Hill towns are a vital slice of the Italian pizza—crumbly crust with a thick gooey culture. Leave the train lines. Take the bus, hitch, or rent a car for a few days. (Many hill towns have a train station nearby. Your ticket includes a bus shuttle that begins its winding climb shortly after your train arrives.) If you're using a rail-and-drive pass, this is car country. Don't just chase down my favorites or your guidebook's recommendations. Somewhere in the social slumber of Umbria and the human texture of Tuscany the ultimate hill town awaits your visit.

3. Cività di Bagnoregio

People who've been there just say "Cività" (chee-vee-TA) with warmth and love. This precious chip of Italy, a traffic-free community with a grow-it-in-the-valley economy, has so far escaped the ravages of modernity. Please approach it with the same respect and sensitivity you would a dying relative, because—in a sense—that's Cività.

Fifteen people still live here. There's no car traffic. A man with a donkey works all day ferrying the town's goods across the long umbilical bridge that connects the town with a small distant parking lot and the rest of Italy. Rome, just 60 miles to the south, might as well be on the other side of the moon.

The perfect hill town, Cività di Bagnoregio

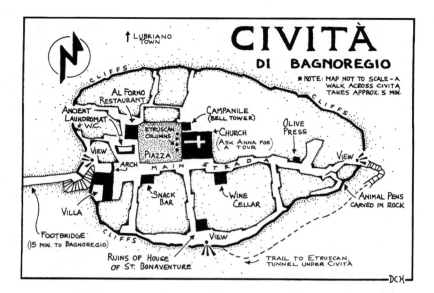

Civltà's charms are subtle, and many tourists wouldn't know what to do in a town without arcade tourism. No English menus, lists of attractions, orientation tours, or museum hours. Just Italy.

Sit in the piazza. Smile and nod at each local who passes by. It's a social jigsaw puzzle, and each person fits. The old woman hanging out the window monitors gossip. A tiny hunchback lady is everyone's daughter. And cats, the only growing segment of the population, scratch an itch on ancient pillars that stick up like bar stools in front of the church. Two thousand five hundred years ago these graced the facade of an Etruscan temple here.

Civltà's population is revised downward with each edition of this book. As old people get frail, they move into apartments in nearby Bagnoregio. Most of the young people are gone, lured away by the dazzle of today to grab their place in Italy's cosmopolitan parade.

Today, Civltà's social pie has three slices: the aging, full-time resident community; the rich Italians from Rome and Milan who are slowly buying up the place for their country escape (the Ferrari family owns the house next to the town gate—and Civltà's only Jacuzzi); and a small University of Washington architecture program headed by Professor Astra Zarina, who owns a villa in Civltà. When in session, ten to 20 UW students live and study here. Over the years, alumni and their families have made Civltà their Italian retreat, and you'll often find a Seattle-ite or two enjoying *la dolce far niente* (the sweetness of doing nothing).

Explore Città. Maria introduces you to a baby donkey as if it were her child. Anna is the keeper of the church. The heartbeat and pride of the village, this is where festivals and processions start, visitors are escorted, and the town's past is honored. Enjoy paintings by students of famous artists; relics of the hometown boy-made-saint Bonaventure; a dried floral decoration spread across the floor; and a cool, quiet moment in a pew.

Città is a man-gripped pinnacle in a vast canyon. Wind and erosion rule the valley. Victoria, numb to her eye-boggling view, showed me the latest in a 2,000-year line of olive presses which have filled her ancient Etruscan cave. Just around the corner from the church is Domenica's cantina. Pull up a stump and enjoy a glass of her family wine. The white has a taste reminiscent of dirty socks, the red tastes cleaner. But it's made right here. That donkey brought up the grapes. Climb down into her ancient cellar. Grab the stick and thunk on the kegs to measure their fullness. Even on a blistering day those caves are always cool, and an endless supply of local Città wine is kept chilled, awaiting future fun.

Città has one restaurant. You can see its green door and handmade sign from the piazza. At Al Forno (the oven), you eat what's cooking. Mom and Pop slice and quarter happily through the day. Spaghetti, salad and wine, on the Al Forno patio, cuddled by Città—I wouldn't trade it for all-you-can-eat at Maxim's.

Spend the evening. Sit on the church steps with people who've done exactly that for 60 years. Al Forno serves late. Children play on the piazza until midnight. As you walk back to your car—that scourge of the modern world that enabled you to get here—stop under a lamp on the donkey path, listen to the canyon . . . distant voices . . . fortissimo crickets.

Città is an artist's dream, a town in the nude. Each lane and footpath holds a surprise. Horses pose, the warm stone walls glow, each stairway is dessert to a sketch pad or camera, and the Grand Canyon moat does its best to keep things that way. It's changing, however, as the persistent battering ram of our modern world pounds on these rare strongholds of the past. With recent exposure in German and French travel magazines, Città sees up to 200 tourists a day on summer weekends. Città will be great for years but never as great as today.

You won't find Città on your map. Take the train to Orvieto and catch a bus to Bagnoregio. From Bagnoregio you walk 20 minutes to Città.

Città has no hotel. Bagnoregio has two. The more colorful is a 20-minute walk out of town. Ask for al Boschetto di Angelino

Catarcia. Angelino is a character who runs through life like a hyper child in a wading pool. Have an English-speaking Italian call him for you (tel. 0761/792369; address: Strada Monterado, Bagnoregio, Viterbo, Italy).

Romans travel to Bagnoregio just to eat at Angelino's. Everything here is sensuously homegrown—figs, fruit, wine, pasta, and rabbit. Bunny is the house specialty. Try the sweet dessert wine.

Angelino is Bacchus squared and he's raised his sons, Dominico and Franco, well. Descend into the fragrant bowels of their wine cellar as if it were a Venus's flytrap. There are no rules unless female participants set them. (Women readers have reported that solo women should avoid the place.) Music and vino kill the language barrier in *la cantina* where Angelino will teach you his theme song, "Trinka, Trinka, Trinka."

4. North Italy Choices: Mountains, Lakes, or Milano

Italy: Venice, Florence, Rome, hill towns, and the Riviera . . . Yes, those are the first targets but there's much more. My favorite European country is a grab bag of cultural, artistic, edible, and natural thrills. I enjoyed researching some of these while writing my *Best of Italy* guidebook.

Italy intensifies as you plunge deeper. If you like it as far south as Rome, go further—it gets better. But, for many, after seven days of *"buon giorno"* and *"grazie,"* Switzerland starts looking better and better. If you've yet to satisfy your appetite for cappuccino, gelato, and people-watching, but Italy's starting to grab you the wrong way, you'll find a milder Italy in the North. North Italy's charms come in three packages: Alpine Dolomites, romantic lakes, and urban Milano. All are within three hours of Venice, Florence, and each other.

The Dolomites, Italy's dramatic limestone rooftop, combine Alpine thrills with Italian sunshine. The famous valleys and towns of the well-developed Dolomites suffer from an après-ski fever, but the bold snow-flecked mountains and green meadows offer great hikes. The cost for reliably good weather is a drained-reservoir feeling. Lovers of the Alps may miss the lushness that comes with the unpredictable weather farther north.

A hard-fought history has left this part of Italy bicultural and bilingual with der emphasis on the Deutsche. Locals speak German first and some wish they were still Austrian. In the Middle Ages the region faced north, part of the Holy Roman Empire. Later it was firmly in

North Italy

the Austrian Hapsburg realm. By losing World War I, Austria's South Tirol became Italy's Alto Adige. Mussolini did what he could to Italianize the region, including giving each town an Italian name. The government has wooed cranky German-speaking locals with economic breaks that make this one of Italy's richest areas (as local prices attest). Today, signs and literature in the autonomous province of Sud Tirol/Alto Adige are in both languages.

In spite of all the glamorous ski resorts and busy construction cranes, local color survives in a warm, blue-aproned, ruddy-faced, long-white-bearded way. There's yogurt and yodeling for breakfast. Culturally as much as geographically, the area feels Austrian. (The western part of Austria is named after Tirol, a village that is now actually in Italy.)

Lifts, good trails, outdoor activity-oriented tourist offices, and a decent bus system make the region especially accessible. But things are expensive. Most towns have no alternative to $50 doubles in hotels, or $40 doubles in private homes. Beds usually come with a hearty breakfast. If you're low on both money and scruples, Sud Tirolean breakfasts are the only ones in Italy big enough to steal lunch from.

The seasons are brutal. Everything is open, booming, full price and crowded from mid-July through September. After a dreary November, the snow hits and it's busy again until April. May and early June are dead. The most exciting trails are still under snow and the mountain lifts are shut down. Most huts and budget accommodations are closed, as locals are more concerned with preparing for another boom season than catering to the stray off-season tourist.

With limited time and no car, maximize mountain thrills and minimize transportation headaches by taking the train to Bolzano and the public bus from there into the mountains.

By car, circle north from Venice and drive the breathtaking Great Dolomite Road (130 miles: Belluno-Cortina-Pordoi Pass-Sella Pass-Val di Fassa-Bolzano). In the spring and early summer, passes labeled "Closed" are often bare, dry, and, as far as local drivers are concerned, wide open. Conveniently for local tour operators, no direct public transportation route covers the Great Dolomite Road.

If Bolzano (Bozen to its German-speaking locals) weren't so sunny, you could be in Innsbruck. This arcaded old town of 100,000, with a great open-air market (Piazza Erbe), is worth a Tirolean stroll and a stop at its Dolomite information center.

Tourist offices in any town are a wealth of information. Before choosing a hike, get their advice. Ideally, pick a hike with an overnight in a hut and make a telephone reservation. Most huts, called *refugios*, offer reasonable doubles, cheaper dorm (*lager*) beds, and good inexpensive meals.

Many are tempted to wimp out on the Dolomites and admire the spires from a distance. They take the cable car into the hills above Bolzano to the cute but very touristy village of Oberbozan. Don't. Bus into the Dolomites instead. Three great destinations, just an hour or two from Bolzano, are the Val di Fassa, Val Gardena, and, best of all, the Alpe di Suisi.

The Alpe di Suisi, Europe's largest alpine meadow, is a car-free natural preserve with a park bus service and well-marked trails fanning out below the ultimate Dolomite peaks, Sassolunga and the Sella group.

Kastelruth, with good bus connections and more village character than any town around, makes a charming home base. Gasthof zum Turm (tel. 0471/706349) and Gasthof zum Wolf (tel. 0471/706332) are each a few cobbles from the church and offer $50 doubles with breakfast.

The Italian Lakes, at the base of Italy's Alps, are a romantic and popular destination for Italians and their European neighbors. The million-lire question is: "Which lake?" For the best mix of handiness, scenery, and offbeatness, giving you a complete dose of Italian-lakes wonder and aristocratic old-days romance, visit Lake Como.

Lined with elegant nineteenth-century villas, crowned by snow-capped mountains, buzzing with ferries, hydrofoils, and little passenger ships, this is a good place to take a break from the intensity and obligatory turnstile-culture of central Italy. It seems half the travelers you'll meet on Lago di Como have tossed their itineraries overboard and are actually relaxing. The area's isolation and flat economy have left it pretty much the way the nineteenth-century romantic poets described it.

While you can easily drive around the lake, the road is narrow, congested, and lined by privacy-seeking walls, hedges, and tall fences. This is train-and-boat country. Regular train departures whisk you from intense Milan into the serenity of Lago di Como in an hour. The lake is well-served by pricey little boats. When you consider the included scenery, the $3 per one-stop hop isn't quite so expensive.

The town of Bellagio, "the Pearl of the Lake," is a classy combination of tidiness and Old World elegance. If you don't mind that tramp-in-a-palace feeling, it's a fine place to surround yourself with the more adventurous of the soft travelers and shop for umbrellas and ties. The heavy curtains between the arcades keep these tourists and their poodles from sweating.

One hop away by ferry, the town of Varenna offers the best of all lake worlds. On the less-driven side of the lake, with a romantic promenade, a tiny harbor, narrow lanes and its own villa, Varenna is the right place to savor a *cappuccino* and ponder the place where Italy is welded to the Alps. The town is quiet at night. The *passerella* (lakeside walk) is adorned with caryatid lovers pressing silently against each other in the shadows.

Menaggio, directly across the lake from Varenna and just 8 miles from Lugano in Switzerland, feels more like a real town than its neighbors. Since the lake is too dirty for swimming, consider its fine public pool.

Finding a room on Lake Como is tight in August, snug in July, and wide open most of the rest of the year. Varenna's Albergo Olivedo is a neat old hotel (lumpy old beds and a glorious little lake-view balcony overlooking the ferry dock, tel. 0341/830115, $40 to $70 doubles). Albergo Milano—friendlier, more comfortable, and right in the old town, with a magnificent breakfast terrace—is your best Varenna splurge (tel. 0341/830298, $80 doubles).

Mennagio's La Primula Youth Hostel is a rare hostel. Family-run for ten years by Ty and Paola, it caters to a quiet, savor-the-lakes crowd and offers the only cheap beds in the region. Located just south of the Menaggio dock, it has a view terrace, lots of games, a members' kitchen, washing machine, bike rentals, easy parking, and a creative, hard-working staff. Ty and Paola print a newsletter to advertise their activities programs: inexpensive 14-day Italian language courses, 3- to 7-day hikes, bike trips, and cooking classes. (Ostello "La Primula", $10 per night in 4 to 6-bed rooms with sheets, breakfast, and a souvenir cookbook, also hearty $10 dinners with wine and flair, 22017 Menaggio, tel. and fax 0344/32356.)

Milan is where you experience Italy of the '90s. The economic success of modern Italy (which now has a higher per-capita income than Britain) can be blamed on cities like Milan. As the saying goes, for every church in Rome there's a bank in Milan. Italy's second city, Milan (population 2 million), is a hard-working, fashion-conscious, time-is-money melting pot of people and history. Its industriousness may come from the region's Austrian heritage. This city of publicists and pasta power lunches is Italy's industrial, banking, TV, publishing, and convention capital. Just describing it is exhausting.

Much of Milan is ugly with a recently bombed-out feeling (WWII). Its huge financial buildings are as manicured as its parks are shaggy. As if to make up for its harsh concrete shell, its people and windows are works of art. Milan is an international fashion capital. Cigarettes are still chic and even the cheese is gift-wrapped.

While many tourists come to Italy for the past, Milan is today's Italy. No Italian trip is complete without seeing it. Milan is hot and muggy in August when locals who can, vacate, leaving the city just about dead. Those visiting in August will find many shops closed and nightlife pretty quiet.

Milan's public-relations expertise has made it a fashion and finance winner. While not big on the tourist circuit, Milan has plenty to see, it's no more expensive than other Italian cities, and its organization is more Milanese than Italian.

Milan's cathedral, the city's centerpiece, is the third-largest church in Europe. At 480 feet long, 280 feet wide, and forested with 52 150-foot-tall sequoia pillars and over 2,000 statues, the place can seat over 10,000 worshippers. Hike up to the rooftop, a fancy crown of spires with great views of the city, the square, and on clear days, even the Swiss Alps.

The cathedral square, Piazza Duomo, is a classic European scene.

Professionals scurry, label-conscious kids loiter, young thieves peruse. Facing the square, the Galleria Vittorio Emanuele, Milan's great four-story-high, glass-domed arcade, invites you in to shop or enjoy a cafe. This is the place to turn a too-expensive cup of coffee into a good value with some of Europe's hottest people-watching. For good luck, locals step on the testicles of the mosaic Taurus on the floor's Zodiac design. Two local girls explained that it works better if you actually give a twirl.

La Scala, possibly the world's most prestigious opera house, is just a holler away. While tickets are as hard to get as they are expensive, anyone can peek into the theater from the museum. Opera buffs will love the museum's extensive collection of things that would mean absolutely nothing to the MTV crowd: Verdi's top-hat, Rossini's eye-glasses, Toscanini's baton, Fettucini's pesto, and the original scores, busts, portraits, and death masks of great composers and musicians.

The Brera Art Gallery, Milan's top collection of paintings, is world class. But you'll see better in Rome and Florence. The immense Sforza Castle, Milan's much-bombed and rebuilt brick fortress, is exhausting at first sight. But its courtyard has a great lawn for picnics and siestas. Its free museum features interesting medieval armor, furniture, Lombard art, and a Michelangelo statue with no crowds—his unfinished *Rondanini Pietà*.

Leonardo da Vinci's ill-fated *Last Supper* is flecking off the refectory wall of the nearby church of Santa Maria delle Grazie. The fresco suffers from Leonardo's experimental use of oil. Decay began within six years of its completion. It's undergone more restoration work than Liz Taylor and that work continues. Most of the original paint is gone, but tourists are still encouraged to pay $8 to peer through the scaffolds to see what's left.

More of Leonardo's spirit survives in Italy's answer to the Smithsonian, the National Leonardo da Vinci Science and Technology Museum. While most tourists visit for the hall of Leonardo designs illustrated in wooden models, the rest of this immense collection of industrial cleverness is just as fascinating. There is plenty of push-button action displaying the development of trains, the evolution of radios, old musical instruments, computers, batteries, telephones, and chunks of the first transatlantic cable. Unfortunately, English descriptions are rare.

At Europe Through the Back Door, where I work, Italy is considered the greatest country in Europe. If all you have is ten days, then do Venice, Florence, Rome, the hill towns, and the Riviera. If you have more time, for intensity head south. But to round out your itinerary with all the best of Italy and none of the chaos, splice in a little of the Dolomites, the lakes, and Milan.

5. Palermo, Sicily's Urban Carnival

It took me seven trips to get down past Italy's "boot." The Sicilians (along with the Irish and except for the street thieves) are the warmest and friendliest Europeans I've met.

Palermo is intense—Italy in the extreme—with lots of purse-snatchers, lousy showers, and grueling heat. It's generally run-down and chaotic, but if you want exotic, urban Italian thrills, Italy's football is a kick. The overnight train ride south from Rome or Naples drops you right into this rich culture, which lives in peaceful oblivion to the touristic bustle that takes such a toll on Venice, Florence, and Rome.

Eating and sleeping stylishly and affordably with no reservations is easy. From the Palermo train station, walk straight down Via Roma

Travelers in search of back-street treats

for your choice of many hotels. (My favorite is the Hotel Moderno, Via Roma 276.)

Eating in Palermo is a treat. Colorful street markets make shopping for picnics a joy. Pizzeria Bellini on Piazza Bellini, near the landmark "four corners" in downtown Palermo, was my dinnertime hangout. Over the course of several meals, I ate my way through their menu, discovering for myself why Italians like to eat. Their fanciest pizza, Quatro Gusti con Fungi, rates as the best $7 I've ever spent in Italy.

One reason Palermo lacks tourist crowds is that it has very few tourist sights, as such. It does have a way of life that, in its own way, offers the tourist more than any monument or museum ever could. Don't tour Palermo—live in it.

Thriving marketplaces abound in nearly every neighborhood. If you've ever wondered what it would be like to be a celebrity, go on a photo-safari through the urban jungles of Palermo. The warmth and excitement will give you smile wrinkles. Scores of merchants, housewives, and children compete for your attention. Cries of "Photo?" come from all corners as you venture down busy alleys.

Visit a vertical neighborhood. Small apartments stack high above the side streets. If you stop to chat, six floors of balconies will fill up, each with its own waving family. I found a wobbly stack of tenements facing one another, a faded rainbow with lots of laundry and people hanging out. One wave worked wonders. Walking around, craning my neck upward, I felt like a victorious politician among hordes of supporters. They called out for pictures and wouldn't let me go until I had filmed each window and balcony full of people: mothers held up babies; sisters posed arm-in-arm; a wild pregnant woman stood on a fruit crate, holding her bulging stomach; and an old, wrinkled woman filled her paint-starved window frame with a toothy grin. I was showered with scraps of paper, each with an address on it. A contagious energy filled the air. It hurt to say *ciao*.

For a strange journey through an eerie cellar of the dead, visit the Catacombs of the Capuchin Monks (Convento di Cappuccini). This dark and dreary basement is decorated with the skeletal remains of 8,000 monks, many clothed and hanging on its walls. With their strange but meaningful habit, this order of monks reminds us that in the middle of our busy vacation or workaday scramble, in a cosmic heartbeat, none of our earthly concerns may matter.

While you're there, notice how much the monks (those still alive) look like that wonderful cup of cappuccino with which you start your

Italian day. Their rich brown cowls with the frothy white tops gave the coffee its name.

For a more typical tourist attraction and a respite from Palermo's swelter-skelter, bus inland to the soothing mountain town of Monreale. Inside Monreale's Benedictine church, you'll find a collection of mosaics that rival Ravenna's. Dozens of Bible scenes wallpaper the church. Since I was wearing shorts, I was given a blanket to wear as a skirt. With my hairy, unholy legs covered, I worked my way, scene by scene, through the Bible.

Apart from Monreale, Palermo has no must-see museum and nothing to compete with Pisa's tipsy tower or Big Ben. Palermo lets you become a temporary Sicilian. That's reason enough to visit.

Portugal
and Spain

6. Lisbon's Gold Still Shines

Barely elegant outdoor cafés, glittering art, entertaining museums, and the saltiest sailors' quarter in Europe, all at bargain basement prices, make Lisbon an Iberian highlight. Portugal's capital is a wonderful mix of Now and Then. Old wooden trolleys shiver up and down its hills, bird-stained statues guard grand squares, and people sip coffee in art nouveau cafés.

Fish market in Lisbon's Alfama

Present-day Lisbon is explained by its past. Her glory days were the fifteenth and sixteenth centuries, when explorers like Vasco da Gama opened up new trade routes, making Lisbon the queen of Europe. Later, the riches of Brazil boosted Lisbon even higher. Then, in 1755, an earthquake leveled the city, killing over 20 percent of its people.

Lisbon was rebuilt on a strict grid plan, symmetrical, with broad boulevards and square squares. The grandeur of pre-earthquake Lisbon survives only in Belem, the Alfama, and the Bairro Alto districts.

While the earthquake flattened a lot of buildings, and its colonial empire is long gone, Lisbon's heritage survives. Follow me through a day in Lisbon.

After breakfast, taxi to the Alfama, the city's colorful sailors' quarter. This was the center of Visigothic Lisbon, a rich district during the Arabic period and now the shiver-me-timbers home of Lisbon's fisherfolk. One of the few areas to survive the 1755 earthquake, the Alfama is a cobbled cornucopia of Old World color. Visit during the busy midmorning market time or in the late afternoon and early evening when the streets chatter with activity.

Wander deep. This urban jungle's roads are squeezed into tangled stairways and confused alleys. Bent houses comfort each other in their romantic shabbiness, and the air drips with laundry and the smell of clams and raw fish. Get lost. Poke aimlessly, sample ample grapes, avoid rabid-looking dogs, peek through windows. Make a friend, pet a chicken. Taste the *blanco seco*—the local dry wine.

Gradually, zigzag your way up the castle-crowned hill until you reach a little green square called Maradouro de Santa Luzia. Rest here and enjoy the lovely view of the Alfama below you. By now it's noon, and you should be quite hungry (unless you took more than photos in the Alfama market). A block behind Maradouro de Santa Luzia is Largo Rodrigues Freitas, a square with several scruffy, cheap, and very local eateries. Treat yourself to a plate of boiled clams and cockles.

If you climb a few more blocks to the top of the hill, you'll find the ruins of Castelo de São Jorge. From this fortress, which has dominated the city for over a thousand years, you enjoy a commanding view of Portugal's capital city.

After lunch, grab a tram or taxi to Torre de Belem (the Belem Tower). The Belem District, 4 miles from downtown, is a pincushion of important sights from Portugal's Golden Age, when Vasco da Gama and company made her Europe's richest power.

The Belem Tower, built in Manueline style (ornate Portuguese Renaissance) has guarded Lisbon's harbor since 1555. Today it symbolizes the voyages that made her powerful. This was the last sight sailors saw as they left and the first one they'd see when they returned, loaded down with gold, diamonds, and venereal diseases.

Nearby, the giant Monument to the Discoveries honors Portugal's King Henry the Navigator and the country's leading explorers. Across the street, the Monastery of Jeronimos is Portugal's most exciting building—my favorite cloister in Europe. The Manueline style of this giant church and cloister combines Gothic and Renaissance features with motifs from the sea—the source of the wealth that made this art possible.

Spend the evening at a Portuguese bullfight. It's a brutal sport, but the bull lives through it and so will you. The fight starts with an equestrian duel—fast bull against graceful horse and rider. Then the fun starts. A colorfully clad eight-man team enters the ring strung out in a line as if to play leapfrog. The leader taunts El Toro noisily and, with testosterone sloshing everywhere, the bull and the man charge each other. The speeding bull plows into the leader head-on. Then— thud, thud, thud—the raging bull picks up the entire charging crew. The horns are wrapped so no one gets gored—just mashed.

The crew wrestles the bull, who by this time must be wondering where these lemming idiots came from, to a standstill, and one man grabs the bull's tail. Victory is complete when the team leaps off the bull and the man still hanging onto the tail "waterskis" behind the

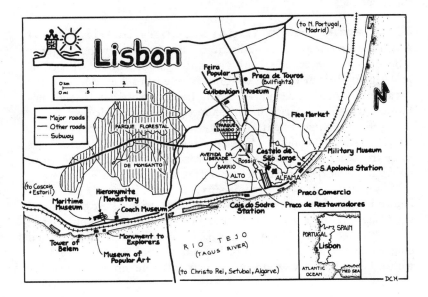

bull. This thrilling display of insanity is repeated with six bulls. After each round, the bruised and battered leader limps a victory lap around the ring. Portugal's top bullring is Lisbon's Capo Pequeño (fights on Thursdays, July-September, other arenas advertise fights most Sundays from Easter to October.)

These are the usual sights; cultural can-cans you can find in any guidebook. But with some imagination, your sightseeing can also include Portugal in action.

Go into a bar as if your poetry teacher sent you there on assignment. Observe, write, talk, try to understand and appreciate; send your senses on a scavenger hunt. The eating, drinking, and socializing rituals are fascinating.

My favorite Lisbon evening was at the Feira Popular, which rages nightly until 1:00 a.m. from May through September (on Ave. da Republica at the Entrecampos metro stop). This popular fair bustles with Portuguese families at play. I ate dinner surrounded by chattering Portuguese families ignoring the ever-present TVs while great platters of fish, meat, fries, salad, and lots of wine paraded frantically in every direction. A 7-year-old boy stood on a chair and sang hauntingly emotional folk songs. With his own dogged clapping, he dragged applause out of the less-than-interested crowd and then passed his shabby hat. All the while, fried ducks drip, barbecues spit, dogs squirt the legs of chairs, and somehow local lovers ignore everything but each other's eyes.

7. Salema, on Portugal's Sunny South Coast

Any place famous as a "last undiscovered tourist frontier" no longer is. The Algarve, Portugal's south coast, disappoints many who come looking for fun in the sun on undeveloped beaches. Most of the Algarve is whitewashed houses, sandy beaches, vacant lots, and sunburned tourists simmering in carbon monoxide and traffic noise.

But the lucky, persistent, or savvy traveler can find places that lack fame, crowds, and condos. There are a few towns where colorful boats share the beach with a colony of sun-worshipers who relax with gusto far from the tacky souvenir racks and package-tour rat race.

The Algarve of your dreams survives—just barely. To catch it before it goes, find a fringe. It took me three tries. West of Lagos, I tried Lux and Burgano, both offering only a corpse of a fishing village, bikini-strangled and Nivea-creamed. Then, just as darkness turned couples into peaceful silhouettes, I found Salema. Any Algarve town with a beach will have tourism, but few mix tourism and realism as

Salema. Catch the Algarve before it's gone.

well as little Salema. Tucked away where a dirt road hits the beach between Lagos and Cape Sagres on Portugal's southwestern tip, Salema is an easy 15-mile bus ride or hitch from the closest train station in Lagos. Don't let the ladies hawking rooms in Lagos waylay you into staying in their city by telling you Salema is full.

Salema has a split personality. Half is a whitewashed old town of scruffy dogs, wide-eyed kids, and fishermen who've seen it all. The other half was built for tourists. The parking lot that separates the jogging shorts from the black shawls becomes a morning market with the horn-tooting arrival of the trucks: a fruit-and-veggies mobile, a rolling meat-and-cheese shop, and the clothing van.

The two worlds pursue a policy of peaceful coexistence. Tractors pull in and push out the fishing boats, 2-year-olds toddle in the waves, topless women read German fashion mags, and old men really do mend the nets. Tourists laze in the sun while locals grab the shade. Dogs roam like they own the place, and a dark, withered granny shells almonds with a railroad spike.

Salema is my kind of beach resort—four restaurants specializing in fresh fish and *vinho verde* (green wine), three hotels, lots of *quartos* (Portuguese bed and breakfasts), the beach, and sun. It's being quietly discovered by British, German, and Back Door connoisseurs of lethargy.

Those in need of activity can hire a local for a 3-hour fishing-boat trip from Salema to Sagres and back with possible swimming stops at desolate beaches along the way (ask John at Pension Mare for specifics). Or, for the best secluded beach in the region, drive to Praia

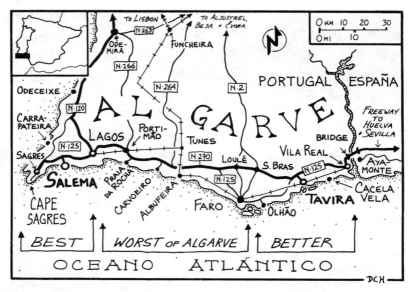

da Castelejo, just north of Cape Sagres (from Villa do Bispo, turn inland and follow the signs for 15 minutes).

So often tourism chases quaint folksiness. And the quaint folks can survive only with the help of tourist dollars. One way a fishing family boosts its income is to rent out a spare bedroom to the ever-growing stream of tan fans from the drizzly north. I arrived at 7:00 p.m. with a group of nine people and saw no "B&B" signs anywhere. I asked some locals, "*Quarto?*" Eyes perked, heads nodded, and I got ten beds in three homes at $10 per person. Quartos line the lane running left from the village center as you face the beach. For specifics, check the Appendix; but it's more fun to ask at the bar. Our rooms were simple, with showers, springy beds, and glorious views of pure paradise. Friendly local smiles assured us that this was the place to be.

As the sun sets, a man catches short fish with a long pole. Behind him is Cape Sagres—the edge of the world 500 years ago. As far as the gang sipping port and piling olive pits in the beachside bar is concerned, it still is.

8. Southern Spain's Pueblos Blancos: Andalusia's Route of the White Villages

When tourists head south from Madrid, it's generally with Granada, Córdoba, Seville, or the Costa del Sol in mind. These big cities have their urban charms but the Costa del Sol is a concrete nightmare,

Estepa, southern Spain

worthwhile only as a bad example. The most Spanish thing about the south coast is the sunshine—but that's everywhere. For something different and more authentic, try exploring the interior of Andalusia along the "route of the white villages."

Make this an exercise in going where no tourist has gone before. If you don't know where you are, you've arrived. I spent several days driving aimlessly from town to village on the back roads of southern Spain, enjoying untouched Spanish culture.

Ronda, straddling an impressive gorge while cradling lots of history, is an entertaining starting point. Nearby you'll find the prehistoric Pileta Caves (open 9:00 a.m.-2:00 p.m. and 4:00-7:00 p.m., a rocky drive or a 2-hour uphill hike from the nearest train station).

Southern Spain

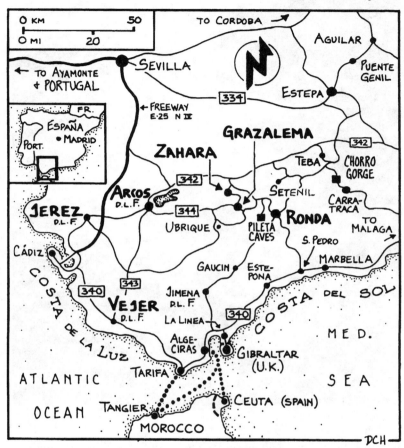

Follow signs to the caves past groves of cork trees to the desolate parking lot. If no one's there, a sign says (in four languages) to "call." Holler down into the valley, and the old man will mosey up, unlock the caves, light the lanterns, and take you on a memorable, hour-long, half-mile journey through the caves. He is a master at hurdling the language barrier, and you'll get a good look at countless natural formations and paintings done by prehistoric *hombres* 25,000 years ago. (That's five times as old as the oldest Egyptian pyramid.) These are crude and faint, but since the famous caves at Altamira are closed, these are the best original Neolithic paintings you'll see in Spain.

From Ronda, the road to Arcos de la Frontera is a charm bracelet of whitewashed villages. In Zahara, climb the ruined castle for a view that would knock Sancho Panza off his ass. Grazalema is ideal for a picnic on its Grand Canyon balcony.

Arcos de la Frontera is a more substantial town with a labyrinthine Old Quarter overlooking a vast plain. Driving through Arcos is about as easy as threading a needle while you're giggling. Spend the night. Climb the church bell tower (possibly with a picnic for the summit). You'll walk right through the caretaker's living room, get the key, leave a tip, and climb to the top. Cover your ears when the giant old clappers whip into action.

Estepa was my Spanish treasure chest. Below a hill crowned with a castle and a convent spreads a freshly-washed and very happy town that fit my dreams of southern Spain.

Situated halfway between Córdoba and Málaga (a 7-mile hitch from the La Roda train station), but light years away from either, Estepa hugs a small hill. Atop the hill is the convent of Santa Clara, worth three stars in any guidebook but found in none. Enjoy the territorial view from the summit, then step into the quiet, spiritual perfection of the church. (If it's locked, find someone with a key.)

The evening is prime time in Estepa. The promenade begins as everyone gravitates to the central square. The spotless streets are polished nightly by the feet of ice-cream-licking strollers. The whole town strolls—it's like "cruising" without cars. Buy an "ice-cream bocadillo" and join in. The town barber, whose shop faces the square, is an artist.

Good information on small-town Andalusia is rare. Little is written on the "Pueblos Blancos." The Michelin Guide, usually invaluable, skips the Andalusian countryside. This area is unvisited, so tourist facilities are limited. Get the best map you can find, ask locals for tips on hotels and touring suggestions, and pick up the *Route of the White Towns* booklet in Seville or at any major Spanish tourist office. (See the Appendix for hotel listings.)

This Andalusian adventure is best by car. Hitching is dreary, and public transportation is pretty bad. Hit the back roads and find that perfect village.

France

9. Alsace and Colmar

The French province of Alsace stands like a flower-child referee between Germany and France. Bounded by the Rhine River on the east and the well-worn Vosges Mountains on the west, this is a lush land of villages, vineyards, ruined castles, twentieth-century war memorials, and an almost naïve cheeriness.

Because of its location, natural wealth, naked vulnerability, and the fact that Germany thinks the mountains are the natural border and France thinks the Rhine River is, nearly every Alsatian generation has weathered an invasion. Centuries as a political pawn between Germany and France has given the Alsace a hybrid culture. Alsatian French is peppered with German words. On doorways of homes, you'll see names like Jacques Schmidt or Dietrich Le Beau. Most locals can swear bilingually. Half-timbered restaurants serve sauerkraut with fine sauces.

Wine is the primary industry, topic of conversation, dominant mouthwash, and perfect excuse for countless festivals, and a tradition providing the foundation for the rest of the Alsatian folk culture.

Alsace's wine road, the Route du Vin, is an asphalt ribbon tying 90 miles of vineyards, villages, and feudal fortresses into an understandably popular tourist package. The dry and sunny climate has produced good wine and happy tourists since Roman days.

During the October harvest season, all Alsace erupts into a carnival of colorful folk costumes, traditional good-time music, and Dionysian smiles. I felt as welcome as a local grape-picker, and my tight sightseeing plans became as hard to follow as a straight line.

If you can pick grapes you can get a job in October. For a hard day in the vineyards, you'll get room and board, $30, and an intimate Alsatian social experience lubricated liberally, logically, by the local wine.

Wine-tasting is popular throughout the year. Roadside *degustation* signs invite you into the wine "caves," where a local producer will serve you all seven Alsatian wines from dry to sweet, with educational commentary if requested. Try Cremant, the Alsatian champagne. Cave-hopping is a great way to spend an afternoon on the Route du Vin. With free tasting and fine $5 bottles, French wine-tasting can be an affordable sport.

Alsace

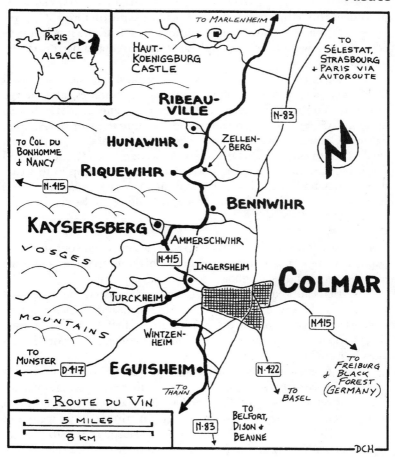

The small caves are fun, but be sure to tour a larger wine co-op. Beer-drinking Germans completely flattened many Alsatian towns in 1944. The small family-run vineyards of these villages sprang back as large, modern, and efficient cooperatives. In the village of Bennwihr, a co-op of 211 people is proud to show you its facilities which can crush 600 tons of grapes a day and turn out 14,000 bottles an hour. No tour ends without taking full advantage of the tasting room. Bennwihr has a wine tradition going back to Roman times. Its name is from the Latin *Benonis Villare*, or "Beno's estate"—and Beno served up a great Riesling.

There's more to Alsace than meets the palate. Those centuries of successful wine production built prosperous and colorful villages. Countless castles capped hilltops to defend the much-invaded plain, and wine wasn't the only art form loved and patronized by local connoisseurs.

Alsatian towns are historic mosaics of gables, fountains, medieval bell towers and gateways, ancient ramparts, churches, and cheery old inns. You'll find plenty of budget one- and two-star hotels (around $35 per double) and ample opportunity to savor the Alsatian cuisine. Colmar is the best home base city. Kaysersberg is the best small town to call home. (Dr. Albert Schweitzer did.) Riquewihr and Eguisheim are the cutest storybook towns to visit. Drop in to a castle or two. Climb the tallest tower and survey Alsace, looking as it has for centuries—a valley of endless vineyards along the Route du Vin.

COLMAR

Colmar, my favorite city in Alsace, sees few American tourists but is popular with Germans and the French. This well-preserved old town of 70,000 is a handy springboard for Alsatian explorations.

Historic beauty, usually a poor excuse to be spared the ravages of World War II, saved Colmar. The American and British military were careful not to bomb the old burghers' half-timbered houses, characteristic red- and green-tiled roofs, and cobbled lanes of Alsace's most beautiful city.

Today Colmar not only survives, it thrives—with historic buildings, impressive art treasures, and a cuisine that attracts eager palates from all over Europe. And Colmar has that special French talent of being great but cozy at the same time. Antique shops welcome browsers, and hotel managers run down the sleepy streets to pick up fresh croissants in time for breakfast. Schoolgirls park their rickety horse-carriages in front of the city hall, ready to give visitors a $4 clip-clop tour of the old town.

Colmar offers heavyweight sights in a warm, small-town package. By the end of the Middle Ages, the walled town was a thriving trade center filled with rich old houses. The wonderfully restored tanners' quarters is a quiver of tall, narrow, half-timbered buildings. Its confused rooftops struggled erratically to get enough sun to dry their animal skins. Nearby you'll find "La Petite Venise," complete with canals and a pizzeria.

Colmar combines its abundance of art with a knack for showing it off. The artistic geniuses Grunewald, Schongauer, and Bartholdi all called Colmar home.

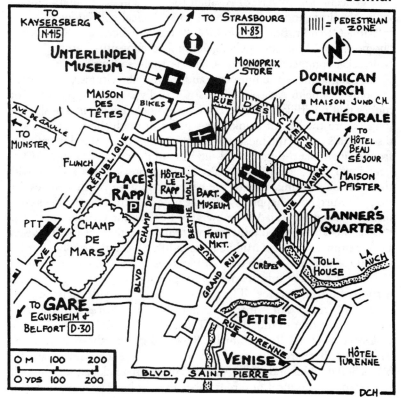

Colmar

Frederic Bartholdi, who created our Statue of Liberty a century ago, adorned his hometown with many fine, if smaller, statues. Don't miss the little Bartholdi museum, offering a good look at the artist's life and some fun Statue of Liberty trivia.

Four hundred years earlier, Martin Schongauer was the leading local artist. His *Virgin of the Rose Garden* could give a state trooper goose bumps. Looking fresh and crisp, it's set magnificently in a Gothic Dominican church. I sat with a dozen people, silently, as if at a symphony, as Schongauer's *Madonna* performed solo on center stage. Lit by fourteenth-century stained glass, its richness and tenderness cradled me in a Gothic sweetness that no textbook could explain. Even if your sightseeing has worked you to the point where you "never want to see another Madonna and Child," give this one a chance.

The Unterlinden Museum, one of my favorite small museums, is housed in a 750-year-old convent next to the tourist office. It has the best collection anywhere of Alsatian folk art and art exhibits ranging from Neolithic and Gallo-Roman archaeological collections to works by Monet, Renoir, Braque, and Picasso. It's a medieval and Renaissance "home show." You can lose yourself in a seventeenth-century Alsatian wine cellar complete with presses, barrels, tools, and aromas.

The highlight of the museum (and for me, the city) is Grunewald's gripping Isenheim Altarpiece. This is actually a series of paintings on hinges that pivot like shutters. Designed to help people in a hospital— long before the age of painkillers—suffer through their horrible skin diseases, it's one of the most powerful paintings ever. Stand petrified in front of it and let the agony and suffering of the crucifixion drag its fingers down your face. Just as you're about to break down and sob with those in the painting, turn to the happy ending—a psychedelic explosion of resurrection happiness. It's like jumping from the dentist's chair directly into a Jacuzzi. We know very little about Grunewald except that his work has played tetherball with human emotions for 500 years. For a reminder that the Middle Ages didn't have a monopoly on grief, stop at the museum's cloth copy of Picasso's famous *Guernica*.

Colmar's tourist information office provides city maps, guides, and a room-finding service. They can also suggest side trips around Alsace's "wine road," into Germany's Black Forest and nearby Freiburg or a tour of the Maginot Line.

I sleep at Hotel-Restaurant Le Rapp (16 rue Berthe-Molly, tel. 89 41 62 10). Bernard, the owner, is a perfect French gentleman. He offers $60 doubles and classy Alsatian cuisine in an elegant dining hall.

For maximum local fun, remember that Colmar goes crazy during its winefest (August) and Sauerkraut Days (two weekends in September). Feasting, dancing, music, and wine—Alsatian-style.

10. From France to Italy over Mt. Blanc

Europe's ultimate mountain lift towers high above the tourist-choked French resort town of Chamonix. Ride the Aiguille du Midi *telepherique* (gondola) to the dizzy 12,600-foot-high tip of a rock needle. As you get in, remind yourself that this thing has been going back and forth now since 1954; surely it'll make it one more time. Chamonix shrinks as trees fly by, soon replaced by whizzing rocks, ice, and snow until you reach the top. Up there, even sunshine is cold. The air is thin. People are giddy. Fun things can happen if you're not too winded to join locals in the Halfway-to-Heaven tango.

Before you spread the Alps. In the distance is the bent little Matterhorn. You can almost reach out and pat the head of Mont Blanc, at 15,781 feet, Europe's highest point.

Alps from atop the Aiguille du Midi, 12,600 feet up

Next, for Europe's most exciting border crossing, get into the tiny red gondola and head south. Dangle silently for 40 minutes as you glide over the glacier to Italy. Squeeze out your porthole, exploring every corner of your view. You're sailing a new sea.

Show your passport at Hellbronner point (11,000 feet) and descend into the remote Italian Valle d'Aosta. It's a whole different world.

Your starting point for this adventure is Chamonix, a convenient overnight train ride from Paris. Chamonix is a resort town—packed and pricey. Like Interlaken, it's a springboard for mountain-worshipers. The town has an efficient and energetic tourist information center and plenty of reasonable beds, including several chalets offering $10 to $15 dorm beds.

From Chamonix, there are days of hikes and cable car rides. The best hikes are opposite the most staggering peaks on the Gran Balcon Sud. Gran Balcon Sud lifts go from Chamonix into a world of pristine lakes, great Mont Blanc range views, and parasailers lunging off the cliff from the Brevent lift station. Watching these daredevils fill the valley like spaced-out butterflies is a thrilling spectator sport. Probably the best easy hike—two hours each way—is from the top of the Flegere lift to Lac Blanc.

If you came only to take the ultimate ride, ride that *telepherique* to the Aiguille du Midi. This lift (about $35 round-trip, daily, 6:00 a.m.-5:00 p.m. in the summer, shorter hours off-season) is Europe's highest

Chamonix and Alpine Crossing from France to Italy

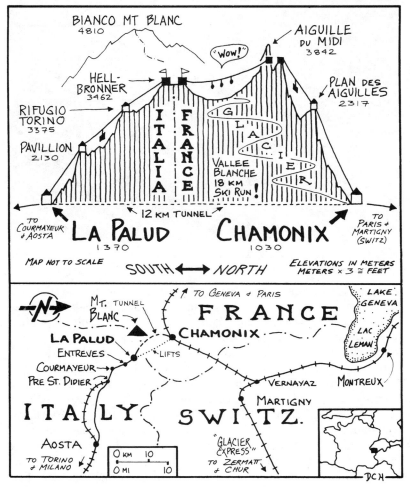

and most spectacular. If the weather is good, forget your budget. (The youth hostel gives 25% discount coupons.) Afternoons are most likely clouded and crowded. In August, the busiest time, ride by 7:00 a.m. to avoid miserable delays. If you plan to dilly-dally, ride directly to your farthest point and do so on your return.

To both save a little money and enjoy a hike, buy a ticket all the way up, but only halfway back down. This gives you a chance to look down at the Alps and over at the summit of Mont Blanc from your

Dangle silently for 40 minutes as you glide over the glacier from France to Italy (Photo by Andrea Hagg)

lofty 12,600-foot lookout. Then you descend to the halfway point, where you're free to frolic in the glaciers and hike back to Chamonix at your leisure.

From the top of Aiguille du Midi, you can continue over the mountain to Italy. It's a long trip; the last departure is at 4:00 p.m. The descent from Hellbronner Point (about $16) takes you into the remote Italian Valle d'Aosta, where a dash of France and a splash of Switzerland blend with the already rich Italian flavor and countless castles to give you an easy-to-like first taste of Italy.

The town of Aosta, your best valley home base, is a 2-hour bus ride (hourly departures, change in Courmayeur) from the base of the lift in La Palud. If a fellow cable-car passenger has a car parked in La Palud, charm yourself a ride to Aosta.

"The Rome of the Alps," as Aosta is called, has many Roman ruins and offers a great introduction to the fine points of Italian life—cappuccino, gelati, and a busy evening stroll or *passegio*. The popular and inexpensive Ulisse Restaurant at Via Ed. Aubert 58 has great pizza. An evening here watching Italy stroll by is a fine way to ease into *la dolce vita*.

Chamonix, Aiguille du Midi, and the Valle d'Aosta—surely a high point in anyone's European vacation.

Germany, Austria, and Switzerland

11. Rothenburg and the Romantic Road: From the Rhine to Bavaria through Germany's Medieval Heartland

Connect the castles of the Rhine and the lederhosen charm of Bavaria by traveling Germany's "Romantische Strasse." Along the Romantic Road (and especially just off it, where no unfamiliar car passes unnoticed and flower boxes decorate the unseen sides of barns), visitors find the Germany most come to see. Church-steeple masts sail seas of rich, rolling farmland, and fragrant villages invite you to slow down. At each village, ignore the signposts and ask an old woman for directions to the next town—just to hear her voice and enjoy the energy in her eyes. Thousands of tourists pass through. Few stop to chat.

The Romantic Road, peppered with pretty towns today because it was such an important and prosperous trade route 600 years ago, is no secret. But even with its crowds, it's a must.

A car gives you complete freedom to explore Germany's medieval heartland—just follow the green Romantische Strasse signs. The most scenic sections are from Bad Mergentheim to Rothenburg (in the north) and from Landsberg to Füssen (in the south). Those without wheels can ride the convenient Europabus tour. From April through October, Romantic Road buses run daily between Frankfurt and Munich, and Frankfurt and Füssen. The ride is free with your Eurailpass. Otherwise, the bus from Munich to Frankfurt costs about $60 (the same as a second-class train ticket). The trip takes 11 hours, including three hours off the bus to explore the fairy-tale towns of Rothenburg and Dinkelsbühl. You can break your journey anywhere along the road and catch the same bus the next day. Ticket reservations are necessary only for summer weekends from Wurzburg or Füssen (tel. 069/790 3256 one day in advance).

Whenever you're traveling, lay the groundwork for your smooth

Germany's Romantic Road

departure upon arrival. For instance, when you get to the Rhine (near Frankfurt), Munich or Füssen, ask at the train or tourist information office exactly where and when the Romantische Strasse bus leaves the next morning and if a reservation is advisable. Then you'll wake up on departure morning and calmly step onto the bus to begin one of the best days of your trip.

The Romantic Road bus drivers are often characters, some likable, some not. Some know everyone they pass, waving and happily greeting people all day long. Others stoke rumors that Eva Braun lives. At Donauworth, as the bus crosses the baby Donau (Danube), the driver will slip in his cassette of "The Blue Danube Waltz." The group on board loosens up, and you have time to talk to the other travelers and build some friendships. This isn't just any bus ride.

ROTHENBURG

Of the many lovable little towns along the Romantic Road, Rothenburg is the most lovable. This is probably the most touristy town in Germany but it's your best possible look at a medieval town. In the Middle Ages, when Frankfurt and Munich were just wide spots in the road, Rothenburg was Germany's second-largest city with a whopping population of 6,000. Today, it's her best-preserved medieval walled town, enjoying tremendous tourist popularity without losing its charm.

Romantic Road bus-tourists get only a short break to roam. Here's Rothenburg's best 90 minutes: the bus drops you at the train station, a few blocks outside the wall. The street from the station leads to the nearest town gate, Rödertor. Climb Rödertor for a fine town view and an interesting display on World War II damage. From there, follow the cobbles to the Market Square (tourist information office). Continue straight down Herrengasse (lined with the mansions of the richest townsmen, or "Herren") to the Castle Garden for fine views of the "Tauber Riviera." You may have a few minutes left to see the Riemenschneider altarpiece in St. Jacob's Church, visit the town history museum under the tower just off the Market Square, or shop.

By this time, any normal person will have decided that, when it comes to Germany's many cute small towns, monogamy is the best policy. Leave the bus, spend the night, and love only Rothenburg. (Rooms are listed in the Appendix.) But if you've got more willpower than common sense, shop and eat your way back through the town center to your bus in time to carry on down the Romantic Road.

Those spending the night in Europe's most exciting medieval town enjoy Rothenburg without its daily hordes of big city day-trippers and risk actually hearing the sounds of the Thirty Years War still echoing through the turrets and clock towers.

Too often, Rothenburg brings out the shopper in visitors before they've had a chance to appreciate the historic city. True, this is a great place to do your German shopping (visit friendly Anneliese Friese's shop, two doors left of the tourist office—10% discount with this book and the best money exchange rates in town), but first see the town. The tourist information office on the Market Square offers guided tours in English (each afternoon at 1:30 and with the more colorful night watchman evenings at 8:00, about $2). A local historian, usually an intriguing character, brings the ramparts alive. A thousand years of history are packed between the cobbles.

After your walking-tour orientation, you'll have plenty of sightseeing ideas. The mile-and-a-half walk around Rothenburg's medieval wall offers great views—especially before breakfast or at sunset. For the best view of the town and surrounding countryside, make the rigorous but rewarding climb to the top of the Town Hall Tower. The friendly ticket-taker on top speaks more Japanese than English, an interesting sign of the touristic times.

Rothenburg's fascinating Medieval Crime and Punishment Museum is full of legal bits and diabolical pieces, instruments of punishment and torture, and even an iron cage—complete with a metal nag gag—all unusually well-explained in English.

St. Jacob's Church contains the one must-see art treasure in town, a glorious 500-year-old altarpiece by Riemenschneider, the Michelangelo of German wood-carvers. Pick up the free brochure that explains the church's art treasures and head upstairs behind the organ for Germany's greatest piece of wood carving.

To hear the birds and smell the cows, take a walk through the Tauber Valley. The trail leads downhill from Rothenburg's idyllic castle gardens to a cute, skinny 600-year-old castle, the summer home of Mayor Toppler. It's intimately furnished and well worth a look. On the top floor, notice the photo of bombed-out 1945 Rothenburg. From here, walk past the covered bridge and trout-filled Tauber to the sleepy village of Detwang, which is actually older than Rothenburg and has a church with another impressive Riemenschneider altarpiece.

Rothenburg's well-preserved medieval sister is Dinkelsbühl, an hour to the south. Old walls, towers, gateways, and the peaceful green waters of the moat defend its medieval architecture from the 20th century. The Romantic Road bus also makes a short stop here to grab a quick bite or to explore, camera in hand, the old cobbled streets. Dinkelsbühl celebrates its colorfully medieval Kinderfest, Children's Festival, in mid-July (from the weekend before the third Monday through the weekend after).

The Romantic Road has much more. If you order now, you'll get Würzburg, with its fine baroque Prince Bishop's Residenz—the Versailles of Franconia—and its oh-wow baroque chapel. You can see another lovely carved altarpiece by Riemenschneider (with the unique thimble museum across the street) a mile from Creglingen. To the south is the flamboyant Wies Church, near Oberammergau, and Mad King Ludwig's Disneyesque Neuschwanstein Castle near Füssen.

The Romantic Road—a quick, comfortable, and inexpensive way to see two of Germany's most beautiful towns—is the best way to connect the Rhine and Bavaria.

12. Hallstatt, in Austria's Commune-with-Nature Lakes District

With the longest life span and one of the shortest work weeks in Europe, Austrians are experts at good living. They focus their free time on the fine points of life: music, a stroll, pastry, and a good cup of coffee. The uniquely Austrian *gemütlichkeit* (as difficult to translate as it is to pronounce, meaning something like a warm, cozy, friendly, focus-on-the-moment feeling) is something even whirlwind tourists pick up in the Salzkammergut Lakes District, where big-city Austrians go to relax.

Far from the urban rat race, though just 60 minutes from Salzburg, this is the perfect place to commune with nature, Austrian-style. The Salzkammergut is a lushly forested playground dotted with cottages. Trains, buses, or boats lead the traveler through gentle mountains and shy lakes, winding from relaxed village to relaxed village.

The Salzkammergut's pride and joy is the town of Hallstatt. The minute it popped into view, I knew Hallstatt was my Alpine Oz. It's just the right size (1,200 people), wonderfully remote—and almost traffic-free. A tiny ferry takes you from the nearest train station across the fjord-like lake and drops you off on the town's storybook square.

Hallstatt, in Austria's Salzkammergut Lakes District (Photo: David C. Hoerlein)

Hallstatt

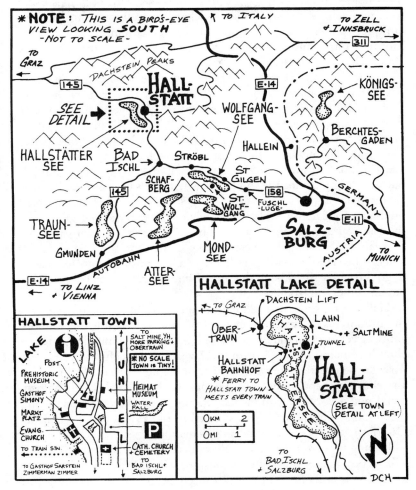

Bullied onto its lakeside ledge by a selfish mountain, Hallstatt seems tinier than it is. Its pint-sized square is surrounded by ivy-covered guest houses and cobbled lanes. It's a toy town. You can tour it on foot in about 10 minutes.

Except in August, when tourist crowds trample most of Hallstatt's charm, there's no shortage of pleasant $15-per-person *Zimmer* (bed and breakfast places). I splurge for an creaky old hotel, spending $50 for a double with breakfast in the Gasthof Simony (tel. 06134/231).

This hotel separates the square from the lake, with balconies over-looking each. My rustic room had hardwood floors, rag rugs, an antique wooden bed with a matching free-standing closet, grand-mother lamps, and a lakeside, flower-decked balcony. The view almost changed my itinerary.

Three thousand years ago, this area was the salt-mining capital of Europe. An economic and cultural boom put this area on the map back in Flintstone times. In fact, an entire 1,000-year chapter in the story of Europe is called "The Hallstatt Period." A humble museum next to the tourist office shows off Hallstatt's salty past. For a better look, you can tour the world's first salt mine, located a thrilling funic-ular ride above downtown Hallstatt. You'll dress up in an old miner's outfit, ride trains into the mountain where the salt was mined, cruise subterranean lakes, scream down long sliver-free banisters, and read brief and dry English explanations while very entertaining guides tell the fascinating story in German. There are several similar salt mine tours in the Salzburg/Innsbruck area. They're fun but cost about $8 and can be crowded with long lines. While they are the major reason to go through a turnstile in this area, I find them marginally worth the money, time, and trouble.

Hallstatt outgrew its little ledge, and many of its buildings climb the mountainside, with street level on one side being three floors above street level on the other. Land is limited—so limited that, in the church cemetery, bones got only 12 years of peaceful subterranean darkness before making way for those of the newly dead. The result is a fascinating chapel of decorated bones. Each skull is lovingly named, dated, and decorated, with the men getting ivy and the women getting rose motifs. This practice was stopped in the 1960s, about when the Catholic Church began permitting cremation.

Passing time in and around Hallstatt is easy. The little tourist office will recommend a hike—the 9,000-foot Mt. Dachstein looms over-head—or a peaceful cruise in a rented canoe. Most people go to Hallstatt simply to relax, eat, shop and stroll. To cloak yourself in the *gemütlich* cobblestones, flowers, and rich blues and greens of Austria's Salzkammergut Lakes District, visit Hallstatt.

13. Hall, in the Shadow of Innsbruck

It's a brisk mountain morning in the Tirolean town of Hall. Merchants in aprons hustle, and roses, peppers, and pears fill their tidy street-side stalls, competing for my photograph. There's not a tourist in sight. They're all 5 miles up the river, in Innsbruck. Just as

The village of Hall near Innsbruck

Hallstatt is the small-town escape from Salzburg, Hall is the place to go if you want the natural surroundings of Innsbruck without the big city.

Hall was a rich salt-mining center when Innsbruck was just a humble bridge (*bruck*) town on the Inn River. Sprawling Innsbruck's tourist industry crowds into its tiny medieval town center. Hall, a tiny village in comparison, actually has a bigger old center. Its rich bundle of old pastel buildings and cobbled streets feels refreshingly real—too real if you're trying to accomplish anything more than a leisurely lunch between noon and 2:00, when everything closes.

The tourist office organizes daily walking tours—in English when necessary. The luxurious Tirolean baroque church, the elegant architecture lining the streets, and 500-year-old mint (which lets visitors make a coin the traditional way) combine to make it clear that in its day, Hall was a local powerhouse.

Back when salt was money, Hall was loaded. You can tour salt mines near Hall in places like Hallein and Hallstatt ("Hall" means salt). Hall has a quicker, cheaper, and easier alternative—its Bergbaumuseum. Tours are given daily of the town's reconstructed salt mine, complete with pits, shafts, drills, tools, and—the climax of any salt mine tour—the slippery wooden slide. It feels like a real mine.

Give your trip a memorable splash by spending a sunny afternoon at Hall's magnificent Freischwimmbad. This huge outdoor swimming

Innsbruck and Hall

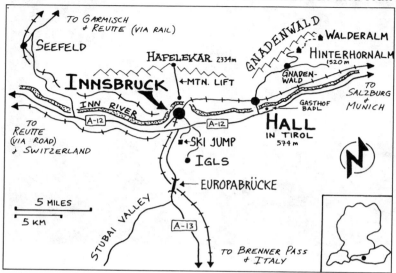

pool has four diving boards, a giant lap pool, and a kiddies' pool bigger than anything in my hometown, bordered by a lush garden, a sauna, a mini-golf course, and lounging locals.

The same mountains that put Innsbruck on the vacation map surround Hall. For a lazy look at life in the high Alps, drive up to 5,000-foot-high Hinterhornalm and walk to a remote working farm.

Begin your ascent in Gnadenwald, a chalet-filled suburb sandwiched between Hall and its Alps. Pay $4 and pick up a brochure at the toll hut. Then wind your way upward, marveling at the crazy amount of energy put into this remote road, to a parking lot at the rustic Hinterhornalm Berg restaurant. This place serves hearty food and offers three simple double rooms ($30) and a precarious dorm hut or "lager" with $10 beds and a cliff-hanger of a view (tel. 05223/2170, crowded on summer weekends, closed by avalanches from November to April). Hinterhornalm is a hang-gliding springboard. On sunny days it's a butterfly nest of thrill-seekers ready to fly.

It's a level 20-minute stroll from the restaurant to the Walderalm farm (see photo in Hiking section, Chapter 3) where you are welcome to wander around a working dairy farm that shares its meadow with the clouds. Cows ramble along ridge-top lanes surrounded by cut-glass peaks. The lady of the farm serves hot soup, Alpine snacks, and drinks (very fresh milk in the afternoon) on rough plank tables. In the distance below, you can almost see the Inn River Valley autobahn bringing all the tour buses into Innsbruck.

14. The Berner Oberland: The Alps in Your Lap

Switzerland offers Europe's most spectacular mountain scenery. There was a time when the only thing higher than those Alpine peaks was the prices you had to pay to see them. Switzerland has enjoyed a very low inflation rate, and today, it's no more expensive than its neighbors. Switzerland does suffer from tourist crowds, however, and you should keep this in mind when you choose your Swiss destination. How do you see the best of the Swiss Alps without enduring traffic jams and congested trails? The answer is twofold: Sleep in Gimmelwald, and ride the lifts and hike around Kleine Scheidegg, the Jungfrau, and the Schilthorn.

KLEINE SCHEIDEGG—THE MONA LISA OF MOUNTAIN VIEWS

I had always considered Interlaken overrated. Now I understand that Interlaken is only a jumping-off point—the gateway to the Alps. Stop in Interlaken for shopping, banking, post, and telephone chores, and to pick up information on the region. Then head south, into the Berner Oberland.

You have several options. Vagabonds who just dropped in on the overnight train (ideal from Paris) you can do a loop trip, going down

Thrill-seeking hang gliders are a common sight on Alpine peaks. Here, an absent-minded hang glider prepares for his last takeoff.

The Berner Oberland

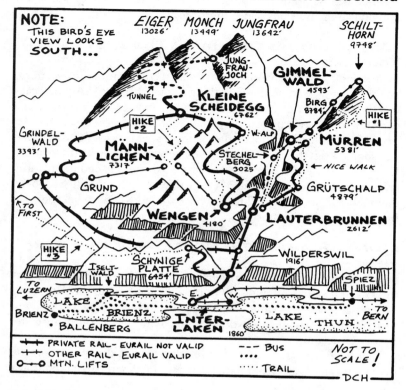

NOTE:
THIS BIRD'S EYE
VIEW LOOKS
SOUTH...

EIGER MONCH JUNGFRAU
13026'   13449'   13642'

SCHILT-
HORN
9748'

JUNG-
FRAU-
JOCH

GIMMEL-
WALD
4593'

TUNNEL

KLEINE
SCHEIDEGG
6762'

BIRG
8784'

HIKE
#1

GRINDEL-
WALD
3393'

MÄNN-
LICHEN
7317'

HIKE
#2

W-ALP

MÜRREN
5381'

← NICE WALK

STECHEL-
BERG
3025

GRUND

GRÜTSCHALP
4879'

→TO
FIRST

WENGEN
+180'

LAUTERBRUNNEN
2612'

HIKE
#3

ISELT-
WALD

SCHYNIGE
PLATTE
6454'

WILDERSWIL
1916'

TO
LUZERN

SPIEZ

LAKE

BRIENZ
BRIENZ

INTER-
LAKEN
1860'

LAKE
THUN

TO
BERN

BALLENBERG

+—+— PRIVATE RAIL- EURAIL NOT VALID
+—+— OTHER RAIL- EURAIL VALID
O—O MTN. LIFTS

— — — BUS
····· TRAIL

NOT TO
SCALE!

—DCH—

Grindelwald Valley, over the Kleine Scheidegg ridge and then into our target, Lauterbrunnen. From there you can head on out by returning to Interlaken or settle into Gimmelwald for the Alpine cuddle after the climax. Those with more time and less energy will get set up in Gimmelwald and ride up to Kleine Scheidegg from Lauterbrunnen, skipping Grindelwald.

Loop trippers should get an early start and catch the private train from the Interlaken East Station (not covered by your Eurailpass) to Grindelwald. Don't sleep in heavily-touristed Grindelwald. Take advantage of its well-informed tourist information office. Browse through the pricey tourist shops. Buy a first-class mountain picnic at the Co-op grocery store. Then ascend by train into a wonderland of powerful white peaks to Kleine Scheidegg, or even higher by gondola to Männlichen (discounted with Eurail). It's an easy 1-hour walk from Männlichen down to Kleine Scheidegg.

Now you have successfully run the gauntlet of tourist traps and reached the ultimate. Before you towers Switzerland's greatest mountain panorama. The Jungfrau, the Mönch, and the Eiger boldly proclaim that they are the greatest. You won't argue.

Like a saddle on the ridge, Kleine Scheidegg gives people something to hang onto. It has a lodge (with cheap dorm bunks) and an outdoor restaurant. People gather here to marvel at tiny rock climbers—many of them quite dead— dangling by ropes halfway up the icy Eiger. You can splurge for the expensive ride from here to the towering Jungfraujoch ($50 round-trip from Kleine Scheidegg; early and late rides are discounted; expect crowd-control problems on sunny summer days, especially after a stretch of bad weather). The ride's impressive, but I couldn't have asked for more than the *Mona Lisa* of mountain views which I enjoyed from Kleine Scheidegg.

From Kleine Scheidegg, start your hike into the less touristed Lauterbrunnen Valley. The hike is not difficult. My gear consisted only of shorts (watch the mountain sun), tennis shoes, a tourist brochure map, and a bib to catch the drool.

It's lunchtime as you hike into your own peaceful mountain world. Find a grassy perch and your picnic will have an alpine ambience that no restaurant could match. Continuing downhill, you may well be all alone and singing to the rhythm of your happy footsteps. The gravelly walk is steep in places, and you can abbreviate it by catching the train at one of two stations you'll pass along the way. As the scenery changes, new mountains replace the ones you've already seen. After two hours, you enter the traffic-free town of Wengen. Avoid the steep, dull hike from Wengen to Lauterbrunnen by taking the $3 train down to the valley floor, where you can continue by bus and gondola or funicular and train to the village of Gimmelwald.

This is the scenic but very roundabout way to Gimmelwald. For a much more direct route, take the train direct from Interlaken-East to Lauterbrunnen. Once you're set up, Gimmelwald becomes your springboard for Alpine fun.

GIMMELWALD—WHERE HEIDI LIVES

The traffic-free village of Gimmelwald hangs nonchalantly on the edge of a cliff high above the floor of the Lauterbrunnen Valley, 30 minutes by car or train south of Interlaken. It's a sleepy village with more cows ringing bells than people. Small avalanches on the almost-touchable mountain wall across the valley look and sound like distant waterfalls. The songs of birds and brooks, and the

Downtown, traffic-free Gimmelwald. "If Heaven isn't what it's cracked up to be, send me back to Gimmelwald."

crunchy march of happy hikers constantly remind you why so many travelers say, "If Heaven isn't what it's cracked up to be, send me back to Gimmelwald."

When told you're visiting Gimmelwald, Swiss people assume you mean the famous resort in the next valley, Grindelwald. When assured that Gimmelwald is your target, they lean forward, widen their eyes, and ask, "Und how do you know about Gimmelvald?"

The village of Gimmelwald, an ignored station on the spectacular Schilthorn gondola (of James Bond fame), should be built up to the hilt. But it's classified "avalanche zone"—too dangerous for serious building projects. So while developers gnash their teeth, sturdy peasants continue milking cows and making hay, surviving in a modern world only by the grace of a government that subsidizes such poor traditional industries. Those who brave the possible avalanches (or visit in the summer when there's no snow) enjoy the Alps in their laps in a Swiss world that looks and lives the way every traveler dreams it might.

Since it allows no cars, there are only two ways to get to Gimmelwald. Drivers park (free and safe) in Stechelberg at the far end of Lauterbrunnen Valley and catch the $3 gondola. Others can catch the bus from Lauterbrunnen to Stechelberg (best choice in the rain). The more scenic but complicated option is to take the

Lauterbrunnen-Grutschalp funicular (a small train) up the steep wall and catch the scenic train (called the *panorama fahrt* in German) to the resort town of Mürren. From Mürren, Gimmelwald is a pleasant 30-minute downhill walk.

Sleep in Gimmelwald's very rugged youth hostel ($6/bed) or at the storybook chalet called Hotel Mittaghorn ($45/double with breakfast). Gimmelwald's shacky hostel is the loosest and friendliest hostel I've ever fallen in love with. Every day its Alps-happy family of hostelers adopts newcomers, filling them with spaghetti and mountain stories. High in the Alps, this relaxed hostel is struggling to survive. Please treat it with loving care, respect its rules (and elderly Lena, who runs the place), and leave it cleaner than when you found it (tel. 036/551704). Since Gimmelwald has no grocery store, you may want to pack in food.

Up the hill is the treasure of Gimmelwald. Walter Mittler, the perfect Swiss gentleman, runs a creaky chalet called Hotel Mittaghorn. It's a classic Alpine-style place with a million-dollar view of the Jungfrau Alps. Walter is careful not to let his place get too hectic or big and enjoys sensitive Back Door travelers. He's a great but occasional cook and runs his hotel alone, keeping it simple but with class. Since he's often booked up, call Walter well in advance at 036/551658. Hotel Mittaghorn is about the last building at the top of the town on the service road to Mürren. (More rooms are listed in the Appendix.)

Evening fun in Gimmelwald is found in the hostel (lots of young Alp-aholic hikers and a good chance to share information on the surrounding mountains) and, depending on Walter's mood, at Hotel Mittaghorn. If you're staying at Walter's, don't miss his dinner or his coffee schnapps. Then sit on the porch and watch the sun lick the mountaintops to bed as the moon rises over the Jungfrau.

From Gimmelwald, ride the gondola up the Schilthorn ($40 round-trip), a 10,000-foot peak capped by Piz Gloria, a revolving restaurant. The early gondola is discounted and includes a hearty continental breakfast. (Walter has special tickets.)

After watching clips from *On Her Majesty's Secret Service*, showing Piz Gloria getting blown up (free, in the theater below the restaurant), go outside for the real thrills. Frolic on the ridge. If you want to hike down, the first 300 yards are the most difficult. The easiest descent is just to the right of the cable car as you face down. The 3-hour hike drops 5,000 feet. If this is too thrilling, ride the gondola back down to Birg (the midway station), and enjoy an easier (but still steep) hike from Birg back to Gimmelwald from there. To leave this Alpine wonderland, take the lift back down to Stechelberg, and catch a bus to Interlaken.

If you're interested in the Alpine cream of Switzerland, it's best seen from Kleine Scheidegg. If you're looking for Heidi and an orchestra of cowbells in a Switzerland that most people think exists only in storybooks—take off your boots in Gimmelwald.

15. Offbeat Alps

Even those who know a Rocky Mountain high find something special about the Alps. In the Alps, nature and civilization mix it up comfortably, as if man and mountain shared the same crib. You can hike from France to Slovenia, finding a hut or remote village for each overnight, and never come out of the mountains. Many times, you'll walk to the haunting accompaniment of long, legato alphorns. And often, just when you need it most, there will be a mechanical lift to whisk you silently and effortlessly—if not cheaply—to the top of that staggering ridge or peak, where your partner can snap a photo of you looking ruggedly triumphant. You'll pass happy yodelers, sturdy grannies, and pony-tailed, dirndl-skirted, singing families. The consistently cheery greetings make passing hikers a fun part of any trek.

While the most famous corners are now solidly in the domain of tour groups, much of the best Alpine charm is folded away in no-name valleys, often just over the ridge from the Holiday Inns and the canned culture on stage.

Here are a few places and activities that will make your Alpine adventures more than a lovely hike.

Extremely remote but accessible by car (barely) is the village of **Taveyanne** in the French-speaking part of Switzerland, 2 miles off the road from Col de la Croix to Villars (or take the footpath from Villars). It's just a jumble of log cabins and snoozing cows stranded all alone at 5,000 feet. The only business in town is the Refuge de Taveyanne, where the Siebenthal family serves hearty meals—great fondue and a delicious *croute au fromage avec oeuf* for $8—in a prize-winning, rustic setting: no electricity, low-beamed ceilings, huge charred fireplace with a cannibal-sized caldron, prehistoric cash register, and well-hung ornamental cowbells. For a memorable experience (and the only rentable beds in the village) consider sleeping in their primitive loft—never full, five mattresses, accessible by a ladder outside, urinate with the cows ($5, May-October, tel. 025/681947).

In western Austria, south of Reutte, lies a treat for those who sus-

There's more than one way to get down an Alp

pect they may have been Kit Carson in a previous life. **Fallerschein** is an isolated log-cabin village, smothered in Alpine goodness. Drop into its flower-speckled world of serene slopes, lazy cows, and musical breezes. Thunderstorms roll down this valley like it's God's bowling alley, but the blissfully simple pint-sized church on the high ground seems to promise that this huddle of houses will remain standing. The people sitting on benches are Austrian vacationers or clandestine lovers who've rented cabins. Fallerschein is notorious as a hideaway for those having affairs. For a rugged chunk of local Alpine peace, spend a night in the local Matratzen lager (simple dorm loft), Almwirtscheft Fallerschein (open June-September, $6 per night, 27 beds and one outhouse, good meals, tel. 05678/5142). Fallerschein is 4,000 feet high at the end of a miserable 1-mile fit-for-jeep-or-rental-car-only gravel road near Namlos on the Berwang road south of Reutte in Austria's Tirol. (To avoid cow damage, park 300 yards below the village at the tiny lot below the bridge.)

The **Sommerrodelbahn** is one of the great Alpine experiences. Several Alpine ski slopes are outfitted with concrete bobsled courses. Local speed demons spend entire summer days riding chair lifts up to "luge" down on oversized skateboards. You sit with a brake stick between your legs. Push to go fast. Pull to stop. There's a Sommerrodelbahn at Chamonix in France, one south of Salzburg, and two in Tirol off the Fernpass road—one halfway between Reutte and Lermoos, the other just past Biberwier in the shadow of the gray and powerful Zugspitze (Germany's tallest mountain). Luge courses are normally open daily in the summer from 8:30 a.m. to 5:00 p.m. unless it's wet. The Biberwier luge is the longest in Austria—4,000 feet. The concrete course banks on the corners and even a first-timer can go very, very fast. Most are careful their first run and really rip on their second. To avoid a slow-healing souvenir, keep both hands on your stick. You'll rumble, windblown and smile-creased, into the finish line with one thought on your mind—"Do it again!"

For a slower but just as invigorating activity, join the people of **Bern** for a midday float through their city on the Aare River. The lunchtime float is a popular tradition in the Swiss capital. Local merchants, legislators, publishers, and students, proud of their clean river and their basic ruddiness, grab every hot summer opportunity to enjoy this wet and refreshing *paseo*. Join the locals in the ritual 20-minute hike upstream from the Swiss National Parliament building, then float playfully or sleepily back down to the excellent and free riverside baths and pool (Aarebad). If the river is a bit much, spectating is fun, and you're welcome to enjoy just the pool.

Switzerland's Appenzell is a region whose forte is cow culture rather than staggering peaks. It has one famous mountain, the 8,200-

A Swiss cliffhanger of a hideaway: Berggasthaus Ascher on Ebenalp

foot-high Sântis Peak. For a fun angle on Alpine culture, go 5 miles south of Appenzell town, to Wasserauen, where you can ride the lift to the top of nearby **Ebenalp** ($12 round-trip). From its summit, enjoy a sweeping view of a major chunk of Switzerland. Then hike down about 15 minutes to a prehistoric cave home (its tiny museum is always open). Wander in and through until you reach a narrow, sunny ledge. Perched here is the Wildkirchli, a 400-year-old cave church, which housed hermit monks from 1658 to 1853, and a 100-year-old guest house, Berggasthaus Ascher, clinging precariously to the cliffside. This rugged guest house was originally built to house those who came here to pray with the hermit monk.

Rather than sleep in the unmemorable town of Appenzell, stay in the Berggasthaus Ascher ($8 per dorm bed, blankets but no sheets required or provided, $7 breakfast, Family Knechtle-Wyss, 9057 Weissbad, 12 minutes by steep trail below top of lift, tel. 071/88 11 42, open May-October). This old house has only rainwater and no shower. The goats live in a neighboring hut. The Berggasthaus is often festive and often quiet. While it can—and on Saturdays, often does—sleep 40 people (four hikers to three mattresses on a crowded night), you'll normally get a small woody dorm to yourself. The hut is actually built onto the cliffside; the back wall is the rock. From the toilet, you can study this Alpine architecture. Sip your coffee on the deck, behind a fairy's curtain of water dripping from the gnarly overhang a hundred yards above. Leave me a note in the guest book, which goes back 50 years.

From this perch you can almost hear the cows munching on the far side of the valley. In the distance, below Sântis, an hour's walk away, is your destination, the Seealpsee (lake) and Wasserauen. Only the parasailers, like neon jellyfish, tag your world "twentieth century."

Along with staggering mountains, Switzerland is loved for its delicious chocolates. All day long, rivers of molten chocolate work their way through factories into small foil packages. While tours are no longer allowed in any Swiss chocolate factories, the **Caillers Chocolate factory** in Broc, just north of Lausanne in French Switzerland, welcomes visitors with a movie and plenty of free samples (May-October, Monday afternoon to Friday morning with shows from 9:00 to 10:00 a.m. and 1:30 to 3:00 p.m., tel. 029/65151).

Imagine a fine baroque church in a Bavarian setting at a monastery that serves hearty food and the best beer in Germany in a carnival setting full of partying locals. That's the **Andechs monastery**, hiding happily between two lakes at the foot of the Alps, just south of

Munich. Come with an appetite, because the food is great and served in medieval proportions: chunks of tender pork chain-sawed especially for you, huge and soft pretzels (best I've had), spiraled white radishes, savory sauerkraut, and Andecher beer that lives up to its reputation.

My favorite map hangs as an 8-foot-by-2-foot poster in my office. It's a pictorial view of the Alps, looking south from an imaginary perch high above Germany, arcing from Vienna to Marseille. As I gaze at it I can almost see, hear, feel, and taste the endless natural and cultural charms that can be called Alpine.

British Isles

16. London: A Warm Look at a Cold City

I've spent more time in London than in any other European city. It lacks the grandeur of Rome, the warmth of Munich, the coffee of Seattle, and the elegance of Paris, but its history, traditions, people, markets, museums, and entertainment keep drawing me back.

London Town has changed dramatically in recent years, and many visitors are surprised to find how "un-English" it is. Whites are a minority in major parts of a city that once symbolized white imperialism. Arabs have nearly bought out the area north of Hyde Park. Chinese take-outs outnumber fish-and-chips shops. Many hotels are run by people with foreign accents, while outlying suburbs are home to huge communities of Indians and Pakistanis. London is learning—sometimes fitfully—to live as a microcosm of its former worldwide empire.

An urban jungle sprawling over 600 square miles with seven million struggling people, a world in itself, a barrage on all the senses, and a first stop for many travelers, London can be overwhelming. On my first visit, I felt very, very small. Here are a few ideas to soften and warm this hard and cold city.

Get oriented by taking the 2-hour London Sightseeing Tour—the best possible fast and cheap introduction to London. Buses leave regularly from Piccadilly Circus, Marble Arch, and Victoria Station. Every other bus comes with a live guide . . . worth waiting for. This $15 open-top double-decker bus tour shows you most of the major landmarks and gives you a feel for the city. While several companies claim to be the "original," it's very competitive and they're all about the same.

On your first evening in London, give yourself a brief "London-by-night" walking tour. If you just flew in, this is an ideal way to fight jet lag. Catch a bus to the first stop across (east of) Westminster Bridge. Walk downstream along the Jubilee Promenade for a capital view. Then, for that "Wow, I'm really in London!" feeling, cross the bridge to view the floodlit Houses of Parliament and Big Ben up close.

Have you tried London, lately?

To thrill your loved ones (or stoke their envy), call home from a pay phone near Big Ben at about three minutes before the hour. As Big Ben chimes, stick the receiver outside the booth and prove you're in London: ding dong ding dong . . . dong ding ding dong.

Then cross Whitehall, noticing the Churchill Statue in the park. (He's electrified to avoid the pigeon problem that stains so many other great statues.) Walk up Whitehall toward Trafalgar Square. Stop at the barricaded and guarded little Downing Street to see #10, home of the British prime minister. Chat with the bored bobby. From Trafalgar, walk to pop-hopping Leicester Square and continue to youth-on-the-rampage Piccadilly, through safely-sleazy Soho (north of Shaftesbury Avenue) up to Oxford Street. From Piccadilly or Oxford Circus you can taxi, bus, or subway home.

To grasp London comfortably, see it as the old town without the modern, congested, and seemingly endless sprawl. After all, most of the visitors' London lies between the Tower of London and Hyde Park—about a 3-mile walk.

Nibble on London one historic snack at a time by taking any of a series of focused, 2-hour walking tours of the city. For about $6, local historians take small groups for a good look at one page of the London story. You can choose from topics such as London's plague, Dickens' London, Roman Londinium, Legal London, the Beatles in London, or Jack the Ripper's London (which, even though guides

Central London

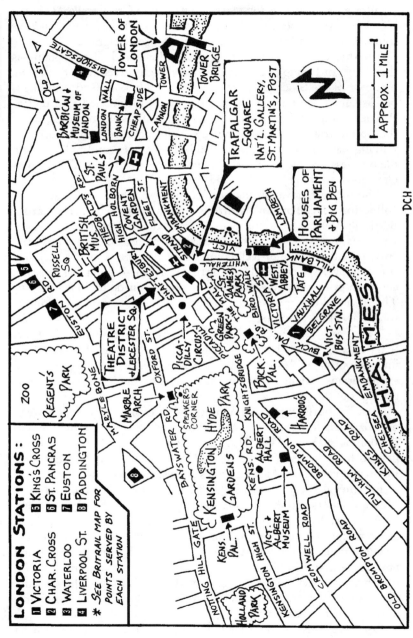

APPROX. 1 MILE

TRAFALGAR SQUARE
NAT'L. GALLERY,
ST. MARTIN'S, POST

HOUSES OF
PARLIAMENT
+ BIG BEN

TOWER OF
LONDON

TOWER
BRIDGE

BARBICAN +
MUSEUM OF
LONDON

LONDON WALL
CHEAPSIDE
BANK

ST.
PAUL'S

BRITISH MUS.

RUSSELL SQ.

COVENT GARDEN

EMBANKMENT

WEST.
ABBEY

TATE

VICT. BUS STN.

BELGRAVE

BUCK. PAL.

KNIGHTSBRIDGE

HARROD'S

ALBERT HALL

VICT. + ALBERT MUSEUM

KENS. PAL.

HOLLAND PARK

THEATRE DISTRICT
+ LEICESTER SQ.

PICCA-DILLY CIRCUS

MARBLE ARCH

SPEAKER'S CORNER

KENSINGTON GARDENS

HYDE PARK

ZOO

REGENT'S PARK

T H A M E S

LONDON STATIONS:

1 VICTORIA   5 KING'S CROSS
2 CHAR. CROSS   6 ST. PANCRAS
3 WATERLOO   7 EUSTON
4 LIVERPOOL ST.   8 PADDINGTON

* SEE BRITRAIL MAP FOR
POINTS SERVED BY
EACH STATION

DCH

admit is a lousy walk, is the most popular). Pub Crawl walks are also a hit. Some walks focus on the various "villages" of London, such as trendy Chelsea and stately, impressed-with-itself Belgravia.

The most central square mile of London—and all of Britain—is the "City" of London. This is London's Wall Street. You can take a free tour of the Stock Exchange. Nearby, traditional British justice is on display at the Central Criminal Courts, nicknamed Old Bailey. Powdered wigs, black capes, and age-old courtesies, my Lord, make the public trials quite entertaining. While churning with briskly-walking black-suited people with tightly-wrapped umbrellas during the business day, almost nobody actually lives in "the City." It's a desolate ghost town on Saturdays and Sundays.

The newly-renovated National Gallery, showing off Britain's top collection of European paintings by masters such as Leonardo, Botticelli, Velazquez, Rembrandt, Turner, the impressionists, and van Gogh, is now one of Europe's classiest galleries. Don't miss the "Micro Gallery," a high-tech computer room even your low-tech dad could enjoy. You can study any artist, style, or topic in the museum and even print out a museum tour map tailor-made to your interests. The National Portrait Gallery, just around the corner, is as exciting as somebody else's yearbook.

The Tate Gallery, with its wonderful collection of British art (particularly works by Blake, Turner, and the pre-Raphaelites), impressionists, and off-the-wall modern art, is a must. Sophisticated art historians patiently take rank beginners by the hand on free tours throughout the day.

History buffs enjoy the Museum of London. It offers a well-organized trip through time—from the swords of Roman Londinium to the bombs of World War II. For more on the war, Churchill's underground headquarters (the Cabinet War Rooms, about 2 blocks from Big Ben) give you a feel for London's darkest days and finest hour.

For megatons of things military, the impressive Imperial War Museum covers the wars of this century. You'll see heavy weaponry, love notes, Varga Girls, Monty's Africa campaign tank, and Schwartzkopf's Desert Storm uniform. Trace the development of the machine gun, push a computer button to watch footage of the first tank battles, and hold your breath through the gruesome "WW I trench experience." You can even buy WW II-era toys. The museum doesn't glorify war, it chronicles the sweeping effects of mankind's most destructive century.

London's latest blockbuster museum, the Museum of the Moving

Image, is just down the road. This high-tech, interactive, hands-on museum traces the story of moving images from the cave man whirling a flaming stick to modern TV. Watch great footage of the earliest movies and TV shows. Turn-of-the-century-clad staff speak as if silent films are the latest marvel.

The British love their gardens, especially the peaceful and relaxing Kew Gardens. Cruise down the Thames or take the subway to Kew for a respite from the city, plants galore, and a good look at the British people. Don't miss the famous Palm House, built of glass and filled with exotic tropical plant life. A walk through this hothouse is a veritable swing through the tropics—in London.

Nearly every morning, you can find a thriving market. There are markets for fish, fruit, used cars, antiques, clothing, and plenty of other things. Portobello Road (antiques on Saturday mornings) and Camden Lock (hip crafts and miscellany, Saturday and Sunday 9:00 a.m. to 6:00 p.m.) are just two of the many colorful markets that offer you great browsing. Don't expect great prices. These days, the only people getting a steal at London's markets are the pickpockets.

On Sunday, enjoy an hour of craziness at Speaker's Corner in Hyde Park. By noon there are usually several soapbox speakers, screamers, singers, communists, or comics performing to the crowd of onlookers. If you catch the London double-decker bus tour from Speaker's Corner at 10:00 Sunday morning, you'll return at noon for the prime-time action. Sundays are otherwise frustrating sightseeing days in London, as most major museums are open only from 2:00 to 5:00 p.m.

No visit to London is complete without spending some time in one of its woody, smoky pubs. They are an integral part of the English culture. You'll find all kinds of pubs, each with its own personality. Taste the different beers. If you don't know what to order, ask the bartender for a half-pint of his or her favorite. Real ale, pumped by hand from the basement (look for the longest handles on the bar), is every connoisseur's choice. For a basic American-type beer, ask for a lager. Children are welcome in most pubs but will not be served alcohol until they are 18. Order some "pub grub" and talk to the people—enjoy a public house.

London's great theater is as good as (and cheaper than) New York's Broadway. Choose from the Royal Shakespeare Company, top musicals, comedy, thrillers, sex farces, and more. Over the years I've enjoyed *Harvey* starring James Stewart, *The King and I* with Yul Brynner, *My Fair Lady*, *A Chorus Line*, *Cats*, *Starlight Express*, and *Les*

Miserables. Performances are nightly except Sunday, usually with one matinee a week. Matinees are cheaper and rarely sell out. Tickets range from about $12 to $40. Most theaters are marked on the tourist maps and cluster in the Piccadilly-Trafalgar area.

Unless you want this year's smash hit, getting a ticket is easy. The "Theater Guide" (free, at any hotel or tourist office) lists everything in town. Once you've decided on a show, call the theater directly, ask about seat availability and prices, and book a ticket using your credit card. Pick up your ticket 20 minutes before show time. You can even book tickets from the U.S. before your trip. Call the British Tourist Authority for the schedule or photocopy it from the London newspaper at your library.

Ticket agencies, which charge a standard 20 to 25 percent booking fee, are scalpers with an address. Agencies are worthwhile only if a show you've just got to see is sold out at the box office. Various ticket agencies scarf up hot tickets, planning to make a killing after the show is otherwise sold out. U.S.A. booking agencies get their tickets from another agency, adding to your expense by involving yet another middleman.

Cheap theater tricks: Most theaters offer cheap returned tickets, matinees, standing room, and senior or student stand-by deals. Picking up a late return can get you a great seat at a cheap-seat price. Standing room costs only a few pounds. If a show's "sold out," there's usually a way to get a seat. Call the theater and ask how. The famous "half-price booth" in Leicester (pronounced "lester") Square sells cheap day-of-the-show tickets to a very limited number of shows on the push list (2:30-6:30 p.m., Monday-Saturday, no phone). I usually buy the second-cheapest tickets directly from the theater box office. Many theaters are so small that there's hardly a bad seat. "Scooting up" later on is less than a capital offense. (Shakespeare did it.)

17. Bath: England at its Elegant and Frivolous Best

Two hundred years ago, this city of 80,000 was the Hollywood of Britain. Today, the former trendsetter of Georgian England invites you to take the 90-minute train ride from London and sample its aristocratic charms. Enjoy violins with your tea, discover the antique of your dreams, and trade your jungle of stress for a stroll through the garden.

If ever a city enjoyed looking in the mirror, Bath's the one. It has more government-protected buildings per capita than any town in England. The entire city is built of a warm-tone limestone it calls

"Bath stone." The use of normal bricks is forbidden, and Bath beams in its cover-girl complexion.

Bath is an architectural chorus line. It's a triumph of the Georgian style (British for Neoclassical), with buildings as competitively elegant as the society they housed. If you look carefully, you'll see false windows built in the name of balance (but not used, in the name of tax avoidance) and classical columns that supported only Georgian egos. Two centuries ago, rich women wore feathered hats atop three-foot hairdos. The very rich stretched their doors and ground floors to accommodate this high fashion. And today, many families have a tough time affording the cost of peeling the soot of the last century from these tall walls.

Few towns combine beauty and hospitality as well as Bath. If you don't visit the tourist office, it'll visit you. A tourist board crew, wearing red, white, and blue "visitor carer" T-shirts, roams the streets in search of tourists to help.

Bath's town square, a quick walk from the bus and train station, is a bouquet of tourist landmarks including the Abbey, the Roman and medieval baths, the royal "Pump Room," and a Georgian flute player, complete with a powdered wig.

Experience the elegance of Bath by staying in one of its top B&Bs. My favorite is Brock's Guest House. This $30-per-person splurge will be the rubber ducky of your Bath time. Marian Dodd, who can say "right-o" and sound natural, just redid her 1765 home. It's quiet and friendly and couldn't be better located at 32 Brock Street, just between the Royal Crescent and the Circus (tel. and fax 0225/338374).

A good day in Bath starts with a tour of the historic baths. Even in Roman times, when the town was called Aquae Sulis, the hot mineral water attracted society's elite. The town's importance peaked in 973 when the first king of England, Edgar, was crowned in Bath's Anglo-Saxon Abbey. Bath reached a low ebb in the mid-1600s when the town was just a huddle of huts around the Abbey and a hot springs with 3,000 residents oblivious to the Roman ruins 18 feet below their dirt floors. Then, in 1687, Queen Mary, fighting infertility, bathed here. Within ten months she gave birth to a son . . . and a new age of popularity for Bath. The town boomed as a spa resort. Ninety percent of the buildings you see today are from the eighteenth century. Local architect John Wood was inspired by the Italian architect Palladio to build a "new Rome." The town bloomed in the Neoclassical style and streets were lined with wide "parades," rather than scrawny sidewalks, upon which the women in their stylishly-wide dresses could spread their fashionable tails.

For a taste of aristocracy, enjoy tea and scones with live classical music in the nearby Pump Room. For the authentic, if repulsive finale, have a sip of the awfully curative Bath water from the elegant fountain. To make as much sense as possible of all this fanciness, catch the free city walking tour which leaves from just outside the Pump Room door. Bath's volunteer guides are as much a part of Bath as its architecture. A walking tour gives your visit a little more intimacy, and you'll feel like you actually have a friend in Bath.

In the afternoon, stroll through three centuries of fashion in the Costume Museum. Follow the evolution of clothing styles, one decade at a time, from the first Elizabeth in the sixteenth century to the second Elizabeth today. The guided tour is excellent—full of fun facts and fascinating trivia. Haven't you always wondered what the line, "Stuck a feather in his cap and called it macaroni," from "Yankee Doodle" means? You'll find the answer (and a lot more) in Bath—the town whose narcissism is justified.

18. York: Vikings to Dickens

Historians run around York like kids in a candy shop. But the city is so fascinating that even non-historians find themselves exploring the past with the same delight they'd give a hall of fun-house mirrors.

York is 200 miles north of London, only 90 minutes on British Rail. Start your visit by taking one of the entertaining and informative guided walking tours. These free walks, leaving morning, afternoon, and summer evenings from the tourist office, offer a practical introduction to the city. To keep the day open for museums and shopping and enjoy a quieter tour (with a splash of ghostly gore), take the evening walk. The excellent guides are likably chatty and opinionated. By the end of the walk, you'll know the latest York city gossip, several ghost stories, and which "monstrosity" the "insensitive" city planners are about to inflict on the public.

With this introductory tour under your belt, you're getting the hang of York and its history. Just as a Boy Scout counts the rings in a tree, you can count the ages of York by the different bricks in the city wall: Roman on the bottom, then Danish, Norman, and the "new" addition—from the fourteenth century.

The pride of the half-timbered town center is the medieval butcher's street called the Shambles, with its rusty old hooks hiding under the eaves. Six hundred years ago, bloody hunks of meat hung

Old World main street, York's Castle Museum

here dripping into the gutter that still marks the middle of the lane. This slaughterhouse of commercial activity gave our language a new word. What was once a "shambles" is now a ye olde tourist shopping mall.

York's four major sights—the York Castle Museum, the Jorvik Viking Museum, the best-in-Europe national Railway Museum, and the huge and historic church, or Minster—can keep a speedy sightseer busy for two days.

York's Castle Museum is a walk with Charles Dickens. The England of the eighteenth and nineteenth centuries is cleverly saved and displayed in a huge collection of craft shops, old stores, living rooms, and other intimate glimpses of those bygone days.

As towns were being modernized in the 1930s, the museum's founder, Dr. Kirk, collected whole shops intact and reassembled them here. On Kirkgate, the museum's most popular section, you can wander through a Lincolnshire butcher's shop, Bath bakery, coppersmith's shop, toy shop, and barbershop.

The shops are actually stocked with the merchandise of the day. Eavesdrop on English grannies as they reminisce their way through the museum's displays. The general store is loaded with groceries and candy, and the sports shop has everything you'd need for a game of nineteenth-century archery, cricket, skittles, or tennis. Anyone for "whiff-whaff" (ping-pong)? In the confectionery, Dr. Kirk beams you into a mouth-watering world of "spice pigs," "togo bullets," "hum bugs," and "conversation lozenges."

In the period rooms, three centuries of Yorkshire living rooms and clothing fashions paint a cozy picture of life centered around the hearth. Ah, a peat fire warming a huge brass kettle and the aroma of fresh baked bread soaking into the heavy, open-beamed ceilings. After walking through the evolution of romantic valentines and un-romantic billy clubs, you can trace the development of early home lighting—from simple waxy sticks into the age of electricity. An early electric heater has a small plaque explaining, "How to light an electric fire: Switch it on!"

Dr. Kirk's "memorable collection of bygones" is the closest thing in Europe to a time-tunnel experience, except perhaps for the Jorvik Viking Exhibit just down the street.

A thousand years ago, York was a thriving Viking settlement called Jorvik. While only traces are left of most Viking settlements, Jorvik is an archaeologist's bonanza, the best-preserved Viking city ever excavated.

The exhibit combines the cleverness of a Disney ride with the abundant harvest of this dig. Rolling backward in a little train car for two, you descend a thousand years in time: past the ghosts and cobwebs of fifty generations. Cromwell . . . Shakespeare . . . Anne Boleyn . . . William the Conqueror . . . and your car flips around. It's A.D. 995. You're in Jorvik.

Slowly you glide through the reconstructed village. Everything—sights, sounds, even smells—has been carefully re-created. You experience a Viking village.

Then your time-traveling train car rolls you into the excavation site, past the actual remains of the reconstructed village you just saw. Stubs of buildings, piles of charred wood, broken pottery—a time-crushed echo of a thriving town.

Your ride ends at the museum filled with artifacts from every aspect of Viking life: clothing, cooking, weapons, clever locks, jewelry, even children's games. The gift shop—the traditional finale of any English museum—capitalized nicely on my newly developed fascination with Vikings in England.

In summer, Jorvik's midday lines are over an hour long. But early or late visitors (last entrance in summer is 7:00 p.m.) usually walk right in. Jorvik's commercial success has spawned a series of similar historic rides that take you into Britain's burly wax-peopled past.

Unless you're a rich kid with nothing else to do, only Jorvik is worthwhile.

York's thunderous National Railway Museum shows 150 fascinating years of British railroad history. Fanning out from a grand roundhouse is an array of historic cars and engines, including Queen Victoria's lavish royal car and the very first "stagecoaches on rails." Even spouses of train buffs will find the exhibits on dining cars, post cars, Pullman cars, and vintage train posters interesting.

York's Minster, or cathedral, is the largest Gothic church in Britain. Henry VIII, in his self-serving religious fervor, destroyed nearly everything that was Catholic—except the great York Minster. Henry needed a northern capital for his Anglican church.

The Minster is a brilliant example of how the high Middle Ages were far from dark. The east window, the largest medieval glass window in existence, is just one of the art treasures explained in the free hour-long tours given throughout the day. The church's undercroft gives you a chance to climb down, archaeologically and physically, through the centuries to see the roots of the much smaller but still huge Norman church (built in A.D. 1100) which stood on this spot and, below that, the Roman excavations. Constantine was proclaimed Roman emperor here in A.D. 306. The undercroft also gives you a look at the modern concrete and stainless-steel save-the-church foundations.

To fully experience the cathedral, go for an evensong service. (No offering plates, no sermon; 5:00 p.m. almost nightly, 4:00 p.m. on Saturday and Sunday; usually spoken, not sung, on Wednesday and Saturday.) Arrive early and ask to be seated in the choir. You're in the middle of a spiritual Oz as 40 boys sing psalms—a red-and-white-robed pillow of praise, raised up by the powerful pipe organ. You've got elephant-sized ears as the beautifully carved choir stalls, functioning as giant sound scoops, magnify the grunting and trumpeting pipes. If you're lucky and the service went well, the organist runs a spiritual musical victory lap as the congregation breaks up.

Thank God for York. Amen.

19. Blackpool: Britain's Coney Island

Blackpool, England's tacky glittering city of fun, with a 6-mile beach promenade, is ignored by American guidebooks. Located on the coast, north of Liverpool, it's the private playground of North England's Anne and Andy Capps.

When I told Brits I was Blackpool-bound, their expressions soured

British trying to have fun in the sun at the beach, Blackpool

and they asked, "Oh God, why?" Because it's the ears-pierced-while-you-wait, tipsy-toupee place that local widows and workers go year after year to escape. Tacky, yes. Lowbrow, okay. But it's as English as can be, and that's what I'm after. Give yourself a vacation from your sightseeing vacation. Spend a day just "muckin' about" in Blackpool.

Blackpool is dominated by the Blackpool Tower—a giant fun center that seems to grunt "have fun." You pay about $10 to get in, and after that the fun is free. Work your way up from the bottom through layer after layer of noisy entertainment: circus, bug zone, space world, dinosaur center, aquarium, and the silly house of horrors. Have a coffee break in the elegant ballroom festooned with golden oldies barely dancing to barely live music. The finale at the tip of this 500-foot-tall symbol of Blackpool is a smashing view, especially at sunset. The Tower, a stubby version of its more famous Parisian cousin, was painted gold in 1994 to celebrate its 100th birthday.

Hop a vintage trolley car to survey Blackpool's beach promenade. The cars, which rattle constantly up and down the waterfront, are more fun than driving. Each of the three amusement piers has its own personality. Are you feeling sedate (north pier), young and frisky (central pier) or like a cowboy dragging a wagon full of children (south pier)?

Stroll the Promenade. A million greedy doors try every trick to get you inside. Huge arcade halls advertise free toilets and broadcast bingo numbers into the streets. The wind machine under a wax Marilyn Monroe blows at a steady gale, and the smell of fries, tobacco, and sugared popcorn billows everywhere. Milk comes in raspberry or banana in this land where people under incredibly bad wigs look normal. I was told I mustn't leave without having my fortune told by a Gypsy-type spiritualist, but at $4 per palm I'll read them myself.

Don't miss an evening at an old-time variety show. Blackpool always has a few razzle-dazzle music, dancing girl, racy humor, magic and tumbling shows ($7 to $15 tickets at the door). I enjoy the "old-time music hall" shows. The shows are corny—neither hip nor polished—but it's fascinating to be surrounded by hundreds of partying British seniors, swooning again and waving their hankies to the predictable beat. Busloads of happy widows come from all corners of North England to giggle at jokes I'd never tell my grandma.

Blackpool's "Illuminations" are the talk of England every late September and October. Blackpool (the first city in England to "go electric") stretches its season by illuminating its 6-mile waterfront with countless blinking and twinkling lights. The American inside me kept saying "I've seen bigger and I've seen better" but I stuffed him with cotton candy and just had some simple fun like everyone else on my specially decorated tram.

For a fun forest of amusements, "Pleasure Beach" is tops. These 42 acres of rides (more than 80, including "the best selection of white-knuckle rides in Europe"), ice-skating shows, cabarets and amusements attract six million people a year, making Pleasure Beach England's most popular single attraction. Their new roller coaster is the world's highest (235 feet), fastest (85 mph), and least likely to have me on board.

For me, Blackpool's top sight is its people. You'll see England here like nowhere else. Grab someone's hand and a big stick of "candy floss" (cotton candy) and stroll. Ponder the thought that legions of English dream of actually retiring here to spend their last years, day after day, dog-paddling through this urban cesspool of fun, wearing hats with built-in ponytails.

Blackpool is in the business of accommodating the English who can't afford to go to Spain. Its 140,000 residents provide 120,000 beds in 3,500 mostly dumpy, cheap, nondescript hotels and B&Bs. Almost all have the same design—minimal character, maximum number of springy beds—and charge $15 to $20 per person including "a plate of cardiac arrest" for breakfast (see Appendix for a few uncharacteristically cozy places).

Blackpool is a scary thing to recommend. Maybe I overrate Blackpool. Many people (ignoring the "50 million flies can't all be wrong" logic) think I do. If you're not into kitsch and greasy spoons (especially if you're a nature-lover and the weather's good), skip Blackpool and spend more time in nearby North Wales or England's Lakes District. But if you're traveling with kids—or still are one yourself—visit Blackpool, Britain's fun puddle where every Englishman goes—but none will admit it.

20. The Cotswold Villages: Inventors of Quaint

Travel writers tend to overuse the word "quaint." I save that word for England's Cotswold villages. These sleepy towns are the film-gobbling epitome of quaint . . . almost edible. Cuddled by woodlands, pastures, and grazing sheep, and cradled by the rolling Cotswold Hills, this 50-by-25-mile part of Gloucestershire is just two hours by train west of London. "Cotswold" is Saxon for "the hills of the sheep's coats."

Stow-on-the-Wold is a good home base town. Located in the heart of the region, any Cotswold site is within easy reach of Stow. Eight roads converge on Stow but none interrupts the peacefulness of its main square. The town has no real sights other than itself. There are several good pubs, plenty of B&Bs, some pleasant shops and a handy little walking tour brochure called "Town Trail."

Cotswold village signpost

The Cotswolds

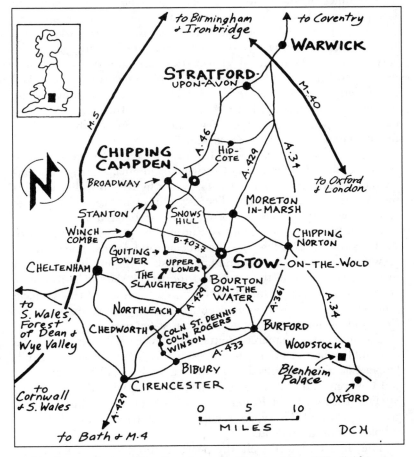

to Birmingham
& Ironbridge

to Coventry

WARWICK

STRATFORD-
UPON-AVON

M·40

M·5

A·46

HID-
COTE

**CHIPPING
CAMPDEN**

A·429

A·34

to Oxford
& London

BROADWAY →

SNOWS
HILL

**MORETON
IN-MARSH**

STANTON

WINCH
COMBE →

B·4077

**CHIPPING
NORTON**

GUITING →
POWER

UPPER
LOWER →

CHELTENHAM

THE
SLAUGHTERS

STOW-ON-THE-WOLD

BOURTON
ON-THE-
WATER

A·424

A·361

A·34

to
S. Wales,
Forest
of Dean &
Wye Valley

NORTHLEACH

CHEDWORTH

COLN ST. DENNIS
COLN ROGERS
WINSON

BURFORD

A·433

WOODSTOCK

BIBURY

Blenheim
Palace

to
Cornwall
& S. Wales

A·429

CIRENCESTER

OXFORD

to Bath & M·4

0   5   10

MILES

DCH

To the south, just 20 miles along the Roman "Foss Way" (this century's A-429), is Cirencester. Two thousand years ago, when Cirencester was called Corinium, five Roman roads met here. This was the second biggest city in Roman Britain, after Londinium. As you wander through Cirencester's fine Roman museum and explore the nearby Chedworth Roman Villa with its impressive ancient mosaics, you'll know why they say, "if you scratch Gloucestershire, you'll find Rome."

In Cirencester's crafts center, traditional craftspeople weave, bake and pot creative odds and old-fashioned ends. Cirencester bustles during its Friday market.

Ten miles north of Stow is another great home base, Chipping Campden, a rich old town that refuses to forget that it was once the center of this region's wool trade. Like any important market town, Chipping Campden has a wide main street. Much of the old wealth survives, giving the town a garden-party feel. Rich widows open their gardens to the public for a donation to their favorite charity. And locals, led by the women in the worthless but entertaining tourist office, gossip about this or that eccentric. In May, Chipping Campden's peasants host the rowdy "Dover Games" which include fun, if painful, events like "shin-kicking."

Just a bit down the road is Broadway, a pleasant but over-crowded town. Climb its hill for a great Cotswold panorama. Nearby Bourton-on-the-Water is even more touristy. I can't figure out if they call this the "Venice of the Cotswolds" because of its quaint canals or its miserable crowds. It's too cute—worth a drive through but no more.

Like many fairy-tale regions of Europe, the present-day beauty of the Cotswolds is explained by economic ups and downs. The residents grew rich on the wool trade and built lavish towns and houses. Then foreign markets stole the trade and the towns slumped—too poor even to be knocked down. Those forgotten time-passed villages have now been rediscovered by us twentieth-century romantics, and the Cotswold villages are enjoying a new tourist-fed prosperity.

To escape the commercial clutter, find a village. The charm of the Cotswolds is best savored in the tiniest towns, like Stanton, Snowshill, Upper Slaughter and its sister, Lower Slaughter (all between Stow and Chipping Campden). These villages, along with Winson, Coln St. Dennis, and Coln Rogers near the entertaining but money-grubbing town of Bibury, are my finalists for the most thatch-happy, cobbled towns in England.

The British love to walk the peaceful footpaths that Cotswold shepherds walked back when "polyester" meant two girls. England has a time-honored tradition of the walker's right of way. Once a year the national hikers' association goes out in force throughout England to be sure no fence-happy landlord is barring the hiker's sacred right to pass. Most of the land is privately owned and fenced in, but you're always welcome (and legally entitled) to pass through, using the various photogenic steps and sheep-stopping turnstiles provided at each stone wall. You must experience a "kissing gate."

Enjoying all this rural beauty is hard work. Just when your weary body needs it most, a village complete with a thirst-quenching and spirit-lifting pub seems to appear. Pubs welcome (but don't serve beer to) children. Most offer hearty and traditional hot lunches for around $6. Quality varies. Good local pub grub advice is abundant and worth seeking.

The Cotswolds have plenty of inns, guest houses, youth hostels, and B&Bs. You can drop into any town before dinner and make yourself at home in a B&B ($22 a night per person, including a hearty breakfast). Unfortunately, the Cotswolds are poorly served by England's trains and buses. A quick visit is frustrating without a car or a willingness to hike, hitch, or bike. Travelers without cars can get a taste of the Cotswolds at Moreton-on-Marsh. It has a train station, a bus connection to Chipping Campden, and a colorful Tuesday market. And several tour companies run inexpensive day trips from Bath to Lacock and Castle Combe, towns on the southern cusp of Cotswold cuteness.

After a well-executed visit, you'll remember everything about the Cotswolds—the walks, churches, pubs, B&Bs, thatched roofs, gates, tourist offices, and even the sheep—as quaint.

21. Mysterious Britain

Stonehenge, Holy Grail, Avalon, Loch Ness . . . there's a mysterious side of Britain steeped in lies, legends, and at least a little truth. Haunted ghost walks and Nessie the Monster stories are profitable tourist gimmicks. But the cultural soil that gives us Beowolf, Shakespeare, and God Save the Queen is fertilized with a murky story that goes back to 3000 B.C., predating Egypt's first pyramids. As today's sightseers zip from castle to pub, they pass countless stone circles, forgotten tombs, man-made hills, and figures carved into hillsides whose stories will never be fully understood. Of course, certain traveling Druids skip the Beefeater tours and zero right in on this side of Britain. They're literate in these things. But with a little background on this slice of the British pie, even the complete skeptic or novice can appreciate Britain's historic aura.

Britain is crisscrossed by lines connecting prehistoric Stonehenge-type sights. Apparently prehistoric tribes intentionally built sites along this huge network of lines, called ley lines, which may somehow have functioned together as a cosmic relay or circuit.

Glastonbury, two hours west of London and located on England's most powerful ley line, gurgles with a thought-provoking mix of history and mystery. As you climb the legend-soaked, conical hill called Glastonbury Tor, notice the remains of the labyrinth that made the hill a challenge to climb 5,000 years ago.

Mysterious Britain

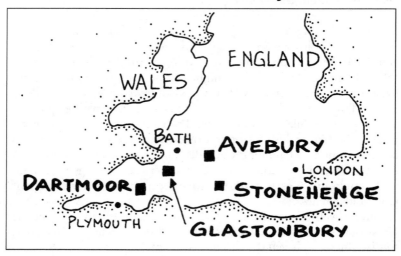

In A.D. 37, Joseph of Arimathea brought vessels containing the blood and sweat of Jesus to Glastonbury, and with that, Christianity to England. While this is "proven" by fourth-century writings and accepted by the Church, the Holy Grail legend which sprang from this in the Middle Ages isn't.

In the twelfth century, England needed a morale-boosting folk hero to inspire its people during a war with France. The ruins of a fifth-century Celtic timber fort at Glastonbury were considered proof enough of the greatness of the obscure fifth-century warlord Arthur. After his supposed remains were found buried in the Abbey, Glastonbury became linked with King Arthur and his knights. Arthur's search for the Holy Grail, the chalice used at the Last Supper, could be mere legend. But many people think the Grail trail ends at the bottom of the "Chalice Well," a natural spring at the base of Glastonbury Tor.

In the sixteenth century, Henry VIII recognized the powerful Glastonbury Abbey as a bastion of the church he fought, so he destroyed the abbey. For emphasis, he hung and quartered the Abbot, sending the parts of his body to four different towns. While that was it for the Abbot, two centuries later, Glastonbury rebounded. In an eighteenth-century tourism campaign, thousands signed affidavits stating that water from the "Chalice Well" healed them, and once again Glastonbury was on the tourist map.

Today Glastonbury and its Tor are a center for searchers, too creepy for the mainstream church but just right for those looking for a place to charge their crystals. Since the society that built the labyrinth worshipped a mother goddess, the hill or tor is seen by many today as a Mother Goddess symbol.

After climbing the Tor (great view, easy parking, always open) visit the Chalice Well at its base. Then tour the evocative ruins of the abbey with its informative visitor center and, in the chapter house, a model of the church before Henry got to it. Don't leave without a browse through the town. The Rainbow's End Café (two minutes from the Abbey on High Street) is a fine place for salads and New Age people-watching. Read the notice board for the latest on midwives and male-bonding.

From Glastonbury, as you drive across southern England, you'll see giant figures carved on hillsides. The white chalk cliffs of Dover stretch across the south of England, and almost anywhere you dig, you hit chalk. While most of the giant figures are creations of eighteenth- and nineteenth-century humanists reacting against the coldness of the industrial age, three Celtic figures (the Long Man of Willmington, the White Horse of Uffington, and the Cerne Abbas Giant) have, as far as history is concerned, always been there.

The Cerne Abbas Giant is armed with a big club and an erection. For centuries, people fighting infertility would sleep on Cerne Abbas. And, as my English friend explained, "maidens can still be seen leaping over his willy."

Stonehenge, England's most famous stone circle, is an hour's drive from Glastonbury. Built between 3100 and 1100 B.C. with huge stones brought all the way from Wales or Ireland, it still functions as a remarkably accurate celestial calendar. A recent study of over 300 similar circles in Britain found that each was designed to calculate the movement of the sun, moon, and stars, and even to predict eclipses in order to help these early societies know when to plant, harvest, and party. Even today, as the summer solstice sun sets in just the right slot at Stonehenge, Druids boogie. Modern-day tourists and Druids are kept at a distance by a fence, but if you're driving, Stonehenge is just off the highway and worth a stop ($4). Even a free look from the road is impressive.

Why didn't the builders of Stonehenge use what seem like perfectly adequate stones nearby? There's no doubt that the particular "blue stones" used in parts of Stonehenge were found only in (and therefore brought from) Wales or Ireland. Think about the ley lines. Ponder the fact that many experts accept none of the explanations of how

Stonehenge is surrounded by barbed wire. This is as close as you'll get.

these giant stones were transported. Then imagine congregations gathering here 4,000 years ago, raising thought levels, creating a powerful life force transmitted along the ley lines. Maybe a particular kind of stone was essential for maximum energy transmission. Maybe the stones were levitated here. Maybe psychics really do create powerful vibes. Maybe not. It's as unbelievable as electricity used to be.

The nearby stone circle at Avebury, 16 times the size of Stonehenge, is one-sixteenth as touristy. You're free to wander among a hundred stones, ditches, mounds, and curious patterns from the past, as well as the village of Avebury, which grew up in the middle of this 1,400-foot-wide Neolithic circle.

Spend some time at Avebury. Take the mile-long walk around the circle. Visit the fine little archaeology museum and pleasant Stones café next to the National Trust store. The Red Lion Pub (also within the circle) has good, inexpensive pub grub. As you leave, notice the pyramid-shaped Silbury Hill. This man-made mound, nearly 5,000 years old, is a reminder that you've only scratched the surface of Britain's fascinating prehistoric and religious landscape.

A fine way to mix Neolithic wonders and nature is to explore one of England's many turnstile-free moors. You can get lost in these stark and sparsely populated time-passed commons, which have changed over the centuries about as much as the long-haired sheep that seem to gnaw on moss in their sleep. Directions are difficult to keep. It's cold and gloomy, as nature rises like a slow tide against human constructions. A crumpled castle loses itself in lush overgrowth. A church grows shorter as tall weeds eat at the stone crosses and bent tombstones.

Dartmoor is the wildest moor—a wonderland of green and powerfully quiet rolling hills in the southwest near the tourist centers of Devon and Cornwall. Crossed by only two or three main roads, most of the land is either unused or shared by its 30,000 villagers as a common grazing land—a tradition since feudal days. Dartmoor is best toured by car, but it can be explored by bike, rental horse, thumb, or foot. Bus service is meager. Several National Park centers provide maps and information. Settle into a small-town B&B or youth hostel. This is one of England's most remote corners—and it feels that way.

Dartmoor, with more Bronze Age stone circles and huts than any other chunk of England, is perfect for those who dream of enjoying their own private Stonehenge sans barbed wire, policemen, parking lots, tourists, and port-a-loos (English sani-cans). The local Ordnance Survey maps show the moor peppered with bits of England's mysterious past. Hator Down and Gidleigh are especially thought-provoking.

Word of the wonders lurking just a bit deeper into the moors tempted me away from my Gidleigh B&B. Venturing in, I sank into the powerful, mystical moorland. Climbing over a hill, surrounded by hateful but sleeping towers of ragged granite, I was swallowed up. Hills followed hills followed hills—green, growing gray in the murk.

Where was that 4,000-year-old circle of stone? I wandered in a world of greenery, eerie wind, white rocks, and birds singing but unseen. Then the stones appeared, frozen in a forever game of statue-maker. For endless centuries, they had waited, patiently, for me to come. Still and silent, they entertained.

I sit on a fallen stone, holding the leash as my imagination runs wild, pondering the people who roamed England so long before written history was around to tell their story. Grabbing the moment to write, I take out my journal. The moor, the distant town, the chill, this circle of stones. I dip my pen into the cry of the birds and write.

22. Dingle Peninsula: A Gaelic Bike Ride

Be warned: Ireland is seductive. In many areas, the old culture seems to be winning its battle with the twentieth century. Stress is a foreign word. I fell in love with the friendliest land this side of Sicily. It all happened in a Gaeltacht.

Gaeltachts are national parks for culture, where the government is protecting the old Irish ways. Shaded green on many maps, these regions brighten the west coast of the Emerald Isle. "Gaeltacht" means a place where Gaelic (or old Irish) is spoken. You'll find the Gaelic culture alive, not only in the language, but tilling the rocky fields, singing in the pubs, and illuminating the weathered faces of the traditionally dark-clad Irish who live there.

A Gaeltacht is where schoolkids take their field trips to learn the old folk dances. Many signposts are in Gaelic only, with the old Irish lettering. If your map is in English . . . good luck. The old-timers are a proud bunch. Often, when the signposts are in English and Gaelic, the English is spray-painted out. And Irish yuppies report that in the 1990s, Gaelic is cool and on the rise.

Dingle Peninsula—green, rugged, and untouched—is my favorite Gaeltacht. It's Ireland's western-most point, quietly living the way it wants to. While nearby Killarney and the famous "Ring of Kerry" bustle with noisy tourists, Dingle ages peacefully, offering an escape into pure Ireland.

The most memorable approach to Dingle town is over the rugged and scenic Connor pass, Ireland's highest mountain pass. Depending on the weather, you'll be dazzled by the lush views, or you'll creep slowly through milky fog, seeing nothing but ghostly sheep as you descend into Dingle.

Dingle town is quiet, salty, easygoing, and very Gaelic. A weather-beaten Dingle friendliness will warm you, even on the coldest of wet mornings.

Ireland's top attraction—the friendliest people in Europe

Dingle Peninsula

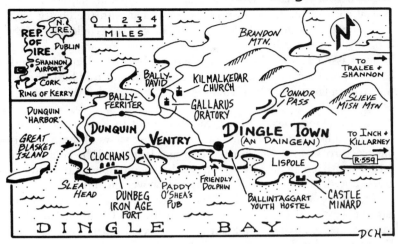

Warm up in a good bed-and-breakfast. I enjoy the peat-fire hospitality of Mrs. Kathleen Farrell's Corner House (a block from the town center, at Dykegate St., Dingle, County Kerry, tel. 066/51516). Any resident of Dingle can direct you to a good B&B like Mrs. Farrell's. A cozy bed, a huge breakfast, and lots of tea shouldn't cost you more than $18. (The Dingle tourist office, tel. 066/51188, is helpful.)

Those traveling on a shoestring can take advantage of one of Ireland's many fine unofficial hostels. Dingle's best is the Ballintaggart House Hostel, in a 300-year-old hunting lodge, a 5-minute walk from town on the road to Killarney. Ignoring its ghost stories, Paddy Fenton filled it with beds in clean coed dorms. There's a big fire in the reading room, a TV and game room, and a guests' kitchen (bed and breakfast for $8, tel. 066/51454). Paddy meets each Tralee-Dingle bus in town or, if you request, the bus will stop right at the hostel.

In the hostel's courtyard are several rentable horses, stacks of old bowls, a 150-year-old soup caldron, and a history lesson. This was a Protestant soup line during the terrible potato famine of 1848. Becoming a Protestant was a meal ticket for starving Catholics during the famine.

Wherever you're staying, find a bike to rent. For $3 a wheel, you're mobile for the day. Pack a picnic, your camera, and a raincoat. The weather on this distant tip of Ireland is often misty, foggy, and rainy. The Emerald Isle didn't get its nickname by basking in the sun.

Pedal your rented bike 20 miles around the peninsula. Follow the coastal road to the little town of Ventry. Chat with the chatty Irish you'll meet along the roadside. An elfish, black-clad Gaelic man might brogue about his arthritis, point out a landmark, or sing you a song. When I asked a local if he was born here, he breathed deeply and said, "No, it was about six miles down the road." When I told him where I was from, a faraway smile filled his eyes and he sighed, "Ah, the shores of Americay."

Bicycle along toward Slea Head, the point in Europe closest to America. The rugged coastline offers smashing views of the treacherous black-rock cliffs. Crashing surf, distant boats, and the countryside (lush and barren all at once) complete this memorable picture. Sheep graze, bored, as clouds quietly cover and uncover the hills.

The wet sod of Dingle is soaked with medieval history. In the darkest depths of the Dark Ages, when literate life almost died in Europe, peace-loving, bookwormish monks fled the chaos of the Continent and its Barbarian raids. They sailed to this drizzly fringe of the known world and lived their monastic lives in the lonely stone igloos or "beehive huts" which you'll see dotting the landscape.

Several groups of these huts, or clochans, line the road, each accessible for a small charge. The Fahan group is best. These mysterious stone huts were built without mortar by seventh-century monks in search of solitude. The huts are especially exciting when you're all alone in one surrounded by dank mist and the realization that it was these monks who kept literacy alive in Europe. To give you an idea of their importance, Charlemagne, who ruled much of Europe in the year 800, imported Irish monks to be his scribes.

It was from this peninsula that St. Brendan, the semi-mythical priest-explorer, is said to have set sail in the sixth century in search of a legendary western paradise. Some think he beat Columbus to North America . . . by nearly a thousand years!

For a more modest but possibly equally frightening voyage, sail to Great Blasket Island on a tiny ferry. Actually an oversized dinghy, with a plywood shield making the bow taller than it is, the boat can soak 12 travelers and still not sink. Great Blasket hosted a tiny community for centuries. The islanders were famed for their vivid stories of life on this fringe of Ireland. Since their harvest came from the sea rather than the land, they were the only Irish people who were spared the famine of 1848.

Today Great Blasket is quiet as can be—rabbits, ruffled sheep, abandoned stone homes, a sometimes hostel, local seals—and ideal for wind-blown but peaceful walks. Visitors can cross by irregular ferry service (several 30-minute crossings a day, weather permitting and passengers demanding, $20 round-trip, from a desperate wad of concrete called "Dunquin harbor").

Back on the mainland, pedal on to Dunquin. To complete the circle, head up the hill past Gallarus Oratory (a 1,000-year-old church with the best mortar-free stonework you'll ever see), and coast home into Dingle town.

With fifty pubs for its 1,500 people, Dingle is a pub crawl waiting to happen. You'll find a pub for every taste—six or eight feature live folk music. O'Flaherty's, right downtown with folk music every night (they pull out all the stops on Tuesdays), is noisy and touristy but a good bet for a sing-along. Murphy's, along the waterfront, offers fine music and less rowdiness. And Dick Mack's Pub on Green Street is also good. But follow your own drummer.

If you have wheels and want a Gaelic "Cheers" run by an Irish "Mayday" Malone, drive 3 miles to Ventry and enjoy the nightly folk music at Paddy O'Shea's (Paidi o'Se in Gaelic). He's a household word in Ireland, a famous Gaelic football player who now runs a local pub.

A few Irish pub tips: When you say "a beer, please" in Ireland, you get a full pint of Guinness, the national drink. If you want a small beer, ask for a "glass," which means a half-pint. Never rush your bartender when he's pouring a Guinness. It's a slow process and you may be very thirsty, but it's bad form not to understand that it's worth the wait. In an Irish pub, you're a guest on your first night; after that you're a regular. Women traveling alone need not worry—you'll become part of the pub family in no time.

Dingle's the place to enjoy traditional music that has not yet been bastardized for the tourist. A tin whistle, a fiddle, a flute, goatskin drums, and bad voices that sound better as the night goes on will awaken the leprechaun in you. Make yourself right at home. Even the shy visitor can join in, drumming the table or playing the ten-pence coins. Inhale the atmosphere, thick as the head on your Guinness.

It's a tradition to buy your table a round, and then for each person at the table to reciprocate. Good thing no one needs a car for a Dingle pub crawl. If an Irishman buys you a drink, you might offer him a toast in Irish. Lift your glass and say, "Slayn-tuh!" Learn some Gaelic. You've got a room full of Gaelic speakers who will remind you that every year five languages go extinct. They'd love to teach you a few words of their favorite language. Before you leave, be sure to thank them by saying, "Guh rev mah a gut."

THE ARAN ISLANDS—ANOTHER GAELTACHT

Another Gaelic treat along Ireland's west coast is the Aran Islands. Even more remote than Dingle, this is Ireland in the extreme, where everyone seems to be typecast for an Irish movie. The three Aran Islands are a 20-minute flight or two-hour boat ride from Galway, the only sizable town in western Ireland. The largest island, Inishmore, is 8 miles long, with one sleepy town, a few farming hamlets, and a wind-blown charm.

As in Dingle, local homes rent rooms inexpensively. Rent a bike or hire a horse and buggy, and explore. Like the rest of Ireland, the Aran Islands have a deep and mysterious history.

The island's famous Iron Age fortress, Dun Aengus, is the most impressive of its kind in all of Europe. For twenty centuries angry waves have battered away at its black foundation, 300 feet straight down. Even with nothing to guard it still stands strong, overlooking the sea from a cliff-edge perch so thrilling that just typing its description gives me travel flutters.

More history can be read into the stones of Inishmore. This tiny island, which looks like alligator skin from the air, is a maze of stone fences. Poor people cleared the stony land to make it arable. With colonial finesse, the British required Irish families to divide their land among all heirs. This doomed even the largest estates to fragmentation, shrinking lots to sizes just large enough to starve a family. Ultimately, of course, the land ended up in the possession of British absentee landlords. The tiny rock-fenced lots that carve up the treeless landscape remind the farmers of the structural poverty that shaped their history. And weary farmers have never bothered with gates. Even today, they take a hunk of wall down, let their sheep pass, and stack the rocks again.

Imagine Ireland back in its heyday, before the Protestants came and before the potato famine and before so many of its best and brightest emigrated to America. The population of this island was 8 million. During the Great Hunger of 1845-1848, a million people starved and more left in "coffin ships," so called because many departed so weak from hunger that they died en route. Today, Ireland's population is only 5 million. It's been a struggle. Ireland is called the Terrible Beauty. And through all its hard times, the people of this "island of saints and scholars" remain its most endearing attraction.

23. Northern Ireland

Travelers come home from Europe marveling about the art of Italy, the grandeur of the Alps, the autobahns of Germany, the tidiness of Holland, and the friendly people of Ireland. The smiles of Ireland are most vivid when fringed by the darkness of Protestant and Catholic extremism in the North.

So many people are working so hard to bring Ireland together. And a browse through any North Ireland city gives a visitor more faith in people than despair over headlines. This is a time of hope, as creative grassroots efforts to grow peace are taking hold. With a Mothers Against Drunk Driving zeal, local groups are making progress with efforts such as cross-cultural summer camps. You'll be entertained by Catholic/Protestant teenybopper jazz combos in the streets of Belfast. And London is chipping in more than soldiers. Every North Ireland town seems to have an impressive new leisure center, courtesy of a government that wants to see Britain great, not bloody. The message is: even if the short term looks like blood, toil, sweat, and tears, in the long run peace will prevail.

Make your visit to Ireland complete by including Northern Ireland, the British-controlled six-county section of a nine-county area of Ireland called Ulster. Only two hours by train from Dublin, it offers the tourist a very different and still very Irish world.

Most of the tourist industry ignores "war-torn" Northern Ireland. The media blow the trouble out of proportion, leading people to believe that nowhere in the area is there peace. That's exciting but false. The British-ruled counties of Northern Ireland are a secret enjoyed and toured mainly by its own inhabitants.

Of course, people are being killed in Northern Ireland—but not as many as in New York City. Car accidents kill more Northern Irishmen than do bombs or guns.

Armored cars, political graffiti, and bomb-damage clearance sales tell the story of the ongoing troubles. Friends you meet may show you the remains of a bombed-out customs house or the flowers that mark a spot where someone was assassinated. But, with common sense, travel in Northern Ireland is safe. About 40,000 Americans travel through Northern Ireland each year, and no American has ever been injured by "the troubles." Travelers give Northern Ireland rave reviews.

Here's a two-day plan that will introduce you to a capital city of 400,000, Ireland's best open-air folk museum, a once-prosperous and now rather sleepy beach resort, and some powerful, if subtle,

*With this Union Jack Bulldog street mural, a Belfast Protestant neighbor-
hood makes its Unionist feelings pitbull-clear*

mountain beauty complete with villages, ancient stone walls, and shepherds. At the same time, you'll get a firsthand look at "the Irish problem"—a tragedy in a potentially happy land. You'll meet some of the friendliest people on earth and learn firsthand about their struggle.

Since trains leave from both cities several times a day, you could even make Belfast a day-trip from Dublin. (Northern Ireland is not covered by the Eurailpass. That segment of the journey costs about $10 each way. North Ireland has a tourist office on Dublin's Nassau Street.) Belfast is also a good stopover en route to Scotland, with daily bus/ferry connections to Glasgow.

A strange peace dominates Belfast. Surrounded by checkpoints, the pedestrians-only "safe zone" in the modern mall-like city center bustles along, oblivious to the problem. Away from the center, many streets reek of the Industrial Revolution. Buildings most tempting to the IRA are protected by heavy metal screens. Religion is preached on billboards and bullhorns promise of a better life through Jesus. Patrolling British soldiers add to this strange urban stew. Only the visitor gawks at troops in bulletproof vests. Before leaving the city center, pick up some information and a map at the tourist office in North Street.

Enjoy the walk to Queen's University past the City Hall, with its massive exterior and impressive interior. Near the university, visit the

Botanical Gardens and the Ulster Museum. The museum has some interesting traditional Irish and contemporary art and a good exhibition teaching the history of Ulster—with a Protestant slant.

West Belfast is where sectarian troubles boil over. To feel the passion that fuels the problem, ride a shared cab from downtown up Falls Road. A huge lot full of well-worn big black cabs shuttle locals, in batches of six or seven, cheaply to and from downtown. Sit next to the cabby and talk with him as you make the whole circle. Get out at the cemetery and wander over to the "Republican" corner. Surrounded by a small green fence are the gravestones of the IRA soldiers killed in this civil war and a memorial to those who died in hunger strikes. It's thought-provoking to see Belfast through a sea of Celtic crosses, each a posthumous statement for a united and independent Ireland.

Falls Road is working-class Catholic. Irish flags are lashed to light poles, political wall murals make loud statements in primary colors, churches protect their windows with grates, an army post looms big

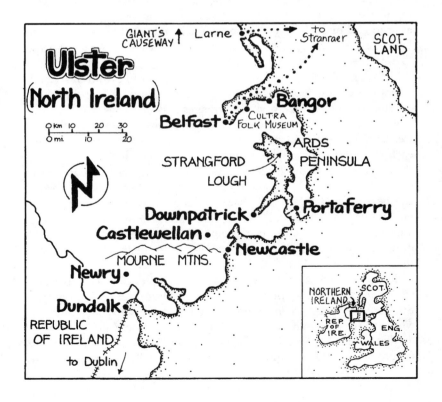

and black at the neighborhood's main intersection, and helicopters drone constantly overhead.

In working-class Protestant neighborhoods, which look just like their Catholic counterparts except for the flags, commitment to the opposite side is just as strong.

As the battle grows more sophisticated, with more powerful weapons and more-carefully targeted victims, most of Ireland has grown disillusioned by the violence. The Irish Republican Army (IRA) and Ulster Volunteer Force (UVF) are now seen by most as rival groups of terrorists who actually work together in Mafia style to run free and wild in their established territories. Maybe the solution can be found in the mellowness of Ulster retirement homes, where old "Papishes" with their rosaries and old "Prods" with their prayer books sit side by side talking to the same heavenly father. But that kind of peace is elusive. Recently an Ulster Protestant on holiday in England told me with a weary sigh, "Tomorrow I go back to my tribe."

Belfast is a busy industrial city, as the world's largest cranes towering over the harbor attest. Plan to see it quickly and get out by mid-afternoon. For a trip into a cozier age, take the 20-minute bus ride to Cultra's Ulster Folk Museum. Buses leave twice an hour from the Oxford Street station near the train station.

The Ulster Folk Museum, the best museum of its kind in Ireland, offers the closest look possible at old and traditional Irish lifestyles. Assembled in one huge park are cottages and buildings from all over Ireland. Only here can you actually walk into an old schoolhouse, weaver's cottage, farmhouse—in fact, an entire old Irish village—with each structure traditionally furnished and warmed by a turf fire. Buy the guidebook, wander for three hours, and you'll learn a lot about the culture of old Ireland. Any questions your guidebook doesn't answer can be answered by the attendant stationed in each building, who'll talk about leprechauns or simply chat about the weather or sports. The neighboring Transport Museum specializes in turf sleds, horse-drawn carriages, and old cars. When you've finished the museum, ride the bus 10 minutes into Bangor.

Formerly a stylish resort town, Bangor is a pleasant place to spend the evening. Take one of the bed-and-breakfast places ($20) right on the waterfront on Queen's Parade. My host made certain I knew just where to find the pubs, dancing, and outdoor gospel singing. I ended up discussing—and solving—the problems of the world with my new friends until 2:00 that morning. For an especially good look at the

Irish, a touch of politics, and a service you can understand, go to church on Sunday morning.

After Bangor, travel south down the Ards Peninsula along the Strangford Lough, a haven for migratory birds that welcomes people. At Portaferry, take the little ferry across the bay and continue south to Castlewellan or Newcastle. You'll pass through Downpatrick, where St. Patrick lies under a large but unimpressive stone.

Now you've reached the mysterious and beautiful Mourne Mountains. Explore the villages and the soft, green rolling "mountains" of 3,000 feet. It's a land rich in folk history and tradition, and equally rich in hospitality. Ask questions. As is so common in Ireland, many of the answers come in song lyrics. From nearby Newry, a train will zip you back to Dublin's fair city, where the weather's so. . . .

Scandinavia and the Baltics

24. Oslo

On May 17, Norway's national holiday, Oslo bursts with flags, bands, and parades. Blond toddlers are dressed up in colorful ribbons, traditional pewter, and wool. But Oslo has plenty to offer the visitor even without its annual patriotic bash. Oslo is fresh, not too big, surrounded by forests, near mountains, and on a fjord. And Oslo's charm doesn't stop there. Norway's largest city, capital, and cultural hub is a smorgasbord of history, sights, art, and Nordic fun.

An exciting cluster of sights is just a 10-minute ferry ride from the city hall. The Bygdoy area reflects the Norwegian mastery of the sea. Some of Scandinavia's best-preserved Viking ships are on display here. Rape, pillage, and—ya sure yu betcha—plunder was the rage 1,000 years ago in Norway. There was a time when much of a frightened Western Europe closed every prayer with, "And deliver us from the Vikings, amen." Gazing up at the prow of one of those sleek, time-stained vessels, you can almost hear the shrieks and smell the armpits of those redheads on the rampage.

Nearby, Thor Heyerdahl's balsa raft *Kon-Tiki* and the polar ship *Fram* exhibit Viking energy channeled in more productive directions. The *Fram*, serving both Nansen and Amundsen, ventured farther north and south than any other ship.

Just a harpoon-toss away is Oslo's open-air folk museum. The Scandinavians were leaders in the development of these cultural parks that are now so popular around Europe. Over 150 historic log cabins and buildings from every corner of the country are gathered together in this huge folk museum. Inside each house, a person in local dress is happy to answer questions about traditional life in that part of Norway. Don't miss the thousand-year-old wooden stave church.

Oslo's avant-garde city hall, built 40 years ago, was a communal effort of Norway's greatest artists and designers. Tour the interior.

Vigeland's Monolith of Life, Frogner Park

Over 2,000 square yards of bold, colorful murals are a journey through the collective mind of modern Norway.

Norway has given the world two outstanding modern artists: Edvard Munch and Gustav Vigeland. After visiting Oslo, many tourists become Vigeland fans—or even "Munchies." Frogner Park, behind the royal palace, features 150 bronze and granite sculptures representing 30 years of Vigeland creativity. The centerpiece is the impressive 60-foot-tall totem pole of bodies known as the "Monolith of Life." This, along with the neighboring Vigeland Museum, is a must on any list of Oslo sights.

Oslo's Munch Museum is a joy. It's small, displaying an impressive collection of one man's work rather than stoning your powers of absorption with art by countless artists from countless periods. You leave the Munch Museum with a smile, feeling like you've learned something about one artist, his culture, and his particular artistic "ism"—expressionism. Don't miss *The Scream*, which captures the exasperation many feel as our human "race" does just that.

You can explore Oslo's 700-year-old Akershus Castle. Its "Freedom Museum," a fascinating Nazi-resistance museum, shows how one country's spirit cannot be crushed, regardless of how thoroughly it's occupied by a foreign power. The castle itself is interesting only with a guided tour.

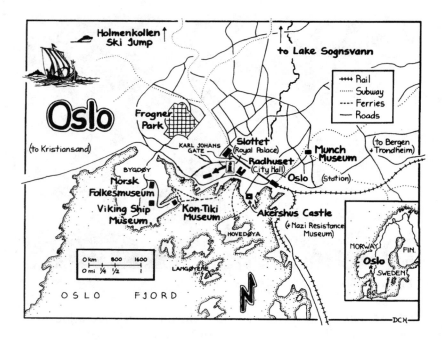

Oslo has been called Europe's most expensive city. I'll buy that. Without local relatives, life on a budget is possible only if you have a good guidebook and take advantage of money-saving options. Remember: budget tricks like picnicking and sleeping in dormitory-type accommodations offer the most exciting savings in the most expensive cities.

If you opt for hotels, you have no choice but to buy rooms that are efficient, clean, and pleasant. It's a kind of forced luxury. Know your budget alternatives, bring a little extra money, and enjoy it.

Language problems are few. The Norwegians speak better English than any people on the Continent. My cousin attends the University of Oslo. In her language studies, she had to stipulate English or American. She learned American—and can slang me under the table.

ONE DAY FOR THE FJORDS?

If you go to Oslo and don't get out to the fjords, you should have your passport revoked. Norway's greatest claim to scenic fame is her deep and lush fjords. "Norway in a Nutshell," a series of well-organized train, ferry, and bus connections, lays this most beautiful fjord country spread-eagle on a scenic platter.

Every morning, northern Europe's most spectacular train ride leaves Oslo (at 7:30) for Bergen. Cameras smoke as this super-scenic railroad roars over Norway's mountainous spine. The barren, windswept heaths, glaciers, deep forests, countless lakes, and a few rugged ski resorts create a harsh beauty. The railroad is an amazing engineering feat. Completed in 1909, it's 300 miles long and peaks at 4,266 feet (which, at this Alaskan latitude is far above the tree line). You'll go under 18 miles of snow sheds, over 300 bridges, and through 200 tunnels in just under 7 hours ($70).

At Myrdal, a 12-mile spur line drops you 2,800 breath-taking feet in 50 minutes to the village of Flam for Norway's ultimate natural thrill, Sognefjord. This is a party train. The conductor even stops the train for photographs at a particularly picturesque waterfall.

The cruise segment of "Norway in a Nutshell" is no longer done by ferry. With the completion of the new 11-kilometer-long tunnel from Flam to Gudvangen (part of the new mountain-blasting Oslo-Bergen highway), the romantic post boat no longer takes mail and tourists on this most scenic of fjord cruises. But sightseeing trips leave throughout the day in smaller, more expensive boats ($15, half off with a train pass, student card or full-fare spouse). These boats get you right into the mist of the many fjord waterfalls and close to the goats, sheep, and awesome cliffs. For 90 minutes, camera-clicking tourists scurry on the drool-stained deck like nervous roosters scratching fitfully for a photo to catch the magic. Waterfalls turn the black-rock cliffs into a bridal fair. You can nearly reach out and touch the sheer towering walls. The ride is one of those fine times, like being high on the tip of an Alp, when a warm camaraderie spontaneously combusts between the strangers who came together for the experience. The boat takes you up one narrow arm (Aurlandsfjord) and down the next (Naeroyfjord) to the nothing-to-stop-for town of Gudvangen, where waiting buses shuttle you ($10) back to the main train line at Voss. From Voss, return to Oslo or carry on into Bergen for the evening.

Bergen, Norway's second city and historic capital is an entertaining place to finish the day and enjoy an evening before catching the overnight train back to Oslo. As you yawn and stretch and rummage around for a cup of coffee back in Oslo's station it'll hit you: you were gone for 24 hours, spent very little, experienced the fjord wonder of Europe, and saw Bergen to boot.

25. Stalking Stockholm

If I had to call one European city "home," it would be Stockholm. Green, clean, efficient, and surrounded by as much water as land, Sweden's stunning capital is underrated by most tourists, ranking just above Bordeaux, Brussels, and Bucharest on their checklists.

While progressive and marching briskly into the future, Stockholm respects its heritage. Every day, mounted bands strut through the heart of town to the royal palace, announcing the changing of the guard and turning even the most dignified tourist into a scampering kid. The Gamla Stan (Old Town) celebrates the Midsummer Festivities (June 21, 22) with the down-home vigor of a rural village, forgetting that it's the core of a gleaming twentieth-century metropolis.

Start your visit with a stop at Europe's most energetic tourist information office, The Sweden House (Sverigehuset), three blocks from the station. This organization will do everything short of whipping you with birch twigs in the sauna. They have an English library and reading room, free pamphlets on every aspect of Swedish culture, and daily walking tours through the old town. Pick up the usual lists of sights and maps as well as the handy *This Week in Stockholm*, a periodical entertainment guide in English.

Stockholm is a place to "do" as well as see. The culture and vitality of Sweden is best felt at Skansen. On a wooded island near the town

Stockholm's floating youth hostel, the af Chapman

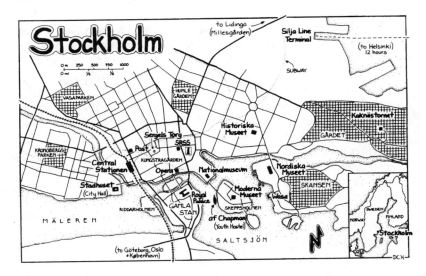

center, this is a huge park of traditional and historic houses, schools, and churches transplanted from all over Sweden. Skansen entertains with live folk music, dancing, pop concerts, a zoo, restaurants, peasant-craft workshops, and endless amusements. It's a cultural treat enjoyed by tourists and locals alike.

Nearby is the *Wasa*, the royal flagship that sank ten minutes into her maiden voyage 350 years ago. While not a good example of Viking seaworthiness, the *Wasa* is incredibly intact in her super-humidified display house and a highlight on any sailor's itinerary.

The Carl Milles Garden is filled with the work of Sweden's favorite sculptor. Strong, pure, expressive, and Nordic, Milles's individual style takes even the most uninterested by surprise. Hanging on a cliff overlooking the city, this sculpture park is perfect for a picnic.

A sauna, Sweden's answer to support hose and a face-lift, is as important as a smorgasbord in your Swedish experience. "Simmer down" with the local students, retired folks, and busy executives. Try cooking as calmly as the Swedes. Just before you become edible, go into the shower room. There's no "luke-cold," only one button, bringing a Niagara of liquid ice. Suddenly your shower stall becomes the Cape Canaveral launch pad, and your body scatters to every corner of the universe. A moment later you're back together, rejoining the Swedes in the slow cooker, this time with their relaxed confidence and a small but knowing smile. More exhilaration is just around the corner. Only rarely will you feel so good.

Stockholm is notoriously expensive. But with a few tips, you can manage fine on a budget. Land a budget bed by calling ahead or arriving in the morning. Train travelers coming from Oslo or Copenhagen should take an overnight train and rent a *couchette*. Scandinavia, always thinking ahead, located its capitals convenient 10-hour train rides apart. Scandinavian *couchettes* (beds on trains), at $15, are a great deal.

Take advantage of your guidebook's listing of budget accommodations. Stockholm's *af Chapman* youth hostel is a classic "cutter ship" permanently moored 5 minutes from downtown. The *af Chapman*, with $10 bunks, is one of Europe's most popular hostels. It holds 30 beds every morning for drop-ins, and these are usually taken by mid-morning. For a good, basic, and friendly hotel near the center, a 15-minute walk from the train station, I stay at the Queen's Hotel (Drottninggatan 71A, tel. 08/249460).

Finally, take advantage of $10-a-day tourist transportation passes which give you free run of Stockholm's excellent bus and subway system as well as unlimited entrance to Skansen. A more expensive 24-hour pass, giving you entrance to all the sights and free use of the public transit, virtually pays for itself as soon as you take the entertaining (and included) boat tour of the city center.

While most visitors side-trip to the too-cute town of Sigtuna, a quick visit to Helsinki is more exciting. Finland's capital, just an overnight boat ride away, is Scandinavian only by geography. Its language is completely unrelated, and culturally, there's nothing "ya sure yu betcha" about Finland.

Getting to Helsinki is a joy. The daily or nightly ships (as little as $130 round-trip with smorgasbord breakfast, dinner, and a stateroom bed each way, or free with a Eurailpass if you rent a bed) feature lavish buffets, dancing, duty-free bingeing, gambling, and the most enchanting island scenery in Europe. A 36-hour "mini-cruise" gives you a day to tour Helsinki and two nights on Scandinavia's biggest "luxury hotel."

26. Aero, Denmark's Ship-in-a-Bottle Island

Few visitors to Scandinavia even notice Aero, a sleepy, 6-by-22-mile island on the south edge of Denmark. Aero has a salty charm. Its tombstones say things like, "Here lies Christian Hansen at anchor with his wife. He'll not weigh until he stands before God." It's a peaceful and homey island, where baskets of new potatoes sit in front of farmhouses—for sale on the honor system.

Aero's capital, Aeroskobing, makes a fine home base. Temple Fielding said it's "one of five places in the world that you must see." The many Danes who wash up the cobbled main drag in waves with the landing of each ferry agree. In fact, this is the only town in Denmark that is entirely protected and preserved by law.

Aeroskobing is a town-in-a-bottle kind of place. Wander down lanes right out of the 1680s, when the town was the wealthy home port of over 100 windjammers. The post office dates to 1749, and cast-iron gas lights still shine each evening. Windjammers gone, the harbor now caters to German and Danish holiday yachts. On midnight low tides, you can almost hear the crabs playing cards.

The Hammerich House, full of old junk, is a turn-of-the-century garage sale open daily in summer. The "Bottle Peter" museum on Smedegade is a fascinating house with a fleet of 750 different bottled ships. Old Peter Jacobsen died in 1960 (probably buried in a glass coffin) leaving a lifetime of his tedious little creations for us visitors to squint and marvel at.

Denmark's Aero Island Bike Ride

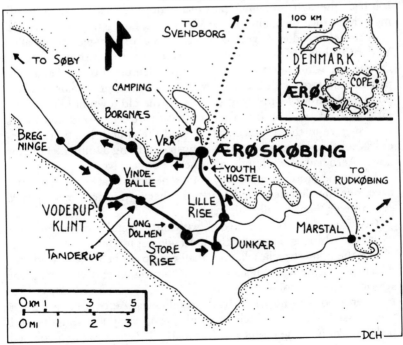

Touring Aero by car is like sampling chocolates with a snow shovel. Enjoy a breezy 18-mile tour of Aero's subtle charms by bike. Borrow a bike from your hotel or rent one from the Esso station on the road behind the tourist office. On Aero, there are no deposits and no locks. If you leave in the morning, you'll can be home in time for a hearty lunch. Ready? As I think the old biker's blessing goes, "May the wind always be at your back, and if it's not, make some."

Leave Aeroskobing west on the road to Vra past many U-shaped farms, typical of this island. The three sides block the wind and are used for storing cows, hay, and people. *Gaard* (meaning "farm") shows up in many local names. Bike along the coast in the protection of the dike, which turned the once-salty swampland to your left into farmable land. Pedal past a sleek modern windmill and Borgnaes, a pleasant cluster of mostly modern summer cottages. (At this point, wimps on one-speeds can shortcut directly to Vindeballe.)

After passing a secluded beach, the best you'll see on Aero, climb uphill over the island's summit to Bregninge. Unless you're tired of thatched and half-timbered cottages, turn right and roll through Denmark's "second longest village" to the church. Peek inside. Then roll back through Bregninge past many more U-shaped *gaards*, heading a mile down the main road to Vindeballe, taking the Voderup exit.

A straight road leads you to an ancient site on a rugged bluff called Voderup Klint. If I were a pagan, I'd stop here to worship too. Savor the sea, the wind, and the chilling view. Then pedal on to Tanderup, past the old farm with the cows with the green hearing aids, a lovely pond, and a row of wind-bent stumps. At the old town of Olde, you'll hit the main road. Turn right toward Store Rise—marked by its church spire in the distance. Just behind the church is a 5,000-year-old Neolithic burial place, the Tingstedet Long Dolmen. Hunker down. Aero had over a hundred of these. Few survive.

Inside the Store Rise church, notice the little boats hanging in the nave, the fine altarpiece, and Martin Luther in the stern making sure everything's theologically shipshape.

Continue down the main road, with the hopeful forest of modern windmills whirring on your right, until you get to Dunkaer.

For the homestretch, take the small road past the topless windmill. Except for "Lille Rise," it's all downhill as you coast home past great sea views to Aeroskobing.

After a power tour of big-city Scandinavia, Aero offers a perfect time-passed island in which to wind down, enjoy the seagulls, and pedal a bike into the essence of Denmark. Take a break in a cobbled world of sailors who, after someone connected a steam engine to a propeller, decided "maybe building ships in bottles is more our style."

27. The Baltics and St. Petersburg: Scandinavia's Rough-and-Tumble Backyard

The Baltic States and St. Petersburg, an easier-than-ever boat ride away from Helsinki or Stockholm, offer a tremendous load of travel thrills. A swing through a couple of Baltic capitals to spice up your Scandinavian adventure is globe-trotting kid stuff. Including Russia ups the ante and, for many, is plenty rewarding. Luckily, with dollars you're powerful and with information you can travel smart. Good guidebooks give you the step-by-step. Here's a brief intro to the four most accessible and comfortable cities in what was the Soviet Union.

ST. PETERSBURG, RUSSIA

Once an imperial showpiece of aristocratic opulence, now draped in the grimy cobwebs of socialism, St. Petersburg is Russia's most tourist-worthy city. Standing on Palace Square, you'll shiver and think "The Russian revolution started here." (You may also shiver and think, "I'm as far north as Alaska.") Romanov palaces, statue-maker gardens, and arched bridges over graceful canals bring back the time of the czars. The cultural cherry on top is the Hermitage Palace. Filled with the czars' art collection, this is one of the world's finest art galleries.

From comrades to Cokes

The Baltics

St. Petersburg's artistic and historical splendor is soaked in the sweet-and-sour sauce of modern Russia with its streets of legless beggars, Mafia-controlled kiosks, wheezing buses, shabby bread stores, broken signs, exhaust-stained facades, and pornography dealers. Hammers and sickles teeter tentatively on Stalin-gothic buildings, not quite sure it's safe to be torn down.

Compared to Moscow, St. Petersburg is compact, walkable, friendly, manageable, and architecturally intact. Save a sunny day just to walk. Keep your head up: ugly Soviet shops mar the first floor of nearly every building, but the upper facades have managed to stay above the squalor.

Nevsky Prospekt, St. Petersburg's main drag, with the most commerce, most landmarks, and safest feeling, is the natural walk. But make a point to explore the back streets along the canals. Take a Romanov stroll through the Summer Gardens. Climb St. Isaac's Cathedral to count the tired smokestacks through the urban haze.

While the subway is a fire hose of a people-mover, the easiest way to get around downtown is by taxi. Two dollars turns nearly any car into a taxi. Just point to the asphalt and within a few seconds a car will stop. Tell him where you want to go (you might have a postcard to point to), let him know you have two dollars for the fare, and you're on your way.

Ready for some culture beyond what was growing on your lunch? How about arguably the best ballet on earth? In St. Petersburg, as in Moscow, tourists can get tickets from scalpers on the side walk a few minutes before each performance for $10. Inside the theater, the brow-beaten despair and dog-eared chaos of today's Russia fades as the cultural spirit of old Russia swirls around the chandeliers. First World-by-the-tail tourists suddenly become gawking bumpkins as babushkas in gowns heap bouquets on the conductor who stands tall in Rimsky-Korsakov's place.

Ushers sell naïve western tourists surplus programs to long-finished performances and prepare tiny two-for-a-dollar black-caviar sandwiches. As the wall of faint hammers and sickles embroidered into the red stage curtain is pulled aside, the riches of Russia are resurrected in music and dance.

Down the street, well-scrubbed agents of the latest revolution—with fast-food arches rather than the hammer and cycle on their caps—eagerly raise their hands, calling customers over to order. Attendants stand guard with mops. Shadowy managers patrol the gleaming quarters enforcing a radical new notion—the customer is king. Serve him fast and serve him with a smile. Yuppie locals (car radios safely at their side) video each other munching hot apple turnovers and slurping shakes. You can get a cheeseburger, fries, and tea for $2—a day's wages for the babushka perusing garbage cans across the street. Downstairs are the best toilets in Russia, so good you wish you had a bigger job.

Bolshoi, begging, Mafia, burgers, hope, and despair—nobody knows where Russia's going. But now, anyone can visit.

TALLINN, ESTONIA

Visiting Tallinn fills us with hope for the future of the ex-Soviet Union. Tallinners, after years of watching Finnish television beamed across the gulf from Helsinki, knew exactly what a Western economy should look like. Since 1991 they've been putting one together with unprecedented speed.

Tallinn, with 29 pointy-roofed medieval towers ringing its easy-to-fortify castle-crowned hill, is a toy city. It feels strangely Scandinavian but ramshackle and cheap.

Tallinn has real grocery stores now, where you pick food off the shelves yourself instead of asking clerks behind a counter to do it. Estonian design has recovered from Sovietism: colorful, simple, Scandinavian-type layout is showing up in yogurt packaging, monthly bus-pass design, and window displays. Estonia is producing goods that actually look competitive on the world market. Uppity Tallinn food stores (whose Moscow counterparts would snort at carrying Russian-made products) are proud to carry Estonian butter and cheese. Pharmacies carry attractively presented, Estonian-made toothpaste alongside the imported tubes of Colgate.

Tallinn looks a little dilapidated but perfectly normal if you come on the boat from Helsinki. Arriving in Tallinn from Russia or one of the other Baltic capitals, its success is shinier. Do Tallinn last.

Estonians consider their country a Nordic nation of solid, hard-working Protestant folk like those who made Scandinavia a showcase of order, propriety, and comfort. They're quick to point out that Finland and Estonia both gained independence from Russia after World War I and that as late as 1938, Estonia's living standard was equal to Finland's. Estonians would have kept pace had it not been for a couple hundred Russian tanks.

RIGA, LATVIA

Tall nineteenth- and twentieth-century buildings give Riga a cosmopolitan feel and a vertical accent unique among the Baltic capitals. Riga has always been the Baltics' closest thing to a metropolis. German merchants and Teutonic knights made Riga the center of Baltic Christianization, commercialization, and colonization in the Middle Ages. Under the czars, the city was the Russian Empire's busiest commercial port. Under Soviet rule, Riga became first an important military center and later, because of its high standard of living, one of the favored places for high-ranking military officers to retire to. (They could choose anywhere in the USSR except Moscow, Kiev, and Leningrad.)

Riga's old town is about to wake up. When it does it will have as much medieval ambience as any old-town center in northern Europe. It's got the requisite gas lamps and cobbles—now all it needs is customers. It's a construction zone by day and a trendy cafe and bar scene by night. But the heavy-duty commerce of Riga is a few blocks away in the new town.

Modern Riga straddles a breezy park. It seems to make a six-story prayer circle around its freedom monument, which rises like an exclamation point high above a puddle of people. The modern city's grand architecture, and the lingering effects of poor Soviet use of space, give Riga the courtly feeling of an elegant old building which no longer has quite enough warmth and life to fill its high-ceilinged rooms.

VILNIUS, LITHUANIA

Sprawling and disorganized, a Catholic church on every corner, Vilnius is the homiest and coziest of the three Baltic capitals, and also the most unsophisticated and run-down. A restful, horizontal city, Vilnius's one- and two-story buildings and its arches and courtyards are more reminiscent of a friendly Polish provincial capital than of the tall, German-influenced architecture in Riga or the Hanseatic frosting-cake feel of Tallinn.

Vilnius's old town, dating largely from the 17th and 18th centuries, is huge and amazingly dilapidated. Burned-out windows, crumbling wooden shutters, cracked plaster, and patchwork roofs cry out for millions of dollars' worth of restoration work while certain Soviet "improvements," like the central telephone office, cry out for the wrecking ball.

The fact that Vilnius is falling apart gives the visitor a heightened sense of possibility. Every paneless window and paintless shutter makes you think of what could be there: a family, a shop, a sewing machine, candles on the table, children in the street.

Vilnius's ramshackle desolation challenges you to explore. The old town is full of cozy cafes and fascinating galleries and shops. Many of them don't have any signs; you have to duck through archways into courtyards, open gates and doors, and slowly learn your way from nook to cranny. Otherwise the city may seem so dead you'll wonder if it wasn't the accidental target of a Soviet neutron bomb.

The city museums have more babushka guards than visitors. Apparently labor is cheaper than a light bulb, so the exhibit rooms are kept dark and you walk through the museum with your own personal light switcher.

As the only inland Baltic capital, Vilnius was always politically and economically closer to its Slavic neighbors (Russia and Poland) than to Scandinavia. This survives: as in Russia, politicians are comic, bombastic, and bumpkinesque. And Lithuania's economy lags behind Estonia and Latvia. Lithuania can still seem like a part of the Soviet Union. The cause is not so much the harsh, urban Sovietism that still survives in Riga, but the provincial inertia that at the same time makes Vilnius endearing.

GETTING YOUR VISAS

American travelers need a visa to visit Lithuania and Latvia. A visa for either country works in both. Estonia no longer requires a visa of American tourists. The cheapest and easiest way to get your Baltics visa is from the Latvian embassy in Washington, D.C. (tel. 202/726-8213). You can also stop by any Latvian or Lithuanian embassy in any European capital and usually get your visa the same day, often for free.

Russian visas are more difficult. The St. Petersburg Youth Hostel is the best simple and reliable option. Nobody else in Russia is so well set-up and so capable of combining a low per-night price with efficient visa support. The hostel's American office is at 409 N. Pacific Coast Highway, Bldg. #106, Suite 390, Redondo Beach, CA 90277, tel. 310/379-4316, fax 310/379-8420. In Finland or Eastern Europe, you can work directly through the hostel (tel. 7/812/277-0569, fax 7/812/277-5102, English always spoken).

Call, write, or fax the California office and they will mail you an information package. The cost of obtaining your Russian visa is a $10 reservation fee, a $30 visa service fee, and $40 for your visa (processed within three weeks, quicker with baksheesh). You'll also pay $16 for each night you plan to stay at the hostel. This is a great value. You should work at least four weeks in advance; faster processing is possible but more expensive.

For much more information, *Rick Steves' Best of the Baltics and Russia* (with Ian Watson, John Muir Publications) offers the most up-to-date rundown on budget independent travel in the Baltics, St. Petersburg, and Moscow.

Greece

28. Peloponnesian Highlights: Overlooked Greece

The Peloponnesian Peninsula stretches south from Athens. This antiquity-studded land of ancient Olympia, Corinth, and Sparta offers plenty of fun in the eternal Greek sun with pleasant fishing villages, sandy beaches, bathtub-warm water, and none of the tourist crowds that plague the much-scrambled-after Greek Isles.

The Peloponnesian port town of Nafplion, two hours southwest of Athens by car or bus, is small, cozy, and strollable. It's a welcome relief after the black-hanky intensity of smoggy Athens. Not only is Nafplion itself fun, but it's a handy home base for exploring two of Greece's greatest ancient sights.

Nafplion's harbor is guarded by two castles, one on a small island and the other capping the hill above the town. Both are wonderfully floodlit at night. Just looking from the town up to its castle makes you need a tall iced tea. But this old Venetian outpost, from the days when Venice was the economical ruler of Europe, is the best-preserved castle of its kind in Greece and well worth the 999-step climb. From the

Epidavros, state-of-the-art acoustics

highest ramparts you'll see several Aegean islands (great day-trips by boat from Nafplion) and deep into the mountainous interior of the Peloponnesian Peninsula. Below you lies an enticing beach.

Nafplion has plenty of hotels, and its harbor is lined with restaurants specializing in fresh seafood. An octopus dinner cost me $8—succulent!

The infamous resin-flavored *retsina* wine is a drink you'll want to experience—once. Maybe with octopus. The first glass is like drinking wood. The third glass is dangerous: it starts to taste good. If you drink any more, you'll smell like it all the next day.

On another night, I left Nafplion's popular waterfront district and had a memorable meal in a hole-in-the-wall joint. There was no menu, just an entertaining local crowd and a nearsighted man who, in a relaxed frenzy, ran the whole show. He scurried about, greeting eaters, slicing, dicing, laughing, singing to himself, cooking, serving, and billing. Potato stew, meatballs, a plate of about 30 tiny fried fish with lime, and unlimited wine cost $15 for two—and could have fed four.

Nafplion is just a short drive from two important classical sights: Epidavros and Mycenae.

Epidavros, 18 miles northeast, is the best-preserved ancient Greek theater. It was built 2,500 years ago to seat 14,000. Today it's kept busy reviving the greatest plays of antiquity. You can catch performances of ancient Greek comedies and tragedies on weekends from mid-June through September. Try to see Epidavros either early or late in the day. The theater's marvelous acoustics are best enjoyed in near-solitude. From the most distant seat you can hear the *retsina* rumbling in your partner's stomach down on the theater floor.

Thirty minutes in the other direction from Nafplion are the ruins of Mycenae. This was the capital of the Mycenaeans who won the Trojan War and dominated Greece 1,000 years before the age of Socrates.

As you tour this fascinating fortified citadel, remember that these people were as awesome to the ancient Greeks of Socrates' day as those Greeks are to us. The classical Greeks marveled at the huge stones and workmanship of the Mycenaean ruins. They figured that only a race of giant Cyclopes could build with such colossal rocks. They called it "Cyclopean" architecture.

Visitors today can gape at the Lion's Gate, climb deep into a cool ancient cistern, and explore the giant *tholos* tombs. The tombs, built in 1500 B.C., stand like huge stone igloos with smooth subterranean domes 40 feet wide and 40 feet tall. The most important Mycenaean artifacts, like the golden "Mask of Agamemnon," are in the National Museum in Athens.

FINIKOUNDAS

The prize-winning Peloponnesian hideaway is the remote village of Finikoundas. Located on the southwest tip of the peninsula between the twin Venetian fortress towns of Koroni and Methoni (2 hours by public bus from Kalamata), Finikoundas is big enough to have a good selection of restaurants, pensions and a few shops, but it's small enough to escape the typical resort traffic, crowds, and noise. It's just right for a sleepy Greek sabbatical.

Finikoundas has plenty of private rooms, or *dhomatia*, for rent. Plan to spend $20 for a simple double a few steps from the beach. The little bay just east of the rock breakwater was the best beach I found, and the swimming was fine—even in October.

You can be a guest of honor at a Greek wedding festival

After a little Apollo-worshipping, I wandered through town in search of Dionysus at just the right waterfront restaurant. The place I found couldn't have been more "waterfront." Since the fishing village had no dock, its Lilliputian fishing boats were actually anchored to the restaurant. I settled my chair comfortably into the sand and the salty atmosphere, as weak wavelets licked my table's legs. I dined amid rusty four-hooker anchors, honorably retired old ropes, and peely dinghies. A naked 20-watt bulb dangled from the straw roof, which rotted unnoticed by Greeks and a few perpetually off-season Germans who seemed to be regulars.

Cuisine in a village like this is predictable. I enjoyed fresh seafood, Greek salad, and local wine. After a few days in Greece, you become a connoisseur of the salad, appreciating the wonderful tomatoes, rich feta cheese, and even the olive-oil drenching.

Almost within splashing distance of my table, young Greek men, in swimsuits not much bigger than a rat's hammock, gathered around a bucketful of just-caught octopi. They were tenderizing the poor things to death by whipping them like wet rags over and over on a big flat rock. They'd be featured momentarily on someone's dinner plate—someone else's.

Evening was a predictable but pleasant routine of strolling and socializing. The streets buzz with take-it-easy action. Dice chatter on dozens of backgammon boards, entrepreneurial dogs and goal-oriented children busy themselves as a tethered goat chews on something inedible in its low-profile corner. From the other end of town comes the happy music of a christening party. Dancing women fill the building while their children mimic them in the street. Farther down, two elderly, black-clad women sit like tired dogs on the curb.

Succumbing to the lure of the pastry shop, I sat down for my day-end ritual, honey-soaked baklava. I told the cook I was American. "Oh," he said, shaking his head with sadness and pity, "You work too hard." I answered, "Right. But not today."

29. Crete's Gorge of Samaria

Swarms of tourists flock to the Greek island of Crete. Many leave, disappointed by the crowds. Try to avoid peak season and the crowded cities. Hike through the rugged interior instead and find a remote corner of the south coast. While ridiculously crowded in the height of summer, the 10-mile hike through the Gorge of Samaria can be a Cretan highlight.

Your home base for this loop trip is Hania, a city on Crete's north coast serviced frequently by the overnight boat from Athens. Catch the earliest bus from Hania to Xyloskalo to beat the heat and midday crowds. After a scenic 25-mile bus ride, you'll be standing high above the wild Gorge of Samaria. Xyloskalo is a small lodge, the end of the road, and the beginning of the trail. The bus will be full of hikers; no one else would come here at this hour. The air is crisp, the fresh blue

Photo (not of Rick Steves) by Andrea Hagg

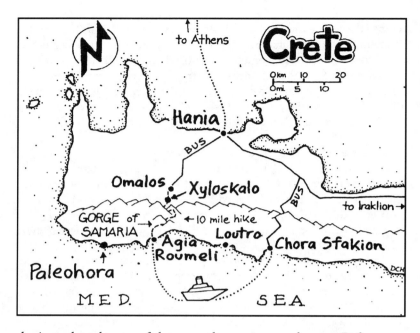

sky is cool, and most of the gorge has yet to see the sun. Before you lies a 10-mile downhill trek, dropping 5,000 feet through some of the most spectacular scenery anywhere in Greece to a black-sand beach on the south coast. (The hike takes 4 to 6 hours, the gorge is open from May through October and costs about $5 to enter.)

Pack light but bring a hearty picnic lunch, a water bottle, and extra film. Food can't be bought in this wonderfully wild gorge, and things get pretty dry and dusty in the summer. There are several springs and you follow a pure mountain stream through much of the gorge. Wear light clothes, but bring a jacket for the cool morning at the top. Come prepared to swim in one of the stream's many refreshing swimming holes.

Descend to the floor of the gorge down an hour of steep switchbacks where you'll reach the stream, a great place for your picnic brunch. A leisurely meal here will bolster your energy, lighten your load, and bring you peace, as this break will let most of the other hikers get ahead of you. If the crowds just won't let up, find solitude by following a stream up a side gorge.

Between you and the Libyan Sea on Crete's southern shore are about 8 miles of gently sloping downhill trails. Hiking along the cool creek, you'll pass an occasional deserted farmhouse, lazy goats, and a small ghost-town with a well. In the middle of the hike, you'll come to the narrowest (and most photographed) point in the gorge, where only three yards separate the 1,000-foot-high cliffs. Keep your eyes peeled for the nimble, cliff-climbing agrimi, the wild Cretan mountain goats.

Finally, by mid-afternoon, signs of Greek civilization begin peeking through the bushes. An oleander chorus cheers you along the last leg of your hike to the coast. You'll find a tiny community with a small restaurant and a few cheap places to stay. The town, Agia Roumeli, is accessible only by foot or boat. Three to six times a day, a small boat picks up the hikers and ferries them to Chora Sfakion (last ride is usually around 6:00 p.m.). Before you begin your hike, confirm when the last boat leaves so you can pace yourself.

While you're waiting for the boat (after you buy your ticket), take a dip in the bathtub-warm, crystal-clear waters of the Libyan Sea. Africa is out there somewhere. The black-sand beach absorbs the heat, so wear your shoes right to the water's edge. A free shower is available on the beach.

The hour-long boat ride (or 8-hour hike) to Chora Sfakion passes some of Crete's best beaches and stops briefly at the pleasant fishing village of Loutro (with several pensions). Buses meet each boat at Chora Sfakion to return you to Hania. The untouristy village of Paleohora (west of Agia Roumeli) has great beaches and a bus connection to Hania. In crossing the island of Crete, the bus goes through some dramatic scenery and several untouched villages inhabited by high-booted, long-mustachioed, espresso-drinking Cretans.

Throughout Europe

30. Dungeons and Dragons: Europe's Nine Most Medieval Castle Experiences

Castles excite Americans. Medieval fortresses are rotting away on hilltops from Ireland to Israel, from Sweden to Spain, lining the Loire and guarding harbors throughout the Mediterranean. From the west coast of Portugal to the crusader city of Rhodes, you'll find castle thrills lurking in every direction.

Most of Europe's castles have been discovered, but some are forgotten, unblemished by turnstiles, postcard racks, and coffee shops, and ignored by guidebooks. Since they're free, nobody promotes them. The aggressive traveler finds them by tapping local sources, like the town tourist office and the friendly manager of your hotel or pension.

Here are nine medieval castles, some forgotten, some discovered, where the winds of the past really howl.

Europe is full of fortified fantasies. One of Sweden's best is Kalmar Castle.

Europe's Nine Best Castles

CARCASSONNE, FRANCE

Before me lies Carcassonne, the perfect medieval city. Like a fish that everyone thought was extinct, Europe's greatest Romanesque fortress-city has somehow survived the centuries.

I was supposed to be gone yesterday, but here I sit—imprisoned by choice—curled in a cranny on top of the wall. The moat is one foot over and 100 feet down. Small plants and moss upholster my throne. The wind blows away the sounds of today and my imagination "medievals" me.

Twelve hundred years ago, Charlemagne stood below with his troops—besieging the town for several years. Just as food was running out, a cunning townsperson had a great idea. She fed the town's last bits of grain to the last pig and tossed him over the wall. Splat. Charlemagne's restless forces, amazed that the town still had enough food to throw fat party pigs over the wall, decided they'd never succeed

Eltz Castle near Cochem on Germany's Mosel River

in starving the people out. They ended the siege and the city was saved. Today, the walls that stopped Charlemagne open wide for visitors.

Located in southwest France, Carcassonne is a medieval fantasy of towers, turrets, and cobbled alleys. It's a castle and a walled city rolled into one—and a refreshing break after the touristic merry-go-round of the French Riviera and Paris.

WARWICK CASTLE, ENGLAND
From Land's End to John O'Groats, I searched for the best castle in Britain. I found it. Warwick Castle is a medieval festival wrapped in a fairy-tale exterior. Even with its crowds of modern-day barbarians and its robber-baron entry fee, it's worthwhile.

Like nearby Stratford, Warwick is "upon the Avon" (which is Celtic for "river"—any river). Once you get past its moat, now a lush green park, Warwick (pronounced "war-ick") will entertain you from lookout to dungeon. Knaves, nobles, jesters, and damsels will all find something interesting: a fine and educational armory, a terrible torture chamber, a knight in shining armor posing on a horse, a Madame Tussaud re-creation of a royal weekend party—an 1898 game of statue-maker—and a grand garden park patrolled by peacocks who welcome picnickers.

ELTZ CASTLE, GERMANY

Germany's best medieval castle experience is the Eltz Castle, above the Mosel River between Cochem and Koblenz. One of the very few Rhine/Mosel-area castles to escape destruction under the French, Burg Eltz is incredibly well preserved and elegantly furnished. The approach to Burg Eltz is part of the thrill. From the car park, you'll hike through a mysterious forest long enough to get in a medieval mood, and then all of a sudden it appears, all alone—the past engulfed in nature—Burg Eltz. It's an hour's steep hike from the nearest train station, Moselkern. Drivers, following a roundabout road from the Mosel, can get within a 15-minute walk or quick shuttle-bus ride from the castle. Call 02672/1300 and ask if there's a scheduled English tour that you can join. Here you'll learn how the lives of even the Middle Age's rich and famous were "nasty, brutish, and short."

RHEINFELS CASTLE, GERMANY'S RHINELAND

Once the mightiest of all the Rhine castles, today Rheinfels is an intriguing ruin overlooking the pleasant medieval town of St. Goar. (Rooms listed in the Appendix.) Study the helpful English information sheet and map before diving in. Check out the classic dungeon with its ceiling-only access. The well (tour guides report) was dug by death-row-type prisoners who were promised freedom if they hit water. Prisoners spent months toiling at the dark bottom of the hole. When they finally succeeded and were lifted wet and happy up into the daylight, they were immediately blinded by the bright sunlight. Ponder life in the Middle Ages as you enjoy a glorious Rhine view from the tallest turret.

A flashlight is handy if you want to explore some of Rheinfels' several miles of spooky tunnels. The museum has a reconstruction of the castle showing how it looked before the French flattened it. Louis XIV destroyed all but one of the castles that line Germany's Rhine. (That castle is Marksburg, which is great; but it lies on the inconvenient side of the river and requires visitors to take a guided tour, offered only in German.)

Germany's Rhine River is lined with castle-crowned hills. There's even a castle built in the middle of the river (called Pfalz, accessible by tiny ferry, but not worth touring). These can be enjoyed conveniently by train, car, or boat. The best 50-mile stretch is between Koblenz and Mainz. The best one-hour cruise is from St. Goar to Bacharach.

CHÂTEAU CHILLON, SWITZERLAND

Set romantically at the edge of Lake Geneva near Montreux, this wonderfully preserved thirteenth-century castle is worth a side trip from anywhere in southwest Switzerland. Follow the English brochure, which takes you on a self-guided tour from tingly perch-on-the-medieval-windowsill views through fascinatingly furnished rooms. The dank dungeon, mean weapons, and 700-year-old toilets will excite even the dullest travel partner. A handy but too-close-to-the-train-tracks youth hostel is a 10-minute stroll down the lakeside promenade toward Montreux (tel. 021/9634934). Attack or escape the castle by ferry (free with your train pass).

REIFENSTEIN CASTLE, ITALY

For an incredibly medieval kick in the pants, get off the autobahn one hour south of Innsbruck at the Italian town of Vipiteno (called Sterzing by residents who prefer German). With her time-pocked sister just opposite, Reifenstein bottled up this strategic valley leading to the easiest way to cross the Alps. It offers castle connoisseurs the best-preserved original medieval castle interior I've ever seen. The lady who lives in Reifenstein Castle takes groups through in Italian, German, and *un poco* English (tel. 0472/765879 in Italy, 0039/472/765879 from Austria, tours normally at 9:30 and 10:30 a.m., 2:00 and 3:00 p.m., closed Friday). You'll discover the mossy past as she explains how the cistern collected water, how drunken lords managed to get their keys into the keyholes, and how prisoners were left to rot in the dungeon (you'll look down the typical only-way-out hole in the ceiling). In the only surviving original knights' sleeping quarters (rough-hewn plank boxes lined with hay), you'll see how knights spent their nights. Lancelot would cry a lot.

The amazing little fortified town of Glurns hunkers down about an hour west of Reifenstein Castle (on the high road to Lake Como). Glurns still lives within its square wall on the Adige River, with a church bell-tower that has a thing about ringing, and real farms, rather than boutiques, filling the town courtyards. You can sleep with the family Hofer near the church, just outside of town (tel. 0473/81597).

MOORISH RUINS OF SINTRA, PORTUGAL

The desolate ruins of an 800-year-old Moorish (Moslem) castle overlook the sea and the town of Sintra just west of Lisbon. Ignored by most of the tourists who flock to the glitzy Pena Palace (a castle capping a neighboring hilltop), the ruins of Sintra offer scramble-up-and-down-the-ramparts fun, atmospheric picnic perches, views, and an enchanted forest. With a little imagination, it's 1,000 years ago, and you're under attack.

CASTLE DAY: NEUSCHWANSTEIN (BAVARIA) AND THE EHRENBERG RUINS (REUTTE IN TIROL)

Four of my favorite castles—two famous, two unknown—can be seen in one busy day. "Castle Day" takes you to Germany's Disney-like Neuschwanstein Castle, the more stately Hohenschwangau castle at its foot, and the much older Ehrenberg Ruins (actually two castles) across the Austrian border in Reutte.

Home base is the small Austrian town of Reutte (just over the German border, three Alp-happy hours by train west of Innsbruck). Reutte has a helpful tourist information office with a room-finding service that can set you up in a private home "any day of the year" for $15 (open until 6:00 p.m., tel. 05672/ 2336).

From Reutte, catch the early bus across the border to touristy Füssen, the German town nearest to Neuschwanstein. (Planning ahead, note times buses return to Reutte.) From there you can walk, pedal a rented bike, or ride a local bus to Neuschwanstein.

Run with the winds of the past in Europe's countless ruined castles. Here, with a little imagination, you're under attack a thousand years ago in Portugal.

"Mad" King Ludwig's Neuschwanstein Castle

Neuschwanstein is the greatest of King Ludwig II's fairy-tale castles. His extravagance and romanticism earned this Bavarian king the title "Mad King Ludwig" (and an early death). His castle is one of Europe's most popular attractions. Get there early. The doors open at 8:30 a.m., an hour before the tour groups from Munich attack.

Take the fascinating (and required) English tour. This castle, about as old as the Eiffel Tower, is a textbook example of 19th-century romanticism. To insult the Middle Ages, people who were glad they were finally out of them named that culture "Gothic" or barbarian. Then, all of a sudden, in the 1800s it was hip to be square, and neo-Gothic became the rage. Throughout Europe, old castles were restored and new ones built—wallpapered with chivalry. King Ludwig II put his medieval fantasy on the hilltop not for defensive reasons but because he liked the view.

The lavish interior, covered with damsels in distress, dragons, and knights in gleaming armor, is enchanting. (A little knowledge of Wagner's operas goes a long way in bringing these stories to life.) Ludwig had great taste—for a mad king. Read up on this political misfit—a poet, hippie king in the "realpolitik" age of Bismarck. He was found dead in a lake, never to enjoy his medieval fantasy come true. After the tour, climb farther up the hill to Mary's Bridge for the best view of this crazy yet elegant castle.

Ludwig's boyhood home, the Hohenschwangau Castle at the foot of the hill, offers a better look at Ludwig's life and far fewer crowds. Like its more famous neighbor, it costs about $5 and takes an hour to tour.

This is a busy day. By lunchtime, catch the bus back to Reutte and get ready for a completely different castle experience.

Pack a picnic and your camera, and with the help of some local directions, walk 30 minutes out of town to the brooding Ehrenberg Ruins. You'll see a small hill crowned by a ruined castle and a larger hill that conceals its ruins.

The Kleine Schloss (small castle), on the smaller hill, is really ruined but wonderfully free of anything from the twentieth century—except for a fine view of Reutte sleeping peacefully in the valley below.

Highlights of Southern Bavaria and Tirol

The Grosse Schloss (large castle) perched atop the bigger hill is eerily overgrown and ruined beyond recognition. This strenuous hike (possible only when the trail isn't washed out) above the small castle is worthwhile if you have time to get romantic. When cloaked in a cloud shroud you can peer into the spooky mist and almost see medieval knights in distress and damsels in shining armor. You have your own castle. Grab a sword fern, lower your hair, and unfetter that imagination.

Back in the twentieth century, you'll find Ehrenberg's castles reconstructed on Reutte's restaurant walls. Ask at your hotel where you can find a folk evening full of slap-dancing and yodel foolery. A hearty dinner and an evening of local Tirolean entertainment is a fitting way to raise the drawbridge on your memorable "Castle Day."

31. Sobering Sights of Nazi Europe

Fondue, nutcrackers, Monet, Big Ben . . . gas chambers. A trip to once-upon-a-time Europe can be a fairy tale. It can also help tell the story of Europe's twentieth-century fascist nightmare. While few travelers go to Europe to dwell on the horrors of Nazism, most value visiting the memorials of fascism's reign of terror and honoring the wish of its survivors—"Forgive but never forget."

Of the countless concentration camps, **Dachau**, just outside of Munich, is most visited. While some visitors complain that it's too

Memorial at the Dachau concentration camp

Nazi Sights

"prettied-up," it gives a plenty powerful look at how these camps worked. Built in 1933, this first Nazi concentration camp is a compelling voice from our recent, grisly past, warning and pleading "Never Again"—the memorial's theme. On arrival, pick up the mini-guide and check when the next documentary film in English will be shown. The museum, the movie, the chilling camp-inspired art, the reconstructed barracks, the gas chambers (never used), the cremation ovens, and the memorial shrines will chisel into you the hidden meaning of fascism. (Dachau is free, open 9:00 a.m. to 5:00 p.m. and closed Mondays.)

Auschwitz (or Oswiecim), near Krakow in Poland, and Mäthausen, near Linz on the Danube in Austria, are more powerful and less touristed. While many camps were slave-labor camps, Auschwitz, the dreaded destination of the Polish Jews such as those on

Schindler's list, was built to exterminate. View the horrifying film shot
by the Russians who liberated the camp in early 1945. Don't miss the
museum. The simple yet emotionally powerful display of prisoners'
shoes, hairbrushes, and suitcases puts lumps in even the most stoic
throats. Allow plenty of time to wander and ponder.

A second Auschwitz camp, **Birkenau**, is 2 miles away. This bleak
ghost camp, an orderly pile of abandoned barracks and watch-towers
overlooking an ash-gray lake, is left as if no one after the war had the
nerve to even enter the place. Today, pilgrims do. Auschwitz is just 90
minutes by train from the wonder of Krakow, Poland's best-preserved
medieval city.

Mäthausen town sits cute and prim on the romantic Danube at
the start of the very scenic trip downstream to Vienna. But nearby,
atop a now-still quarry, linger the memories of a horrible slave-labor
camp. Less tourist-oriented than Dachau, Mäthausen is a solemn
place of meditation and continuous mourning. Fresh flowers adorn
yellowed photos of lost loved ones. The home country of each victim
has erected a gripping monument. You'll find yourself in an artistic
gallery of grief, resting on a foundation of Never Forget. Mäthausen
(open daily, 8:00 a.m. to 5:00 p.m.) offers an English booklet, an
English movie, and a painful but necessary museum.

Paris and Amsterdam also have their Nazi sights: the **Memorial de
la Deportation** in Paris and **Anne Frank's house** in Amsterdam. To
commemorate the 200,000 French victims of Hitler's camps, Paris
built an evocative memorial on the tip of the Ile de la Cité just behind
Notre-Dame. A visit to this memorial is like entering a work of art.
Walk down the claustrophobic stairs into a world of concrete, iron
bars, water, and sky. Inside the structure the 200,000 crystals—one for
each lost person—eternal flame, triangular niches containing soil
from various concentration camps, and powerful quotes will etch the
message on your mind.

Anne Frank's house, made famous by her diary, gives the cold,
mind-boggling statistics of fascism the all-important intimacy of a
young girl who lived through it and died from it. Even bah-humbug
types, who are dragged in because it's raining and their spouses read
the diary, find themselves caught up.

Before you leave Anne's beyond-the-hidden-staircase world, you'll
get an update on fascism today in Europe. The committed volun-
teers at the Anne Frank house know that the only way fascism
will leave its loony fringe is if we get complacent and think it could
never happen again.

While Hitler controlled Europe, each country had a courageous if small resistance movement. All over Europe, you'll find streets and squares named after the martyrs of the resistance. Any history buff or champion of the underdog will find the courageous patriotism documented in the **Oslo and Copenhagen Nazi resistance museums** thrilling.

Since destruction and death are fascist fortes, only relatively insignificant bits and pieces of Hitler's Germany survive. **Berlin**, now that its Wall is history, is giving its Nazi chapter a little more attention. Several new Nazi-related museums and memorials are in the works. Berlin's Reichstag building (which mysteriously burned down, giving Hitler the excuse every fascist needs to blame the Commies and supersede the law) offers an interesting exhibit on "Questions in German History." You might also visit Berlin's Great Synagogue (which was burned on Kristallnacht in 1938), the site of Hitler's bunker (where he committed suicide in the last days of the war), the Topography of Terror exhibit (near what was Checkpoint Charlie, illustrating SS tactics), and four small "mountains" made from the rubble of the bombed-out city.

Munich's most Hitleresque building is the stony, bold **Haus der Kunst**. Hitler's house of art is now filled with the stuff he hated most . . . modern art. Dali. Picasso. Kandinski. Take that!

In **Nuremberg**, the ghosts of Hitler's showy propaganda rallies still rustle in the Rally Grounds (now Dutzendteich Park), down the Great Road, and through the New Congress Hall. The local tourist office has a handy booklet entitled *Nuremberg 1933 to 1945*.

The town of **Berchtesgaden**, near the Austrian border, is any German's choice for a great mountain hideaway—including Hitler's. The remains of Hitler's Obersalzburg headquarters, with its extensive tunnel system, thrill some World War II buffs but are so scant that most visitors are impressed only by the view.

Knowing you can't take on the world without a great freeway system, Hitler started Germany's autobahn system. **Hitler's first autobahn rest stop** is on the lake called Herrenchiemsee between Munich and Salzburg. Now a lakeside hotel for U.S. military personnel, it's still frescoed with "Deutschland über alles" themes. Take the Feldon exit and politely wander around the hotel. The dining room has the best "love your Aryan heritage and work hard for the state" art.

Your best opportunity to experience Fascist architecture is in Rome, where you can wander through Mussolini's futuristic suburb called **E.U.R.** and the bold pink houses of Fascist Italy's Olympic Village. South of Rome, on the coastal road to Naples, are several towns built in the Mussolini era (such as Latina, Sabaudia, Pontinia, and Aprilia) which are interesting for their stocky colonnades and the intentional sterility of their piazzas.

After completing his "final solution," Hitler had hoped to build a grand museum of the "decadent" Jewish culture in **Prague**. Today Prague's State Jewish Museum (Statni Zidovske Muzeum), in a complex of old synagogues, contains artifacts the Nazis assembled from that city's once-thriving Jewish community.

Just outside of Prague is the **Terezin concentration camp**. This particularly insidious place was dolled up as a model camp for Red Cross inspection purposes. Displays show how the inmates had their own newspaper and how the children put on cute plays. But after the camp passed its inspection, life returned to slave labor and death. A touching collection of Jewish children's art reflects their experience during this Nazi nightmare.

Possibly the most moving sight of all is the martyred village of **Oradour-sur-Glane** in central France. This town, 15 miles northwest of Limoges, was machine-gunned and burned in 1944 by Nazi SS troops. Seeking revenge for the killing of one of their officers, they left 642 townspeople dead in a blackened crust of a town under a silent blanket of ashes. The poignant ruins of Oradour-sur-Glane— scorched sewing machines, pots, pans, bikes, and cars—have been preserved as an eternal reminder of the reality of war. When you visit, you'll see the simple sign that greets every pilgrim who enters: "*Souviens-toi* . . . remember."

32. Europe's Best-Preserved Little Towns

Every once in a while as you travel, you stumble onto a town that somehow missed the 20th-century bus. Ironically, many of these wonderfully preserved towns are so full of Old World charm because, for various reasons, their economies failed. The towns became so poor that no one even bothered to tear them down to build more modern towns. The Cotswolds lost their export market. Bruges' harbor silted up. Stranded-in-the-past Dutch fishing towns were left high and dry as the sea around them was reclaimed. Toledo lost its position as Spain's capital city.

Today, many of these towns enjoy a renewed prosperity as "tourist dreams come true." Others slumber on, quietly keeping their secrets. When the Old World is not performing on big-city stages, it huddles in the pubs and gossips in the markets of Europe's villages. Here are a few of my favorites. (Hotels are listed in the Appendix.)

Óbidos, Portugal's medieval walled gem, is a short drive north of Lisbon. Its city wall circles a clutter of cobbled paths, alleys, flower-decked homes, and a castle, now one of Portugal's popular *pousadas* (historic government-run hotels). While several queens used the town as a dowry, today's Óbidos is used by the Portuguese tourist board to lure tourists. Like a glazed tile, it's beautiful but dead.

Toledo, so historic and well-preserved that the entire city is protected as a national monument, is Spain's historic, artistic, and spiritual capital. Toledo is filled with tourists day-tripping from Madrid, 90 minutes to the north. Miss the bus and spend the night! After dark, Toledo is much more medieval—almost haunted in some corners. Explore its back streets and marvel at the great cathedral with a sacristy full of El Greco masterpieces. Munch on communion wafer-like cookies the size of a paper plate. End your day with a feast of roast suckling pig somewhere in the dark tangle of nighttime Toledo.

The small resorts of the French Riviera line the beach, like prostitutes on bar stools, waiting for tourists in search of a good time. But **Collioures**, just before the Spanish border, aims its charms at its own people and a few savvy passersby. And while most of France's Mediterranean coast is condo city, the stretch just south of Perpignon is more like camping village. Collioures offers an ideal small town-without-the-glitz alternative to the more famous stretch. Like a child trying to entertain, it offers 31 flavors of pastel cheering up its crowded port-town lanes; six scooped-out, sandy little beaches; a craggy coastline promenade; and a winking lighthouse. With all this under a once-mighty castle and in the shade of the Pyrenees, it's no wonder painters and local families feel no need to struggle with the Cannes-fusion that grabs the typical Riviera-bound visitor. In a district called Catalane, flying a flag looking just like Barcelona's over its tiny bull-ring, and greeting you with its own accent, in some ways Collioures has turned its cobbled back on France. But the ambience of Collioures is what was so charming about the Cote d'Azur back before the introduction of the paid vacation made the Riviera France's holiday beach. Collioures is about 2 hours by car or train from Avignon, Carcassonne, and Barcelona. And by car, you're an hour's climb to Peyrepertuse, the most impressive castle ruin of the many that dot the Pyrenees. For cheap, airy, and comfortable rooms a block past the stream bed in the old town, call "Chambres," 20 rue Pasteur, tel. 68 82 15 31.

Bruges (pronounced BROOZH, in French), or Brugge (pronounced BROO-guh, in Flemish), is Belgium's medieval wonderland.

Bruges has enough art to make a big city proud. Let a local guide show you the town's treasures: fun modern art, an impressive collection of Flemish paintings, a leaning tower, and the only finished Michelangelo statue in Northern Europe. Like so many small-town wonders, Bruges is well pickled because its economy went sour. Formerly a textiles trading center riding high on the prosperity of the Northern Renaissance, its harbor silted up, the shipping was lost, and Bruges was forgotten—until rediscovered by modern-day tourists. Once again, Bruges thrives. Just 15 minutes from Oostende, where boats dock from Dover, Bruges makes a fine first night on the Continent for travelers coming over from England.

The Netherlands will tempt you with splashy tourist towns— communities of clichés where women with the ruddiest cheeks are paid to stand on doorsteps wearing wooden shoes, lace aprons, and smiles. A local boy peels eels, there's enough cheese to make another moon, and some kid somewhere must have his finger in a dike. These towns (such as Volendam, Monnickendam, and Marken) are designed to be fun, and they are. But make an effort to find a purely Dutch town that is true to itself, not to tourism. Rent a bike and enjoy exploring this tiny, flat country with your own wheels. In Holland, you can rent a bike at one train station and leave it at nearly any other. My favorite village is little **Hindeloopen** (near Sneek). Silent behind its dike, it's right out of a Vermeer painting—hard-core Holland. The towns of Haarlem, Delft, and Edam are pleasant small-town bases for easy day-tripping into often-sleazy Amsterdam.

England loves quaintness. Every year she holds most-beautiful-town contests, and all over the country cobbles are scrubbed, flowers are planted, and hedges shaved. With such spirit, it's not surprising that England is freckled with more small-town cuteness than any country in Europe. The "ye olde" pubs and markets, combined with townspeople who happily eat, breathe, and sleep their history, make any rural part of England a fine setting to enjoy tea and scones or a pint of beer.

While you're likely to find a small, prize-winning town just about anywhere in England, the **Cotswold Hills** and the southeast coast tuck away some of the best. Both regions were once rich, but shifting seas and industrial low tides left them high and dry. Today, their chief export is coziness with a British accent. The southeast coast has five former ports, the "Cinque Ports," that now harbor tourists for a living. One of them, Rye, is commonly overrated as England's most photogenic village. England's many moors hide away time-passed villages that have refused to join the modern parade. **Staithes**, Captain Cook's boyhood town, just north of Whitby near the York Moors, is a salty jumble of ancient buildings bunny-hopping down a ravine to a cramped little harbor.

Europe has become a scavenger hunt for tourists, and most of the prizes have been found. But there are many towns that time forgot and tourists neglect. Passau in Germany, Hall in Tirol, Rouen in France, Sighisoara in Romania, and Erice in Sicily are just a few. Even with tourist crowds, which are now a standard feature in the summer months, the smaller towns of Europe give the traveler the best look at Europe's old culture.

33. Bad Towns and Tourist Traps

It's generally not considered "in good style" to write negatively about tourist destinations. But since I'm the kind of tour guide who burps with the mike on, I'd like to give you my opinion on Europe's dullest places. Chances are that you have too many stops on your trip wish list and not enough time. To make your planning a little easier, take my advice and skip the places described here.

Zurich and Geneva are two of Switzerland's largest and most sterile cities. Both are pleasantly situated on a lake—like Buffalo and Cleveland. And both are famous, but name familiarity is a rotten reason to go somewhere. If you want a Swiss city, see Bern, but it's almost criminal to spend a sunny Swiss day anywhere but high in the Alps.

Bordeaux must mean "boredom" in some ancient language. If I were offered a free trip to that town, I'd stay home and clean the fridge. Connoisseurs visit for the wine, but Bordeaux wine country and Bordeaux city are as different as night and night soil. There's a wine-tourist information bureau in Bordeaux which, for a price, will bus you out of town into the more interesting wine country nearby.

Andorra, a small country in the Pyrenees between France and Spain, is as scenic as any other chunk of those mountains. People from all over Europe flock to Andorra to take advantage of its famous duty-free shopping. As far as Americans are concerned, Andorra is just a big Spanish-speaking Radio Shack. There are no bargains here that you can't get at home. Enjoy the Pyrenees with less traffic elsewhere.

Germany's famous Black Forest disappoints more people than it excites. If that's all Germany offered, it would be worth seeing. For Europeans, any large forest is a popular attraction. But I'd say the average American visitor who's seen more than three trees in one place would prefer Germany's Romantic Road and Bavaria to the east, the Rhine and Mosel country to the north, the Swiss Alps to the south, and France's Alsace region to the west—all high points that cut the Black Forest down to stumps.

Norway's Stavanger, famous for nearby fjords and its status as an oil-boom town, is a large port that's about as exciting as, well, put it this way . . . emigrants left it in droves to move to the wilds of Minnesota. Time in western Norway is better spent in and around Bergen.

Bucharest, the capital of Romania, has little to offer. Its top-selling postcard is of the Intercontinental Hotel. If you're heading from eastern Europe to Greece, skip Thessaloníki, which deserves its place in the Bible but doesn't belong in travel guidebooks.

Athens, while worth visiting, is probably the most overrated city in Europe. A hundred years ago, Athens was a sleepy town of 8,000 people with a pile of ruins in its backyard. Today it's a giant mix of concrete, smog, noise, tourists, and four million Greeks. See the four major attractions (the Acropolis, the Agora, the Plaka, and the great National Archaeological Museum) and get out to the islands or countryside.

Extra caution is merited in southwest England, a minefield of tourist traps. The British are masters at milking every conceivable tourist attraction for all it's worth. Here are some booby traps worth avoiding if you're traveling on limited time or money:

Cornwall, England's southernmost region, has more than its share of cotton-candy fluff when it comes to tourism. I'll never forget driving down the road past signs prepping me for the "Devil's Toenail." "Only 5 miles—The Devil's Toenail." Then, "The Devil's Toenail—next left!" Well, I figured I'd only be here once, so I better check it out. I pulled into the parking lot. Paid to park. Paid again to pass through the turnstile. Walked to the bottom of the ravine. And there it was, a rock the size of a watermelon, that looked just like . . . a toenail. Disappointed and a bit embarrassed, I took a quick picture and hiked back to my car, promising myself never again to fall for such a sly snare.

Predictably, Land's End, the far southwest tip of England, is geared up to attract—and does attract—hordes of tourists. You pay to park, pay again to enter, walk out to the point for a photo to prove you were there, grab a postcard, and leave.

On the north Cornwall coast, above Land's End, are two more tourist magnets. Tintagel is famous for its castle—the legendary birthplace of King Arthur. The castle's exciting windswept and wave-beaten ruins are well worth exploring. Meanwhile, the town does everything in its little power to exploit the profitable Arthurian legend. There's even a pub in town called the Excali Bar.

Just up the coast is Clovelly. I had it circled in my guidebook years before I ever got there. It sounded so cute—"daintily clinging to the rocky coast, desperately trying not to plunge into the wicked seas." But when you arrive, reality rules. You'll pay to park your car 100 yards away and join the crowds funneling into the little town's one street. You can shop your way down one side to the waterfront and up the other side past cute knickknack shops, all selling just about the same goodies—like "clotted cream that you can mail home." Don't let tourist traps get between you and the real beauties of England.

The towns and places I've mentioned here are worth skipping only because they're surrounded by so many places much more worthy of the average traveler's limited vacation time. If you have a villa in Andorra or a cuckoo-clock shop in the Black Forest, no offense is meant. Just remember to distinguish carefully between entrepreneurial ventures and legitimate sightseeing attractions.

Beyond Europe

34. Morocco: Plunge Deep

Walking through the various *souks* of the labyrinthine *medina*, I found sights you could only dream of in America. Dodging blind men and club-feet, I was stoned by smells, sounds, sights, and feelings. People came in all colors, sizes, temperaments, and varieties of deformities. Milky eyes, charismatic beggars, stumps of limbs, sticks of children, tattooed women, walking mummies, grabbing salesmen, teasing craftsmen, seductive scents, half-bald dogs, and little boys on rooftops were reaching out from all directions.

Ooo! Morocco! Slices of Morocco make the *Star Wars* bar scene look bland. And it's just a quick cruise from Spain. You can't, however, experience Morocco in a day-trip from the Costa del Sol. Plunge deep and your journal will read like a Dali painting. While Morocco is not easy traveling, it gets rave reviews from those who plug this Islamic detour into their European vacation.

In Spain, catch a boat to Tangier from Algeciras or the more pleasant town of Tarifa. Don't linger in Tangier and Tetuan, the Moroccan Tijuanas of the north coast. Tangier is not really Morocco—it's a city full of con men who thrive on green tourists. Find the quickest connections south to Rabat. Power your way off the boat, then shove through the shysters to the nearby train station. They'll tell you there's no train until tomorrow, or "Rabat is closed on Thursdays," anything to get you to stay in Tangier. Believe nothing. Be rude if you have to. Tangier can give you only grief, while the real Morocco lies to the south. Try to make friends with a Moroccan traveler on the boat, who won't be a con man and who'll usually be happy to help you slip through his embarrassingly stressful port of entry.

Rabat, Morocco's capital, is a good first stop. This comfortable most-European-city-in-Morocco lacks the high-pressure tourism of the towns on the north coast. Or, for a pleasant break on the beach and a relaxing way to break into Morocco, spend a day at Asilah, between Tangier and Larache.

Taxis are cheap and a real bargain when you consider the comfort, speed, and convenience they provide in these hot, dusty, and confus-

Moroccan road sign: Beware of toboggans

ing cities. Eat and drink carefully in Morocco. Bottled water and bottled soft drinks are safe. The extra cautious might have "well-cooked" written in Arabic on a scrap of paper and flash it when you order meat. I found the couscous disappointing but the tajine and omelets uniformly good. The Arabs use different number symbols. Learn them. You can practice on license plates which list the number twice. Morocco was a French colony, so French is more widely understood than English. A French phrase book is handy. Travel very light in Morocco. You can leave most of your luggage at your last Spanish hotel for free if you plan to spend a night there on your return from Africa.

After Rabat, pass through Casablanca (great movie, dull city) and catch the Marrakech Express south. You'll hang your head out the window of that romantic old train and sing to the passing desert.

Marrakech is the epitome of exotic. Take a horse-drawn carriage from the station to downtown and find a hotel near the Djemaa el Fna, the central square of Marrakech, where the action is. Desert musicians, magicians, storytellers, acrobats, snake charmers, gamblers, and tricksters gather crowds of tribespeople who have come to Marrakech to do their market chores. As a tourist, you'll fit in like a clown at a funeral. Be very careful, don't gamble, and hang onto your wallet. You're in another world, and you're not clever here. Spend an entire day in the colorful medina wandering aimlessly from *souk* to

Morocco

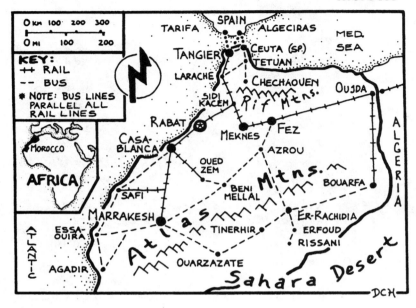

souk. There's a *souk* for each trade, such as the dyers' *souk*, the leather *souk*, and the carpet *souk*.

In the medina, you'll be badgered—or "guided"—by small boys all claiming to be "a friend who wants to practice English." They are after money, nothing else. If you don't want their services, make two things crystal clear: you have no money for them and you want no guide. Then completely ignore them. Remember that while you're with a guide, he'll get commissions for anything you buy. Throughout Morocco, you'll be pestered by these obnoxious hustler-guides.

I often hire a young and easy-to-control boy who speaks enough English to serve as my interpreter. It seems that if I'm "taken," the other guides leave me alone. And that in itself is worth the small price of a guide.

The market is a shopper's delight. Bargain hard, shop around, and you'll come home with some great souvenirs. Government emporiums usually have the same items you find in the market, priced fairly. If you get sick of *souks*, shop there and you'll get the fair price—haggle-free.

From Marrakech, consider getting to Fez indirectly by taking an exciting 7-day loop to the south. While buses are reliable and efficient throughout Morocco, this tour is best by car, and it's easy to rent a car in Marrakech and drop it off in Fez. (Car rentals are cheaper from the U.S.A.)

Drive or catch the bus south, over the rugged Atlas Mountains, to Saharan Morocco. Explore the isolated oasis towns of Ouarzazate, Tinerhir, and Er-Rachidia. If time permits, the trip from Ouarzazate to Zagora is an exotic mud-brick pie. These towns each have a weekly "market day" when the tribespeople gather to do their shopping. This is your chance to stock up on honeydew melons and goats' heads. Stay in Tinerhir's Hotel du Todra and climb to the roof for a great view of the busy marketplace below.

Venture out of town into the lush fields where you'll tumble into an almost Biblical world. Sit on a rock and dissect the silence. A weary donkey carrying a bearded old man in a white robe and turban might clip-clop slowly past you. Suddenly, six Botticelli maidens flit like watercolor confetti across your trail and giggle out of sight. Stay tuned. The show goes on.

Bus rides in this part of Morocco are intriguing. I could write pages about experiences I've had on Moroccan buses—good and bad—but I don't want to spoil the surprise. Just ride them with a spirit of adventure, fingers crossed, and your bag not on the rooftop.

SAHARAN ADVENTURE

Heading south from Er-Rachidia, a series of mud-brick villages bunny-hop down a lush river valley and into the Sahara. Finally, the road melts into the sand and the next stop is, literally, Timbuktu.

The strangeness of this Alice in a sandy Wonderland world, untempered, can be overwhelming—even frightening. The finest hotel in Erfoud, the region's major town, will provide a much-needed refuge, keeping out the sand, heat waves, and street kids and providing safe-to-eat and tasty local food, reliable information, and a good affordable bed.

But the hotel is only your canteen and springboard. Explore! If you plan to go deep into the desert, hire a guide. Choose one you can understand and tolerate, set a price for his services, and, before dawn, head for the dunes.

You'll drive to the last town, Rissani (market days: Tuesday, Thursday, Sunday), and then farther south over 15 miles of natural asphalt to the oasis village of Merzouga. There's plenty of tourist traffic at sunrise and in the early evening, so hitching is fairly easy. A couple of places in Merzouga rent spots on their terrace for those who spend the night. If a civil war is still smoldering in the desert, you may have to show your passport.

Before you glows a chain of sand-dune mountains. Climb one. It's not easy. I seemed to slide farther backward with each step. Hike along a cool and crusty ridge. Observe bugs and their tracks. Watch small sand avalanches you started all by yourself. From the great virgin summit, savor the Sahara view orchestrated by a powerful silence. Your life sticks out like a lone star in a black sky. Tumble, roll, and slosh down your dune. Look back and see the temporary damage one person can inflict on that formerly perfect slope. Then get back in your car before the summer sun turns the sand into a steaming griddle and you into an omelet. Off-season, the midday desert sun is surprisingly mild.

Merzouga is full of very poor people. The village children hang out at the ruins of an old palace. A ragtag percussion group gave us an impromptu concert. The children gathered around us tighter and tighter as the musicians picked up the tempo. We shared smiles, warmth, and sadness. A little Moroccan Judy Garland saw out of one eye, the other cloudy as rice pudding. One gleaming 6-year-old carried a tiny brother slung, sleeping, on her back. His crusty little fly-covered face was too tired to flinch. We had a bag of candy to share and tried to get 40 kids into an orderly line to march past one by one. Impossible. The line degenerated into a free-for-all and our bag became a piñata.

Only through the mercy of your guide can you find your way back to Rissani. Camels loiter nonchalantly, looking very lost and not caring. Cool lakes flirt, a distant mirage, and the black hardpan road stretches endlessly in all directions.

Then with a sigh we were back in Rissani, where the road starts up again. For us, it was breakfast time, and Rissani offered little more than some very thought-provoking irony. My friends and I could find no "acceptable" place to eat. Awkwardly, we drank germ-free Cokes with pursed lips, balanced bread on upturned bottle caps, and swatted laughing legions of flies. We were by far the wealthiest people in the valley—and the only ones unable to enjoy an abundant variety of good but strange food.

Observing the scene from our humble rusted table, we saw a busy girl rhythmically smashing date seeds; three stoic, robed elders with horseshoe beards; and a prophet wandering through with a message for all that he was telling to nobody.

Er-Rachidia was as dull and comforting as home. Back at the hotel, we shared the Walkman and enjoyed the pool, resting and recharging before our next Saharan plunge.

SAHARAN NIGHTLIFE

Desert dwellers and smart tourists know the value of a siesta during the hottest part of the day. But a Saharan evening is the perfect time for a traveler to get out and experience the vibrancy of North African village life. We drove 10 miles north of Erfoud to a fortified mud-brick oasis village. There was no paint, no electricity, no cars—only people, adobe walls, and palm trees. Absolutely nothing other than the nearby two-lane highway hinted of the twentieth century.

We entered like Lewis and Clark without Sacajawea, knowing instantly we were in for a rich experience. A wedding feast was erupting and the whole town buzzed with excitement, all decked out in colorful robes and their best smiles. We felt very welcome.

The teeming street emptied through the medieval gate onto the field, where a band was playing squawky oboe-like instruments and drums. A circle of 20 ornately-dressed women made high siren noises with tongues flapping like party favors. Rising dust diffused the lantern light, giving everything the grainy feel of an old photo. The darkness focused our attention on a relay of seductively beautiful, snake-thin dancers. A flirtatious atmosphere raged, cloaked safely in the impossibility of anything transpiring beyond coy smiles and teasing twists.

Then the village's leading family summoned us for dinner. Pillows, blankets, a lantern, and a large round filigreed table turned a stone cave into a warm lounge. The men of this family had traveled to Europe and spoke some English. For over two hours, the women prepared dinner and the men proudly entertained their first-world guests. First was the ritualistic tea ceremony. Like a mad chemist, the tea specialist mixed it just right. With a thirsty gleam in his eye and a large spike in his hand, he hacked off a chunk of sugar from a coffee can-sized lump and watched it melt into Morocco's basic beverage. He sipped it, as if testing a fine wine, added more sugar, and offered me a taste. When no more sugar could be absorbed, we drank it with cookies and dates. Then, with the fanfare of a pack of Juicy Fruit, the men passed around a hashish pipe. Our shocked look was curious to them. Next, a tape deck brought a tiny clutter of music, from Arab and tribal Berber music to James Brown, reggae, and twangy Moroccan pop. The men danced splendidly.

Finally the meal came. Fourteen people sat on the floor, circling two round tables. Nearby, a child silently waved a palm branch fan, keeping the flies away. A portable washbasin and towel were passed around to start and finish the meal. With our fingers and gravy-soaked slabs of bread, we grabbed spicy meat and vegetables.

Everyone dipped eagerly into the delicious central bowl of couscous.

So far, the Moroccan men dominated. Young girls took turns peeking around the corner and dashing off—much like teeny-boppers anywhere. Two older women in striking, black-jeweled outfits were squatting attentively in the corner, keeping their distance and a very low profile. Then one pointed to me and motioned in charades, indicating long hair, a backpack, and a smaller partner. I had been in this same village in the '70s. I had longer hair and a backpack and was traveling with a short partner. Did she remember us? I scribbled "1978" on a scrap of paper. She scratched it out and wrote "1979." Wow! She remembered my 20-minute visit so long ago! People in remote lands enjoy a visiting tourist and find the occasion at least as memorable as we do. So many more doors open to the traveler who knocks.

After a proud tour of their schoolhouse, we were escorted across the field back to our car, which had been guarded by a silent, white-robed man. We drove away, reeling with the feeling that the memories of this evening would be the prize souvenir of our trip.

35. Turkey's Hot

Turkey is a proud new country. It was born in 1923, when Ataturk, the father of modern Turkey, rescued it from the buffet line of European colonialism. He divided church and state, liberated (at least on paper) women, replaced the Arabic script with Europe's alphabet, and gave the battle-torn, corrupt, and demoralized remnants of the Ottoman empire the foundation of a modern nation. Because of Ataturk, today's 60 million Turks have a flag—and reason to wave it. For a generation, many young Turkish women actually worried that they'd never be able to really love a man because of their love for the father of their country.

At the same time, Turkey is a musty archeological attic with dusty civilization stacked upon civilization. The more they dig, the more they learn that Turkey, not Mesopotamia, is the cradle of Western civilization.

I find Turkey even tastier, friendlier, cheaper, and richer in culture and history than Greece. But the average Turk looks like a character the average American mother would tell her child to run from. Dark and unshaven . . . Turks can't help it if they look like someone who could assassinate the Pope. It's important that we see past our visual hang-ups and recognize Turks as the sincere and friendly people they are.

Turkey would love to meet you

Those who haven't been to Turkey wonder why anyone would choose to go there. Those who've been, dream of returning. Turkey is being discovered. Tourists are learning that the image of the terrible Turk is false, created to a great degree by its unfriendly neighbors. Turks are quick to remind visitors that, surrounded by Syria, Iraq, Iran, Armenia, Georgia, Bulgaria, and Greece, they're not living in Mr. Rogers' neighborhood.

Many Americans know Turkey only from the thrilling but unrealistic movie *Midnight Express*. The movie was paid for, produced, and performed by Armenians and Greeks (historically unfriendly neighbors). It says nothing about the Turks or Turkey today. Also, many visitors are put off by Turkey's "rifles on every corner" image. Turkey is not a police state. Its NATO commitment is to maintain nearly a million-man army. Except in the far east, where they are dealing with the Kurds and Iraq, these soldiers have little to do but "patrol" and "guard"—basically loiter, in uniform.

Today, Turkey is on the move. It's looking West and getting there. You can travel cheaply throughout the country on Turkey's great bus system. Buses seem to go from nearly all points to nearly all points nearly all the time. Telephones work. Hotels have FAX machines. I recently had a forgotten plane ticket expressed across the country in 24 hours for $3. Fifty percent of Turkey's 42,000 villages had electricity in 1980. Now all do. Does all this modernization threaten the beautiful things that make Turkish culture so Turkish? An old village woman assured me, "We can survive TV and tourism because we have deep and strong cultural roots."

English is ever more widely spoken, and tourism is booming. Business everywhere seems brisk but inflation is so bad that most hotels list their prices in deutsche marks or dollars. With around 35,000 Turkish liras to the dollar, shoppers carry calculators to keep track of the zeros.

Travel in Turkey is cheap. Good, comfortable, double rooms with private showers cost $20. Vagabonds order high on menus. And buses, which offer none of the romantic chaos of earlier years, take travelers anywhere in the country smoothly for about $2 an hour.

Turkey knows it's on the fence between the rising wealth and power of a soon-to-be-united Europe and a forever-fragile-and-messy Middle East. Turks know the threat of the rising tide of Islamic fundamentalism and, while the country is 98 percent Muslim, they want nothing of the Khomeni-style rule that steadily blows the dust of religious discontent over their border. But fundamentalists are making inroads. As they walk by, veiled women in tow, modern-minded Turks grumble—a bit nervously. On Ataturk Day, stadiums around the country are filled with students shouting in thunderous unison, "We are a secular nation."

Two months after the Gulf War, I enjoyed my ninth trip through Turkey, this time with 22 travel partners and a Turkish co-guide. We had a life-changing 15 days together, enjoyed a level-headed look at Islam, took a peek at a hard-working, developing country with its act impressively together, and learned how our mass media can wrongly shape America's assessment of faraway lands. No survey was necessary to know that we all brought home a better understanding of our world. But a survey did show that fourteen people bought carpets (mostly under $1,000, one for $3,000), eight people had diarrhea (seven for under two days, one for six days), and nine of us learned to play backgammon well enough to actually beat a Turk in a smoky teahouse. For $5, you can buy tea for 20 new friends, play backgammon until the smoke doesn't bother you, and rock to the pulse of Turkey. Oh, those tiny handmade dice . . . cockeyed dots in a land where time is not money.

Turkey reshuffles your cards. A beautiful girl is called a pistachio, especially if she's a 90-60-90 (metric). To insult someone, tell them they have the face of a Maltese plum—the ugliest fruit you'll ever enjoy. Industrious boys break large chocolate bars into small pieces to sell for a profit. For two dollars, a Gypsy's bear will do a show called "your mother-in-law dancing in a Turkish bath."

Much of Turkey is scrambling into the modern Western world but the Turkish way of life is painted onto this land with an indelible cultural ink. If you're able to put your guidebook aside and follow your wanderlust, you'll still find sleepy goats playing Bambi on rocks overlooking a nomad's black tent. High above on the hillside, the lone but happy song of the goatherd's flute plays golden oldies. The mother bakes bread and minds the children, knowing her man is near.

Riding the waves of Turkey is like abstract art, a riveting movie without a plot, a melody of people, culture, and landscape you just can't stop whistling.

GÜZELYURT—CAPPADOCIA WITHOUT TOURISTS

Cappadocia is rightly famous as the most bizarre and fascinating bit of central Turkey that accepts bank cards. The most exciting discovery I made on my last trip was a town on the edge of Cappadocia called Güzelyurt.

Güzelyurt means "beautiful land." It's best known in Turkey as the town where historic enemies—Greeks, Turks, Kurds, and Bulgarians—live in peace. The town is a harmony of cultures, history, architecture, and religions. Walk down streets that residents 3,000 years ago might recognize, past homes carved into the rocks, past friendly greetings of *merhaba*. Scowling sheepdogs, caged behind ten-foot-high troglodyte rockeries, give the scene just enough tension.

Walk to a viewpoint at the far side of town (above the Sivisli church) toward the snowy slopes of the Fuji-like volcano that rules the horizon. Before you is a lush and living gorge. The cliff rising from the gorge is stacked with building styles: upon the 1,600-year-old church sit troglodyte caves, Selcuk arches, and Ottoman facades. And on the horizon gleams the tin dome of the twentieth-century mosque, with its twin minarets giving you a constant visual call to prayer. The honey that holds this architectural baklava together is people.

Put your camera away, shut your mouth, and sit silently in the sounds of 1000 B.C Children play, birds chirp, roosters crow, shepherds chase goats, and mothers cackle. (Ignore that distant motorbike.)

Below you, sleeping in the greens and wet browns of this tidepool of simple living, is the church of St. Gregorius. Built in 385, it's the birthplace of church music, specifically the Gregorian chant. Its single minaret indicates that it's preserved as a mosque today in a valley where people call god Allah.

Who needs three-star sights and tourist information offices? In Güzelyurt, we dropped by the city hall. The mayor scampered across town to arrange a lunch for us in his home. He welcomed us Christians, explaining, "We believe in the four books"—the local way of saying, "It doesn't matter what you call Him, as long as you call Him." He showed us the names of his Greek Christian friends, kept as safe and sacred as good friends could be in his most precious and holy possession, the family Koran bag.

The lady of the house made tea. Overlapping carpets gave the place a cozy bug-in-a-rug feeling. As the lady cranked up the music, we all began to dance like charmed snakes. It was very safe sex until our fingers could snap no more. A small girl showed me a handful of almonds and said, "Buy dem." *Badam* is Turkish for almond, and this was her gift to me. Enjoying her munchies, I reciprocated with a handful of Pop Rocks. As the tiny candies exploded in her mouth, her surprised eyes became even more beautiful.

The town's name is spelled proudly across its volcanic backdrop. The black bust of Ataturk seems to loom just as high over the small modern market square. The streets are alive with the relaxed click of victorious *tavla* pieces (backgammon). The men of the town, who seem to be enjoying one eternal cigarette break, proudly make a point not to stare at the stare-worthy American visitors searching for postcards in a town with no tourism.

Güzelyurt, in central Turkey, is 35 miles from Nevsehir and a short bus ride from Aksaray. It's near the Peristrema Valley, famous for its 7-mile hike through a lush valley of poplar groves, eagles, vultures, and early Christian churches. The town has one rustic but classy hotel (Hotel Karballa, Güzelyurt, Aksaray, tel. 382/451-2103, $40 doubles with dinner and breakfast) and one pension (Pansion Gelveri, run by Kadir Gok who speaks German, one block off the town square, $7 for bed and a great local-style breakfast, tel. 382/451-2166).

Belisirma, a village near Güzelyurt, is even more remote. With a population of "100 homes," Belisirma zigzags down to its river, which rushes through a poplar forest past the tiny Belisirma Walley Wellkome Camping (one bungalow). A group of bangled women in lush purple wash their laundry in the river under the watchful eyes of men who seem to have only a ceremonial function. Children on donkeys offer to show off the troglodyte church carved into the hill just past the long, narrow, farm plots. A lady, face framed in the dangling jewelry of her shawl, her net worth hanging in gold around her neck, points to my postcard, a picture of a little girl holding a baby sheep. The girl is her niece. They call the card, "Two Lambs."

14 DAYS IN TURKEY

Turkey offers the most enjoyable culture shock within striking distance of Europe. But it's a rich brew, and for most, two weeks is enough. Here's my recommendation for the best two-week look at Turkey.

Flying to Istanbul is about as tough as flying to Paris. For instance, if you fly SAS, both are about a 2-hour flight from your Copenhagen hub. When planning your trip, remember that flying "open jaws" into Istanbul and home from Athens is about $70 cheaper than flying in and out of Istanbul . . . and makes for a more diverse and efficient itinerary.

Spend your first two days in Istanbul. Take the taxi ($12) from the airport to the Hippodrome near the Blue Mosque where you'll find several decent small hotels and pensions. My choice would be the Turkoman Hotel ($55 doubles, Asmali Cesme Sokak #2, 34400 Sultanahmet, tel. 516-2956, fax 516-2957). Cheaper and also good in the neighborhood are the Optimist Guesthouse (Atmeydani 68, tel. 516-2398, $35 doubles) and the Hippodrome Pansiyon (Ucler Sokak #9, Sultanahmet, tel. 516-0902, very simple, $16 doubles).

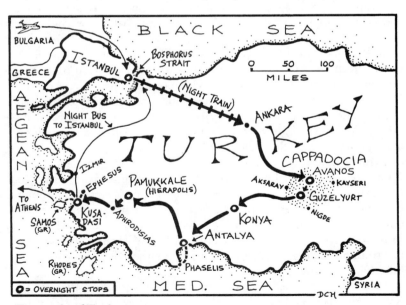

Two weeks of Turkey

For an easygoing first evening, walk over to the Blue Mosque and enjoy the free sound and light show in the park. Spend the next day doing the historic biggies: Topkapi Palace, Blue Mosque and the Aya Sofya church. The latter was built in 537, when Istanbul was called Constantinople and was the leading city in Christendom. It was the largest domed building in Europe until Brunelleschi built Florence's great dome in the Renaissance, nearly a thousand years later.

Bone up on Anatolian folk life in the Islamic Arts Center (just off the old Roman racetrack called the Hippodrome), then taxi to the modern center of bustling Istanbul for dinner in the "Flower Passage," where Istanbul's beautiful people and tourists alike enjoy the funky elegance. If you like baklava, stroll the city's main drag, Istiklal Street, in search of a pastry shop. From the heartbeat of Istanbul, Taksim Square, catch a cab home. A less touristy dinner option is the Kumkapi, a fishermen's-wharf district teeming with seafood restaurants and happy locals (a pleasant walk from the Hippodrome).

The next morning, browse the bizarre bazaar and Spice Market. After lunch take an intercontinental cruise up the Bosphorus. If you disembark in Asian Istanbul you can taxi quickly to the station to catch your overnight train to Ankara.

This, the only reliable train in Asian Turkey, gets you to the country's capital by 8:00 a.m.. As you munch feta cheese, olives, tomatoes, and cucumbers for breakfast in the dining car, you know you're far from home.

Ankara has two blockbuster sights. The Museum of Anatolian Civilizations is a prerequisite for meaningful explorations of the ancient ruins that litter the Turkish countryside. The Ataturk Mausoleum shines a light on the recent and dramatic birth of modern Turkey and gives you an appreciation of that country's love of its George Washington. For a happening scene, a great view, and a look at modern Turkey, ride to the top of the Ankara tower.

From Ankara, it's a 4-hour bus ride to exotic and evocative Cappadocia, an eroded wonderland of cave dwellings that go back to the early Christian days when the faithful fled persecution by hiding in Cappadocian caves. Cappadocia gives you a time-tunnel experience, with its horse carts, troglodytes, strangely eroded mini-Matterhorns called "fairy chimneys," traditional crafts, and labyrinthine underground cities. Don't miss the Back Door town of Güzelyurt (see above).

From mysterious Cappadocia, cross the Anatolian Plateau to Konya, the most conservative and orthodox Muslim city in Turkey, home of the Mevlana order and the Whirling Dervishes. The dance of the dervish connects a giving god with our world. One hand is gracefully raised, the other is a loving spout, as he whirls faster and faster in a trance the modern American attention span would be hard-pressed to understand.

Then follow the steps of St. Paul over the Taurus Mountains to the Mediterranean resort of Antalya. You can hire a yacht to sail the Mediterranean coast to your choice of several beachside ruins. After a free day on the beach, travel inland to explore the ruins of Aphrodisias and that site's excellent museum.

Nearby is Pamukkale, a touristy village and Turkey's premier mineral spa. Soak among broken ancient columns in a mineral spring and wander the acres and acres of terraced steamy mineral pools. Hop like a frisky sparrow through a kaleidoscope of white birdbaths.

For the final leg of your two-week swing through Turkey, head west to the coastal resort of Kusadasi. Nearby is my favorite ancient site, the ruins of Ephesus. For a relaxing finale, take a Turkish Hamam (bath with massage) in Kusadasi before catching the daily boat to the entertaining island of Samos in Greece (see below). Boats and planes take travelers from Samos to other Greek islands and on to Athens.

SOME HINTS TO MAKE TURKEY EASIER

Good information is rare in Turkey, especially in the East. Bring a guidebook from home. Take advantage of Tom Brosnahan's guidebook to Turkey (Lonely Planet, 1993 edition). Maps are easy to get in Turkey.

Eat carefully. Find a cafeteria-style restaurant and point. Choose your food personally by tasting and pointing to what you like. Joke around with the cooks. They'll love you for it. Bottled water, soft drinks, *chai* (tea), and coffee are cheap and generally safe. Watermelons are a great source of safe liquid. If you order a glass of tea, your waiter will be happy to "process" your melon, giving it to you peeled and in little chunks on a big plate.

Learn to play backgammon before you visit Turkey. Backgammon, the local pastime, is played by all the men in this part of the world. Join in. It's a great way to instantly become a contributing member of the local teahouse scene.

Really get away from it all. Catch a *dolmus* (shared taxi) into the middle of nowhere. Get off at a small village. If the bus driver thinks you must be mistaken or lost to be getting off there, you've found the right place. Explore the town, befriend the children, trade national dance lessons. Act like an old friend returning after a ten-year absence, and you'll be treated like one.

You'll be stared at all day long. Preserve your sanity with a sense of humor. Joke with the Turks. Talk to them, even if there's no hope of communication. One afternoon, in the town of Ercis, I was waiting for a bus and writing in my journal. A dozen people gathered around me, staring with intense curiosity. I felt that they needed entertainment. I sang the Hoagy Carmichael classic, "Huggin' and a-Chalkin'." When the bus came, my friend and I danced our way on board, waving good-bye to the cheering fans. From then on, my singing entertained most of eastern Turkey.

Make invitations happen and accept them boldly. While exploring villages with no tourism, I loiter near the property of a large family. Very often the patriarch, proud to have a foreign visitor, will invite me to join him cross-legged on his large, bright carpet in the shade. The women of the household bring tea, then peer at us from around a distant corner. Shake hands, jabber away in English, play show-and-tell, show photos from home, take photos of the family, and get their addresses so you can mail them copies. They'll always remember your visit. And so will you.

ISLAM IN A PISTACHIO SHELL

Five times a day, God enjoys a global wave as the call to prayer sweeps at the speed of the sun from the Philippines to Morocco. The muezzin chants: "There is only one God and Mohammed is one of his prophets."

Islam is the fastest-growing religion on earth. Unbiased listings place Mohammed above Jesus on Guinness-type listings of all-time most influential people. For us to understand Islam by studying Khadafy and Hussein would be like a Turk understanding capitalism and Christianity by studying Hitler and Reagan.

Your journeying may give you the opportunity to travel in, and therefore better understand, Islam. Just as it helps to know about spires, feudalism, and the saints to understand your European sightseeing, a few basics on Islam help make your sightseeing in Moslem countries more meaningful. Here they are.

The Islamic equivalent of the Christian bell tower is a minaret, which the muezzin climbed to chant the call to prayer. In a kind of architectural Darwinism, the minarets have shrunk as calls to prayer have been electronically amplified; their height is no longer necessary or worth the expense. Many small modern mosques have one tin mini-minaret about as awesome as your little toe.

Worshipers pray toward Mecca, which, from Turkey, is about in the same direction as Jerusalem, but not quite. In Istanbul, Aya Sofya was built 1,400 years ago as a church, its altar niche facing Jerusalem. Since it became an out-of-sync-with-Mecca mosque, the Moslem focus-of-prayers niche is to the side of what was the altar.

Ah, the smell of socks. A mosque is a shoes-off place. Westerners are welcome to drop in. The small stairway seeming to go nowhere is symbolic of the growth of Islam. Mohammed had to stand higher and higher to talk to his growing following. Today every mosque will have one of these as a kind of pulpit. No priest ever stands on the top stair. That is symbolically reserved for Mohammed.

The "five pillars" of Islam are basic to an understanding of a religious force that is bound to fill our headlines for years to come. Followers of Islam should:

1. Say and believe, "There is only one God and Mohammed is one of his prophets."

2. Visit Mecca. This is interpreted by some Muslims as a command to travel. Mohammed said, "Don't tell me how educated you are, tell me how much you've traveled."

3. Give to the poor (one-fortieth of your wealth, if you are not in debt).

4. Fast during daylight hours through the month of Ramadan. Fasting is a great social equalizer and it helps everyone to feel the hunger of the poor.

5. Pray five times a day. Modern Muslims explain that it's important to wash, exercise, stretch, and think of God. The ritual of Muslim prayer works this into every day—five times.

You'll notice women worship in back of the mosque. For the same reason I find it hard to concentrate on God at aerobics classes, Muslim men decided prayer would go better without the enjoyable but problematic distraction of bent-over women between them and Mecca.

How Muslims can have more than one wife is a bigamistry to many. While polygamy is illegal in Turkey, Islam does allow a man to have as many wives (up to four) as he can love and care for equally. This originated as Mohammed's pragmatic answer to the problem of too many unattached women caused by the death of so many men in the many wars of his day. Religious wars have been as common in Islam as they have been in Christendom.

These basics are a simplistic but honest attempt by a non-Muslim to help travelers from the Christian West understand an often-misunderstood but very rich culture worthy of our respect. And these days, when those who profit from arms sales are so clever at riding the bloody coattails of religious conflict, we need all the understanding we can muster.

THE BEST WAY FROM ATHENS TO TURKEY

The best thing about Athens is the boat to Turkey. Athens is a crowded, over-rated, and polluted tourist trap. See what's important (Acropolis, Agora, Plaka, and National Museum) and leave! Catch a boat ($20, 12 hours) or plane ($70, 1 hour) to Samos, Rhodes, or Kos. Each of these islands is connected daily by boat ($25, 2 hours) to Turkey. This short boat ride gives you more cultural change than the flight from the United States to Athens.

Leaving Greece via Samos gives you a look at one my favorite Greek Islands and drops you in Kusadasi, a pleasant place to enter Turkey and a 20-minute drive from Ephesus.

Samos—green, mountainous, diverse, and friendly—has tourist crowds but not as bad as other Greek islands. Bus transportation on the island is fine. And for $12 a day you can crisscross Samos on your

Greek and Turkish travel agencies are more reliable and helpful than they look

own moped. Pounding over potholes, dodging trucks, stopping to dream across the sea at the hills of Turkey, spanked happily by the prickly wind and Greek sun, a moped ride around Samos is my annual jackhammer of youth.

The tourist map shows plenty of obscure sights on Samos. Gambling that the Spiliani monastery was worth the detour, I traded potholes for gravel and wound up the hill. The road ended at a tiny church overlooking the sunburnt island.

Behind the church was the mouth of a cave, with whitewashed columns carved like teeth into the rock. I wandering into the drippy, dank darkness, cool and quiet as another world. Sitting still, I could almost hear the drip-by-drip growth of the stalagmites and the purr of my brain. The only motion was the slight flicker of slender candles and me ready to venture out of Christendom and into Islam.

36. Eastern Turkey

While Istanbul and the western Turkish coast are rapidly moving toward European-style mainstream tourism (yet still fascinating, cheap, and eager to please), inland Anatolia offers the most cultural thrills. To tour Turkey with abandon, go east, using Ankara as a springboard. From here, buses fan out regularly, transporting you to the region, culture, and era of your choice.

Find a town that has yet to master the business of tourism, like Kastamonu (5 hours northeast of Ankara). Business hotels are comfortable ($15 doubles), but not slick. I handed a postcard to the boy at the desk, hoping he could mail it for me. He looked it over a couple of times on both sides, complimented me, and politely handed it back. As I left, he raised his right hand like a cigar-store Indian and said, "Hello." While changing money, I was spotted by the bank manager, who invited me into his office for tea. I was his first American customer.

Wandering in and out of small crafts shops I met an 85-year-old white-bearded wood-carver, who bragged that his work decorated prayer niches in mosques all over Iran. As he sized up just the right chunk of wood, he held up his chisel and said with a twinkle in his eye, "*This* is the greatest factory in the world."

A few minutes and a pile of wood shavings later, the man gave me a carved floral decoration with his signature in swirling Arabic. When I

In Turkey, you don't need museums; they're living in the streets

offered to pay, he refused. At his age, he explained, if I appreciated his art, that was all he needed.

Outside, a gaggle of men wearing grays, blacks, and browns were shuffling quietly down the street. A casket floated over them as each man jostled to the front to pay his respects by "giving it a shoulder."

Turkey is a land of ceremonies. Rather than relying on a list of festivals, travel with sharp eyes, flexibility, and some knowledge of the folk culture. Local life here is punctuated with colorful, meaningful events. As the dust from the funeral procession clears, you may see a proud 8-year-old boy dressed like a prince or a sultan. He's celebrating his circumcision, a rite of passage that some claim is an echo from the days of matriarchal Amazon rule, when entry into the priesthood required c-c-c-castration. This is a great day for the boy and his family. Turks like to call it the "happiest wedding," because there are no in-laws.

Having an interpreter helps you explore and mingle with meaning, but it's not required. Many older Turks speak German. The friendliness of Turkey is legendary among those who have traveled beyond the cruise ports. While relatively few small-town Turks speak English, their eagerness to help makes the language barrier an often enjoyable headache.

Enjoy jabbering with the people you meet. If Turkish sounds tough to you, remember, it's the same in reverse. Certain sounds, like our "th," are tricky. My friend Ruth was entertained by the tortured attempts Turks made at pronouncing her name. Any English-speaking Turk can remember spending long hours looking into the mirror, slowly enunciating: "This and these are hard to say. I think about them every day. My mouth and my teeth, I think you see, help me say them easily."

Throughout Turkey, travelers often lament over the ugly, unfinished construction that scars nearly every town with rusty tangles of steel rebar waiting to reinforce future concrete walls. But in Turkey, unfinished buildings are family savings accounts. Inflation here is ruinous. Any local in need of a hedge against inflation keeps a building under construction. Whenever there's a little extra cash, rather than watch it evaporate in the bank, Ahmed will invest in the next stage of construction. It's the goal of any Turkish parent to provide each child with a house or apartment with which to start adult life. A popular saying is, "rebar holds the family together."

If you're looking for a rain forest in Turkey, go to the northeast, along the Black Sea coast, where it rains 320 days a year. This is the world's top hazelnut-producing region, and home of the Laz people. A highlight of one tour (which I co-guide through Eastern Turkey with 22 American travelers and a Turkish guide) was spending an evening and a night with a Laz family. Actually the families of three brothers, they all live in one large three-layered house provided them by the now-elderly parents.

Our group was the first Americans that the 16 people who live here had ever seen. We were treated to a feast. In Turkey it's next to impossible to turn down this kind of hospitality. As we praised the stuffed peppers, members of our group discreetly passed Pepto Bismol tablets around under the table. (The pouring tea didn't quite mask the sound of ripping cellophane.)

After dinner we paid our respects to the grandma. Looking like a veiled angel in white, she and her family knew she would soon suc-cumb to her cancer. But for now, she was overjoyed to see such a happy evening filling her family's home.

When we wondered about having an extended family under one roof, the sons assured us: "If a day goes by when we don't see each other, we are very sad." To assure harmony in the family, the three brothers married three sisters from another family. They also assured us that entertaining our group of 22 was no problem. If we weren't there, they'd have had as many of their neighbors in.

No Turkish gathering is complete without dancing, and anyone who can snap his or her fingers and swing a hula-hoop can be com-fortable on the living room dance floor of new Turkish friends. Two aunts, deaf and mute from meningitis, brought the house down with their shoulders fluttering like butterflies. We danced and talked with four generations until after midnight.

Stepping into the late-night breeze, I noticed what had seemed to be a forested hillside was now a spangled banner of lights shining through windows, each representing a "third world" home filled with as much "family values" as the one we were a part of tonight. So much for my stereotypical image of fanatical Muslim hordes. Before leaving, the next morning, our friends tossed a gunnysack of hazelnuts into our bus.

For decades this eastern end of Turkey's Black Sea coast was a dead-end, butting up against the closed border of Soviet Georgia. But today the former USSR is ringed by sprawling "Russian markets" rather than foreboding guard posts.

From Finland to Turkey you'll find boxy Lada automobiles over-loaded with the lowest class of garage-sale junk, careening toward the nearest border on a desperate mission to scrape together a little hard cash. In the Turkish coastal town of Trabzon, 300 yards of motley tarps and blankets displayed grandpa's tools, pink and yellow "champagnski" ($1.50 a bottle), Caspian caviar (the blue lid is best, $3), battered samovars, fur hats, and nightmarish Rube Goldbergian electrical gadgetry. A Georgian babushka lady with a linebacker build, caked-on makeup, and bleached blonde hair, offered us a wide selection of Soviet pins, garish plastic flowers, and now-worthless ruble coins.

To satisfy my group's strange appetite for Godforsaken border crossings, we drove out to the Georgian border. No one knew if we could cross or not. As far as the Turkish official was concerned, "No problem." We were escorted through the mud, past pushcarts bound for flea markets and huge mired-in-red-tape trucks. In this strange economic no-man's land, the relative prosperity of Muslim Turkey was clear. Just a prayer call away from Georgia, a sharp little Turkish mosque with an exclamation-point minaret seemed to holler, "you sorry losers, let us help you onto our boat." Young Georgian soldiers with hardly a button on their uniforms checked identity cards, as those who qualified squeezed past the barbed wire and through the barely open gate. The soldier told us we couldn't pass. In search of a second opinion, we fetched an officer who said, "Visa no, problem"— a negative which, for a second, I misinterpreted as a positive.

Driving inland from the Black Sea under 10,000-foot peaks, our bus crawled up onto the burnt, barren, 5,000-foot-high Anatolian

In eastern Turkey, the village children will turn out to greet you

plateau to Erzurum, the main city of Eastern Turkey (24 hours by bus from Istanbul). Life is hard here. Blood feuds, a holdover from feudal justice under the Ottomans, are a leading cause of imprisonment. Winters are below-zero killers. Villages spread out onto the plateau like brown weeds, each with the same economy: ducks, dung, and hay. But Allah has given this land some pleasant surprises. The parched plain hides lush valleys where rooftops sport colorful patches of sun-dried apricots, where shepherd children still play the flute, and where teenage boys prefer girls who dress modestly. And you can crack the sweet, thin-skinned hazelnuts with your teeth.

Entering a village, we passed under the banner announcing, "No love is better than the love for your land and your nation." Another hay-duck-and-dung town, it took us warmly into its callused hands. Each house wore a tall hat of hay—food for the cattle and insulation for the winter. The mountains of cow pies were neatly-stacked promises of warmth and cooking fuel for six months of snowed-in winter that was on its way. A man with a donkey cart wheeled us through town. Veiled mothers strained to look through our video camera's viewfinder to see their children's mugging faces. The town's annually elected policeman bragged that he keeps the place safe from terrorists. Children scampered around women beating raw wool with sticks—a rainbow of browns that would one day be woven into a carpet to soften a stone sofa, warm up a mud brick wall, or serve as a daughter's dowry.

Driving east from Erzurum, we set our sights on 18,000-foot Mount Ararat, rising like Mount Fuji out of a tie-dyed landscape. Villages growing between ancient rivers of lava expertly milk the land for a subsistence living. After a quick re-read of the flood story in Genesis, I couldn't help but think that this powerful, sun-drenched, windswept land had changed little since Noah docked.

Turkey is in the middle of a small war in the east. Forty thousand Kurdish guerrillas (terrorists or freedom fighters, depending on your politics) are "in the mountains," while ten million Turkish Kurds, leading more normal lives, help provide their base of support. The guerrillas have not targeted tourists, perhaps because of the American relief for their beleaguered comrades in nearby Iraq, or because their quarrel is with the Turkish army, not with visitors. On a ridge high above our bus, I could make out the figure of a lone man silhouetted against a bright blue sky, waving to us as we rolled by.

When I got up early the next morning to see the sunrise over Mount Ararat, I could make out a long convoy of Turkish army vehicles. It reminded me that these days it takes more than forty days of rain to fix things. Our world is a complicated place where the nightly news is just a shadow play of reality. To give it depth you need to travel.

37. The Treasures of Luxor, Egypt

With my travel spirit flapping happily in the breeze, I pedal through Luxor on my rented one-speed, catching the cool shade and leaving the stifling heat with the pesky baksheesh-beggar kids in the dusty distance.

I load onto the old ferry, the man in the engine room hits the groaning motor into gear with a rock, and in a few minutes, the noisy city life is gone and the Nile takes me into a lush brown and green world of reeds, sugarcane, date palms, mud huts, and a village world amazingly untouched by the touristic bustle of modern Luxor.

I like the far side of the Nile. An irrigation ditch leads me into a village, where I am truly big news on two wheels. People scurry, grabbing their families to see the American who chose them over Tut. It was a royal welcome. They would have given me the Key to the Village, but there were no locks.

From Athens, Cairo is just a 90-minute flight or a day at sea away. And you're in a whole new world. Economy or student boat and plane tickets from Athens to Egypt are reasonable. For the best possible price, buy your ticket in Athens. Budget fares are not advertised outside of Greece.

I spent more time in and around Luxor than in any European small town, and I could have stayed longer. On top of the village thrills,

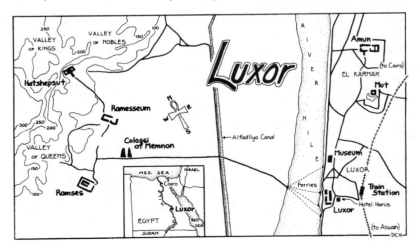

there are tremendous ancient ruins. The East Bank offers the tourist two famous sites: the Temples of Amun, Mut, and Khonsu at Karnak, 1 mile north of Luxor, and the Temple of Luxor, which dominates the town of Luxor.

And the West Bank, because of an ancient Egyptian belief, has all the funerary art, tombs, and pyramids. To the ancient Egyptian, the world was a lush green ribbon cutting north and south through the desert. It was only logical to live on the East Bank, where the sun rises, and bury your dead on the West Bank, where the sun is buried each evening. Across the Nile from Luxor is an area rich in tombs, temples, and ruins. The Temple of Queen Hatshepsut, Deir el-Medina, the Ramseseum, the Colossi of Memnon, and the Valleys of the Kings, Queens, and Nobles are among the many monuments from Egypt's ancient past that await you. Be selective, buying tickets for the most important sights at the ticket office near the ferry landing. You may become jaded, probably sooner than you think. So don't waste your powers of absorption on anything mediocre.

Luxor town itself has plenty to offer. Explore the market. You can get an inexpensive custom-made caftan with your name sewn on in arty Arabic. I found the merchants who pester the tourists at the tombs across the Nile had the best prices on handicrafts and instant antiques. A trip out to the camel market is always fun (and you can pick up a camel for half the U.S. price).

For me, five days in a small town is asking for boredom. But Luxor fills five days like no town its size. Here's a good plan.

FIVE DAYS IN LUXOR

Day 1. Your overnight train from Cairo arrives at 5:00 a.m. If it's too early to check in, leave your bags at a hotel, telling them you'll return later to inspect the room. Hop a horse carriage to the temples at Karnak while it's still cool. These comfortable early hours should never be wasted. Check into a hotel by midmorning. Explore Luxor town. Enjoy a *felucca* ride on the Nile at sunset.

Day 2. Cross the Nile and rent a taxi for the day. It's easy to gather other tourists and split the transportation costs. If you're selective and start early, you'll be able to see the best sites and finish by noon. That's a lot of work, and you'll enjoy a quiet afternoon back in Luxor.

Day 3. Through your hotel, arrange an all-day minibus trip to visit Aswan, the Aswan Dam, and the important temples (especially Edfu) south of Luxor. With six or eight tourists filling the minibus, this day should not cost over $12 per person.

Day 4. Rent bikes and explore the time-passed villages on the west side of the Nile. Bring water, your camera, and a bold spirit of adventure. This was my best Egyptian day.

Day 5. Enjoy Luxor town. Tour the excellent Luxor museum. Take advantage of the great shopping opportunities. Catch the overnight train back to Cairo.

Egypt seems distant and, to many, frightening. It's actually quite accessible, and with a few tips, there's a reasonable chance you'll survive and even enjoy your visit.

The overnight train ride from Cairo to Luxor is posh and scenic—a fun experience itself. A second-class air-conditioned sleeping car provides comfortable two-bed compartments, fresh linen, a wash basin, and wake-up service. Make a reservation for this ride at least three days in advance, both ways. In the crazy Cairo ticket office, be patient and persistent. Tip (bribe) if necessary.

In the cool months (peak season), it's wise to make hotel reservations. Off-season, in the sweltering summer heat, plenty of rooms lie vacant. Air-conditioning is found in moderate hotels. Budget hotels with a private shower, fan, and balcony offer doubles for around $20. A cot in the youth hostel, for a couple of dollars, is rock bottom in price—and comfort. The Hotel Horus has a central location, showers, fans, a good clean restaurant, a friendly and helpful staff, a

One of the most interesting ways to see Egypt

priceless (i.e., safe to drink) cold-water machine, and a good budget price ($25 doubles, Maabed El Karnak Street, tel. 095/2165). Hotel Horus is just across the street from the impressive Temple of Luxor and a 3-minute camel ride from the Nile.

Egypt is not a place where you should save money at the expense of comfort and health. A little extra expense buys a lot of comfort.

Eat well and carefully. With the terrible heat, your body requires plenty of liquids. Some Luxor water (i.e., that served in good restaurants) is safe to drink. Pepsi and the local cola, Sico, are safe and cheap. Watermelons are cheap, safe, and thirst-quenching. Cool your melon in your hotel's refrigerator. Choose a clean restaurant. Hotels generally have restaurants comparable to their class and price range.

To survive the summer heat, follow a few hints. The sightseeing day lasts from 5:00 a.m. until noon. The summer heat, which they say can melt car tires to the asphalt, is unbearable and dangerous after noon. Those early hours are prime time: the temperature is comfortable, the light is crisp and fresh, and the Egyptian tourist hustlers are still sleeping. Spend afternoons in the shade. Wear a white hat (on sale there) and carry water. An Egypt guidebook is a shield proving to unwanted human guides that you need no help.

Stay on the budgetary defense. No tip will ever be enough. Tip what you believe is fair by local standards and ignore the inevitable plea for more. Unfortunately, if you ever leave them satisfied—you were ripped off. Consider carrying candies or little gifts for the myriad children constantly screaming *"Baksheesh!"* ("Give me a gift!") Hoard small change in a special pocket so you'll have tip money readily available. Getting change back from your large bill is tough.

Transportation in and around Luxor is a treat. The local taxis are horse-drawn carriages. These are romantic—but, as usual in Egypt, drive a hard bargain and settle on a price before departing. The "Tourist Fary," as the sign reads, crosses the Nile from dawn until late at night and costs only pennies. Sit on the roof and enjoy the view with the local crowd.

Transportation on the West Bank of the Nile (opposite Luxor) consists of donkeys, bicycles, and automobile taxis. You can rent donkeys for the romantic approach to the tombs and temples of West Thebes. But the sun melts the romance fast, and your trusty dusty donkey will become a curse, or worse. Bikes work for the cheap and hardy. An automobile taxi is the quickest and most comfortable way to explore the tombs and ruins. When split between four tourists, a taxi for the "day" (6:00 a.m.-noon) is a reasonable way to go. To save money and make friends, assemble a little tour group at your hotel. You'll enjoy the quick meet-you-at-the-ferry-landing service of the taxi and, in one long morning, adequately cover Luxor's West Bank sights.

Take an evening cruise on the Nile in a *felucca*, the traditional sail-boat of this area, for just a few dollars an hour. Lounging like Cleopatra in your private felucca in the cool beauty of a Nile sunset is a romantic way to end the day and start the night.

A New Enlightenment Through Travel

Thomas Jefferson said, "Travel makes you wiser but less happy." I think he was right. And "less happy" is a good thing. It's the growing pains of a broadening perspective. After exposure to new ways of thinking and finding truths that didn't match those I always assumed were "self-evident" and "God-given," coming home gave me culture shock in reverse. I've shared with you a whole book on my love of travel. Here are a few thoughts on my most valuable souvenir—a new way of thinking.

The "land of the free" has a powerful religion—materialism. Its sophisticated priesthood (business, media, military and political leaders) makes its goal unsustainable growth. The Platinum Rule of "have it all" supersedes the Golden Rule. Contentment and simplicity are sins. Mellow is evil. The devil is anything steering you away from being a good producer/consumer.

Sure, greater wealth would be wonderful. But 4 percent of the planet's people (the U.S.A.) now control about 25 percent of the global economic pie. And the only way to get a bigger slice (or even maintain what we already have) is to get more and more aggressive—with ourselves, the environment, and the poor world (both at home and abroad). The meekest victim is the future.

Whoa! What happened to me? The young Republican traveled. And, like the early astronauts, I saw a planet with no boundaries. It's a single, tender organism painted with the faces of six billion equally precious people. And by traveling I've seen humankind as one body, which somehow must tell its fat cells to cool it because half the body is starving and the whole thing is threatened.

To continue traveling after you get home, explore new ideas. Intellectual shock can be as broadening as culture shock.

A new enlightenment is needed. Just as the French Enlightenment led us into the modern age of science and democracy, this new Enlightenment will teach us the necessity of sustainable affluence, peaceful co-existence with other economic models, controlling nature by obeying her, and measuring standard of living by something more human than material consumption.

I hope that your travels will give you a fun and relaxing vacation or adventure, and also that they'll make you an active patriot of our planet.

—*Rick Steves*

Send Me a Postcard—Drop Me a Line

Thousands of trips are shaped by this book. That's a heavy responsibility, and I do my conscientious best to keep every page up-to-date. Things do change, however, and travelers are always making new discoveries. I would really appreciate any corrections, additional ideas and discoveries, comments, criticisms, and feedback of any kind. All readers who correspond with us will receive a subscription to our *Back Door Travel Newsletter* (it's free, anyway).

If you would like to share your discoveries with other *Back Door* readers or help to improve the next edition of *ETBD*, please send a card to Europe Through the Back Door, Box 2009, 120 4th North, Edmonds, WA 98020. Our free computer bulletin board travel information service is at 206-771-1902, 1200 or 2400, 8/N/1. Thanks and happy travels!

Asia Through the Back Door

New, completely rewritten 4th edition.

Done Europe? Asia is the logical next step for the globe-trotter who's seen Europe and is ready for even more cultural thrills. Rick Steves and Bob Effertz have pooled a lifetime of travel experience into this handbook in hopes that their readers can learn from Rick's and Bob's mistakes—rather than their own. If *Europe Through the Back Door* gives you some good travels, you'll enjoy its Asian sister.

The first half of *Asia Through the Back Door* covers all the necessary skills for footloose and fancy-free Asian travel. Chapters cover everything from how to communicate without speaking the language, to eating and sleeping cheap, to understanding the local religions, to staying healthy, to tips for women traveling alone (written by a woman traveler). In the last half, the authors share their 30 favorite discoveries, their Back Doors to the very best that Asia has to offer.

Anyone equipped with good information, who expects to travel smart, can. This book is the best first step for great Asian travels.

Appendix

37 Back Doors: Recommended Accommodations

This book is not written as a directory-type guidebook. Nonetheless, here are a few specific recommendations to help you plug the 37 Back Doors featured in this book into your trip. While many rip out this appendix section and use it to navigate by, I have covered nearly all of the back doors much more thoroughly with my various country guidebooks. For a complete rundown on good places to eat and sleep, please navigate by one of my seven "Best of" country guidebooks (updated annually, published by John Muir Publications). While I've normally listed only prices for double rooms, most places have singles and triples. Prices may vary with plumbing and season. In the interest of brevity, I've been lean with descriptions here. Assume you get what you pay for.

1. Cinque Terre: Italy's Traffic-Free Riviera

I sleep in **Vernazza**. **Trattoria Gianni** (doubles-L75,000-L85,000, CC-VMA, Piazza Marconi 5, 19018 Vernazza, reception at restaurant on harbor square, tel. and fax 0187/812228, tel. 821003, closed January 6-March 6), the best value in town, has 14 small, simple, comfortable doubles, artfully decorated a la shipwreck, up lots of tight, winding, spiral stairs under the castle with great views. **Pension Sorriso** is the only real pension in town (doubles-L80,000-L90,000, including breakfast, summertime dinner is required and a room with dinner and breakfast costs L65,000 per person; CC-VM; 19018 Vernazza, Cinque Terre, La Spezia, 50 yards up from train station, tel. 0187/812224; while train sounds rumble through the front rooms of the main building, the annex up the street is quieter). Of Vernazza's many private rooms and apartments for rent, these offer six or eight cheap rooms year around: **Affitta Camere da Nicolina** (L30,000 per person, great views, right over the harbor but close to the noisy church bell tower, ask at the Vulnetia restaurant/pizzeria, tel. 0187/821193). **Affitta Camere da Filippo** (doubles-L60,000, triples-L70,000, quads-L80,000, no views less noise, ask at Trattoria da Sandro, tel. 812244). **Affitta Camere da Franco** (four quiet rooms, doubles-L55,000, with bath and view-L60,000, going down the main street, turn right at the pharmacy, climb via Carattino to #64, tel. 821082).
In **Riomaggiore: Youth Hostel Mama Rosa** is run with a splash of John Belushi and a pinch of Mother Theresa by Rosa Ricci (an almost-too-effervescent and friendly character who welcomes backpackers at the train station), her husband Carmine, and their English-speaking son, Silvio. This informal hostel is a chaotic but manageable jumble with the ambiance of a YMCA locker room (with a cat-pee aroma and nearly outdoor toilets and showers behind scanty curtains) filled with bunk beds. (L20,000 beds, price guaranteed through 1995, Piazza Unita 2, tel. 0187/920173, just show up without a reservation, no curfew.)

2. The Hill Towns of Tuscany and Umbria

Orvieto: Hotel Duomo (doubles-L48,000-L76,000, Via di Maurizio 7, tel. 0763/41887) and **Albergo Posta** (doubles-L55,000-L75,000, Via Luca Signorelli 18, Orvieto, tel. 0763/41909) offer old, well-worn elegance in the center of the hill town, a 2-minute walk from the cathedral. **Albergo Picchio** (doubles-L40,000-L60,000, Via G. Salvatori 17, 05019 Orvieto Scalo, tel. 0763/90246), a shiny, modern, concrete and marble place, more comfortable and family-run but with less character, is in the lower, ugly part of town, 3 minutes from the train station. **Siena: Pension Bernini** (a small, family-run place with a view terrace, doubles-L60,000, Via Sapienza 15, tel. 0577/289047) and **Alma Domus** (a strictly but wonderfully nun-run convent-style hotel, doubles-L50,000-L60,000, Via Camporegio 37, tel. 0577/44177) are both near San Domenico church. **Assisi: Albergo Italia** (doubles-L42,000-L65,000, overlooking the main square at Vicolo della Fortezza, tel. 075/812625) or the new, modern hostel Della Pace (L15,000 beds, just below the town at San Pietro Campagna, tel. 075/816767).

3. Città Di Bagnoregio
Bagnoregio has no private rooms but two good hotels: **Al Boschetto** (doubles-L60,000, Strada Monterado, Bagnoregio/Viterbo, Italy, tel. 0761/792369) is a family circus of Italian culture. **Hotel Fidanza** (doubles-L78,000, Via Fidanza 25, Bagnoregio/Viterbo, tel. and fax 0761/793444) is modern, comfortable, normal, and right in town. (Rooms 206 and 207 have views of Città.)

4. North Italy Choices: Mountains, Lakes, or Milano
Kastelruth: Gasthof Zum Turm (doubles-L90,000, Kofelgasse 8, tel. 0471/706349) and **Gasthof Zum Wolf** (Wolkenstein strasse 5, tel. 0471/706332) are good.
Varenna: Albergo Olivedo (doubles-L50,000-L85,000, just across from the ferry dock, tel. 0341/830115, Laura speaks English) and **Albergo Milano** (doubles-L110,000, great for honeymoons, in the village center, tel. and fax 0341/830298) are each a good value.
Across the lake in **Menaggio: La Primula Youth Hostel** (L14,000 per dorm bed, tel. 0344/32356) offers the only cheap beds in the area.
Milan: To be downtown, stay at **Hotel Speronari** (doubles-L60,000-L80,000, near the cathedral square at Via Speronari 4, 20123 Milano, tel. 02/864-61125, fax 720-03178). Near the station, **The Best Hotel** is best (doubles-L80,000, Via B. Marcello 83, 20124 Milan, tel. 02/294-04757, fax 201966).

5. Palermo, Sicily's Urban Carnival

6. Lisbon's Gold Still Shines
Sleeping Downtown in **Baixa: Albergaria Residencial Insulana** (doubles-8,000$ with breakfast, CC:VMA, elevator, all with air-conditioning, Rua da Assuncao 52, tel. 01/342-3131) is very professional with 32 quiet and comfortable (if a bit smokey) rooms. **Pensao Aljubarrata** (doubles-3,000$, Rua da Assuncao 53-4, tel. 346-0112) is a family-run sleepable bargain bet if you can handle the many stairs and the bubbly black vinyl flooring. Once on top you'll have cute tiny balconies from which to survey the Rua Augusta scene. **Pensao Residencial 13 da Sorte** (doubles-6,000$, elevator, Rua do Salitre 13, tel. 353-9746, fax 395-6946), the cheeriest of all places I found, has big full bathrooms in each of its 24 thoughtfully appointed rooms and bright small town tiles throughout (up Ave Liberdade, around the corner from Hotel Plaza, back rooms are quieter).
Baírro Alto: Residencial Nova Silva (doubles-4,500$-5,500$, Rua Victor Cordón 11, 1200 Lisboa, tel. 01/342-4371, fax 342-7770) is a quiet, ramshackle place with a fine location on the crest of the Baírro Alto overlooking the river. **Pensão Duque** (doubles-3,000$, also cheaper no-window rooms, Calçada do Duque 53, tel. 346-3444), with an ancient tangle of steep stairways, tacky vinyl floors, yellow paint, and dim lights, is too seedy for most, but the price, location, hard beds, and saggy ancient atmosphere make it a prize for some.

7. Salema, on Portugal's Sunny South Coast

There are plenty of **private homes** renting rooms along the town's residential street, which runs left from the village center as you face the beach. Building #64 on the left is the home of Romeu and Ercilia Viegas (7 doubles-2,500$, none with sinks, but a kitchenette and bathroom on the pleasant sun terrace, tel. 082/65128). The **Casa Duarte**, farther up the street and on a side alley closer to the water at #7 is more expensive but a little more elegant with beach views and a kitchenette (doubles-3,500$, tel. 082/65206). Vagabonds sleep free on the beach (public showers available in the town center). **Pension Mare** (doubles-6,000$ with a fine breakfast, Praia de Salema, Vila do Bispo 8650, Algarve, tel. 082/65165), a blue-and-white building overlooking the village, is run by an Englishman, John, who offers five rooms with private showers and a tidy paradise for British sun-seekers.

8. Southern Spain's Pueblos Blancos: Andalusia's Route of the White Villages

You can sleep very cheaply in any town in a **private home.** Just ask around for *camas* or *casas particular*. You may want to spend the night in one of these places:
Zahara: Hostal Marques de Zahara, doubles-$30, classy, tel. 956/137261, or the homier **Pension Gonzalo** next door at tel. 956/137217.
Arcos de la Frontera: Hotel Los Olivos (doubles-6,000-7,500 ptas, San Miguel 2, tel. 956/700811, fax 702018) is a bright, cool, and airy place with a fine courtyard, roof garden, bar, view, friendly English-speaking folks, and easy parking. **Hotel Restaurant El Convento** (doubles-5,000 ptas, all with shower, Maldonado 2, tel. 956/702333) just beyond the parador deep in the old town, is cozier and cheaper than Los Olivos and has a fine restaurant. Tourist office, open 9:00-15:00, 10:00-14:00 Saturday and Sunday, tel. 956/702264.

9. Alsace and Colmar

Colmar: Hotel la Rapp (rue Berthe-Molly 16, tel. 89-41-62-10) is my favorite. For a fine private room right downtown call the funky and flowery **Chambre d'Hote** at 12 rue de l'Ange, tel. 89-41-58-72.

10. From France to Italy Over Mt. Blanc

Chamonix: Simple, central, clean, and inexpensive accommodations include **Hotel de l'Arve** (classy, 50-53-02-31), **Hotel Marronniers** (Alpine funky, 50-53-05-73), **Hotel Asia** (basic, 50-55-99-25). **Dorms: Les Grands Charmoz** (50-53-45-57), **Ski Station** (50-53-20-25), **La Montagne** (50-53-11-60), **Le Chamoniard** (50-53-14-09), and the **Youth Hostel** (50-53-14-52).

For those trying to chose between the Gimmelwald/Jungfrau region and the Chamonix/Mont Blanc region, I'd choose Gimmelwald because it is less touristy, offers more diverse activities, and is more fun if the weather turns bad. With limited time in Chamonix, skip the Mer de Glace (unless you're dying to see a dirty old glacier).

11. Rothenburg and the Romantic Road: From the Rhine to Bavaria through Germany's Medieval Heartland

Schedule tips: Best segment of Rhine Cruise (free with Eurail) is one hour from Bacharach (castle youth hostel) to St. Goar (great Rheinfels castle). The most interesting quick Germany crossing is to butt the Rhine (Koblenz to Mainz by train with above cruise spliced in) up against the Romantic Road bus tour (leaving the Frankfurt train station at 8:00 a.m.). If you miss the bus, ride the trains to

Rothenburg (3 hours, Frankfurt, changing at Würzburg, changing again at Steinach), spend the night and catch the bus early tomorrow afternoon. The bus tour gets you into Munich at about 7:00 p.m., no problem since the train station tourist information office is open until at least 9:00 p.m. The bus to Füssen arrives at 8:00 p.m. after its TI closes, and after the last bus to Reutte, so call ahead for a room in Füssen. Going north, connect the Romantic Road bus tour, ending in Frankfurt, with a late train into the Rhineland.

Bacharach: Bacharach's castle youth hostel, **Jugendherberge Stahleck**, is Germany's most impregnable youth hostel (closed from 9:00 to 15:00, IYHF members of all ages welcome, 20 DM dorm beds, 5 DM for sheets, normally places are available but call and leave your name, tel. 06743-1266, English spoken, with barracks-like dorms, hearty and very cheap meals). **Hotel Kranenturm** (doubles-80 DM with this book, Langstrasse 30, tel. 06743/1308, fax 1021) for hotel privacy with Zimmer warmth, central location, and medieval atmosphere. **Frau Amann** (doubles-50 DM, Oberstrasse 13, in the old center on a side lane a few yards off the main street, tel. 06743/1271) rents 2 rooms in her quiet, homey, and traditional place with a cushy living room, a self-serve kitchen, and free loaner bikes.

Rothenburg: Hotel Goldener Rose (doubles-60 DM-80 DM, Spitalgasse 28, 8803 Rothenburg, tel. 09861/4638); **Herr und Frau Moser** (30 DM per person, one double and one triple, Spitalgasse 12, tel. 5971, for the best real with-a-local-family, comfortable and homey experience); Rothenburg's fine youth hostel, the **Rossmühle** (18 DM beds, 5 DM sheets, 8 DM dinners, tel. 09861/4510, reception open 7:00-9:00, 17:00-19:00, 20:00-22:00, will hold rooms until 18:00 if you call).

12. Hallstatt, in Austria's Commune-with-Nature Lakes District

Best beds are at **Gasthoff Simony** (doubles-500-800 AS, 4830 Hallstatt, tel. 06134/8231), right on the square with a lake view, balconies, creaky wood floors, slip-slidey rag rugs, antique furniture, and a huge breakfast. **Pension Sarstein** (doubles-400-600 AS, Gosaumühlstrasse 83, tel. 06134/8217) is a modern building, a few minutes' walk along the lake from the center, run by friendly Frau Fisher. Her sister, **Frau Zimmermann** (180 AS B&B, Gosaumühlstrasse 69, tel. 06134/8309) runs a small *Zimmer* just down the street in a 500-year-old house with low beams, time-polished wood, and fine lake views. **The Gasthaus Mühle Naturfreunde-Herberge** (145 AS per bed in co-ed dorms with breakfast, cheaper with a hostel sheet, run by Ferdinand, Kirchenweg 36, just below the tunnel car park, tel. 8318) is a good value with three- to six-bed rooms and hearty food. Ferdinand runs a Pizzeria in the Gasthaus providing the cheapest dinners in town.

13. Hall, in the Shadow of Innsbruck

Sleep at friendly Frau Steiner's **Gasthof Badl** (doubles-660 AS, Innsbruck 4, A-6060, Hall in Tirol, tel. 05223/56784) just off the autobahn. Tourist office tel. 05223/6269.

14. The Berner Oberland: The Alps in Your Lap

Gimmelwald: The **Mountain Hostel** is simple, less than clean, rowdy, cheap, and very friendly (tel. 036/551704, 9 SF per bed in 2- to 15-bed rooms, 2 SF for sheets, open all year). One block from the lift station, the hostel has low ceilings, a self-serve kitchen, co-ed washrooms, and enough hot water for only ten (1 SF, five minute) hot showers a day. Next door, the **Pension Gimmelwald** (with a dorm on its top floor and decent 90 SF doubles, two-night minimum, tel. 55 17 30) serves meals. Walter Mittler's **Hotel Mittaghorn**, up the hill, is the treasure of Gimmelwald (doubles-60 SF with breakfast, triples-85 SF, quads and quints-105 SF, loft beds with breakfast are 25 SF, 3826 Gimmelwald, Bern, tel. 036/551658, make phone reservations and reconfirm a day in advance). It's a classic, creaky, Alpine-style place with memorable beds, a million-dollar view of the Jungfrau Alps, and a single communal shower. To some, Hotel Mittaghorn is a fire just waiting to happen, with a kitchen that would never pass code, terrible beds, and nowhere near enough plumbing, run by an eccentric man. These people enjoy Interlaken, Wengen or Mürren and that's where they should sleep. Be warned, you may meet more of my readers than you hoped for, but it's a fun crowd—an extended family.

15. Off-beat Alps
Accommodations are listed in the chapter.

16. London: A Warm Look at a Cold City
The first three places are on the north edge of Holland Park, just west of Hyde Park (tube: Nottinghill Gate). **Hotel Ravna Gora** (doubles-$75, 29 Holland Park Avenue, WII, tel. 071/727-7725, well-worn, friendly, a bit eccentric, cheapest decent rooms in town), **Holland Park Hotel** (doubles-$100, 6 Ladbrook Terrace, WII 3PG, tel. 071/792-0216, hotelesque), **Vicarage Private Hotel** (doubles-$80, 10 Vicarage Gate, tel. 071/229-4030, classy-cozy too), **Cambria House** (an amazing, comfortable Salvation Army hotel, doubles-$50, near Russell Square at 37 Hunter Street, tel. 071/837-1654), **Woodville House** (doubles-$85, near Victoria, small-town friendly, 107 Ebury Street, tel. 071/730-1048), **Mary Ward's Guest House** (doubles-$30, friendly, homey, very simple but better than the youth hostel, south of the Thames, 98 Hambalt Rd., Clapham Common, London, tel. 081/673-1077).

17. Bath: England at its Elegant and Frivolous Best
Brock's Guest House (elegant in all ways, doubles-$70, Marion Dodd, 32 Brock Street, tel. 0225/338374, fax 334245), the **Woodville House** (doubles-$42, two-night minimum, no smoking, 4 Marlborough Lane, tel. 0225/319335), and the **Holly Villa Guest House** (doubles-$45, 6 Henry Street, tel. 0225/424052) are each fine values.

18. York: Vikings to Dickens
These small bed-and-breakfast places are a short walk from the train station, tourist office, and town center, and charge around $25 per person with a huge breakfast. In York, sleep at the **Airden House** (snug and traditional, run by Susan and Keith Burrows, 1 St. Mary's, York YO3 7DD, tel. 0904/638915). Nearby, the **Sycamore** (19 Sycamore Place, tel. 0904/624712) is also good. For downtown funkiness, sleep above the **Golden Fleece** bar (tel. 0904/625171).

19. Blackpool: Britain's Coney Island
The **Robin Hood Hotel** is a super place, cheery, no smoking, family-run, easy parking, with a big welcoming living room and 12 newly and tastefully refurbished rooms with the only real firm beds I found (doubles-$60 with breakfast, 1.5 miles north of Tower across from peaceful stretch of beach at 100 Queens Promenade, North Shore FY2 9NS, tel. 0253/351599, Pam Webster). **The Sheralea**, a few doors down, is similar (86 Queens Promenade, tel. 0253/357694, Ruth and Brian Catlow). **The Prefect Hotel** is all smiles and pink flamingo-pretty. (Divine

would've loved it.) It's shabby but spacious-for-Blackpool with all the fun touches (doubles-$40, 2 miles north of Tower at 204 Queens Promenade, FY2 9JS, tel. 0253/352699, Bill and Pauline Acton).

20. The Cotswold Villages: Inventors of Quaint
Sleeping in **Stow-on-the-Wold**, the best regional home base: The **Croyde B&B** (Norm and Barbara Axon, Evesham Road, Stow-on-the-Wold, Nr. Cheltenham, Glos., GL54 1EJ, tel. 0451/831711), the **West Deyne B&B** (tel. 0451/831011), and the **Limes** (in the old town, tel. 830034) are all good.

21. Mysterious Britain

22. Dingle Peninsula: A Gaelic Bike Ride
Sleep cozy in the town at Kathleen Farrell's **Corner House B&B** (tel. 066/51516) or cheap just out of town on the Tralee Road at the **Ballintaggart House Hostel** (tel. 066/51454). Eileen and Paddy Cleary's **Skellig View B&B**, three rooms for rent, 1 kilometer east of Ventry, 5 minutes from Dingle town, is a happy, story-ridden place, a wonderful cultural experience with a harbor view. For good Dingle eating, try **Doyle's Seafood Bar** (John St, tel 066-51174) or the **Half Door.** Many restaurants have a special menu before 19:00. Tour Dingle Peninsula with John Moran's **Slea Head Tours** (3-hour minibus tours, tel. 066/51155). For an archaeological tour of the peninsula or a historical walk through the town, take a Sciuird tour (fine value, daily from the TI, tel. 51937).

23. Northern Ireland
Sleep in Bangor near Belfast at **Battersea Guest House** (Jacque Hanna, 47 Queens Parade, Bangor, BT20 3BH, tel. 0247/461643, room #3 is best).

24. Oslo
In Oslo, the season dictates the best deals. In low season (July through mid-August, and Friday, Saturday, and Sunday the rest of the year) fancy hotels are the best value for softies with 600 kr for a double with breakfast. In high season (business days outside of summer), your affordable choices are dumpy-for-Scandinavia (but still nice by European standards) hotel doubles (300 kr to 400 kr) and 270 kr doubles in private homes. For experience and economy (but not convenience), go for a private home. Oslo's two hostels are far from the center, expensive (160 kr per bed), and usually full. Summer vagabonds sleep cheap (100 kr) at the downtown sleep-in. **Sjomannshjem** (doubles-300 to 400 kr, enter on Fred Olsengate, at Tollbugt 4, 0152 Oslo, tel. 22 41 20 05) is a "retired seaman's hotel," plain, clean, simple and shipshape. **City Hotel**, clean, basic, homey, with a wonderful lounge, originated 100 years ago as a cheap place for Norwegians to sleep while they waited to sail to their new homes in America. It now serves the opposite purpose. (doubles-500 kr to 800 kr, depending on season, Skippergatan 19, tel. 22 41 36 10, fax 22 42 24 29.) **Rainbow Hotel Astoria** (Twins-500 kr to 685 kr, three blocks in front of the station, 50 yards off Karl Johans Gate at Dronningensgate 21, 0154 Oslo, tel. 22 42 00 10, fax 22 42 57 65) is a modern comfortable place.
Private Homes: The **Caspari family** rents three comfortable rooms in their home (doubles-270 kr, 60 kr extra for one night stay, at the Heggeli T-bana stop, Heggeliveien 55, tel. 22 14 57 70). This woodsy, peaceful suburb is a place you'd like to raise your kids in—or call home for a couple of days in Oslo. **Mr. Naess** (doubles-250 kr, walk 20 minutes from the station or take bus 27 or 56 five stops to Olaf Ryes Place, facing a park at Toftestrasse 45, tel. 22 37 58 94) offers big,

homey old rooms overlooking a park and a fully-loaded kitchen. More urban, this place is a flat in a big old building with plenty of work-a-day shops and eateries nearby.

25. Stalking Stockholm

Peak season for Stockholm's expensive hotels is business time—workdays outside of summer. Rates drop by 30 to 50 percent in the summer or on weekends. The Tourist Office sorts through all of this for you. Their **Stockholm Package** offers business-class doubles with buffet breakfasts for 700 kr, includes two free Stockholm Cards, and lets children up to age 18 sleep for free. This is limited to mid-June through mid-August and Friday and Saturdays throughout the year. Assuming you'll be getting two Stockholm cards anyway (350 kr), this gives you a $200 hotel double for about $50. This is for real (summertime is that dead for business hotels). Arriving without reservations in July is never a problem. It gets tight during the Water Festival (ten days in early August) and during a convention stretch for a few days in late June.

Queen's Hotel, cheery, clean, and just a 10-minute walk from the station, this is probably the best cheap hotel in town (summer rates: doubles-435-585 kr, 640-845 kr in winter, CC:VMA, Drottninggatan 71A, tel. 24 94 60, fax 21 76 20).

Bentley's Hotel is an interesting option with an old English flair (summer rates include winter Sundays: small doubles-500 kr, CC:VMA, a block up the street from Queen's at Drottninggatan 77, 11160 Stockholm, tel. 14 13 95, fax 21 24 92) and a pile of decent but simple doubles with no sinks, plumbing, or breakfast at 400 kr.

Rooms in Private Homes: Mrs. Lindstrom rents out three doubles with access to a kitchenette in her comfortable home (doubles-300 kr, near the Drottningholm Palace, a 7-minute walk from T-bana: Islandstorget, at Danavagen 39 in the Bromma district, tel. 371608). **Else Mari Sundin** (doubles-400 kr with breakfast, bus 47 or 69 to Torstenssonsgatan 7, go through courtyard to "garden house" and up to 2nd floor, tel. 665-3348, or at her country home, 036/45151) is an effervescent retired actress who rents two rooms in her very homey place, beautifully located just two blocks from the bridge to Djurgarden.

Youth Hostels: *af Chapman* **(IYHF),** Europe's most famous youth hostel, is the permanently moored cutter ship *af Chapman.* Just a 5-minute walk from downtown, with 140 beds, two to eight per stateroom (Skeppsholmen, 11149 Stockholm, tel. 679-5015). **Zinken Hostel** is a big, basic hostel with plenty of doubles, a launderette, and kitchen facilities (T-bana: Zinkensdamm, Zinkens Vag 20, tel. 668-5786). If you want a 180 kr double (extra for sheets and non-members), sleep here.

26. Aero, Denmark's Ship-in-a-Bottle Island

In Aeroskobing, sleep at the **Pension Vestergade** (a quirky 200-year old home warmly run by Phyllis Packnass, Vestergade 44, 5970 Aeroskobing, tel. 62 52 22 98), **Det Lille Hotel** (a friendly and ship-shape 19th-century captain's home at Smedegade 33, tel. 62 52 23 00), or the local **youth hostel** (tel. 62 52 10 44). Tourist information tel. 62 52 13 00.

27. The Baltics and St. Petersburg

The latest edition of *Rick Steves' Best of the Baltics and Russia* (by Ian Watson) is filled with all the nitty-gritty necessary to make an independent budget trip through the region smooth and affordable.

28. Peloponnesian Highlights: Overlooked Greece

29. Crete's Gorge of Samaria

30. Dungeons and Dragons: Europe's Nine Most Medieval Castle Experiences

Carcassonne: Right in the old center, **Hotel des Ramparts** (place de Grands-Puits, tel. 68-71-27-72) is best. The **youth hostel** is very good and accepts non-members (in the old town, tel. 68-25-23-16). Also good are **Hotel Montmorency** (tel. 68-25-19-92) and **Hotel du Donjon** (tel. 68-71-08-80). Near the Rheinfels castle, sleep in **St. Goar**'s **Hotel Montag** (doubles-130 DM, tel. 06741/1629, fax 2086), the private home of **Frau Kurz** (doubles-60-70 DM, minimum two nights, near station, Ulmenhof 11, tel. 06741/459), or the **youth hostel**, right under the castle (15 DM beds, tel. 388). **Reutte** (tourist office tel. 05672/2336): There are two fine **hostels**; in town (small and modern, summer only, tel. 05672/71479), or Frau Reyman's **Jugendgastehaus Graben** (130 AS beds, across the river in a more traditional old building, tel. 05672/2644), **Hotel Goldener Hirsch** (doubles-820 AS, smoky, Old World elegance near station, right downtown, tel. 05672/2508, fax 2508100), **Hotel Maximilian** (doubles-840 AS, in nearby Ehenbichl village, a classy splurge, tel. 05672/2585, fax 258554), and **Hotel Schluxen** (doubles-800 AS, rustic, in the meadow, super quiet and traditional, tel. 05677/8903, fax 890323). Closer to Ludwig's castles, you might stay in **Füssen**: great private rooms at **Haus Peters** (doubles-70 DM, near station, Augustenstr. 5-1/2, tel. 08362/7171).

31. Sobering Sights of Nazi Europe

32. Europe's Best Preserved Little Towns

Bruges: Stay fancy at **Hansa Hotel** (doubles-3,400 BF, N. Desparsstraat 11, tel. 050/338444), comfortable at **Hans Memling Hotel** (doubles-2,300 BF, Kuiperstr 18, 8000 Bruges, tel. 050/332096) or cozy with the **Dieltiens family** (doubles-1,250-1,600 BF, St. Walburgastraat 14, tel. 050/334294).
Obidos: **Casa do Poco** (doubles-9,000$, tel. 062/959358) or the **Albergasia Rainha Santa Isabel** (doubles-10,000$, tel. 062/959115). Tourist office tel. 062/959231).
Toledo: **Hostal de Cardenal** (splurge, tel. 925/222490) or **Fonda Segovia** (cheap, tel. 925/211124).

33. Bad Towns and Tourist Traps
Sleep elsewhere.

34. Morocco: Plunge Deep

35. Turkey's Hot
Samos: Stay at **Hotel Mariana** (Kalomiris Street 22, 3 minutes from the boat dock, tel. 273/27369) or **Hotel Samos** (doubles-$30, across from the dock, 11 Th. Sofoulis, Samos, tel. 0273/28377).
Kusadasi: Stay at the family-run **Konak Hotel** (doubles-$25, Yildirim Caddesi #55, Kusadasi 09400, tel. 9-636/16318, fax 51/147301). Varan and Ulusoy are the best bus companies for overnight rides from Kusadasi to Istanbul.

36. Eastern Turkey

37. The Treasures of Luxor, Egypt

Sample 22 Days European Regional Itineraries

The destinations proposed in each of these "best 22 days" itineraries are featured in the Rick Steves country guidebook for that area.

22 Days in Europe
Day 1 - Depart U.S. for Amsterdam
Day 2 - Arrive in Amsterdam
Day 3 - Amsterdam
Day 4 - From Holland to the Rhine
Day 5 - The Rhine to Rothenburg
Day 6 - Rothenburg ob der Tauber
Day 7 - Romantic Road, Dachau, Tirol
Day 8 - Bavaria and Castle Day
Day 9 - Over Alps to Venice
Day 10 - Venice
Day 11 - Florence
Day 12 - Rome
Day 13 - Rome
Day 14 - Italian hill towns
Day 15 - Drive the Italian Riviera
Day 16 - Free on Cinque Terre beach
Day 17 - Drive to the Alps
Day 18 - Alps hike day, Gimmelwald
Day 19 - Free in Alps; evening to France
Day 20 - Colmar, Alsatian villages, wine
Day 21 - On to Paris, stop at Reims
Day 22 - Paris
For all the specifics, see *Rick Steves' Best of Europe*

22 Days in France
Day 1 - Arrive in Paris
Day 2 - Paris
Day 3 - Paris
Day 4 - Paris
Day 5 - Into Normandy via Rouen
Day 6 - Bayeux, D-Day beaches
Day 7 - Mont St. Michel, Brittany, and to the Loire Valley
Day 8 - Loire Chateau hopping
Day 9 - Sarlat, the Dordogne Valley
Day 10 - Dordogne Valley
Day 11 - Sarlat, Albi, and Carcassonne
Day 12 - From Carcassonne to Arles
Day 13 - La Crême de Provence
Day 14 - From the Rhone to the Riviera
Day 15 - Beaches on the Côte d'Azur
Day 16 - From Riviera to Alps
Day 17 - Alps Admiration
Day 18 - From Chamonix to Chardonnay
Day 19 - A Taste of Burgundy
Day 20 - From Burgundy to Alsace—Beaune to Colmar via Dijon
Day 21 - Colmar and the Route du Vin
Day 22 - Back to Paris, Verdun, and Reims
For all the specifics, see *Rick Steves' Best of France, Belgium and the Netherlands*

22 Days in Germany, Austria, and Switzerland
Day 1 - Arrive Frankfurt, to Rothenburg
Day 2 - Rothenburg
Day 3 - Romantic Road to Tirol

Day 4 - Bavarian highlights, castle day
Day 5 - Bavaria to Munich
Day 6 - Munich, capital of Bavaria
Day 7 - Munich to Salzburg
Day 8 - Salzburg, Lakes District
Day 9 - Hallstatt to Vienna
Day 10 - Vienna—Paris's eastern rival
Day 11 - Vienna to Hall in Tirol
Day 12 - Innsbruck and into Switzerland
Day 13 - Interlaken and up into the Alps
Day 14 - Alps hike day, Gimmelwald
Day 15 - Free time in Alps, French Switzerland
Day 16 - Cheese and chocolate, Mürten
Day 17 - Bern, drive into Germany
Day 18 - Black Forest
Day 19 - Baden-Baden to the Rhineland
Day 20 - The Rhine and its Castles
Day 21 - Mosel Valley, Köln, Bonn
Day 22 - Berlin
For all the specifics, see *Rick Steves' Best of Germany, Austria, and Switzerland*

22 Days in Great Britain
Day 1 - Arrive and set up in London
Day 2 - London
Day 3 - London
Day 4 - Salisbury, Stonehenge, Bath
Day 5 - Bath
Day 6 - Side trip to Glastonbury, Wells
Day 7 - South Wales, Folk Museum
Day 8 - Cotswold villages, Blenheim
Day 9 - Stratford, Warwick Castle, Coventry Cathedral
Day 10 - Industrial Revolution Museum
Day 11 - North Wales, Snowdon National Park, Caenarfon Castle, Medieval Banquet
Day 12 - Blackpool
Day 13 - Windermere Lake District
Day 14 - Hike and explore Lake District
Day 15 - Loch Lomond, Scottish West Coast
Day 16 - Scottish Highlands, Loch Ness
Day 17 - Edinburgh
Day 18 - Edinburgh
Day 19 - Hadrian's Wall, Durham Cathedral, Beamish Folk Museum
Day 20 - North York Moors, York
Day 21 - York
Day 22 - Cambridge, evening to London
For all the specifics, see *Rick Steves' Best of Great Britain*

22 Days in Italy
Day 1 - Arrive in Milan
Day 2 - Sightsee Milan
Day 3 - Train to Riviera
Day 4 - All Day in Cinque Terre
Day 5 - Pisa, Florence
Day 6 - Florence
Day 7 - Florence, Siena
Day 8 - Siena
Day 9 - Orvieto, Città
Day 10 - Hill Towns to Rome
Day 11 - Rome
Day 12 - Rome
Day 13 - Rome
Day 14 - Rome, Naples, Sorrento

Day 15 - Amalfi, Paestum, night train
Day 16 - Venice
Day 17 - Venice, Side-Trips
Day 18 - Dolomites
Day 19 - Dolomites
Day 20 - Dolomites to the Lakes
Day 21 - Lake Como, Varenna
Day 22 - Return to Milan, Trip Over
For all the specifics, see *Rick Steves' Best of Italy*

22 Days in Scandinavia
Day 1 - Arrive in Copenhagen
Day 2 - Sightsee in Copenhagen
Day 3 - Sightsee in Copenhagen
Day 4 - Frederiksborg Castle, N. Zealand
Day 5 - Vaxjo, Kalmar, glass country
Day 6 - Pass Gota Canal to Stockholm
Day 7 - Sightsee in Stockholm
Day 8 - Sightsee in Stockholm, evening cruise
Day 9 - Helsinki, Finland
Day 10 - Stockholm, Uppsala, to Oslo
Day 11 - Sightsee Oslo
Day 12 - Sightsee Oslo
Day 13 - Gudbrandsdalen, Peer Gynt country
Day 14 - Glacier hike, Sognefjord
Day 15 - Fjord cruise to Gudvangen—"Norway in a Nutshell"
Day 16 - Sightsee in Bergen
Day 17 - Drive from Bergen to Setesdal
Day 18 - Traditional Setesdal valley, evening sail to Denmark
Day 19 - Jutland, Arhus
Day 20 - Aero Island
Day 21 - Aero, Odense, Roskilde, Copenhagen
Day 22 - Fly home from Copenhagen
For all the specifics, see *Rick Steves' Best of Scandinavia*

22 Days in Spain and Portugal
Day 1 - Arrive in Madrid and set up
Day 2 - Madrid
Day 3 - Madrid
Day 4 - Segovia
Day 5 - Salamanca to Coimbra, Portugal
Day 6 - Nazaré
Day 7 - Nazaré, beach day
Day 8 - Obidos and on to Lisbon
Day 9 - Lisbon
Day 10 - Lisbon and nearby beach towns
Day 11 - Salema
Day 12 - Salema and nearby beaches
Day 13 - Seville
Day 1? -Seville
Day 15 - Arcos de la Frontera, Tarifa
Day 16 - Tarifa
Day 17 - Morocco
Day 18 - Gibraltar
Day 19 - Costa del Sol and Granada
Day 20 - Granada and Moorish Alhambra
Day 21 - Toledo
Day 22 - Madrid
For all the specifics, see *Rick Steves' Best of Spain and Portugal*

European Weather

Here is a list of average temperatures and days of no rain. This can be helpful in planning your itinerary, but I have never found European weather to be particularly predictable.

1st line, avg. daily low; 2nd line, avg. daily high; 3rd line, days of no rain

	J	F	M	A	M	J	J	A	S	O	N	D
AUSTRIA	26°	28°	34°	41°	50°	56°	59°	58°	52°	44°	36°	30°
Vienna	34°	38°	47°	57°	66°	71°	75°	73°	66°	55°	44°	37°
	23	21	24	21	22	21	22	21	23	23	22	22
BELGIUM	31°	31°	35°	39°	46°	50°	54°	54°	50°	44°	36°	33°
Brussels	42°	43°	49°	56°	65°	70°	73°	72°	67°	58°	47°	42°
	19	18	20	18	21	19	20	20	19	19	18	18
DENMARK	29°	28°	31°	37°	44°	51°	55°	54°	49°	42°	35°	32°
Copenhagen	36°	36°	41°	50°	61°	67°	72°	69°	63°	53°	43°	38°
	22	21	23	21	23	22	22	19	22	22	20	20
EGYPT	42°	44°	50°	59°	69°	70°	73°	73°	71°	65°	54°	45°
Luxor	74°	79°	86°	95°	104°	106°	107°	106°	103°	98°	87°ᵇ	78°
	31	28	31	30	31	30	31	31	30	31	30	31
FINLAND	17°	15°	22°	31°	41°	49°	58°	55°	46°	37°	30°	22°
Helsinki	27°	26°	32°	43°	55°	63°	71°	66°	57°	45°	37°	31°
	20	20	23	22	23	21	23	19	19	19	19	20
FRANCE	32°	34°	36°	41°	47°	52°	55°	55°	50°	44°	38°	33°
Paris	42°	45°	52°	60°	67°	73°	76°	75°	69°	59°	49°	43°
	16	15	16	16	18	19	19	19	19	17	15	14
	40°	41°	45°	49°	56°	62°	66°	66°	62°	55°	48°	43°
Nice	56°	56°	59°	64°	69°	76°	81°	81°	77°	70°	62°	58°
	23	20	23	23	23	25	29	26	24	22	23	23
GERMANY	29°	31°	35°	41°	48°	53°	56°	55°	51°	43°	36°	31°
Frankfurt	37°	42°	49°	58°	67°	72°	75°	74°	67°	56°	45°	39°
	22	19	22	21	22	21	21	21	21	22	21	20
GREAT BRITAIN	35°	35°	37°	40°	45°	51°	55°	54°	51°	44°	39°	36°
London	44°	45°	51°	56°	63°	69°	73°	72°	67°	58°	49°	45°
	14	15	20	16	18	19	18	18	17	17	14	15
GREECE	42°	43°	46°	52°	60°	67°	72°	72°	66°	60°	52°	46°
Athens	54°	55°	60°	67°	77°	85°	90°	90°	83°	74°	64°	57°
	24	22	26	27	28	28	30	30	28	27	24	24
IRELAND	35°	35°	36°	38°	42°	48°	51°	51°	47°	43°	38°	36°
Dublin	47°	47°	51°	54°	59°	65°	67°	67°	63°	57°	51°	47°
	18	17	21	19	20	19	18	18	18	19	18	18
ITALY	39°	39°	42°	46°	55°	60°	64°	64°	61°	53°	46°	41°
Rome	54°	56°	62°	68°	74°	82°	88°	88°	83°	73°	63°	56°
	23	17	26	24	25	28	29	28	24	22	22	22
PORTUGAL	47°	57°	50°	52°	56°	60°	64°	65°	62°	58°	52°	48°
(Lagos/Algarve)	61°	61°	63°	67°	73°	77°	83°	84°	80°	73°	66°	62°
	22	19	20	24	27	29	31	31	28	26	22	22
	46°	47°	49°	52°	56°	60°	63°	64°	62°	57°	52°	47°
Lisbon	56°	58°	61°	64°	69°	75°	79°	80°	76°	69°	62°	57°
	22	20	21	23	25	28	30	30	26	24	20	21

1st line, avg. daily low; 2nd line, avg. daily high; 3rd line, days of no rain

	J	F	M	A	M	J	J	A	S	O	N	D
MOROCCO Marrakesh	40°	43°	48°	52°	57°	62°	67°	68°	63°	57°	49°	52°
	65°	68°	74°	79°	84°	92°	101°	100°	92°	83°	3°	66°
	24	23	25	24	29	29	30	30	27	27	27	24
Tangiers	47°	48°	50°	51°	56°	60°	64°	65°	63°	59°	52°	48°
	60°	61°	63°	65°	71°	76°	80°	82°	78°	72°	65°	61°
	21	18	21	22	26	27	31	31	27	23	20	21
NETHERLANDS Amsterdam	34°	34°	37°	43°	50°	55°	59°	59°	56°	48°	41°	35°
	40°	41°	46°	52°	60°	65°	69°	68°	64°	56°	47°	41°
	12	13	18	16	19	18	17	17	15	13	11	12
NORWAY Oslo	20°	20°	25°	34°	43°	51°	56°	53°	45°	37°	29°	24°
	30°	32°	40°	50°	62°	69°	73°	69°	60°	49°	37°	31°
	23	21	24	23	24	22	21	20	22	21	21	21
SPAIN Madrid	33°	35°	40°	44°	50°	57°	62°	52°	56°	48°	40°	35°
	47°	51°	57°	64°	71°	80°	87°	86°	77°	66°	54°	48°
	22	19	20	21	22	24	28	29	24	23	20	22
Barcelona	42°	44°	47°	51°	57°	63°	69°	69°	65°	58°	50°	44°
	56°	57°	61°	64°	71°	77°	81°	82°	67°	61°	62°	57°
	26	21	24	22	23	25	27	26	23	23	23	25
Malaga	47°	48°	51°	55°	60°	66°	70°	72°	68°	61°	53°	48°
	61°	62°	64°	69°	74°	80°	84°	85°	81°	74°	67°	62°
	25	22	23	25	28	29	31	30	28	27	22	25
SWEDEN Stockholm	23°	22°	26°	32°	41°	49°	55°	53°	46°	39°	31°	26°
	31°	31°	37°	45°	57°	65°	70°	66°	58°	48°	38°	33°
	23	21	24	24	23	23	22	21	22	22	21	22
SWITZERLAND Geneva	29°	30°	35°	41°	48°	55°	58°	57°	52°	44°	37°	31°
	39°	43°	51°	58°	66°	73°	77°	76°	69°	58°	47°	40°
	20	19	21	19	19	19	22	21	20	20	19	21
TURKEY Antakya area	39°	41°	45°	51°	59°	66°	71°	72°	66°	58°	51°	43°
	57°	59°	66°	74°	83°	89°	93°	94°	91°	84°	73°	61°
	23	21	25	25	27	28	30	30	29	28	25	24
YUGOSLAVIA Belgrade	27°	27°	35°	45°	53°	58°	61°	60°	55°	47°	39°	30°
	37°	41°	53°	64°	74°	79°	84°	83°	76°	65°	52°	40°
	23	22	24	21	22	21	25	24	24	23	23	22
Dubrovnik	42°	43°	47°	51°	58°	64°	69°	69°	65°	58°	51°	46°
	52°	53°	57°	63°	71°	78°	83°	83°	76°	69°	60°	55°
	23	21	23	23	26	26	28	28	25	23	21	21

Metric Conversion Table

1 inch	=	25 millimeters	1 ounce	=	28 grams
1 foot	=	0.3 meter	1 pound	=	0.45 kilogram
1 yard	=	0.9 meter	Temp. (F.)	=	9/5 C+32°
1 mile	=	1.6 kilometers	1 kilogram	=	2.2 lbs.
1 sq. yd.	=	0.8 square meter	1 kilometer	=	62 mile
1 acre	=	0.4 hectare	1 centimeter	=	0.4 inch
1 quart	=	0.95 liter	1 meter	=	39.4 inches

RICK STEVES' 1995 BACK DOOR GUIDE TO
EUROPEAN RAILPASSES

When I started traveling in the early 70s, the Eurailpass was king...cheap, simple, and the obvious best deal. My choices were kindergarten-simple: one month or two? Now, twenty years later, travelers exploring Europe have an exciting but confusing multitude of railpass options to sort through: all-Europe, the mix-n-match three-to-nine-country "Europass," regional, country-specific, rail, rail/drive, rail/drive/fly, consecutive-day, flexi, saver-for-twosomes, youth passes, and point-to-point tickets -- not to mention the many kinds of passes that are sold only on the other side of the Atlantic. This, coupled with the fact that an increasing number of Americans are taking regionally-focused rather than whirlwind trips, means that smart budget travelers need to be more informed than ever in order to make the best choice. While many agents out there have had access to information to help them sell railpasses, no one has gathered, organized, and analyzed the information necessary *for the traveler* to assess all the options and make the smart decision on which pass, if any, to buy. Until now.

I hope this chapter helps you sort through your European transportation options and find the best deal for a great trip.

HOW TO USE THIS INFORMATION

This guide explains your railpass options and compares buying railpasses to buying individual tickets. It does not describe the legal fine points of each railpass. The full legal conditions and instructions come with each pass. For simplicity, I've made generalizations that may not be correct for every kind of railpass.

Most railpasses are only available outside of Europe. Some are only available in their home country. And some can be purchased either here or in Europe. In this chapter, any time you see a pass price in foreign currency (followed by $ equivalents), you can assume that the pass should (or must) be purchased in Europe. Unless otherwise noted, if you see only a dollar price listed for a pass, you can assume that the pass is not available in its country and should be purchased in the USA before you depart. Prices listed in this guide should be good through Dec. 31, 1995, but all prices and conditions are subject to change. European railpasses can be purchased through most American travel agents, or through my Europe Through the Back Door travel company.

LIFE IN THE PASS LANE

If you're thinking of traveling in Europe with a railpass, a good first step is to learn about the basic features that are common to most railpasses...

Consecutive day railpasses. The standard railpass allows you unlimited train travel for the duration of the pass (e.g., you can travel 15 consecutive days with your 15-day pass).

Flexipasses. Most countries now offer cheaper flexipasses which allow you to travel a shorter number of days within a longer period (e.g., any 10 days within a 2 month period). When you look at the flexipass, you'll see a string of boxes, one for each travel day available to you. Before boarding the train (or bus or boat covered by your pass), you simply fill in that day's date in ink in one of the boxes. You can take as many separate trips as you like within each travel day.

On major flexipasses (Eurail, French, German, Scandinavian), an overnight journey uses up only one of your travel days. If you're catching an overnight train (or boat) that leaves after 7 p.m., you'll write in the next day's date on your pass. If the very first use of your flexipass is for an overnight train ride, you'll still write in the next day's date, but your pass will be validated for the actual date you board. Although this decreases your pass' total validity period by two days, you're still "using up" just one "flexi" travel day for the overnight trip. All rides must be started and completed within the pass's validity period.

Flexipass or consecutive day pass? If you want to travel nearly every day and cover a lot of ground, a consecutive day pass is the right choice for you. If you like to stop for a few days at various places, a flexipass is generally the better choice.

Flexipasses are a popular budget option. But before buying a flexipass, divide the money saved by the number of days you'll go without train travel. For example, if you're planning a 21-day trip, you can choose between a $648 21-day consecutive day Eurailpass or a cheaper $560 ten-days-out-of-two-months flexipass. The flexipass option saves you $88. But you'll go without train travel for 11 days. For many travelers, the more expensive 21 consecutive day pass is actually a better deal because it provides 11 more days of first class train travel for only $8 a day. Of course, if you're sure you don't need the extra days, go with the cheaper flexipass.

First or second class pass? In the case of Eurailpasses, the choice is made for you if you're age 26 or older -- you must buy a first class Eurailpass. Only those under 26 have the choice of buying either a second or a first class Eurailpass. BritRail and most special country passes offer discounted second class passes to travelers of any age.

Wrestling with the choice between first and second class? Remember, nearly every train has both first and second class cars, each going precisely the same speed. First class railpasses, like point-to-point tickets, cost 50% more than second class. If you're rugged and on a tight budget, go second class. If you have the extra money, riding first class is less crowded and more comfortable (although in much of Europe, the new second class cars, which predominate, are more comfortable than the old first class cars). In most countries, the first class compartments are configured with six seats (three facing three) and the second class compartments have six to eight seats (three or four facing three or four). In the open-style cars, first class has three seats per row (two on one side and a single on the other) and second class cars have four skinnier seats separated by the aisle. Back Door travelers know that nuns and soldiers are partying in second class. First class is filled with Eurail travelers over 25 who had no choice and local people who paid 50% extra in hopes that they wouldn't have to sit with you and me.

Those with first class passes can travel in second class. Those with second class passes must pay the difference (50% more than the second class fare for each trip) to upgrade to first class.

Longer or shorter pass? Notice how the longer railpasses get cheaper per day. For a $498 15-day "consecutive day" Eurailpass, you're paying $33 a day. For a $1398 three-month pass, the cost is about $15 a day. (Most one-hour train rides cost more than that.) Consider the difference between a one-month pass for $798 and a two-month pass for $1098. You get an extra month of train travel for just $300, or $10 a day. When you ponder getting a longer pass, consider its cheaper cost per day, not whether you'll use the pass the entire duration. With two long train rides (e.g., Paris-Munich, $170 each way first class), a 35-day trip can justify a two-month railpass.

With some thoughtful juggling, a longer trip can be squeezed into a shorter, cheaper pass. For example, if you're starting and finishing in London, start your continental travels in Paris and finish in Amsterdam. Pay for the $35 Calais-Paris train ride and start your pass 4 days later as you leave Paris. Plan for your pass to expire as you arrive in Amsterdam where you can easily spend 4 days with short cheap day trips that don't merit the use of a railpass. This 30-day trip could be done on a 21-day pass (saving $150 over the cost of a one-month pass). Your net savings here, after the trip into Paris from the harbor and the little day-trip tickets might be $50--considerable but probably not enough to crimp your traveling style.

If you're taking a long trip of over three months, you might consider buying two passes to cover the length of your journey.

Youth passes. To be eligible for a youth pass, you must be under 26 (according to your passport) the day you validate the pass. Generally, children from 4 to 11 get passes for half the adult pass prices and those under 4 travel free. These ages vary a bit among different country passes.

RAILPASS GLOSSARY

Bonus: A bus or boat ride covered by a railpass.

Car day: A 24-hour period of car rental.

CDW: Collision damage waiver (supplemental insurance to get zero $ deductible in case there's damage to your rental car).

Class A, B, C, and D: Refers to size of rental car, from class A (smallest) to class D (largest, or in some places automatics).

Flexipass: Allows a specified number of days of travel within a longer period (such as any 5 days of travel in 2 months).

Issue date: Stamped on a railpass by the issuing agent, used as the official date of purchase.

Period of validity: The total number of days or months that a pass is active for use.

Point-to-point tickets: Individual tickets you purchase as you go (no pass involved).

Rail 'n drive pass: Offers a combination of train travel and car rental.

Special country pass: a railpass (but not a Eurailpass) covering a specific country or region.

Standard class: Britain's term for 2nd class.

Supplement: Additional charge beyond the ticket price for certain trains and boat rides.

Validation: The activation of a railpass by a railway official. Once validated, the pass's clock starts ticking.

Youth railpass: Discounted pass available only to youths (Eurail defines youth as under 26).

Validation. A pass must be validated before its first use and within six months of its issue date (e.g., if May 24 is stamped on your pass you must validate--or start-- the pass by November 23). Validation is free, quick and easy at any European train station. If you're riding a train into Eurail country from a non-Eurail country (like from Poland into Germany), you can get your pass validated for free on the train. Otherwise, conductors charge a $5 to $12 penalty in local currency to validate passes on board. Let's say you have a French railpass, you're heading from Amsterdam to Paris by train, and you want the French portion of your route to be covered with your French railpass. At the Amsterdam train station you would buy a ticket to the French border, and at the same time validate your French pass. This way you won't need to get off the train at the first stop in France (and you won't be at the conductor's mercy if you stay on board). Never write anything on your pass before it's been validated. All trips and bonuses must be started and finished within the valid life of your pass. Since passes usually go up in price on January 1st, those traveling in the first six months of a year can travel on last year's prices by buying in late December.

What is a railpass "day" and "month"? A railpass day runs from midnight to midnight. A railpass month runs, for example, from April 26 through May 25. One-month passes last longest when started in a 31-day month.

Sleeping. Whenever I can, I sleep on the train. Every night spent riding the rails gives me an extra day to sightsee, saves me the cost of a hotel, and allows me to arrive early before the budget alternatives to expensive hotels fill up. The scenery missed generally is insignificant when you consider the time you gain—a whole day to bike in Holland, hike in the Alps, or sunbathe on a Greek beach — taking your longest train trips at night makes sense.

You can sleep for free on the trains by miserably sitting up all night if the compartment is crowded or by lying down comfortably on seats that fold out into a free bed. Considering the frequent interruptions as people come in late and the vulnerability of your possessions as you sleep, one of Europe's great bargains is the $15 couchette ($24 if you buy it through your state-side travel agent). An attendant monitors the couchette compartment and also deals with conductors, thieves, and customs officials on your behalf as you sleep safely and uninterrupted.

A couchette is a bed in a usually lockable compartment with two triple bunks (co-ed, with a blanket, pillow, clean linen, and up to five compartment mates). Book your couchettes a few days in advance, either through a European travel agent or at train stations. Unreserved couchettes or sleepers can be rented on the train from train attendants. Some countries offer first class couchettes (four bunk beds per compartment rather than six) for the normal $15 fee to travelers who have first class tickets or railpasses.

A sleeper offers more privacy and comfort than a couchette. You'll pay from $40 to $80 on top of your ticket price for a berth in a still-crowded two- or three-bed sleeper with a tiny sink. Whether you have a ticket or a railpass, you must pay extra for a couchette or sleeper.

Reservations. Railpasses do not include or guarantee reservations for seats, couchettes, or sleepers. Reservations are required for some of Europe's super trains (e.g. TGV), for any train marked with an R in the schedule, on long rides in Spain and Norway, and for couchettes and sleepers. Otherwise (except during some busy holiday periods), reservations are not worth the trouble and expense. Reservations, which cost from $3 to $10, can be made as long as 2 months in advance or as short as a few hours in advance. In 24 years of European train travel, I've never made or needed a reservation before I arrived in Europe.

Supplements. While your railpass covers you on all of a country's national train lines, there are a few "super trains" (and, in Italy, lots of mediocre ones) which charge a supplement. While the Eurailpass covers most supplement trains (such as the IC and TGV), some country passes don't. These are best learned about and paid for in the station, prior to boarding, although any conductor is happy to charge you a small penalty to collect for the supplement en route. Supplements are generally noted in the schedules and are normally in the $10 range.

Refunds. Without insurance, passes are not refundable if lost or stolen. Unused and unvalidated passes are 85% refundable if returned to the place of purchase within six months; or within one year for Eurailpasses. Most refunds take 6 to 8 weeks. Some unused passes can be exchanged for a more expensive pass free of charge. There is a 15% penalty for "downgrading" from a longer pass to a shorter cheaper pass. Travelers who have a good medical excuse, supported by documentation, can sometimes get a refund on an unused portion of their pass.

Buying your pass. Most railpasses must be purchased in the USA before your trip, and are not sold in Europe. There are some exceptions: Eurailpasses are now available at major European railway stations for about 20% more than the USA price; and there are several cases, notably in Great Britain, Scandinavia, Switzerland, Austria, and Belgium, in which you have good, completely-legal-for-Yankees railpasses sold in Europe at some savings compared the prices you'll find in the USA. And some passes or versions of passes are only available locally in Europe (I'll identify these in each country-by-country analysis later on).

Your neighborhood travel agent can sell you most of the passes listed in this guide. Agents that don't do a lot of independent European travel may need your help in understanding what's available. You need a good steady relationship with a good travel agent. When you find one, keep your travel eggs in one basket...be loyal...take good care of him or her...they have a tough job. You can't expect a normal agent to get excited about selling the small stuff (like a railpass or car rental) without some big stuff (a plane ticket). Lately most agencies (but not ETBD) have tacked on a $10 "handling fee" for railpasses.

If you have a good agent, stick with him or her. If your agent can't handle your needs, find someone who specializes in budget Europe. But if you need a real railpass expert, we at ETBD live, eat and sleep railpasses (ask our spouses). Railpasses are our specialty, and we'd love to help you out (see page 460).

WHERE TO CALL FOR RAILPASS INFORMATION

DER (German Rail, carries all European passes) 1-800-782-2424

RailEurope (France Rail, carries all European passes) 1-800-438-7245

BritRail (BritRail, BritFrance and BritGerman passes only) 1-800-677-8585

Europe Through the Back Door (carries all passes) 1-206-771-8303

Express delivery of passes to Europe: It's easy for travelers in Europe to have a friend buy them a railpass in the USA and mail it to Europe. All your friend needs is your legal name and money. DHL Worldwide Express and UPS each have reliable and reasonable two-day delivery services to most of Europe.

COMMON FEATURES OF RAIL 'N DRIVE PASSES

Most countries now offer a rail 'n drive pass that gives travelers a set number of days of car rental to mix in with a set number of days of train travel (e.g., any 4 rail days and 3 car days out of a 2-month period).

Given the high cost of short-term car rentals, and the fun of delving into certain areas with your own wheels, rail 'n drive passes can be a great option. Train days are best spent on long hauls and going from big city to big city. Car days are most enjoyable when scouring the countryside.

These days, renting a car and driving in Europe is very similar to driving in the USA. All you need is your US driver's license (except in Hungary and Spain, which require an international driver's license), a major credit card, and 23 years of life experience. Car rental offices are located in virtually every sizeable European city (often next to the train station). If your rail 'n drive pass gives you a choice of Hertz or Avis, you must stick with the company you choose. (For a lot more on renting cars and driving in Europe, see p. 74.)

Ordering a rail 'n drive pass. When you order your pass, you must state your date of first use (although you aren't required to actually begin your travel on that date). This date will appear on your pass as the first day of your pass's period of validity. For example, a EurailDrive pass has a period of validity of two months (during which time you can use 4 rail days and 3 car days). If your trip is shorter than the period of validity of your pass, give your arrival date in Europe as your date of first use. This will allow you maximum flexibility in using your pass.

Rail 'n drive passes often give you the opportunity to purchase additional car and/or rail days at a specified cost per day. If you want to add car or rail days, you must do so at the time you purchase the pass.

Your pass gives you a voucher for each day of car travel, allowing you unlimited mileage for 24 hours in whatever class of car you choose, free drop-off privileges to other offices within that country (and occasionally in the neighboring country), all taxes, and legal minimum insurance. You may want to buy the deductible away (which is normally the value of the car) by purchasing the Collision Damage Waiver supplement (CDW, $8 to $14 a day).

Prices for rail n' drive passes vary with the car model chosen. For the sake of brevity, I've listed these pass prices generally per person with two people traveling together in the smallest car available. Other group members pile into the car for free and just buy the equivalent rail flexipass. Children 4-11 pay half the cost of an adult rail flexipass, and ride along in the rental car for free. For all the price specifics, contact your travel agent.

Some rail n' drive passes come pre-validated. Those that aren't need to be validated at a train station even if you begin your travel with a car day. One principal driver's name appears on the pass but others can be added in Europe for a small fee.

Car reservations. Rail 'n drive travelers should reserve their first day of car rental a week before leaving the USA by calling Hertz (1-800-654-3001) or Avis (1-800-331-1084). Without advance reservation, cars are subject to availability.

Choosing the size of a car. Class A category cars are small, Ford Fiesta-type cars, okay for two small/cheap adults. Class B cars are less-small, Ford Escort-type cars, comfortable for two adults and more fun on the autobahn. Families should probably opt for the class C Ford Sierra/Mondeo-type cars. Gas is expensive in Europe at $3 to $4 a gallon. Smaller cars get better mileage. Automatics are available, but those who can't handle a stick shift pay dearly (Hertz won't reserve an automatic, but may allow you to upgrade once you're in Europe). For details, see my handy car size chart on page 77.

BUYING POINT-TO-POINT TICKETS IN EUROPE

Probably one out of ten Eurailpass travelers would have traveled smarter and cheaper by simply buying tickets as they went. While point-to-point tickets are sold by travel agents in the USA, I'd keep my options open and probably save about 10% by buying tickets on my own in Europe.

Railpass shoppers should consider the point-to-point ticket option by using the ticket cost maps (scattered throughout this chapter) to add up the cost of travel they plan to do. The maps show the cost in dollars for second class trips. Remember, first class tickets cost 50% more than second class throughout Europe. While travelers age 26 and older who choose Eurail must buy a first class pass, anyone can buy second class point-to-point tickets.

Connecting the dots:
Point-to-point 2nd class rail fares in $US.

The point-to-point prices used in this chapter are based on the "Eurail Tariff" fares which US travel agents charge for point-to-point tickets. After checking with station ticket offices in many European countries, I've concluded that these fares are generally accurate enough for the comparison purposes of this chapter. Those willing to shop around in Europe and avoid the fast supplement trains will find some cheaper special point-to-point deals in Europe.

Local fares are based on kilometers traveled. Each country has its own "francs per kilometer" type of formula (although some are beginning to charge more during peak use times). Rules vary with most tickets, allowing anywhere from one day to two months to complete a journey with unlimited stop-overs along the route.

Point-to-point tickets for youth. Travelers under 26 can buy discounted tickets (30-50% off, usually called "BIJ" or "Twen-Tours" tickets) throughout Europe at student travel agencies such as Eurotrain and Wasteels (tel. 407/351-2537 in USA), which has over 200 branches in eastern and western Europe. *Let's Go* guidebooks list budget travel offices in each city, usually located in or near major train stations. BIJ tickets are good for about 90% of international departures (all but the express trains) and allow unlimited stop-overs for two months along the route. They offer a further discount of about 10% on round-trip tickets. Sample one-way BIJ fares:

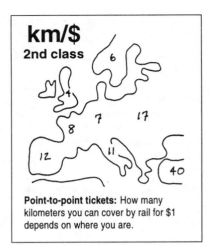

Point-to-point tickets: How many kilometers you can cover by rail for $1 depends on where you are.

◆   London-Rome, £97 ($160, 40% off the regular $240 fare).
◆   London-Amsterdam, £33 ($55, 50% off the regular $100 fare).
◆   London-Paris, £47 ($78, 40% off).

Point-to-point prices of international boat crossings. Some boat crossings are covered by railpasses, but if you're buying point-to-point tickets, you'll need to know the prices (which aren't always predictable on some routes, so we're giving you a best-case-worst-case range)...

◆   Brindisi, Italy to Patras, Greece: 18 hrs, $45 to $160, free with Eurailpass, except for a peak season surcharge of $20 from mid-July to mid-August.
◆   Wales to Ireland: 4 hrs, $30 to $50 (free if you can talk your way into a car, which is allowed four free passengers).
◆   Ireland to France: 14 hrs, daily, $90 to $170 (free with Eurailpass).
◆   Newcastle, England to Bergen, Norway: 21 hrs, $50 to $150.
◆   Calais, France to Dover, England: 1-2 hrs, daily, $35 (free with BritFrance pass). The long-awaited English Channel Tunnel (the "Chunnel") is now open for business. This cuts the London-Paris train trip from 6 hours to just over 3 hours, but costs more than the slower train-boat-train ride.

Eurail tariff prices vs. reality. Most of the point-to-point ticket prices in this chapter come from the official Eurail Tariff listing. When it comes to certain boat crossings in Europe, you should take these "official" prices with a hefty grain of salt. For example, the Eurail Tariff tell us that tickets for the boat connecting Brindisi, Italy and Patras, Greece should sell for $138 to $163. But many travelers are able to get these same tickets from local agents in Greece and Italy for less than $50, depending on whether it's a buyer's or seller's market that week.

A plug for my railpass video. I've produced an hour-long video called "How to get the most from your railpass" that explains lots of the ins and outs of rail travel in Europe. You can order a copy from my Europe Through the Back Door travel company for $15, or get one free if you buy a Eurailpass from us.

EURAIL AND EUROPASSES

17 Eurailpass countries

FIRST CLASS CONSECUTIVE DAY EURAILPASS

15-day	$498
21-day	648
1-month	798
2-months	1098
3-months	1398

Children 4-11 pay half fare, those under 4 ride free.

FIRST CLASS EURAIL FLEXIPASS

Any 5 days in 2 months	$348
Any 10 days in 2 months	560
Any 15 days in 2 months	740

Kids 4 - 11 pay half fare, those under 4 ride free.

SECOND CLASS EURAIL YOUTHPASS

For travelers under age 26 only.

15 consecutive days	$398
1 month of consecutive days	578
2 months of consecutive days	768
Any 5 days out of 2 months	255
Any 10 days out of 2 months	398
Any 15 days out of 2 months	540

The granddaddy of European railpasses, Eurail gives you unlimited rail travel on the national trains of 17 European countries. That's 100,000 miles of track through all of western Europe including Ireland, Germany, Greece and Hungary (excluding Great Britain and eastern Europe). The pass includes many bonuses such as boat rides on the Rhine, Mosel, Danube, lakes of Switzerland, several international ferries (Ireland-France, Sweden-Finland, Germany-Denmark, Italy-Greece), buses in many countries, and the Romantic Road bus tour through Germany. Eurail also has a money-saving, scaled-down 3 to 9 country flexi "Europass" (described on the following pages).

FIRST CLASS EURAIL SAVERPASS

15-day Saverpass	$430 per person
21-day Saverpass	$550 per person
1-month Saverpass	$678 per person

Groups of 3 or more people traveling together at any time of year can buy a Saverpass. Two people traveling together can buy the pass only if all their train travel occurs within the months October through March. Just one pass is issued to the entire Saverpass traveling group. All or part of the group may travel with the pass during the period of validity. Children aged 4-11 pay half the adult saverpass fare with one or more full-fare adults.

FIRST CLASS EURAILDRIVE PASS

Any 4 days of rail and 3 days of car in a 2 month period.

Car categories (Hertz or Avis)	2 adults	1 adult	extra car day
A-Economy (like Ford Fiesta)	$299	$385	$49 (per car)
B-Compact (like Ford Escort)	339	429	65
C-Intermediate (like Ford Sierra)	359	465	75

Prices are approximate per person. Third and fourth persons sharing car get a 4-day out of 2-month railpass for $249. You can add on up to 5 additional days of rail ($49 a day per person) and of car (see above).

EUROPASSES

	1st. class	"Partner"	Youth 2nd.
3 adjacent countries (from France, Ger, Switz, Italy, Spain):			
5 days in 2 months	$280	$140	$198*
6 days in 2 months	318	159	226*
7 days in 2 months	356	178	254*
4 adjacent countries (from France, Ger, Switz, Italy, Spain):			
8 days in 2 months	$394	$197	$282
9 days in 2 months	432	216	310
10 days in 2 months	470	235	338
All 5 countries (France, Germany, Switz, Italy, Spain):			
11 days in 2 months	$508	$254	$366
12 days in 2 months	546	273	394
13 days in 2 months	584	292	422
14 days in 2 months	622	311	450
15 days in 2 months	660	330	478
Extra-cost add-ons available for Europasses:			
Austria:	$35	$35	$25
Belgium & Luxembourg:	22	22	16
Portugal:	22	22	16

3 to 8 Europass countries

Europasses are good for use only in the countries shown above. Countries of use must be adjacent to one another (for instance, you cannot buy a 3-country pass for Germany, Italy and Spain). Choosing "extra-cost add-ons" does not increase your number of days.

Europass "partner" deal: When one traveler buys a first class Europass at full fare, anyone traveling with that person can buy the same pass for half price. Partners must traveler together at all times. (e.g. Marco Polo pays $280 for a 5-day pass, Mary Polo gets the same pass for $140. If they bring the little Polos, they also go for $140 each.) No "partner" discounts for youth passes.
* These Youthpasses include 4 countries, not 3.

EUROPASS DRIVE

5 first class rail days and 3 car days out of 2 months, with extra car and rail days as an option

car categories	2 adults	1 adult	extra car days
A-Economy	$345	$429	$45
B-Compact	379	475	59
C-Intermediate	399	509	69
Each add'l rail day	38	38	

Prices are approximate per person. Adding more rail days can add more countries, as with regular Europasses.

COMPARING PASSES WITH FIVE FLEXI RAIL DAYS

	1st cl.	2nd. cl.
France only	$245	$205
Germany only	260	178
Spain only	250	200
3-country Europass	280	N/A
17-country Eurailpass	348	N/A

EURAIL VS. A PATCHWORK OF COUNTRY PASSES

If you're covering several countries on your trip, Eurail is generally the best deal. You'll find that a patchwork of individual country passes is usually more expensive and restrictive than the basic Eurailpass. And if you're limiting your travels to France, Germany, Switzerland, Italy and Spain, the new "Europass" is hard to beat. However, if your trip is limited to a single country, an individual country railpass is a better deal.

ESTIMATING PASS SAVINGS

Use the point-to-point fare maps in this chapter to add up the cost of your journey and compare it to the cost of a railpass (see p. 61 for an all-Europe fare map). If the costs are equivalent, it makes sense to buy a pass, unless you enjoy waiting in lines to buy tickets.

CHOOSING BETWEEN A EUROPASS AND EURAIL FLEXIPASS

The more focused Europass will save you money if your travels are limited to between three and five adjacent countries: Germany, France, Italy, Switzerland, and Spain (with the option to add Belgium/Lux, Austria and/or Portugal for a small extra fee). In addition, a Europass offers more "flexi-ness" than a Flexipass, by letting you choose anywhere from 5, 6, 7... up to 15 days of travel within a 2 month period. The more flexi days you choose, the more countries you can include, and your cost per travel day drops. Both passes offer cheaper 2nd class versions for youths, rail/drive deals, and the same non-rail bonuses within each country. Here are some Euro/Eurail comparison numbers to crunch as you plan your trip:

Flexi Days	Europass	Europass "partner"	Eurail Flexipass
	Choose from 5 countries		All 17 countries
5 days	$280, choose 3 countries ($56/day)	$140 ($28/day)	$348 ($70/day)
10 days	$470, choose 4 countries ($47/day)	$235 ($24/day)	$560 ($56/day)
15 days	$660, all five countries ($44/day)	$330 ($22/day)	$740 ($49/day)

The Europass is an option that can make sense for the right trip, especially if two or more travelers can take advantage of the "partner" deal. But notice that the single-traveler price difference between the Europass and the Eurail Flexipass isn't huge. If you're a solo traveler with an indefinite itinerary, you may be better off buying the full-blown Eurail Flexipass to give you the freedom to travel in any of the 17 countries. With either pass, when you travel a lot, the savings over buying tickets as-you-go can be substantial. Consider these sample trips:

Frankfurt-Paris-Madrid-Rome-Vienna-Berlin-Frankfurt

A: 11 days in 2 months first class Europass plus Austria (6 countries, 6 overnight trips, 5 extra rail days) $508 + $35 = ... $543

B: Same as A with 2 traveling together ($543 + 35) + ($254 + $35) = $832/2 = per person: . $416

C: 10 days in 2 months 17-country 1st class Eurail flexipass: $560

D: 1st class tickets purchased as-you-go in Europe: $945

E: 2nd class tickets purchased as-you-go in Europe: $630

Munich-Paris-Geneva-Nice-Venice-Rome

A: 5 days in 2 months 1st class Europass (3 countries, 3 overnight trips): $280

B: Same as A with 2 traveling together ($280 + $140)/2 = per person: $210

C: 5 days in 2 months 17-country Eurail Flexipass: $348

D: 1st class tickets purchased as-you-go in Europe: $520

E: 2nd class tickets purchased as-you-go in Europe: $345

Europass Add-Ons: The Europass allows you to pay a little more to add on up to four extra countries — Austria, Belgium/Lux and Portugal. But be aware that this option adds no extra days of travel. Here's one way to assess their value:

Europass Add-On	Sample 2nd class tickets in that country
$35 for Austria	Salzburg-Vienna, $30; north-south border $25 (e.g. fare through Austria from Munich to Venice via Innsbruck)
$22 for Belgium	Brussels to any border, about $15
$22 for Portugal	Lisbon to Algarve or Spanish border, $20

EURAILPASS ANALYSIS:

Trips covering several countries are usually cheapest with the budget whirlwind traveler's old standby, the Eurailpass (or its companion, the Europass). This is because the more days that are included in a pass, the cheaper your per-day cost is. A group of short country passes will each be high (expensive) on that curve of diminishing per-day costs, while a Eurailpass or Europass with a longer life span will be a better deal overall.

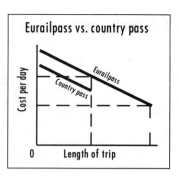

Eurailpass vs. country pass

For an at-a-glance break-even point, remember that a one-month Eurailpass pays for itself ($798) if you're traveling from Amsterdam-Rome-Madrid-Paris on first class or Copenhagen-Berlin-Rome-Madrid-Amsterdam-Copenhagen on second class. A one month Eurail Youthpass ($578) saves you money if you're traveling from Amsterdam to Rome to Madrid and back to Amsterdam. Both first and second class Eurailpasses pay for themselves quicker in the north where the cost per kilometer for rail travel is higher. Of course, when you choose a Eurailpass you're paying for 17 countries. If your plans take you only to the core "Europass" countries, and if a flexi approach works for you, you'll save 15-20% by going with a Europass. The chart two pages back shows you what a bargain a Europass is when compared to its individual country flexipass competitors (made even better with the "partner" deal for friends traveling together).

Remember that nearly all European trains are covered by Eurail and Europasses. Eurail and Europasses include the supplements on all European EC and IC trains, France's TGV, Germany's ICE and Spain's Talgo. Exceptions are: Sweden's X2000 ($20 extra) and the ETR from Milan to Rome ($50 extra, includes a meal). Eurail now covers 85% of Spain's speedy AVE train from Madrid to Seville. There are private scenic mountain trains in Switzerland that are not covered (see the Switzerland section for specifics).

EURAILDRIVE PASS ANALYSIS:

The EurailDrive Pass is a great deal compared to the Eurail Flexipass if two are traveling together and would like 3 days of car rental. When you back out the value of a 4-day flexi railpass ($280 based on 80% of the cost of a $348 five-day pass), the drive option gives a single traveler 3 car days for $100, and 2 traveling together 3 car days for only $20 each. That's $14 a day ($7 per person, not including gas or CDW) — better than the best weekly car rental rate, and with the flexibility of a day here and a day there. Great areas for a day of joyriding include: the Dutch countryside; the Rhine, Mosel, or Bavaria in Germany; the Loire, Burgundy, Alsace, Provence, and the Pyrenees in France; Tuscany, Umbria and the Dolomites in Italy; the white-washed hilltowns of Andalusia in Spain; Norway's fjord country; Ireland's west coast; or "car hiking" in the Austrian or Swiss Alps. When comparing prices, remember that each day of car rental will come with about $30 of extra expenses (CDW insurance, gas, parking) which you'll divide by the number in your party. See "Common features of rail 'n drive passes" earlier in this chapter for more thoughts on rail 'n drive options.

COUNTRY RAILPASSES: GREAT BRITAIN

Britain's BritRail Pass gives you free run of the British train system: 15,000 train departures from 2,400 stations daily in England, Scotland and Wales. It does not cover Northern Ireland or the Republic of Ireland (although the BritIreland pass does). Since Great Britain is not covered on the Eurailpass, BritRail is a big seller.

Britain & Ireland:
Point-to-point 2nd class rail fares in $US.

BRITRAIL PASS

Validity in consec. days	Adult first cl.	Adult standard	over 60 first cl.	over 60 standard	16-25 youth standard
8	$315	$230	$295	$209	$189
15	515	355	479	320	280
22	645	445	585	399	355
1 month	750	520	675	465	415

Standard is the polite British term for second class.
Children 5-15 pay half fare on all varieties of BritRail passes.

BRITRAIL FLEXIPASS

4 days in 1 month	$259	$195	$235	$170	$160
8 days in 1 month	399	275	360	250	225
15 days in 1 month	590	405	535	365	----
15 days in 2 months	----	----	----	----	319

Note: overnight journeys begun on your BritRail pass or flexipass's final night can be completed the day after your pass expires--only BritRail allows this trick. British couchettes cost a steep $40.

BRITRAIL DRIVE PASS

	standard class	first class
Any 3 days by rail + 3 days by car in 1 month:	$290	$340
Any 6 days by rail + 7 days by car in 1 month:	$560	$660

BritRail Drive packages give you rail travel throughout England, Scotland and Wales and use of a Hertz car. Prices listed are approximate per person, with two traveling together for a class B (manual 2-door 4-seat) economy car. Add about $15 for class C and another $15 for class D cars. Drivers must be 21. Seniors over 60 save $20 on these rates. Your travel agent can give you a complete description of this complex program.

ENGLAND/WALES FLEXIPASS

Any 4 days out of 1 month for $155 peasant class or $205 first class (children 5-15 pay half fare).

LONDON VISITOR TRAVELCARD

3 days for $25; 4 days for $32; 7 days for $49. These cover you on all 650 square miles of London's bus and subway (tube) system, including the tube (but not the "Airbus") trip from Heathrow airport and can be used any time during the day. Your travel agent will give you a voucher which you will redeem when you arrive at any major underground or transport office, including Heathrow airport, to get (and validate) your actual pass. Children (5 to 15) get 60% off.

LONDON EXTRA

2 three-day passes for $85, 2 four-day passes for $115, 2 seven-day passes for $175. This offer includes two passes: a flexi 3/8, 4/8 or 7/15-day railpass, and a 3, 4 or 7-consecutive-days London Visitor Travelcard, (described above). The railpass covers sidetrips from London to all of southeast England including Oxford, Cambridge, Salisbury, and Exeter. These passes can be used together or at different times. One "Guide Friday" city bus tour (worth $10) is also included. First class costs about 20% more, kids about 70% less.

FREEDOM OF SCOTLAND TRAVELPASS

8 days	$159
15 days	220
8 days out of 15 flexi	185

Good on all trains, standard class only, and covers Caledonian MacBrayne ferry service to Scotland's most popular islands. The Scots give no discounts for wee kiddies.

Scotland by bus. Backpackers can travel around Scotland for less using "jump on/jump off" bus routes, making a 1000 km circuit with unlimited stops for about $90 (sold at Scottish hostels).

LONDON TRAVELCARD AND LOCAL TUBE PASS ALTERNATIVES:

Many travelers save money by buying their Travelcards or the cheaper options in London. Remember that most sightseeing occurs within or near the Central Zone (much less than 650 square miles!). The passes, easy to buy at any major London tube station, include (with rough dollar costs):

◆ 1 day Central Zone (good for most of downtown, everything within and including the Circle Line, all day, but not before 9:30 a.m. on work days, $4).
◆ Same pass, but for all zones ($6).
◆ 7 Day Central Zone Pass (no 9:30 a.m. limit, $20 and a photo).
◆ LT Card (one day of tube and bus travel in any two zones, all hours, $6).
◆ Punks and skinheads travel free after dark.

BRITISH RAIL DEALS NOT SOLD IN THE USA

While Britain has the most expensive per-kilometer train tickets in Europe, the Brits also offer the most exciting discounts (unfortunately, some are designed to be tough for tourists to take advantage of). In Britain, round-trip "day-return" tickets can cost as little as 10% more than the one-way fares. Britain also offers a great Apex deal for round-trip tickets arranged 1 week in advance, and super cheap Super Apex tickets 2 weeks in advance (on major lines only). For example, while the regular London-Edinburgh one-way fare is £63 ($100), you can get a round-trip apex fare for £ 44 ($70), or a Super Apex fare for only £30 ($47). Blimey!

Britain's **Young Person's Railcard** or **Senior card** costs £16 ($25) and offers a 30% discount on train trips and boat rides to Ireland or Europe for those between 16-23 or over 60. The **Family Card**, available in Britain for £20 ($32), gives parents traveling with kids a 25% discount, and lets kids under 16 travel along for only £2.

To order a BritRail pass you need to include your date of departure from the US. You'll have six months to start your pass. For more information and to request their excellent free "Go BritRail" brochure and the British Rail Pocket Timetable, contact BritRail Travel International, 1500 Broadway #1000, NYC, NY 10036, tel. 800/677-8585. The many hotel and tour deals offered by BritRail are overpriced.

BRITRAIL ANALYSIS:

At only 4 kilometers per dollar, Great Britain has Europe's most expensive train system. While BritRail passes are no steal, they still pay for themselves quickly if you're going to Scotland. The regular London-Edinburgh-London fare costs nearly the same as an 8-day pass ($230). Those on a budget will find that standard class (British for second class) is fine, and first class passes are not worth the extra 40%. In fact, many trains have only standard class cars.

Bus travel will save you money. Before buying a BritRail pass, consider the good rail and bus deals available locally. As explained below, equivalent 8, 15, 22 and 30 day bus passes are 40% less than their second class rail counterparts.

BRITRAIL OR BRITBUS...

While much of Britain is simply not served by trains, travelers can go anywhere just about any time by coach. ("Bus" means city bus. "Coach" is British for any long distance bus). British coach travel is cheaper but slower than rail travel. While some argue you get a closer look at Great Britain through a bus rather than a train window, I'd bus Britain only to save money and to fill gaps in the train system.

Many buses are ideal for daytrips from London. Youths over 59 or under 24 can buy a £7 ($10) discount card in Great Britain (for up to 30% off on all National Express coaches). For more information on British coach travel passes contact the British Travel Associates, Box 299, Elkton, VA 22827, tel. 1-800-327-6097.

COMPARING TRAIN AND COACH TRAVEL IN BRITAIN

From London to:	miles	by train	by coach
Bath	107	25 / 1.25hr / $42	9 per day / 3 hr / £21 ($34)
Cambridge	56	31 / 1hr / $21	13 per day / 1.75hr / £11 ($18)
Cardiff, Wales	145	21 / 1.75 / $56	9 per day / 3.25hr / £24 ($38)
Edinburgh	390	17 / 4hr / $100	2 per day/ 8hr / £34 ($54)
Oxford	60	35 / 1hr / $23	46 per day / 1.75hr / £6 ($10)
Stratford	110	4 / 2hr / $30	3 per day / 3hr / £15 ($24)
York	188	27 / 2hr / $80	4 per day/ 4.25hrs / £17 ($27)

BRITISH TOURIST TRAIL FLEXI BUS PASS

3 consecutive days	£50 ($80)	5 days in 10	£80 ($128)
8 days in 16	£120 ($192)	15 days in 30	£180 ($288)

Allows unlimited bus travel in England, Scotland and Wales on the extensive National Express bus service. These buy-in-Britain prices are about $10 cheaper than the going rate for British bus passes sold in the USA. (The prices above are the approx. cost to buy the passes in Great Britain.) Special youth and senior passes save 20% for those over 59 or under 26.

REPUBLIC OF IRELAND

Ireland's trains fan out from Dublin but neglect much of the countryside. The bus system is better. Your Eurailpass covers the boat from Ireland to France. Here's an assortment of special Irish travel deals:

♦ The **Emerald Isle Card** is Ireland's best transportation pass deal. It gives train and long distance coach (Bus Eireann and Ulster Bus) service throughout all of Ireland (the Republic and the North) including city bus service in major cities: 8 days in 30 for £105 ($170), any 15 days in 30 for £180 ($288). It's sold at CIE Tours in Dublin or Limerick, Ulster Bus in Belfast, or at CIE Tours/

Ireland: Point-to-point 2nd class rail fares in $US.

Irish Rail in the USA (100 Hanover Ave, Box 501, Cedar Knolls, NJ, 07927, 800-243-7687). The USA number is helpful for information but passes cost about $10 more and take longer. You can get them more quickly, and cheaply at any major station in Ireland. Children's passes are half price.

♦ The rail only **Irish Rover** pass gives you 5 rail days in a 15 day period for £70 ($112).

♦ The combo **Irish Explorer** flexipass gives any 8 days of bus or rail travel out of 15 (in the Republic of Ireland only) for £85 ($136), or a rail-only version with 5 out of 15 days for £60 ($96).

♦ For bus travel only, the **Road Rambler**, offering 8 out of 15 days for £65 ($104), is available only in Ireland.

♦ Any student can get 50% off on rail and bus travel with a **Travelsave Stamp** (take your ISIC student I.D. card and $10 to any USIT student travel office in Ireland).

BRITIRELAND PASS

This pass covers the entire British Isles (England, Wales, Scotland, Northern Ireland and the Republic of Ireland) including a round-trip Sealink ferry crossing between Wales or Scotland and the Emerald Isle during the pass's validity (reserve a day in advance).

	1st class	Standard
5 days out of 1 month	$389	$289
10 days out of 1 month	599	419

SEALINK FERRIES CONNECTING BRITAIN AND IRELAND

British port to...	Irish port	crossings daily	hours	cost
Holyhead	Dun Laoghaire	4	3.5	$30
Fishguard	Rosslare	2	3.5	$30
Stranraer	Larne	9	2.25	$30
London (RR/boat)	Dublin	2	10	$60

Travelers from London to Dublin may find it worth $20 extra to catch the quick shuttle flight.

OVER AND UNDER THE ENGLISH CHANNEL

While it's hard to nail down exact prices and options for those traveling from London to Paris or Amsterdam, it's safe to say that these routes are very competitive, and you'll get better prices in London than from agents in the USA. Bus connections are cheapest. Round-trips cost about the same as one-ways. When purchasing a train/boat/train ride from London to points in Europe, you can save about 25% by going overnight (but there is no overnight discount for rides going in the opposite direction). Flying is more reasonable than you might expect, and some airlines now offer a cheap London stopover on flights to Europe. Students can find great deals.

London to Paris:
Bus: £38 O/W (one-way), £55 R/T (round-trip) within 6 months, 10 hours day or overnight on Eurolines (tel. 0171-730-8235) or CitySprint (tel. 01304/240241).
Train: £42 O/W overnight, £57 by day, 7 hours, £65 R/T within 5 days, £85 R/T within 2 months. BritRail Hoverspeed crossing in 6 hours for £60.
Chunnel: The Eurostar connects London and Paris in just over 3 hours. Intro O/W fares: $154 1st cl, $123 2nd cl, $75 2nd cl non-refundable purchased 2 weeks in advance, kids $77 1st cl, $62 2nd cl. Fly: £112.

London to Amsterdam:
Bus: Eurolines £38 O/W, 12 hours day or night, £55 R/T within 6 months, same price to Brussels.
Train: £50 O/W day or night, 12 hours, £63 R/T within 5 days, £83 R/T within 2 months.
Fly: £125 regular.

English ports of Dover, Folkestone, or Harwich to:

	Trips/day	Time	Cost
Calais	31	1 hr	$35 ferry only
Oostende	3	2-4 hrs	$35 ferry only
Hoek v. Holland	2	7 hrs	$100 ferry only

Train connections: London-Dover/Folkestone (2 hrs, $27), London-Harwich (1.5 hrs, $34), Oostende-Brussels (1.5 hrs, $15), Calais-Paris (3.5 hrs, $37), Hoek to Amsterdam (2 hrs, $16).

The Chunnel. Finally... You can take a train under the English Channel — for about what it costs to fly over it. But, if you've got more money than time, this is now the fastest way from Big Ben to the Eiffel Tower. Imagine London to Paris in three hours! Tickets are like plane tickets — with required reservations and prices fluctuating according to season, time, and demand (see above). The traditional train-boat-train alternative will remain completely flexible and substantially cheaper than the new underwater option. Ultimately the Chunnel will save 3 hours on most trips. (But until the high-speed British train line is built, your speed on this leg will be less than breath-taking.) Note that in order to "encourage" you to use the Chunnel (and to recoup their investment quicker), British trains will no longer serve the ferry ports so conveniently. Look for the ferry companies to counter by providing shuttle buses to and from the nearest train station.

BRITFRANCE PASSES

In this rare example of cross-Channel cooperation, the entire British and French rail networks are at your disposal, and you can split your days between countries any way you like. BritFrance Passes no longer include the cross-Channel ferry crossing, but do give discounts on the Eurostar Chunnel crossing.

BRITFRANCE FLEXIPASS

	1st class	2nd class
5 days in month	$359	$259
10 days in a month	539	399

BRITFRANCE RAIL 'N DRIVE PASS

5 days rail and 3 days Avis car out of 1 month

car categories	1st class	2nd class	extra car days (no limit) *
A-Economy	$429	$329	$44
B-Small	465	359	59
C-Medium	485	385	72
D-Small automatic	485	385	72

Prices are approximate per person for two traveling together. Solo travelers will pay $65 to $120 more.
* Price per car/ day, not per person.

BRITFRANCE ANALYSIS:

The BritFrance passes cost about the same as patching together a BritRail pass and a France pass. Your best option may be determined by how many rail days you need. Up to 6 extra days are available on the France Pass at $30 a day. All figuring below is based on second class passes. Results are similar in first class. You'll spend about $35 to walk on to a Channel ferry.

MIXING AND MATCHING BRITRAIL, FRANCE RAIL AND BRITFRANCE PASSES

2nd class pass(es) chosen	Channel crossing	Cost per rail day	Total cost
5 in 30 days BritFrance	$35 extra	$52	$259
4 in 30 days BritRail + 3 in 30 days France	$35 extra	48	340
10 in 30 days BritFrance	$35 extra	40	399
8 in 30 BritRail + 3 in 30 days France	$35 extra	38	420

A plug for my travel slideshow videos: I've produced a series of 2-hour country-specific slideshow videos to help you plan trips using regional railpasses. Each video covers travel skills, and a preview of the sights you may want to visit. These tapes are available for $10 each. For a complete list of tapes and topics, call 206/771-8303 and ask for a free copy of my quarterly travel newsletter/catalog.

FRANCE

France's SNCF, Europe's super train system, offers over 16,000 departures a day around this Texas-sized country. Unlike most countries, point-to-point French ticket prices go up in peak times. Local schedules show blue (quiet), white (normal), and red (holiday) times. Those under 26 and over 60 can buy cards at stations for 50% discounts on blue times.

FRANCE FLEXIPASS

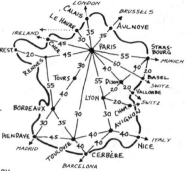

	1st class	2nd class
Any 3 days in a month	$185	$145
Additional days (max 6)	30	30
France Flexi Saver*	150 ea.	115 ea.

*3 days in a month, 2 people traveling together on all journeys, extra days $30 each. Kids 4-11 half fare.

FRANCE RAIL 'N DRIVE PASS

Any 3 days of rail and 3 days of car in a month.

car category	1st class	2nd class	extra car day
A-Economy	$200	$179	$39
B-Small	230	219	55
C-Medium	264	239	75
D-Small automatic	254	219	65

France: Point-to-point 2nd class rail fares in $US.

Rail 'n Drive prices are approximate per person, two traveling together. Solo travelers pay about $100 extra, third and fourth members of a group need only buy the equivalent flexipass. Extra rail days (maximum of 6) cost $30 first class or $30 second class per day.

FRANCE FLY OPTIONS

You can add an Air-Inter flight anywhere within France to your France rail pass for about $85 (in the USA call 1-800-237-2747). Air France is offering a 7 days in 30 flexi fly pass for $299.

FRANCE ANALYSIS:

The France Flexipass is very basic: about $40 a day ($50 in first class) for up to nine days of rail travel on Europe's top train system. You're welcome on the super TGV trains with either a first or second class pass — there's no supplement, but you will need to make a seat reservation ($15 from the U.S., about $3 in France).

The France Rail 'n Drive pass, when compared to the 3 days-in-a-month France Flexipass, is a fine deal for traveling couples, giving you 3 days of tiny car for $34 more per person (or only $15 more per person if you compare the first class passes). Many places in rural France are great for a day in a car, and renting a car by the day would cost you much more than this $10-$25 a day rate (plus $30 a day for gas, tolls and CDW insurance).

If having a car appeals to you, consider the money-saving option of leasing. In France, you can lease a small car for as few as 14 days for around $430 (available through Europe by Car).

ITALY

ITALIAN KILOMETRIC TICKET

Also known as the Biglietto Chilometrico, this features coupons for unlimited trips totalling up to 3,000 kilometers that can be split by up to 5 people for about $279 first class and $171 second class (e.g., a group of five could go the 570 km from Venice to Rome on a Kilometric Ticket for $34 each, a substantial savings over the normal $45 regular ticket price). Like the Go Anywhere pass, this is sold in the USA through the Italian State Railways (1-800-248-8687 for a busy signal) or cheaper and easy in Italy at CIT travel agencies and major train stations.

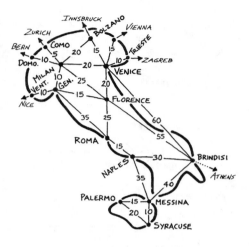

Italy: Point-to-point 2nd class rail fares in $US.

THE ITALIAN "GO ANYWHERE" RAILPASS (BTLC)

	1st cl	2nd cl
8 days	$236	$162
15 days	294	200
21 days	340	230
30 days	406	274
Any 4 days out of 9	186	130
Any 8 days out of 21	268	178
Any 12 days out of 30	334	226

Passes cover all supplements and surcharges except for the very uppity TR450 trains. This is retailed in the USA through travel agents, direct from the Italian State Railways in NYC (1-800-248-8687), or cheaper and easy in Italy at CIT travel agencies and major train stations. Flexi passes are sold only in the USA. The prices above include an extra $10 per pass tacked on by the ISR folks in New York.

ITALY ANALYSIS:

Traveling with point-to-point tickets in Italy is cheap but frustrating because of the long lines, confusing system of supplements (charged for just about any train other than the milk runs), and the predictable language problem when dealing with people in Italian train stations. The Italian BTLC Railpass (like the Eurailpass) is worth a lot more than its point-to-point value for the fact that it covers all the supplements and lets you travel freely without dealing with the station lines and personnel. Unlike the Italian BTLC Railpass (and Eurailpass), the Kilometric Ticket does not cover the extensive, expensive and confusing system of supplements, and with the Kilometric Ticket you still need to wait in line to validate your pass each time you travel.

GERMANY

GERMAN RAILPASS

	1st cl	1st twin	2nd cl	2nd twin	Junior
5 days in a month	$260	$130	$178	$89	$138
10 days in a month	410	205	286	143	188
15 days in a month	530	265	386	193	238

The discounted "twin" pass is for the traveling companion of anyone who buys a regular full price pass in the same class. "Twins" must travel together at all times. Junior passes are for anyone under 26. The German railpass covers all the Eurail bonuses in Germany (boats on the Rhine and Mosel, Romantic Road bus tour, and so on). These passes are available in Germany, but since the 15% VAT (value-added tax) is added on, they are more expensive over there than in the USA.

Germany: Point-to-point 2nd class rail fares in $US.

GERMAN RAIL 'N DRIVE

4 days of rail and 2 days of Hertz car rental in a month. Add up to 4 extra 1st class rail days for around $40/day (around $30/day 2nd class). Prices (except for extra car days) are approximate per person for two traveling together. Solo travelers pay about $40 extra. For specifics, call DER at 1-800-782-2424.

	1st cl	2nd cl	extra car day
A: Ford Fiesta-type car	$238	$178	$48
B: Ford Escort-type car	258	198	62
C: Ford Sierra/Mondeo-type car	268	208	70

BRIT-GERMAN RAILPASS

Finally (but 50 years too late for Rudolf Hess) there is a pass covering the entire British and German rail networks. Split the days as you like, but your pass won't cover the trip between the two countries. $359 gives you any 5 first class flexi days in a month, $566 gives you 10. Kinder 5 - 15 go for halb fare, under 5 go for free.

SOLD ONLY IN GERMANY...

The **Tramper-Monats** ticket offers any traveler under 23 a month of travel throughout Germany on all trains for 465 DM ($290). The no-frills Tramper-Monats ticket (no super ICE trains) costs only 350 DM ($219). The 220 DM ($125) **BahnCard** gives a 50% discount on 2nd class tickets for a year. Those over 59, under 23, students under 27, and spouses (traveling with someone with the 220 DM card) get the same card for 110 DM (children under 18, 50 DM). Families can save even more with the "BahnCard fuer Familien." BahnCards are sold at German train stations. The **Guten Abend** ticket lets you go anywhere in Germany between 7 p.m. and 2 p.m. the next day for about 50 DM (2nd class, buy at German train stations).

AUSTRIA

AUSTRIAN FLEXIPASS

	1st cl	2nd cl
Any 4 days out of 10 days	$165	$111

Children under 7 travel free, 7-15 about half price.
Bonuses include 50% off on Danube ships and on
Lake Constance. These passes are available in the
USA or at train stations in countries outside of Austria.
Prices are about the same in Germany but require you
to get off the train at the border to exchange your voucher for the actual ticket.

Austria: Point-to-point 2nd class rail fares in $US.

Austria's one-month **Bundesnetzkarte** (Network Pass) costs about AS 3,600 ($360) second class or AS 5,400 ($540) first class at Austrian train stations. It offers unlimited travel on Austrian railways, and a 50% discount on boat trips. Groups of up to six travelers can buy and share a discount mileage pass called a **Kilometer-bank** which is good on any train trip of at least 44 miles. 2,000 second class kilometers (1240 miles) cost AS 2,100 ($210) and you can add a thousand kilometers at a cost of AS 1,000 ($100) per thousand (first class kilometers charged at 50% premium, children 6-15 go for half the rate, passes sold only in Austria). Austria offers men over 64 and women over 59 a **senior card** (AS 220 at post offices and train stations) which gives 50% off on all trains for one year.

AUSTRIA ANALYSIS:

A threesome traveling the 320 km from Salzburg to Vienna and back would pay $240 ($40 per second class ticket each way). For about $30 less, they could buy the Kilometerbank ticket, use up about 1920 km for the trip and still have 80 km to play with.

When considering the Austrian Flexipass, remember there is a first class "European East Pass" which gives you any 5 days in 15 for $185 or any 10 days in a month for $299 and covers Austria with the Czech Republic, Slovakia, Hungary and Poland to boot. If you're going to Prague or Budapest, this may actually beat the Austrian pass.

SWITZERLAND

SWISS PASS AND SWISS FLEXIPASS

	1st cl	2nd cl
4 days	$234	$156
8 days	280	196
15 days	328	226
1 month	452	312
3 days in 15 flexipass	234	156

These passes cover all the trains, boats and buses with 25% off on the high mountain rides (such as above Murren and above Kleine Scheidegg). Kids under 16 travel free with a parent.

Switzerland: Point-to-point 2nd class rail fares in $US.

THE SWISS CARD

Sold in America, this $126 first class (or $104 second class) card gives you a round-trip train ride (each direction completed in one day) from any Swiss airport or border point to any point in Switzerland, plus 50% discounts on all Swiss railways, lake steamers, postal buses and most mountain lifts for a month. This is a money-saver for those without a railpass

SWISS RAIL 'N DRIVE PASS

Any 3 days rail and 3 days Avis car out of 15 days:

	1st cl	2nd cl	extra car day
A-Economy	$299	$225	$49
B-Small	345	269	75
C-Medium	369	295	89
D-Small automatic	359	279	79

Prices listed are approximate per person with two traveling together. Solo travelers pay about $100 more. This covers the same extras as the Swiss Pass. Driving in scenic Switzerland makes you want to roll down the window and yodel.

who'll be exploring Switzerland from a homebase. A Swiss Card is basically a one-month Half-Fare Travel Card with a round-trip train fare into and out of the country.

DEALS AVAILABLE ONCE YOU GET TO SWITZERLAND

The **Half-Fare Travel Card** gives you 50% off on all national and private trains, postal buses, and steamers for 150 SF a year (sold at Swiss train stations).

The **Berner Oberland Pass**, allowing any 5 days of free second class travel and 10 days at 50% off in a 15 day period for 175 SF ($145), is the most useful of Switzerland's regional passes. This pass gives you free use of virtually all the trains, boats and lifts in the Bern, Interlaken, Lucerne and Zermatt area. The highest mountain lifts (such as to the Jungfrau from Kleine Scheidegg or to the Schilthorn from Murren) are 50% off with this pass during the five "free travel" days.

The **Swiss Family Card**, available for 20 SF at major stations, allows children under 16 to travel free with their parents. Based on the validity of the parent's ticket or pass, this works even on the high mountain routes. Often called the Swiss Family Robinson Card, this is available for free on request with any Swiss pass ordered in the USA.

SWISS TRAINS AND LIFTS NOT COVERED BY EURAIL

More than any other country, Switzerland has private "panorama" trains that are not national lines and therefore not covered by the Eurailpass. These are covered (either free or discounted) by the various Swiss passes. The most important are:

- ◆ All the trains in the Jungfrau/Schilthorn region south of Interlaken (Interlaken-Grindelwald $5, Interlaken-Gimmelwald $8, Interlaken-Jungfraujoch $80 round-trip);
- ◆ The Brig-Disentis segment of the Glacier Express that scenically crosses mountainous south Switzerland from Martigny to Chur ($35);
- ◆ The private train to see the Matterhorn (Brig-Zermatt $25).

There are, of course, still many super-scenic (non-private) Alpine rides completely covered by the Eurail and Swiss pass. Some of the best are Geneva to Brig, Montreux to Spiez, Interlaken to Lucerne, and Chur to Tirano (Italy).

BENELUX COUNTRIES

BENELUX TOURRAIL PASS

	1st cl	2nd cl	Jr 5-25 2nd cl
Any 5 days out of 30	$230	$153	$115

Covers trains in Belgium, Lux and the Netherlands. This pass is on sale cheaper in Belgium for 4040 BF ($140) 2nd class, 6050 BF ($208) 1st class, 3030 BF ($104) 2nd class jr. It's not for sale in the Netherlands.

Benelux countries: Point-to-point 2nd class fares in $US.

BELGIUM ONLY

Available at train stations in Belgium, the **Belgian Tourrail** pass is a 5 day out of 30 day flexipass offering second class travel in Belgium for 1980 BF ($68) and first class travel for 2970 BF ($102). The **Go Pass** gives youths under 26 any ten trips in Belgium for 1290 BF ($44).

NETHERLANDS ONLY

Domino Passes	1st cl	2nd cl	2nd cl. Jr 12-26 yrs	2nd cl. Child
Any 3 days in a month	$84	$64	$46	$26
Any 5 days in a month	135	100	71	44
Any 10 days in a month	250	178	124	80
7-day Rover Pass	127	85	---	---

The **7-day Public Transport Link** gives you free run of all the urban buses and trolleys in the Dutch cities (including Amsterdam) for $14, sold only with the 7 day Rover Pass. Many travel agents don't offer these, so you may have to go directly through the Netherlands Tourist Board (tel. 1-800-598-8501). There is also a **One-Day Rail Pass** sold at local train stations for about 60 guilders ($36).

BENELUX ANALYSIS:

Most visits don't cover enough miles to justify these passes. This region has more than its share of special local deals. For example, the Amsterdam station offers many round-trip fares for only 25% over the regular one-way fare. Most of the passes listed above can be purchased more cheaply in Europe than here.

SPAIN/PORTUGAL

SPAIN FLEXIPASS

	1st class	2nd class
Any 3 days in 2 months	$175	$137
Extra rail days (max 7)	38	32

Kids 4 - 11 half fare, under 4 cooked and sold as roast suckling pigs.

PORTUGUESE FLEXIPASS

1st Class: Any 4 days out of 15	$99
Any 7 days out of 21	$155

Iberia: Point-to-point 2nd class rail fares in $US.

SPAIN RAIL 'N DRIVE PASS

Any 3 rail days and 3 car days in a month.

	1st cl	2nd cl	extra car day
A-Economy car	$265	$219	$45
B-Small car	279	235	55
C-Medium car	309	265	70
D-Small automatic	339	295	95

Prices are approximate per person for two traveling together. Solo travelers pay about $80 extra. The 3rd and 4th persons sharing the car buy only the railpass. Extra rail days cost $38 1st class, $32 2nd. Drop off car in the same country where you pick it up, either Spain or Portugal.

SPAIN ANALYSIS:

Considering the high cost and lack of imagination offered by Spain's railpasses and the cheap point-to-point bus and train fares, Spain's passes are generally not a very good deal. Spain's flexipass is expensive, costing nearly as much as the 3 country (including Spain) Europass (although Spain offers a second class option you won't find on Eurail). Reservations are required on most long runs. Spain is a good and reasonable place to rent a car (good rates, sparse traffic, frustrating public transportation schedules).

SPAIN AND PORTUGAL BY PUBLIC BUS

Spain and Portugal have extensive and inexpensive bus systems that serve many transportation needs better than the local trains. Consider these connections:

From Madrid to:	by bus	by train
Avila	3/day, 2 hrs, $6	20/day, 2 hrs, $8
Segovia	9/day, 1.5 hrs, $5	10/day, 2 hrs, $5
Toledo	12/day, 1 hr, $4	10/day, 1.5 hrs, $6
Salamanca	12/day, 3 hrs, $13	4/day, 3.5 hrs, $11
Barcelona	4/day, 9 hrs, $22	7/day, 7-10 hrs, $30-50
Sevilla	13/day, 7 hrs, $19	5/day, 4-8 hrs, $50
Granada	5/day, 6 hrs, $24	2/day, 7 hrs, $35

From Lisbon to:	by bus	by train
Algarve	5/day, 5 hrs, $14	7 hrs, $10
Porto	5/day, 5 hrs, $12	5 hrs, $12

While point-to-point train tickets are reasonable in Portugal ($.18 per mile in first class, $.12 in second), trains are slow and frustrating. Buses, while a little more expensive than 2nd class trains, are your handiest bet.

SCANDINAVIA

Scanrail Passes give you unlimited rail travel in Norway, Sweden, Denmark and Finland, and many free or discounted ferry rides.

SCANRAIL PASS, AS SOLD IN THE USA

	1st class	2nd class	2nd class under 26	2nd class over 55!
Any 5 out of 15 days	$199	$159	$119	$140
Any 10 out of 21 days	339	275	206	239
30 consecutive days	499	399	299	349

Trolls 4-11 are half price. 1st class youth and senior passes are available.

SCANRAIL PASS, AS SOLD IN SCANDINAVIA

	1st class	2nd class	1st cl. youth	2nd cl. youth
Any 5 days in 15	DK 1,521 ($270)	DK 1274 ($230)	DK 1,139 ($200)	DK 948 ($170)
21 consecutive days	2,490 (450)	1930 (350)	1930 (350)	1450 (260)

Passes are sold at Scandinavian train stations.

SCANRAIL 'N DRIVE PASS

Any 4 rail days and 3 Avis car days in a 15 day period. Prices are approximate:

	2 adults 1st	2 adults 2nd	1 adult 1st	1 adult 2nd	extra car days (maximum 5)
A-Economy car	$269	$229	$339	$299	$49
B-Compact car	299	259	395	355	59
C-Intermediate car	319	279	435	389	69

NORWAY RAIL PASS

	1st cl	2nd cl
3 days in a month:	182	129
7 consecutive days	235	180
14 consecutive days	315	243

Prices are approximate, and may be 20% less between October and April.

FINNRAIL PASS

	1st class	2nd class
3 days in a month	$139	$95

Children (6-16) are half fare, under 6 are free.

Scandinavia:
Point-to-point 2nd class rail fares in $US.

SOME SCANDINAVIAN COUNTRY SPECIFICS...

Norway: All express trains require a 20NOK ($3) reservation. Sleeping cars have 3 berths and cost 100 NOK ($15), the same as a 6-bed couchette elsewhere in Europe. Norway offers point-to-point ticket discounts for certain "green departures" at off-peak times. Special "green departure mini-price tickets" take travelers from Oslo to any major Norwegian city for about $50 (sold at any station, one day in advance). Seniors over 67 automatically get a 50% discount on tickets purchased in Norway. Students can often fly in Norway for about the price of a train ticket.

Denmark: Offers discounts to seniors over 65 and groups of 3 or more traveling together.

Sweden: Travelers under 16 and over 65 travel for half fare. The **Reslust Card,** which costs about 120 kr ($18), or 50 kr ($7) if you're over 65, gives travelers 50% off on off-peak trains (marked with a red circle in timetables) and 25% off on all Tuesday, Wednesday, Thursday and Saturday trains. SAS offers a standby fare to those under 26 for about 250 kr ($36) per flight.

Finland: The **Bussilomalippu** bus pass gives you 1000 km in 2 weeks for 300 marks ($60). There is a **Finnair Holiday Ticket** which gives you 15 days of air travel in Finland for about $300.

SCANDINAVIA ANALYSIS:

The ScanRail 'n Drive option is handy for those interested in a fjord-country and Norwegian mountain joyride which is not well served by the train. Both kinds of passes go very easy on the first class mark-up. Even though Scandinavian second class is like southern European first class, for $5 a day extra I'd probably spring for first class.

HOW RAILPASSES COVER SCANDINAVIAN INTERNATIONAL BOAT CROSSINGS

from	to	Eurail	Scanrail
Stockholm (Silja)	Helsinki	$20 *	50%
Stolkholm (Viking)	Helsinki	free	30%
Stockholm (Silja)	Turku, Finland	free	50%
Denmark (Helsingor)	Sweden	free	free
Germany (Puttgarten)	Denmark	free	50%
Danish ferries served by trains		free	free
Kristiansand, Norway	Denmark (Hts)	30%	no
Copenhagen	Oslo	20%	no
Bergen fjord trip	Flam	no	50%
Denmark or Sweden	Germany	free	50%
Copenhagen	Malmo	25%	25%
Gothenberg, Sweden	Frederikshavn	free	free

* The Eurailpass covers you on the Silja ship to Helsinki, but you must reserve a berth (figure about $20 per person).

GREECE

GREEK TOURIST CARD

Sold only in Greece at main stations, this pass gives 10 days of unlimited 2nd class train and bus travel for 12,000 drachmas ($57). It's available cheaper for 20 or 30 days or for groups of 2 to 5 travelers. American travel agents also sell a not very exciting Greek Flexi Railpass: 1st class only, 3 days in 1 month for $95, 5 days in 1 month for $136.

GREECE ANALYSIS:

There is little reason for most visitors to buy any kind of railpass in Greece. Train travel in Greece is slow and frustrating. The bus system is much better. Most travelers will spend their time island-hopping. Several companies compete for each island's business, and deck class is never expensive. Ideally, let ferry schedules shape the list of islands you visit. I choose to connect a series of islands on a line served by daily boats rather than cutting across the schedule grain and using routes served only once or twice a week. On nearly any day an Athens "bucket shop" will sell you a cheap plane ticket from Athens to London (and most of Europe) for about $200. For time travelers, the Magic Bus does the heavy trip from Athens to London for $130. Shower first, and bring plenty of snacks.

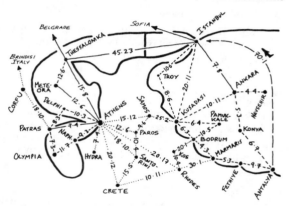

Greece and Western Turkey: Second class cost in $US (first number) and hours of travel (second number) between locations by rail (solid line), boat (dotted line) and bus (dashed line).

TURKEY

Turkey has no railpasses (praise Allah). The only trains worth using in Turkey are the ones from Greece or Bulgaria into Istanbul and the reliable Istanbul-Ankara night train ($32 with a couchette). Buses are a traveler's best friend in Turkey.

A multitude of bus companies compete, connecting any town with just about any other town several times each day for about $1.50 an hour. It's normally worth choosing the more expensive lines. Turkish Airlines runs an extensive domestic service, allowing you to fly from Istanbul to most Turkish cities for $40 to $80. I wouldn't drive in Turkey. It's too cheap, easy and fun to go local on the buses, shared taxis and regular taxis.

EASTERN EUROPE

CENTRAL EUROPE PASS

Any 5 days in 1 month (first class) $296
Covers Germany, Poland, Czech Republic and Slovakia.

EUROPEAN EAST PASS

Any 5 days out of 15 (first class) $185
Any 10 days in a month (first class)   299
Covers Austria, Czech Republic, Slovakia, Hungary and Poland.

Eastern Europe:
Point-to-point 2nd
class rail fares in $US.

HUNGARY PASS

Any 5 days out of 15 (first class) $55
Any 10 days in a month (first class)   69
First class, kids 5-14 half fare, Huns go free.

CZECH REPUBLIC PASS

Any 5 days out of 15 (first class) $69

CZECH PRAGUE OUT PASS

$49 first class, $30 second class, cheaper for those under 26. Good for two train rides: from any Czech border into Prague, and then back from Prague back out of the country through any border crossing, within 7 days. Since most travelers to the Czech Republic just do Prague, this is a handy way to add Prague access to a Eurailpass. For info call EurAid in the USA at 708/420-2343, or in Munich at 089/593889.

EASTERN EUROPE ANALYSIS:

Buying point-to-point tickets is very cheap throughout eastern Europe. The only reason to buy a railpass for any of these countries is to avoid the need to change money and the hassle of buying tickets as you go. Poland, Romania and Bulgaria also offer railpasses.

Train travel in the Baltics and Russia is too cheap for railpasses. Connecting the three Baltic capitals with a night train and a couchette costs less than $5. Over there, Moscow to St. Petersburg tickets with a couchette are around $20. These tickets are much more expensive when arranged from the USA.

THE ALL-EUROPE INTERRAIL PASS

This pass is hard to track. It changes every year. Basically it's a one month 2nd class pass sold to Europeans under 26 covering all the Eurail countries plus Britain, Morocco, all of Eastern Europe except the former USSR and Turkey. It's issued at European stations for about $400 to anyone under 26 who can prove European residency for at least 6 months. (Strictness on this rule varies. Sometimes having a six-month old stamp in your passport or local receipt will work, but don't count on it.) There is a new "zonal" version of this pass offering less terrain for less money. And there's a new 26+ InterRail pass for people of any age (15 days for about $340, 30 days for about $430). Unfortunately this oldster's pass is not accepted by much of Europe (France, Belgium, Switzerland, Italy, Spain, and Portugal). Don't go to Europe planning to get one of these without having a local contact confirm for you the latest prices and availability.

TRANSPORTION OPTIONS FOR SEVEN GREAT 22-DAY TRIPS

Here is a quick analysis of your transportation options for my seven favorite 22-day itineraries as described in my *Rick Steves' Best of...* guidebook for that country or region. My preferred choices, if any, are in bold:

22 DAYS IN EUROPE

Route: Amsterdam-Rhineland-Romantic Road-Tirol-Venice-Florence-Rome-Italian Riviera-Swiss Alps-Beaune-Paris. For this plan, let your dreams rather than the cost dictate your transportation choice:

$450   second class point-to-point
$648   21 day Eurailpass
$560   10 days in 2 months Eurail flexipass
$530   10 days in 4 countries Europass + $60 extra for rides out of Netherlands and through Austria.
$413   Average cost per person for 2 traveling together with 10 days Europass and "partner" plus $60 each for trips out of Netherlands and Austria.
$635   EurailDrive, $590 (+$45 per person for gas and CDW) for 9 rail days and 3 car days (good for two traveling together with an interest in driving a little, in a small car).
$600   Three weeks in a leased car (split by 2, including gas, CDW, tolls and parking in Italy)

22 DAYS IN GREAT BRITAIN

Route: London-Bath-Cardiff-Cotswolds-North Wales-Windermere-Oban-Edinburgh-Durham-York-Cambridge-London.

$350   second class point-to-point
$290   15 days in 30 flexi bus pass
$445   22 days BritRail pass
$405   15 days in a month BritRail flexipass
$500   3 weeks in a leased car ($1000 split by 2)

22 DAYS IN FRANCE

Route: Paris-Normandy-Brittany-Loire-Carcassonne-Provence-Alps-Burgundy-Alsace-Paris.

$365   second class point-to-point
$370   France Rail 'n Drive Pass (9 second class rail days and 3 car days, two people), $323+$45 for gas and CDW.
$648   21 day Eurailpass

22 DAYS IN ITALY

Route: Milan-Cinque Terre-Florence-Siena-Rome-Naples-Paestum-Venice-Dolomites-Como-Milan.

$200   2nd class point-to-point
$334   12 days in a month first class Italian pass
$226   12 days in a month 2nd class Italian pass
$340   21 days first class Italian railpass (worth it)
$230   21 days 2nd class Italian railpass
$648   21 days Eurailpass
$600   3 weeks in a leased car (including Italian extras: theft insurance, extra-strength Tylenol, city parking and autostrada tolls, split by 2)

22 DAYS IN GERMANY, AUSTRIA & SWITZERLAND

Route: Frankfurt-Romantic Road-Reutte-Munich-Salzburg-Hallstatt-Vienna-Innsbruck-Appenzell-Interlaken-Bern-Lausanne-Baden-Baden-Mosel-Rhine-Bonn-Frankfurt.

$550   second class point-to-point
$648   21 day Eurailpass
$590   German 4 rail days and 2 car days ($178+30+$15 gas and CDW), 4 days in ten Austrian Flexipass ($111), Swiss Rail 'n Drive pass with 3 rail days and 3 car days ($225+$45 gas and CDW), best for couples who don't mind second class train and want to do some driving.
$500   3 weeks in a leased car ($1000 split by 2).

22 DAYS IN SPAIN & PORTUGAL

Route: Madrid-Salamanca-Coimbra-Lisbon-Algarve-Seville-Gibraltar-Nerja-Granada-Toledo-Madrid.

$210   2nd class point-to-point (best for tight budgets)
$500   3 weeks in a leased car split by two (a great car trip)
$350   5 days in a month Spain 1st class flexipass and 4 days in 15 days Portugal flexipass
$500   Spain Rail 'n Drive with 3 rail days and 4 car days ($340+60 gas and CDW) plus 4 days in 15 days Portugal flexipass and some extra rides

22 DAYS IN NORWAY, SWEDEN & DENMARK

Route: Copenhagen-Kalmar-Stockholm-Helsinki-Stockholm-Oslo-Fjords-Bergen-Aarhus-Aero-Copenhagen.

$648   21 day first class Eurailpass
$460   2nd class point-to-point
$275   Scanrail 9 days in 21 days 2nd class flexipass
$350   21 consecutive day 2nd class ScanRailpass (buy in Scandinavia)
$450   21 consecutive day 1st class ScanRailpass (buy in Scandinavia)
$700   3 weeks in a leased car (split by 2) plus a round-trip boat to Finland

For more details on these itineraries and the guidebooks that cover them, see pages 420-422.

Index

Other Books from John Muir Publications

Travel Books by Rick Steves

Asia Through the Back Door, 4th ed., 400 pp. $16.95

Europe 101: History, Art, and Culture for the Traveler, 4th ed., 372 pp. $15.95

Mona Winks: Self-Guided Tours of Europe's Top Museums, 2nd ed., 456 pp. $16.95

Rick Steves' Best of the Baltics and Russia, 1995 ed. 144 pp. $9.95

Rick Steves' Best of Europe, 1995 ed., 544 pp. $16.95

Rick Steves' Best of France, Belgium, and the Netherlands, 1995 ed., 240 pp. $12.95

Rick Steves' Best of Germany, Austria, and Switzerland, 1995 ed., 240 pp. $12.95

Rick Steves' Best of Great Britain, 1995 ed., 192 pp. $11.95

Rick Steves' Best of Italy, 1995 ed., 208 pp. $11.95

Rick Steves' Best of Scandinavia, 1995 ed., 192 pp. $11.95

Rick Steves' Best of Spain and Portugal, 1995 ed., 192 pp. $11.95

Rick Steves' Europe Through the Back Door, 13th ed., 480 pp. $17.95

Rick Steves' French Phrase Book, 2nd ed., 112 pp. $4.95

Rick Steves' German Phrase Book, 2nd ed., 112 pp. $4.95

Rick Steves' Italian Phrase Book, 2nd ed., 112 pp. $4.95

Rick Steves' Spanish and Portuguese Phrase Book, 2nd ed., 288 pp. $5.95

Rick Steves' French/German/Italian Phrase Book, 288 pp. $6.95

A Natural Destination Series

Belize: A Natural Destination, 2nd ed., 304 pp. $16.95

Costa Rica: A Natural Destination, 3rd ed., 400 pp. $17.95

Guatemala: A Natural Destination, 336 pp. $16.95

Undiscovered Islands Series

Undiscovered Islands of the Caribbean, 3rd ed., 264 pp. $14.95

Undiscovered Islands of the Mediterranean, 2nd ed., 256 pp. $13.95

Undiscovered Islands of the U.S. and Canadian West Coast, 288 pp. $12.95

For Birding Enthusiasts

The Birder's Guide to Bed and Breakfasts: U.S. and Canada, 288 pp. $15.95

The Visitor's Guide to the Birds of the Central National Parks: U.S. and Canada, 400 pp. $15.95

The Visitor's Guide to the Birds of the Eastern National Parks: U.S. and Canada, 400 pp. $15.95

The Visitor's Guide to the Birds of the Rocky Mountain National Parks: U.S. and Canada, 432 pp. $15.95

Unique Travel Series
Each is 112 pages and $10.95 paper.
Unique Arizona
Unique California
Unique Colorado
Unique Florida

Unique New England
Unique New Mexico
Unique Texas
Unique Washington (available 2/95)

2 to 22 Days Itinerary Planners

2 to 22 Days in the American Southwest, 1995 ed., 192 pp. $11.95

2 to 22 Days in Asia, 192 pp. $10.95

2 to 22 Days in Australia, 192 pp. $10.95

2 to 22 Days in California, 1995 ed., 192 pp. $11.95

2 to 22 Days in Eastern Canada, 1995 ed., 240 pp $11.95

2 to 22 Days in Florida, 1995 ed., 192 pp. $11.95

2 to 22 Days Around the Great Lakes, 1995 ed., 192 pp. $11.95

2 to 22 Days in Hawaii, 1995 ed., 192 pp. $11.95

2 to 22 Days in New England, 1995 ed., 192 pp. $11.95

2 to 22 Days in New Zealand, 192 pp. $10.95

2 to 22 Days in the Pacific Northwest, 1995 ed., 192 pp. $11.95

2 to 22 Days in the Rockies, 1995 ed., 192 pp. $11.95

2 to 22 Days in Texas, 1995 ed., 192 pp. $11.95

2 to 22 Days in Thailand, 192 pp. $10.95

22 Days Around the World, 264 pp. $13.95

Other Terrific Travel Titles

The 100 Best Small Art Towns in America, 224 pp. $12.95

Elderhostels: The Students' Choice, 2nd ed., 304 pp. $15.95

Environmental Vacations: Volunteer Projects to Save the Planet, 2nd ed., 248 pp. $16.95

A Foreign Visitor's Guide to America, 224 pp. $12.95

Great Cities of Eastern Europe, 256 pp. $16.95

Indian America: A Traveler's Companion, 3rd ed., 432 pp. $18.95

Interior Furnishings Southwest, 256 pp. $19.95

Opera! The Guide to Western Europe's Great Houses, 296 pp. $18.95

Paintbrushes and Pistols: How the Taos Artists Sold the West, 288 pp. $17.95

The People's Guide to Mexico, 9th ed., 608 pp. $18.95

Ranch Vacations: The Complete Guide to Guest and Resort, Fly-Fishing, and Cross-Country Skiing Ranches, 3rd ed., 528 pp. $19.95

The Shopper's Guide to Art and Crafts in the Hawaiian Islands, 272 pp. $13.95

The Shopper's Guide to Mexico, 224 pp. $9.95

Understanding Europeans, 272 pp. $14.95

A Viewer's Guide to Art: A Glossary of Gods, People, and Creatures, 144 pp. $10.95

Watch It Made in the U.S.A.: A Visitor's Guide to the Companies that Make Your Favorite Products, 272 pp. $16.95

Parenting Titles

Being a Father: Family, Work, and Self, 176 pp. $12.95

Preconception: A Woman's Guide to Preparing for Pregnancy and Parenthood, 232 pp. $14.95

Schooling at Home: Parents, Kids, and Learning, 264 pp., $14.95

Teens: A Fresh Look, 240 pp. $14.95

Automotive Titles

The Greaseless Guide to Car Care Confidence, 224 pp. $14.95

How to Keep Your Datsun/Nissan Alive, 544 pp. $21.95

How to Keep Your Subaru Alive, 480 pp. $21.95

How to Keep Your Toyota Pickup Alive, 392 pp. $21.95

How to Keep Your VW Alive, 25th Anniversary ed., 464 pp. spiral bound $25

TITLES FOR YOUNG READERS AGES 8 AND UP

American Origins Series
Each is 48 pages and $12.95 hardcover.
Tracing Our English Roots
Tracing Our French Roots (available 5/95)
Tracing Our German Roots
Tracing Our Irish Roots
Tracing Our Italian Roots
Tracing Our Japanese Roots
Tracing Our Jewish Roots
Tracing Our Polish Roots

Bizarre & Beautiful Series
Each is 48 pages, $14.95 hardcover, $9.95 paperback.
Bizarre & Beautiful Ears
Bizarre & Beautiful Eyes
Bizarre & Beautiful Feelers
Bizarre & Beautiful Noses
Bizarre & Beautiful Tongues

Environmental Titles

Habitats: Where the Wild Things Live, 48 pp. $9.95

The Indian Way: Learning to Communicate with Mother Earth, 114 pp. $9.95

Rads, Ergs, and Cheeseburgers: The Kids' Guide to Energy and the Environment, 108 pp. $13.95

The Kids' Environment Book: What's Awry and Why, 192 pp. $13.95

Extremely Weird Series
Each is 48 pages and $9.95 paper, $14.95 hardcover.

Extremely Weird Bats
Extremely Weird Birds
Extremely Weird Endangered Species
Extremely Weird Fishes
Extremely Weird Frogs
Extremely Weird Insects
Extremely Weird Mammals
Extremely Weird Micro Monsters
Extremely Weird Primates
Extremely Weird Reptiles
Extremely Weird Sea Creatures
Extremely Weird Snakes
Extremely Weird Spiders

Kidding Around Travel Series
All are 64 pages and $9.95 paperback, except for *Kidding Around Spain* and *Kidding Around the National Parks of the Southwest*, which are 108 pages and $12.95 paperback.

Kidding Around Atlanta
Kidding Around Boston, 2nd ed.
Kidding Around Chicago, 2nd ed.
Kidding Around the Hawaiian Islands
Kidding Around London
Kidding Around Los Angeles
Kidding Around the National Parks of the Southwest
Kidding Around New York City, 2nd ed.
Kidding Around Paris
Kidding Around Philadelphia

Kidding Around San Diego
Kidding Around San Francisco
Kidding Around Santa Fe
Kidding Around Seattle
Kidding Around Spain
Kidding Around Washington,
D.C., 2nd ed.

Kids Explore Series
Written by kids for kids, all are
$9.95 paper.

Kids Explore America's African
American Heritage, 128 pp.

Kids Explore the Gifts of
Children with Special Needs,
128 pp.

Kids Explore America's
Hispanic Heritage, 112 pp.

Kids Explore America's Japanese American Heritage, 144 pp.

Masters of Motion Series
Each is 48 pages and $9.95 paper.

How to Drive an Indy Race Car
How to Fly a 747
How to Fly the Space Shuttle

Rainbow Warrior Artists Series
Each is 48 pages and $14.95 hard-
cover. ($9.95 paperbacks available
4/95.)

Native Artists of Africa
Native Artists of Europe
Native Artists of North America

Rough and Ready Series
Each is 48 pages and $12.95 hard-
cover. ($9.95 paperbacks available
4/95.)

Rough and Ready Cowboys
Rough and Ready Homesteaders
Rough and Ready Loggers
Rough and Ready Outlaws and
Lawmen
Rough and Ready Prospectors
Rough and Ready Railroaders

X-ray Vision Series
Each is 48 pages and $9.95
paper.

Looking Inside the Brain
Looking Inside Cartoon Animation
Looking Inside Caves and Caverns
Looking Inside Sports Aero-
dynamics
Looking Inside Sunken Treasures
Looking Inside Telescopes and
the Night Sky

Ordering Information
Please check your local bookstore
for our books, or call **1-800-888-7504**
to order direct. All orders are shipped
via UPS; see chart below to calculate
your shipping charge for U.S. destinations. **No post office boxes
please; we must have a street
address to ensure delivery.** If the
book you request is not available, we
will hold your check until we can ship
it. Foreign orders will be shipped surface rate unless otherwise requested; please enclose $3 for the first
item and $1 for each additional item.

For U.S. Orders Totaling	Add
Up to $15.00	$4.25
$15.01 to $45.00	$5.25
$45.01 to $75.00	$6.25
$75.01 or more	$7.25

Methods of Payment
Check, money order, American
Express, MasterCard, or Visa. We
cannot be responsible for cash sent
through the mail. For credit card
orders, include your card number,
expiration date, and your signature,
or call **1-800-888-7504**. American
Express card orders can only be
shipped to billing address of card-
holder. Sorry, no C.O.D.'s.
Residents of sunny New Mexico,
add 6.25% tax to total.

Address all orders and inquiries to:
John Muir Publications
P.O. Box 613
Santa Fe, NM 87504
(505) 982-4078
(800) 888-7504